BEYOND ENLIGHTENMENT

What is enlightenment? For Buddhists it involves the discovery of the truth of *duḥkha*—pain, suffering, and sorrow—followed by the realization that *duḥkha* can be brought to an end. In like manner, Protestant Christians speak of enlightenment as a moment when, touched by God, one becomes aware of one's own escape from eternal damnation. Likewise, European philosophers have imagined an age of Enlightenment, a time of individual freedom and social equality. In all three cases, enlightenment, as insight into reality, is conjoined with enlightenment, as a state of harmony and peace, beyond politics.

Beyond Enlightenment treats the political implications of this apolitical ideal. It is a sophisticated study of some of the assumptions underlying, and ramifications involved in, the study of Buddhism (especially, but not exclusively, in the West), and of the tendency of scholars to ground their study of Buddhism in particular assumptions about the Buddha's enlightenment and a particular understanding of religion, traced back through Western orientalists to the Enlightenment and the Protestant Reformation. Richard Cohen's book will be of interest to buddhologists, indologists, scholars of comparative religion, and intellectual historians.

Richard S. Cohen is Associate Professor of South Asian Religious Literatures at the University of California, San Diego. This is his first book, though he has published numerous articles in such venues as the *Journal of the American Academy of Religion* and *History of Religions*. He is now working on a study of Buddhism and counterculture.

ROUTLEDGE CRITICAL STUDIES
IN BUDDHISM
General Editors: Charles S. Prebish and
Damien Keown

Routledge Critical Studies in Buddhism is a comprehensive study of the Buddhist tradition. The series explores this complex and extensive tradition from a variety of perspectives, using a range of different methodologies.

The series is diverse in its focus, including historical studies, textual translations and commentaries, sociological investigations, bibliographic studies, and considerations of religious practice as an expression of Buddhism's integral religiosity. It also presents materials on modern intellectual historical studies, including the role of Buddhist thought and scholarship in a contemporary, critical context and in the light of current social issues. The series is expansive and imaginative in scope, spanning more than two and a half millennia of Buddhist history. It is receptive to all research works that inform and advance our knowledge and understanding of the Buddhist tradition.

A SURVEY OF VINAYA
LITERATURE
Charles S. Prebish

THE REFLEXIVE NATURE OF
AWARENESS
Paul Williams

ALTRUISM AND REALITY
Paul Williams

BUDDHISM AND HUMAN
RIGHTS
*Edited by Damien Keown, Charles
S. Prebish and Wayne Husted*

WOMEN IN THE FOOTSTEPS
OF THE BUDDHA
Kathryn R. Blackstone

THE RESONANCE OF
EMPTINESS
Gay Watson

AMERICAN BUDDHISM
*Edited by Duncan Ryuken
Williams and
Christopher Queen*

IMAGING WISDOM
Jacob N. Kinnard

PAIN AND ITS
ENDING
Carol S. Anderson

EMPTINESS
APPRAISED
David F. Burton

THE SOUND OF LIBERATING
TRUTH
*Edited by Sallie B. King and
Paul O. Ingram*

BUDDHIST THEOLOGY
*Edited by Roger R. Jackson and
John J. Makransky*

THE GLORIOUS DEEDS OF
PURNA
Joel Tatelman

EARLY BUDDHISM—A NEW
APPROACH
Sue Hamilton

CONTEMPORARY
BUDDHIST ETHICS
Edited by Damien Keown

INNOVATIVE BUDDHIST
WOMEN
Edited by Karma Lekshe Tsomo

TEACHING BUDDHISM
IN THE WEST
*Edited by V.S. Hori, R.P. Hayes and
J.M. Shields*

EMPTY VISION
David L. McMahan

SELF, REALITY AND
REASON IN TIBETAN
PHILOSOPHY
Thupten Jinpa

IN DEFENSE OF
DHARMA
Tessa J. Bartholomeusz

BUDDHIST PHENOMENOLOGY
Dan Lusthaus

RELIGIOUS MOTIVATION
AND THE ORIGINS OF
BUDDHISM
Torkel Brekke

DEVELOPMENTS IN
AUSTRALIAN BUDDHISM
Michelle Spuler

ZEN WAR STORIES
Brian Victoria

THE BUDDHIST
UNCONSCIOUS
William S. Waldron

INDIAN BUDDHIST THEORIES
OF PERSONS
James Duerlinger

ACTION DHARMA
*Edited by Christopher Queen, Charles
S. Prebish and Damien Keown*

TIBETAN AND ZEN BUDDHISM
IN BRITAIN
David N. Kay

THE CONCEPT OF THE
BUDDHA
Guang Xing

THE PHILOSOPHY OF DESIRE
IN THE BUDDHIST PALI
CANON
David Webster

THE NOTION OF *DITTHI* IN
THERAVADA BUDDHISM
Paul Fuller

THE BUDDHIST THEORY OF
SELF-COGNITION
Zhihua Yao

MORAL THEORY IN
ŚANTIDEVA'S
ŚIKṢĀSAMUCCAYA
Barbra R. Clayton

BUDDHIST STUDIES FROM
INDIA TO AMERICA
Edited by Damien Keown

DISCOURSE AND IDEOLOGY
IN MEDIEVAL JAPANESE
BUDDHISM
*Edited by Richard K. Payne and
Taigen Dan Leighton*

BUDDHIST THOUGHT AND
APPLIED PSYCHOLOGICAL
RESEARCH
*Edited by D.K. Nauriyal, Michael
S. Drummond and Y.B. Lal*

BUDDHISM IN CANADA
Edited by Bruce Matthews

BUDDHISM, CONFLICT AND
VIOLENCE IN MODERN
SRI LANKA
Edited by Mahinda Deegalle

THERAVĀDA BUDDHISM
AND THE BRITISH
ENCOUNTER
Religious, missionary and colonial
experience in nineteenth century
Sri Lanka
Elizabeth Harris

BEYOND ENLIGHTENMENT
Buddhism, religion, modernity
Richard S. Cohen

The following titles are published in association with the *Oxford Centre for Buddhist Studies*

 Oxford Centre for Buddhist Studies
a project of The Society for the Wider Understanding of the Buddhist Tradition

The *Oxford Centre for Buddhist Studies* conducts and promotes rigorous teaching and research into all forms of the Buddhist tradition.

EARLY BUDDHIST METAPHYSICS
Noa Ronkin

MIPHAM'S DIALECTICS AND THE DEBATES ON EMPTINESS
Karma Phuntsho

HOW BUDDHISM BEGAN
The conditioned genesis of the early teachings
Richard F. Gombrich

BUDDHIST MEDITATION
An anthology of texts from the Pāli canon
Sarah Shaw

BEYOND ENLIGHTENMENT

Buddhism, religion, modernity

Richard S. Cohen

Routledge
Taylor & Francis Group

LONDON AND NEW YORK

First published 2006
by Routledge
2 Park Square, Milton Park, Abingdon, Oxon OX14 4RN

Simultaneously published in the USA and Canada
by Routledge
270 Madison Ave, New York, NY 10016

*Routledge is an imprint of the Taylor & Francis Group,
an informa business*

Typeset in Times New Roman by
Newgen Imaging Systems (P) Ltd, Chennai, India
Printed and bound in Great Britain by
Antony Rowe Ltd, Chippenham, Wiltshire

British Library Cataloguing in Publication Data
A catalogue record for this book is available
from the British Library

Library of Congress Cataloging in Publication Data
Cohen, Richard, 1963–
Beyond enlightenment : Buddhism, religion,
modernity / Richard Cohen.
p. cm.—(Routledge critical studies in Buddhism)
Includes bibliographical references and index.
1. Enlightenment (Buddhism) 2. Enlightenment. 3. Religious
awakening—Comparative studies. I. Title. II. Series.
BQ4398.C65 2006
294.3'442—dc22   2005025919

ISBN10: 0–415–37294–1
ISBN13: 978–0–415–37294–7

061406/13624 T8

FOR NANCY

Perhaps there is no religion the study of which is likely to be so useful to Europeans as Buddhism. Discarding, as it does, those primary beliefs which we are tempted to regard as the essential ideas of religion generally, Buddhism forces us to reconsider the question to what extent these beliefs can be pronounced universal or necessary ingredients of the religious consciousness of mankind.

(John R. Amberley, "Recent Publications on Buddhism,"
The Theological Review 9 (July 1872): 293)

CONTENTS

ILLUSTRATIONS

Figures

Tables

PREFACE

You are walking down a forest path. You meet a man who positively beams serenity. You ask his teacher's name. He replies,

Nobody is my teacher.
Nobody is comparable to me.
I am the only perfect buddha in the world.
I have attained supreme enlightenment.
I am conqueror over all.
I know everything.
I am not contaminated by anything at all...
I have all the powers of the omniscient.
I am an arhat in the world.
I am unrivaled in all realms, including those of the gods.
I am the victor who conquered Māra.[1]

This happened—so we are told—to a wanderer named Upagu, sometime in the fifth century BCE. Upagu answered with a shrug, "perhaps," and left quickly by a different road. Now we remember Upagu as the fool. He could have been Śākyamuni Buddha's first disciple. But where a wiser man would have recognized the truthful words of a buddha fresh from enlightenment, Upagu heard a megalomaniacal rant: violent words of conquest seemingly at odds with the serene visage of the man who spoke them.

Would you have recognized the man as enlightened? Would you have discerned a spirit of universal peace, beyond politics, in words that valorize hierarchy, celebrate raw power, and speak well of battle? If so, then *Beyond Enlightenment* is a book about you. If, however, you are puzzled that anybody would answer these questions in the affirmative, if you find Upagu's laconic "perhaps" a reasonable response, perhaps too reasonable, then *Beyond Enlightenment* is a book for you.

For me, the book grows out of wonderment at the politics of the apolitical. By *politics* I mean simply the existential situation in which imperfect people, unaware of the full reasons they act as they do and uncertain about the full ramifications of their decisions, nevertheless make choices that ramify upon others. Our everyday world is a political world, for there are inevitable contingencies to how we choose to express our wills. We struggle, we clash, we strive, we harm, we suffer. *Apolitics* describes an alternate existential state, in which power is exercised with autonomy, certainty, stability, supremacy, in sum enlightenment.

Beyond Enlightenment asks how political action comes to be accepted as apolitical; how contingent paths become necessary routes to absolute freedom. To return to Śākyamuni and Upagu, the buddha positively celebrates the fact that he alone dominates the world. But his words also guarantee that this ascendancy is a force for universal good because his power is the power of a fully enlightened being. His omniscience allows him to exercise power completely apart from the contingency of politics. For somebody who takes Śākyamuni at his word, enlightenment functions as something like a philosopher's stone, transmuting the base-metal of political contingency into the certitude of power's apolitical expression.

In common speech, the word "enlightened" can be applied as readily to a group of people as to an individual. Thus it is a truism that there would be no Buddhism if claims for the buddha's enlightenment had gained no social traction, if there were no saṅgha. This truism can be rephrased, however, shifting focus to a matter that is worth further investigation: There would be no Buddhism if the ideological transformation of the political into the apolitical had not been supplemented by the installation of that ideology at the heart of a social order. That is, the study of the political–apolitical is supplemented by the study of *hegemony*. Hegemony is found where one segment of a society proffers its own desires and ideals as universal values bearing on the social whole, necessary for social peace. The erasure of contingency, the disavowal of partisanship, the representation of truths as absolute and experiences as spontaneous—unsullied by arbitrary wants or selfish calculations—are the foundational social acts.

Such are *Beyond Enlightenment's* basic concerns: the political function of the apolitical; enlightenment as an instrument of hegemony. Here now is a brief outline of its structure.

Chapter 1 explains the meaning and import of several abstract nouns—religion, enlightenment, hegemony—and explores linkages among them. It proposes that the Enlightenment of seventeenth- and eighteenth-century Europe provides the political context for understanding Buddhist enlightenment as the simultaneous, coequal, perfection of rationality, religiosity, morality, and humanity, beyond politics.

The next three chapters provide a set of case studies for investigating the hegemonic workings of enlightenment. All three draw their major examples from the Ajanta caves, a western Indian archaeological site dating to the fifth century CE. We might see these three as elements in a postmodern microhistory of Ajanta. The first and fifth chapters, by contrast, mention Ajanta only in passing; the sixth, not at all.

Chapter 2 treats the hegemony of enlightenment—conceived as a source of exceptional universal value—over the discursive construction of Ajanta's spatiality. In 1983 Ajanta was enrolled on UNESCO's list of World Heritage Monuments as a site possessing "exceptional universal value." What was involved in the transvaluation of Ajanta from isolated archaeological site into locus of universality?

Chapter 3 explores the hegemony of intentionality over the discursive construction of Ajanta's temporality. Based upon inscriptions and art created in ancient times, Ajanta is invariably identified as a Buddhist site. This chapter wonders how Ajanta's identity might change if one narrates its history in terms of its graffiti, since graffiteers who scratched their names onto Ajanta's walls demonstrate no interest in Buddhism.

Chapter 4 explores the hegemony of a "scriptural anthropology" (a view of humanity as necessarily and universally religious) over the discursive construction of Ajanta's materiality. In the nineteenth century, archaeologists expected that the distinctions between Buddhism, Hinduism, and Jainism were so thoroughgoing that a few simple criteria might allow them to distinguish instantly Buddhist artifacts from those that are Hindu or Jain. What truth about religion made them think this project could succeed? What truth about humanity?

Chapter 5 integrates the major problems outlined in the first chapter with specific solutions offered in the subsequent three. Thus whereas Chapter 1 considered Enlightenment in its European forms, Chapter 5 considers how contemporary Buddhists assert hegemony through enlightenment-claims. Indeed, many Buddhists today are ambivalent about being called "Buddhists." They observe that the buddha did not teach Buddhism but dharma; and that following dharma is not the same as belonging to a religion. For them, the word "Buddhism" signifies a religion for folk who remain ensnared by a superstitious concern for gods and other mythological errors. Of course, they hold off Buddhism with one hand, only to lay hold on it with the other. In their eyes, they alone are Śākyamuni's true followers. As seekers of dharma who reject the supernatural, these modern Buddhists also represent themselves as empiricists, rationalists, and secularists. And they believe that the dharma, as rational and secular, provides the legitimate groundwork for a universal society of freedom and peace.

A brief conclusion, Chapter 6 proposes that religious tropes and religious institutions are incapable of eradicating the structural conditions that produce conflict; they are also unsuitable guides to managing conflict in a pluralistic world.

ACKNOWLEDGMENTS

This book has been a long time in coming. So many teachers and friends helped me along the way that I cannot acknowledge all by name. Still, several do deserve very special mention. Let me begin with Walter Spink, my Ajanta guru. Walter taught me to see beyond ideas, to the materiality of material objects. Thanks also to Luis Gómez, a master of Buddhism's complexities and nuance. Two friends who deserve my warmest gratitude are Chuck Prebish and John Strong. Neither man has borne a formal institutional obligation to me, yet both have been my constant advocates and benefactors. I would also like to acknowledge their assistance in the creation of *Beyond Enlightenment*: Chuck, as series editor for Routledge, John for his many fine suggestions as a reader.

There is no way *this* book could have been written had I not had the good fortune of being hired into UCSD's (University of California, San Diego) Literature Department. Where else would I have been encouraged to translate the historical study of ancient Buddhist caves into a general critique of the politics of religion? Particular thanks are due to Arthur Droge, Page Dubois, and Lisa Lowe, each of whom encouraged me to think beyond disciplinary boundaries. The university was generous with money and time, as were Mr and Mrs Warren Hellman, benefactors of the fellowship that bears their name. While I'm on the subject, the city of San Diego (or at least the geographical locality) also deserves mention. Most of the book was plotted during long runs along beaches and through parks. When "beyond disciplinary boundaries" veers toward "undisciplined" blame San Diego's sunshine.

Speaking of discipline, my parents David and Bernice Cohen tried to instill it sometimes, but not too often and not too much. Their love, acceptance, and support are the very cornerstones of this work.

Finally, and fully, there's Nancy. By the end of this work, a reader might be wondering whether nothing is sacred to the author. If there is one thing that could fit that category, it would have to be my love for Nancy. But love is not the half of it. I read her intelligent suggestions, her critical acumen, her writerly sensibility, and stylistic excellence on every page.

Yes, I have only myself to blame for the book's infelicities and errors.

1

A BENIGN INTRODUCTION

...at least do no harm.

(Hippocrates, *The Epidemics*, 1.2)

A trip to the bodhi tree

Did you know that approximately 90 percent of books in Los Angeles' Bodhi Tree Bookstore describe the buddha using the word "enlightened" rather than "awakened"?[1] Anyone familiar with English-language writings on Buddhism will already be aware that such a bias exists. But even an avid reader might be surprised by the magnitude of the imbalance. And for a reader of Sanskrit, the preference for "enlightened" must be especially puzzling as well.

I remember learning in graduate school that the basic denotation for *budh*—the Sanskrit root that gives us *buddha* (enlightened or awakened) and *bodhi* (enlightenment or awakening)—is to wake up or to recover consciousness. My professor presented "enlightenment" as an infelicitous translation and instructed his students to use "awakening" instead. This directive later found its way into print: Awakening is preferable to enlightenment because *bodhi* "is not the result of an 'illumination' as much as a process of realization, of coming to understand."[2] However, one should not understand Professor Gómez to be valorizing the literal over the metaphoric, or the real over the imaginary: to awaken to truth is no less metaphorical than to be enlightened by it. The issue, rather, has to do with the materiality of the two metaphors. The event-oriented connotations of enlightenment are less accurate, conceptually and etymologically, than those of process-oriented awakening. Be that as it may, my survey at the Bodhi Tree Bookstore demonstrated that Buddhism continues to be the eponymous religion of enlightenment. This book investigates the political context within which enlightenment holds such discursive power.

Beyond Enlightenment is not an intellectual history of native Indian doctrines concerning the cognitive state we call enlightenment. Nor is it primarily a linguistic history of "bodhi" and "buddha" in Sanskrit sources, or of "enlightenment" and "awakening" in English. What dimension of enlightenment, then, is its focus? Enlightenment is "the very basis on which the whole superstructure of

1

Buddhist developments has been raised," in the words of David Snellgrove, a historian of India and Tibet whose insights I have long valued.[3] This is a study of the ground beneath Snellgrove's architectural metaphor. What kind of bedrock does enlightenment provide for so-called "Buddhist developments"? It does certainly require a solid substratum for tantric antinomianism (e.g., "You should slay living beings; you should speak lying words; you should take what is not given; you should frequent others' wives") to stand steadily next to Pāli moralism (e.g., "The fool who does not perform good actions but commits many sins is reborn in hell after he dies").[4] Enlightenment is that ground. Enlightenment enables disparate and sometimes diametrically opposed doctrines, practices, mythologies, legitimations of power, cosmologies, ethoi, values, narratives, ways of life, and soteriologies to all be called "Buddhist." A discursive analysis of enlightenment brings one to the basis of Buddhism itself.

I was inspired to go to the Bodhi Tree Bookstore, to compare the usage of "enlightenment" and "awakening," after reading one of Jean Calvin's letters in which the theologian declared, "It is God alone who enlightens our minds to perceive His truth."[5] Of course, I had met the verbal root *enlighten* outside a specifically Buddhist context before. But Calvin's words jolted me. To name god as the sole source of enlightenment is hardly a Buddhist notion. Yet here was the translator of Calvin, like Buddhism's translators, using "enlighten" to mark the connection between human knowledge and the ultimate good. Some quick reconnaissance soon showed me that the trope of illumination or enlightenment frequently serves this function in Christian literature. Martin Luther also spoke of being enlightened by the Holy Spirit, and Matthew Tindal's *Christianity as Old as the Creation* described "a clear and distinct Light that enlightens all Men; and which, the Moment they attend to it, makes them perceive those eternal Truths, which are the Foundation of all our Knowledge."[6] That "enlightenment," a word I had long associated with Buddhism's essence, had a prior history is unremarkable. That I had not given this history any thought is, again, hardly noteworthy. That no one else had done so created a nice puzzle to solve.

The results were more intriguing than I could have hoped. Early Indologists had no consensus understanding of *buddha* or, still less, of *bodhi*. The 1801 edition of *Asiatick Researches* provides a nice example. One article that year saw Mr Joinville lament that he "made every inquiry, and [had] been informed that there is no etymology for the word Boudhou in the ancient languages of *Ceylon*."[7] A second writer, Captain Mahony, found better informants. His article teaches, "The word Bhooddha, in the *Palee* and *Singhalai* languages, implies, *Universal Knowledge or Holiness*."[8] Despite Joinville's and Mahony's inability to agree on the etymology of buddha, let alone its spelling, a convention did develop during the first half of the nineteenth century, in which buddha was translated as *intelligent* or *wise* or *sage*.[9] Bodhi, likewise, almost invariably came to be translated as *Intelligence* or *Supreme Intelligence*.[10]

Occasionally, light imagery did peek through. The earliest use of the English "enlighten" in a discussion of Buddhism belongs to the 1835 translation from

French of an article by Charles Neumann. Neumann wrote, "Shákya, having exhausted every species of science, received the name of Buddha, that is, the 'sage' or 'enlightened.' From hence, his followers have been termed Bauddhas, or Buddhists."[11] Likewise the following year, Brian Hodgson rendered a Sanskrit verse praising the primordial buddha, the *ādibuddha*: "By reason of the ten jnánas [i.e., ten types of gnosis], his soul is enlightened. He too is the enlightener of the ten jnánas." Yet in the same article, Hodgson explicitly defined the word "buddha" as "wise."[12]

We have to wait until an 1857 article in *The Times* for a thorough, even pointed, explanation for why "enlightened" is the preferred English translation for "buddha":

> Buddha himself went through the school of the Brahmans. He performed their penances, he studied their philosophy, and he at last claimed the name of "the Buddha," or "the Enlightened," when he threw away the whole ceremonial, with its sacrifices, superstitions, penances, and castes, as worthless, and changed the complicated systems of philosophy into a short doctrine of salvation.[13]

The Times published this article anonymously. In the same year, however, Max Müller reprinted it in a short book under his own name.[14] Müller's book received immediate attention; at least three publications from 1858 cite it. Two of these three also called the buddha "the enlightened," whereas the third called Müller "incompetent" and "not equal to [Buddhism's] severe and seemingly impossible abstractions."[15] After this swift reception, the vogue (if it even deserves that name) for "enlightened" apparently subsided. Then in 1867 Müller released the first volume of his *Chips from a German Workshop*, a collection of previously published articles. *Chips* reprinted *The Times'* piece as well as a second article, from *The Edinburgh Review*, that also directed readers to know the buddha as "the enlightened."[16] By the mid-1870s, it had become commonplace to call the buddha "enlightened." By the end of the 1880s, the terminologies of "enlightened" and "enlightenment" dominated the English-language literature on Buddhism.

Seeing the light in Müller's science of religion

I began my survey of nineteenth-century literature on Buddhism expecting to find that the popularization of *enlightenment* was the result of a gradual, decentralized change in usage rather than a forceful reimagination. Yet the latter is what Max Müller seems to have given us. Granted, no subsequent scholar named Müller as inspiring his use of "enlighten" in the same way that another referred back to Eugène Burnouf for his translation of "bodhi" as "intelligence."[17] There is no smoking gun here—just the publication of an influential book succeeded almost immediately by a sea change in translation. Nevertheless, Müller's preference for "enlightened" is worth thinking about further, not because he was a foremost scholar of Buddhism, but because he dominated the fields of comparative linguistics, comparative mythology, and comparative religion. Buddhism offered Müller *exempli gratia* for his pursuit of science in these disciplines. "Enlightened" is neither etymologically truer to the Sanskrit *buddha*, nor self-evidently better English than "wise," "supremely intelligent," or "awakened." But the imagination of the buddha as enlightened fit perfectly into Müller's science; it seems to have captured the minds of his readers and it has since become our own common sense.[18] Indeed, although Müller now has little direct sway over the study of religion, his indirect influence is patent. The modern study of religion, including Buddhism, works within a conceptual space stabilized by Müller's lifelong project to build a complete science of thought.[19]

This is hardly the place for a close analysis of Müller's life's work, still less the history of the study of religion post-Müller. But a quick summary of his intellectual project will serve as a neat counter against which to represent my own. As with any major thinker, Müller refined and amplified his views over the course of his career. Here I focus upon the preface to the first volume of *Chips from a German Workshop*, since this is the work that seems to have popularized *enlighten* as a Buddhist terminology.

One enters Max Müller's theory of religion by way of his theory of language. Language is the starting point, for Müller defined humanity by its capacity for rational thought: "Man means the thinker, and the first manifestation of thought is speech."[20] Müller believed in essences, but essences as manifest *in* history. That is to say, Müller was not simply a connoisseur of linguistic diversity. Rather, Müller expected that a scholar who could find order in the jumble of tongues would also be able to reach "backward from the most modern to the most ancient strata" at which he would discover "the very elements and roots of human speech...and with them the elements and roots of human thought."[21] Müller desired to reach the common roots and universal dimensions of language (in the singular), although he was resigned to the fact that this ideal, this pure mode of thought, never exists in a pristine form. Particular temporal expressions would be more or less close to the ideal. The ability to judge that degree of purity required the comparative study of multiple languages.

What was true of language, for Müller, held for religion as well. Religion suffused humanity's whole history, from its contemporary forms to the most ancient days, as "a succession of new combinations of the same radical elements."[22] Human beings were religious by nature. Indeed, the science of religion would be absurd unless scholars presupposed that a capacity for religion "formed part of the original dowry of the human soul."[23] If humans could not hear "the tongues of angels" (literally) then "religion itself would have remained an impossibility."[24] Müller saw this elemental religiosity as providing the firm foundation for every religion's special truths. A proper science of religion, accordingly, was dedicated to abstracting natural religion's "truly religious elements" from the "mythological crust" within which they were inevitably embedded: "the foreign worldly elements...and human interests [that] mar the simplicity and

4

purity."[25] Just as the science of language could deduce a fundamental logic and order in every speech, "even the most degraded," so the science of religion would look to the multiplicity of religious forms because through their comparative study the scientist could comprehend the divine purpose. As with languages, some religions were more authentic and pristine than others. And even within the history of a single religion there would be more or less ideally religious moments. Thus Müller articulated a general pattern for religious history: all religions are founded by superior men; all succumb to decay; yet all might be returned to their original purity through a due reformation.

> Without a constant return to its fountain head, every religion, even the most perfect, nay the most perfect on account of its very perfection, more even than others, suffers from its contact with the world, as the purest air suffers from the mere fact of its being breathed.[26]

This is why Müller was at pains to argue that the science of religion's cold, critical gaze must be directed toward Christianity no less than toward any other religion. The science of religion supports the ongoing reformation of Christianity, by giving believers the ability to know how far present forms have fallen from Jesus' pure intentions. But crucially for Müller, the selfsame tests that separate Christian gold from Christian dross could be used to assay Christianity's superiority over other religions. Thus his science was as much a tool for evangelism and missionizing as for reformation. It gave missionaries a language through which to lecture Brahmins and Buddhists, Zoroastrians and Muslims, on the present corruption of their religions too, so divergent from *their* founders' purities. Addressed in the objective language of science, reasonable Brahmins and reasonable Buddhists, reasonable Zoroastrians and reasonable Muslims, would comprehend that the singular source for their disparate revelations was really the one true god. Empowered by this knowledge, "the truth seeking soul," who must choose "between Christ and other Masters," would make the correct choice.[27] In this way, the science of religion would restore "to the whole history of the world, in its unconscious progress toward Christianity, its true and sacred character."[28]

Such is the scientific context within which Müller translated "buddha" as "the enlightened." Müller was a scholar careful about the meanings of words. And he was not stinting in his use of metaphors of light. He would "sweep away the cobwebs of false learning, and let in the light of real knowledge." In his anthropology, humans search after "light and truth." He hoped that his science would give missionaries the ability to find "any spark of true light" in barbarous forms of faith.[29] Seeing the light meant apprehending truth with intellectual clarity. Indeed, in a later work Müller even allowed that "Buddha himself appeals only to what we should call the inner light."[30] But Müller's ecumenism only went so far. For if light was truth, truth had but one single source, or so said Augustine of Hippo as cited by Müller: "What is now called the Christian religion ... was not absent from the beginning of the human race ... from which time [it was] the true religion."[31]

With the second edition of *Chips*, Müller added a citation from Justin Martyr to factor this equation in still more general terms. The italics are Müller's: "*They who have made or make the Logos or Reason the rule of their actions are Christians.*"[32]

Müller's use of "enlighten" made Buddhism more suitably Christian by making it more suitably religious by making it more suitably universal. To extrapolate the preceding discussion: In Müller's science to call the buddha, sitting beneath the Bodhi tree, *enlightened* was

- to imagine that human beings have a natural, innate capacity for religion;
- to imagine that Śākyamuni's fulfillment of that natural capacity transformed him into "the enlightened";
- to imagine that Śākyamuni's transformation belongs to a class of similar events enjoyed by other founders of the ancient religions of the world, all of whom were brimming with noble aspirations and yearning for truth;
- to imagine that this transformative event also holds the essence of Buddhism's own particular religiosity;
- to imagine that this transformative event provides an objective basis for judging the "Buddhistic" purity of Buddhism's historical manifestations;
- to imagine that, as is the case for other ancient religions of the world, the truths realized in this transformative event are often measurably at odds with the practices of those who profess to be his disciples;
- to imagine that the insights that transformed Śākyamuni into a buddha also made him a proto-Christian;
- to imagine that, as a branch of the science of religion, the scientific study of Buddhism would advance the world-historical project of "assign[ing] to Christianity its right place among the religions of the world."[33]

For the language of enlightenment to fulfill its discursive function in Müller's science, Śākyamuni had to be assimilated to Jesus as a religious founder, and Buddhism to Christianity as a religion. For us now, however, the chief problem with Müller's project is not its appropriation of the ideology of scientific objectivity to assert Christian hegemony. In fact, Müller tipped his hand rather quickly. The 1870 lectures that were the basis for his *Introduction to the Science of Religion* described that science as having two parts: comparative theology and theoretic theology.[34] To study man by looking for traces of divinity is hardly the practice of a *human* science. No, the chief problem with Müller's project now is that, leaving aside its Christian teleology, it requires one to presuppose that the category *religion* possesses an integrity and function that enables it to stand apart from Christianity and Buddhism, and thus to mediate between them. For someone who does not accept his discourse of universal, natural religiosity, every one of the other points implied by Müller's calling the buddha "enlightened" is also open to question. Indeed, I wonder about the whole enterprise of constituting religiosity as an object for science, even within the so-called human sciences: as religiosity, so enlightenment; and as religion, so too Buddhism. Given that enlightenment serves as the basis for the imagination of Buddhism as something that has an original integrity and purity, something that can be corrupted, something that can be reformed—must one presuppose the discourse of natural religiosity even to speak about Buddhism as an integral historical object? Can one accept that there is any such thing as Buddhism unless one accepts that human beings *are* religious; that enlightenment is not just a word or idea but a universal human potentiality? Unless one hears angels? Unless one accepts that there are angels to be heard?

At the heart of Müller's science is the quest for purity. Read the following statement: "Whenever we can trace back a religion to its first beginnings, we find it free from many of the blemishes that offend us in its later phases."[35] *Offend us?* With this strange deixis Müller reveals the political context within which *enlightenment* holds discursive power: the valorization of an impossible perfection matched by the repudiation of every all-too noticeable imperfection. Indeed, Buddhists describe the moment of enlightenment as the discovery of four truths, the first of which is *duḥkha*—pain, suffering, sorrow, in short, woeful imperfection. But what is wrong with being blemished and imperfect, with being marked by time, with reinventions that eschew the original? Let us imagine a scholar of religion who is not offended by impurity and thus opts out of Müller's *us*. How will that person study Buddhism beyond enlightenment?

Enlightenment does not translate *Aufklärung*

Max Müller served two gods. We already know of Müller's Christian faith. We also have his word that he fulfilled his professorial duties at Oxford, whether teaching German literature or the Science of Language, by "preaching Kant."[36] Müller confessed this philosophical faith in his preface to a translation of Immanuel Kant's *Critique of Pure Reason*, published in 1881 on its centenary anniversary. The *Critique* had been Müller's "constant companion" since he first read it as a schoolboy. Although Müller did not ask his readers to become "blind worshippers of Kant" themselves, he did name Kant as a seminal figure in the service of that same world-historical project to which Müller himself had dedicated his science of religion. Thus, to convince his English readership of the *Critique's* exceptional value, Müller cited a letter first addressed to Kant in 1789 by a prominent theologian of the day, Johann Heinrich Jung-Stilling:

> You are a great, a very great instrument in the hand of God.... your philosophy will work a far greater, far more general, and far more blessed revolution than Luther's Reform.... Your philosophy must therefore be eternal and unchangeable, and its beneficent effects will bring back the religion of Jesus to its original purity, when its only purpose was—holiness.[37]

Who was this Kant whom Müller worshiped and Jung-Stilling placed second to Jesus as an instrument of holiness? Could he really have been the same philosopher whose architectonic analysis of experience gave us such phrases as "the amphiboly of concepts of reflection" and "the transcendental unity of apperception"? Let us leave Müller for Kant. Using Müller, the previous section introduced *Beyond Enlightenment's* fundamental concern: the politics of natural religiosity as mediated through the term "enlightenment." What is the political context within which enlightenment holds discursive power? Kant will lead us forward. This current section offers some insight into the lexical meaning of "enlightenment." The next section will address the issue of *political context* directly. And the section following that will consider enlightenment's *discursive power*. That will bring us to the midpoint of this benign introduction, after which the focus shifts to Buddhism, India, and the chapters that follow.

In 1783, the *Berlinische Monatsschrift* published an article in which Johan Friedrich Zöllner, a theologian, questioned whether nuptial ceremonies require a religious component or whether they might be purely civil affairs. But it was a question Zöllner posed in a footnote that captured Immanuel Kant's interest: *What is Enlightenment (Aufklärung)?*[38] In the following year, the *Berlinische Monatsschrift* published Kant's reply, a short article that is now an eighteenth-century classic. Kant's answer to Zöllner began with a series of definitions:

> *Enlightenment is the human being's emergence from his self-incurred minority. Minority* is the inability to make use of one's own understanding without direction from another. This minority is *self-incurred* when its cause lies not in lack of understanding but in the lack of resolution and courage to use it without direction from another. *Sapere aude!* Have the courage to make use of your *own* understanding! is thus the motto of Enlightenment.[39]

Among all the forms of self-incurred immaturity, the "most harmful," in Kant's view, was a lack of courage in relation to religious matters.[40] Nothing was more unEnlightened than the unquestioning, puerile acceptance of guidance offered by clergymen and Church.

Kant defined Enlightenment. Müller preached Kant. Müller translated "buddha" as "the enlightened." The chain of reasoning seems clear: by calling the buddha enlightened, Müller was also portraying him as an *Aufklärer*, a man appropriate for the modern age, which Kant himself called an Age of Enlightenment.[41] Indeed, glance back to Müller's 1857 inauguration of this usage (see page 3). Note that the buddha received the name "enlightened" precisely when he rejected the accepted wisdom and established rituals of Brahminism in favor of a doctrine of salvation through self-understanding. For Müller, *sapere aude!* could have been Siddhārtha Gotama's motto as well.

These coincidences noted, however, we should also beware of reading too much into this Kantian connection. First, 1865 was the first year in which *Aufklärung* was translated as Enlightenment, in the sense of the Age of Enlightenment—and there it was used as a term of derision.[42] So when Müller characterized the buddha as enlightened in 1857 he could not have been referring back to this German antecedent, or to eighteenth-century philosophy *in nuce*.[43] To make this point even more clearly, we need only open the 1869 German translation of Müller's *Chips*, authorized by Müller himself. In every case, "the enlightened" is translated as "der Erleuchtete," not "der Aufklärer."[44] Our linguistic inheritance, in short, should not be misconstrued as Müller's linguistic prescience.

The verbs *erleuchten* and *aufklären* are not interchangeable synonyms in German.[45] Still, it is felicitous that both were translated into English as e/Enlighten.[46] For European intellectual developments during the seventeenth and eighteenth centuries did profoundly influence later centuries' scholarship on India's history. It is difficult to say whether David Snellgrove (see page 2) would have metaphorized enlightenment as the ground on which Buddhist developments were built had Enlightenment thinkers not articulated an idea of natural religion, which Müller himself called "eternal religion," and the "rock" on which super-natural religion must be built if it is not to collapse: "Supernatural religion with-out natural religion is a house built on sand."[47] If scholars conceive Śākyamuni's enlightenment as the indispensable antecedent to Buddhist developments, then just as surely the European Enlightenment was indispensable for the genesis of the academic field, Buddhist Studies. For scholars, enlightenment is an Enlightenment phenomenon. To understand what it means to go beyond enlight-enment, accordingly, we must also consider the other shore of the Enlightenment.

What is enlightenment? Political context

Beyond spiritual attainment, the term Enlightenment denotes a period in European intellectual history, reaching from the seventeenth through the eighteenth centuries. At its culmination, the Enlightenment might have been the first instance in which a cohesive body of philosophers and artists represented themselves as standing at the brink of history, aware of their own modernity, motivated as much by an ethical imperative to build the future as by a love for the wisdom of the past. Theirs was an ethics of earth-bound freedom, whose principles are enumerated by historian Peter Gay: "freedom from arbitrary power, freedom of speech, freedom of trade, freedom to realize one's talents, freedom of aesthetic response, freedom, in a word, of moral man to make his own way in the world."[48] As Gay's exuberant description makes clear, the Enlightenment lends itself to metanarrative clichés and yet cannot be easily comprehended within them. The Enlightenment was international, with each country producing unique literary forms and intellectual modalities. Its leading figures held diverse professions; they were journalists and activists, courtiers, econ-omists, physicians, and even philosophers seeking to change the world as well as to understand it. All, perhaps, fancied themselves freethinkers. Thus Diderot and d'Alembert's *Encyclopédie* presents Enlightenment philosophes as men who

> have dared to overthrow the sacred bounds set down by religion and have
> broken the fetters that faith placed on their reason. They are proud of
> having rid themselves of the prejudices concerning religion which their

upbringing instilled in them, and they look with disdain on their fellows as being weak men, slavish spirits and pusillanimous souls who let themselves be frightened by the consequences of unbelief, who dare not for an instant to step outside the circle of established truths or follow new paths, and whose minds are dulled by the yoke of superstition.[49]

Yet reason was not an end in itself. The longer essay from which this passage is extracted stated that for a philosophe "civil society is his only god."[50] The philosophes saw the intellect as an instrument of politics, but there was hardly a consensus on how the mind's light should inflame the body's dynamic. Kant's answer to the question, What is Enlightenment?, concluded, "Argue as much as you will and about whatever you will; only obey!"[51] And Voltaire's *Candide* finished with its hero turning his attention from metaphysics to a grounded determination to cultivate his garden. Yet America's and France's revolutionaries were Enlightenment men. The Declaration of Independence and the *Déclaration des droits de l'homme et du citoyen* both crystallized Enlightenment political thought.

This is not the place for a general introduction to the Enlightenment. I would focus, rather, on the period's political anthropology; in particular, politics tied to the naturalization of religion as a pre-political or apolitical mark of the human essence. Scattered among the previous citations from Kant's short essay, we have glimpsed the limns of that subject. Enlightened man encounters his world with a mature intellect that does not accept truths presented by clergy or king out of mere deference to authority. He reasons by himself toward the universal dicta that are the basis of moral action. He speaks his mind in public but performs his duties without complaint. He is a verbal warrior in defense of the true, the good, and the beautiful: equal parts philosopher, statesman, and saint.

"What is Enlightenment?" offers a cartoon of the Aufklärer. A more fully articulated understanding requires one to open Kant's major works, the *Critique of Pure Reason* and *Critique of Practical Reason*. I take my lead here from Étienne Balibar, a philosopher who, in the course of tracing a genealogy of political-man from the Greek classical to the premodern Christian to the modern secularist, names Kant as the inventor of modern subjectivity.[52] The threshold to modern secularism was crossed when Enlightenment thinkers disentangled political citizenship from theological dicta; or in Balibar's words, "when the principle of a secular and democratic social organization was declared" in the late eighteenth and early nineteenth centuries.[53] If a citizen of Augustine's City of God willingly subjected himself to the soul's commands that spoke to him from inside his own depths, for Kant the political subject himself legislated as a citizen. It was the fact that the law was an expression of the citizen's own will that rendered him obedient to its dictates. Still, as we shall see, the same political anthropology that made the citizen a rational legislator also made him a religious believer. For Kant, secular politics was neither areligious nor irreligious.

Before Kant, epistemologists were vexed by the need to explain how sense faculties apprehend external objects and how the mind can judge whether its own inner objects, that is, ideas, truly correspond to those external things. Kant was satisfied with Locke's and Hume's claims that knowledge begins with contact between the mind and the external world. Yet their explanations of that encounter were wholly unsatisfactory. In fact, Kant saw these empiricists as half wrong. Yes, human knowledge does require sense experience. "But although all our cognition commences *with* experience, yet it does not on that account all arise *from* experience."[54] Sense experience never operates in an unmediated fashion. What seems to be direct perception of worldly objects is, in fact, always already an amalgam of sense impressions *and* intellection.

Kant spent the greater part of the *Critique of Pure Reason* clarifying the preconditions for sense experience: how the human mind must be structured in order to produce the world that it perceives. The details of that structure do not interest us. Here, it is sufficient to recognize that Kant drew a general distinction between *phenomena* and *noumena*. Our mental lives are oriented toward the former: *phenomena* are apparential things and experiences that have been categorized or mentally constructed. *Noumena*, by contrast, are objects of pure understanding; things as they are in-themselves, before they are categorized or mentally constructed. While, in a sense, noumena are real, Kant was careful to point out that they are real as a "boundary concept," delimiting the sphere of the knowable.[55] Human beings lack a mental faculty to intuit noumena directly, and thus noumena can never be valid objects of positive knowledge. Noumena can never be treated as *facts*.

This inability to cognize noumena directly would seem to create a dilemma. For if phenomena are processed before they become objects of knowledge, then there can be no absolute epistemic basis for distinguishing reality (valid phenomena) from fantasy (skewed constructions). How can we reach consensus about the truth or falsity of our ideas and experiences? Solipsism is, in fact, not the norm. For Kant posited that the cognitive structures shaping personal experience are themselves universal and transpersonal. Every person necessarily constructs the world of experience for himself, but every rational person constructs precisely the same world in precisely the same way.

Kant published the *Critique of Pure Reason* in 1781, and revised it in 1787. One year later he published the *Critique of Practical Reason*, which treats *morality* as an entailment of the distinction between noumena and phenomena. The first *Critique* introduced noumena: transcendental objects that we cannot know directly, but that are logically necessary for us to experience a world of external phenomena. The second *Critique* proposed that human beings likewise have a noumenal dimension, a subjective quiddity that also cannot be cognized through the senses. Crucially, although Kant would not allow positive statements of fact about objective noumena, he does make a positive claim about subjective noumena. The fact that we cannot know ourselves in-ourselves means that we *must* understand ourselves to be free. As a noumenon, every individual person is transcendentally *free and unconditioned*. Indeed, Kant goes so far as to call this elemental human freedom, "the *keystone* of the whole structure of a system of pure reason."[56]

Transcendental freedom, in turn, fixes the onus of moral responsibility. For Kant considered the movement from the noumenal to the phenomenal, from human potentiality to concrete reality, to be a matter of volition. Every goal we consciously pursue, every motivated act, is predicated upon *choosing* a principle for action. Morality is another name for that choice. "What is essential in every determination of the will by the moral law is that, as a free will . . . it is determined solely by the law."[57] Morality is the intentional subjection of the individual will to universal rational principles; the elevation of objective duty over subjective happiness in the pursuit of the highest good. A man is moral when he freely allows universal laws derived through reason to determine how he acts. Just as an individual is an epistemic subject insofar as he participates in a transpersonal world of coherent experience, likewise an individual is a moral subject insofar as he engages in a transpersonal world of rational action. Kant attributed the moral law's objectivity to the fact that it is obligatory "for everyone having reason and will."[58]

Here we reach the crucial conjunction: Kant's rational secular man is also *necessarily* a religious man. That is, the *Critique of Pure Reason* stipulates that noumenal entities, such as god and the immortal soul, can never participate in the world of intersubjective facticity, for humans cannot intuit them unmediatedly or experience them mediatedly as phenomena. Nevertheless, the *idea* of god plays a crucial subjective role for practical, moral reason. The belief in god's existence, together with the existence of an immortal soul and transcendentally free will, are necessary, rational beliefs entailed by morality defined as the rational use of the will. "It is morally necessary to assume the existence of God," Kant asserts.[59] Why? Simply put, one cannot direct one's will toward the highest good, that is, act morally, unless one really accepts that such a good exists. "The postulate of the possibility of the *highest derived good* . . . is likewise the postulate of the reality of a *highest original good*, namely the existence of God."[60] This is *not* to say that non-believers can be forced to avow a belief in god (soul; freedom), or be deprived of political rights if they refuse to do so. In fact, one cannot require or legislate that any individual hold any particular belief. To believe or not believe must be a free act. "The human being must make or have made *himself* into whatever he is or should become in a moral sense, good or evil. These two [characters] must be an effect of his free power of choice."[61] But an individual who does not postulate the real existence of god, an immortal soul, and god-given freedom of the will, cannot be a fully moral human being. Lacking these rational beliefs, an individual cannot possibly pursue the ultimate moral aim. Thus, Kant repeated several times, both in *The Critique of Practical Reason* and *Religion Within the Boundaries of Mere Reason*, that "morality . . . inevitably leads to religion, and through religion it extends itself to the idea of a mighty moral lawgiver outside the human being."[62] "The moral law leads . . . to religion"; religion defined as "the recognition of all duties as divine commands."[63]

The scope for religion as described by Kant is greatly circumscribed when compared with its place as envisioned by theologians like Augustine and Calvin. It might appear that the rationally religious man, like his premodern Christian brethren, still subjugates himself before divine ordinances that exist independently of himself. But for Kant, the moral law is treated *as if divine* because it is rational, not accepted as rational because it *really is* divine. Religious claims can be subjective and pragmatic, but never independent, objective, or true matters of fact. Religiosity is allowed to function unimpededly within the Enlightenment's *novus ordo saeculorum* insofar as its power is directed to the private realm of conscience, commitment, and belief. Religious institutions may succor, edify, influence decisions, and suggest answers to ultimate questions. They may not require followers to swear any contract or oath that impedes collective progress toward Enlightenment; they may not require the suspension of doubt or rational public discourse. Nor may they assert control over the coercive instruments of political government. For in the modern world, human beings actualize their humanity, becoming Enlightened subjects, only when they have the wisdom to accept the responsibilities of political citizenship. In return for the privatization of religiosity, no citizen is forced to relinquish or deny his own personal beliefs, even if considerably outside the mainstream. Purely internal, this confessional diversity will not disrupt the regular working of government. The secular state becomes a public sphere within which antagonisms that might arise due to personal distinctions vis-à-vis gender, ethnicity, economic status, philosophy, and of course religious faith or dogma, are set aside in favor of a single shared identity (*citizenship*), and will toward the common good. Secularism thus-conceived is actualized in democratic citizenship, the political harmonization of a pluralistic society.

Kant's citizen is the rational animal who becomes a moral animal who becomes a religious animal. This might seem to be a mere vestigial trace of Christian particularism within his universal schema. In fact, universalization of the Christian-particular is the condition of possibility for Kant's cosmopolitical imaginary. However minimal religion's remaining presence may be, religion remains absolutely necessary. For Kant, one cannot be a full-fledged secular citizen—that is, a knower who freely enters into a cosmopolitical compact for the common good with other knowers—unless one already postulates that an omnipotent, omniscient, omnipresent, omnibeneficent god exists; that this god created human beings with an immortal soul (i.e., "the *existence* and personality of the same rational being continuing *endlessly*"), so that they could progress toward moral perfection; and that this god granted his creatures the freedom to make that progress of their own volition.[64]

When Étienne Balibar describes modern subjectivity as Kant's *invention*, he stands only a step away from the hyperbole of Max Müller and Johann Heinrich Jung-Stilling, for whom Kant was second only to Jesus as an agent of divine truth. One cannot attribute the complex entanglement of reason, morality, religiosity, and politics to Kant alone, yet there can be no doubt of its power from the nineteenth century to the present. Nowhere is this knot more capably disentangled than in Karl Marx's "On the Jewish Question" (1844), a critical review of Bruno Bauer's *Die Judenfrage*. In that day Germany was an expressly Christian state; Jews were required to obey laws born of a theology and tradition they expressly rejected. Bauer thus asked whether Jews deserve special release from state regulations regarding religion. His answer: a clear *no*. For Bauer, all Germans were enchained equally by the politics of religious prejudice. The important work was not to liberate Jews from Christian laws, but to liberate all human beings from religious prejudice—to abolish religion itself. Marx argued, in contrast, that Bauer's solution was superficial: religious freedom does not necessarily translate into political freedom, and the latter is what matters. In the modern secular state (North America being Marx's principal example), religion is not a matter of public regulation but a private concern of each individual. Thus, Marx observed,

> The division of a human being into a *public man* and a *private man*, the *displacement* of religion from the state into civil society, this is not a stage of political emancipation but its *completion*; this emancipation therefore neither abolishes the *real* religiousness of man, nor strives to do so.[65]

Pay particular attention to the fact that Marx himself emphasized the word *real* (*wirkliche*). What does it mean for human beings to have a *real religiousness* that cannot be touched by governmental power? It means that the transition from Christian citizenship—in which the mechanisms of religious and political power are at parity—to that of the Enlightenment ideal—in which the secular public is discontinuous with the religious private—required a reimagination of human interiority. In the modern age, religion is not produced by a transcendent god speaking discipline and truth using a human's inner voice. Through the Reformation, humans were supernaturally religious; with the Enlightenment they became naturally so. Religiosity became an anthropological constant, concomitant with reason, and thus an object suitable for scientific analysis. We have already seen Max Müller's science of religion. His contemporary, Pierre Daniel Chantepie de la Saussaye, described that science's element with great concision: "religion is the specific and common property of mankind."[66] There is no place for a human being outside and apart from a system of religious classification. Thus a contemporary sociologist, Peter Berger, proposes that "an agnostic or even an atheist philosopher may well agree" that the statement, " 'the religious impulse ... has been a perennial feature of humanity' ... is not a theological statement but an anthropological one."[67] Berger uses nice rhetoric: his "may well" softly whispers away any dissent from his position.

In short, Marx's statement that political emancipation does not abolish man's "*real* religiousness" alerts us to the fact that in the Enlightenment humanity itself became a new species, *Homo religiosus*. Enlightened citizenship—secular citizenship—requires that human beings possess an elemental faculty of religiosity closely tied to their faculty of rationality. And since the postulation of god is a necessary precondition for legitimate participation in the political arena, that belief must itself be pre-political or apolitical. *God, properly conceived, is not a political subject/object* — this is an unequivocally politicized articulation of divinity. Indeed, when Marx used the positive statement "*real* religiousness" to characterize the thing preserved in political emancipation, was he not witness to the fact that innate religiosity has become a political form throughly mystified in Enlightenment thought? What irony that even an antireligious thinker would idealize religiosity as apolitical, and hypothesize a politics within which that ideal is actualized?

This is a real problem: the logic whereby real religiousness is idealized as pre-political or apolitical. Now even an atheist must be an inner Christian to be a legitimate citizen of a secular state. Apropos, *The New Yorker* published this short poem of Czeslaw Milosz in tribute upon the writer's death:

> If there is no God,
> Not everything is permitted to man.
> He is still his brother's keeper
> And he is not permitted to sadden his brother,
> By saying that there is no God.[68]

How has the denial of god's existence become a singularly inhuman act, a sin against humanity?

The Enlightenment provides the political context for understanding Buddhist enlightenment, with its theorization of a natural religiosity that has the unsettling political status of being a human characteristic that lies beyond the political. This idea of a generic religiosity that is natural to humanity and is constitutively apolitical is the transcendental condition for a secularism in which religion appears to be *analytically* separable from politics, and politics appears to be *functionally* separable from religion. Enlightenment is the simultaneous, coequal, perfection of rationality, of religiosity, of morality, of humanity—beyond politics. This perceived apoliticality is the political context within which the word "enlightenment" holds discursive power.

What is enlightenment? Discursive power

It is a felicitous accident that although words derived from *aufklären* and *erleuchten* are not synonymous in German they were translated into English with the same verbal root. For the English speaker this makes *e/Enlightenment* a tremendously rich word. Enlightenment's semantic field includes several Sanskritic valences (intellection, wisdom, liberation), other values associated with the Protestant Reformation (anti-clericalism, guiding providence, divine inspiration, salvation), and still others that evoke the European Enlightenment (modernity, rationalism, science, secular emancipation). It would seem that e/Enlightenment is crammed full of significance. In semiological terms, enlightenment is a polyvalent symbol. However, this semantic surfeit allows us to treat it under another rubric, one from the field of poststructuralist discourse theory that I find rather more useful. The word "enlightenment" also functions as what Ernesto Laclau calls an *empty signifier*, "a signifier without a signified."[69] If the previous section explored the matter of enlightenment's political context, it still remains to consider what it would mean for this word to have *discursive power*. This latter entails understanding enlightenment as an empty signifier.

The theorization of empty signifiers is central to the work of Ernesto Laclau, who, over the past two decades, has refined how we think about *hegemony*. For Laclau hegemony "is more than a useful concept: it defines the very terrain in which a political relation is actually constituted."[70] As such it is a matter worth careful attention. What would it mean for enlightenment to be a signifier without a signified? And how might such an odd misconfiguration provide the very groundwork of a political terrain? How does enlightenment establish hegemonic relations? Cognate questions fill Laclau's corpus of writings. But let us take an answer from his short essay, "Why do Empty Signifiers Matter to Politics?"[71]

The essay begins with Laclau's oblique definition of the empty signifier, followed by his protestation that empty signifiers ought not be confused with the more commonly encountered polyvalent symbols, which might be merely equivocal or ambiguous. Polyvalence can be exemplified by a snippet of conversation overheard in a restaurant: "There is a profound connection between enlightenment and freedom." Is this a statement about Zen doctrine, or European history, or the touch of the Holy Spirit? The signified is indefinite here, not because the words enlightenment and freedom lack referents, but because the listener lacks a context within which to be precise in the identification of those referents. Ambiguity in this case is easily remedied: when listening to private conversations at adjoining tables, pay better attention.

When one considers enlightenment as an empty signifier, by contrast, the sound ən'līt°nmənt will still call the listener's ear to the possibility of meaning, but there will be no particular object to which that meaning can be attached. How does this work? Laclau reminds his readers of elementary structural linguistics as articulated by Ferdinand de Saussure. Saussure taught that a word's significance is not determined solely by its correspondence to an object "out there," but by its place within a system of linguistic difference. Linguistic value is relational. One tangible example comes from the game of chess.[72] If a rook is lost from a chess set, another object can be substituted. Any arbitrary thing can be a rook as long as the players agree on the substitution, and as long as this new rook is distinguishable from pawns, kings, and so on. The rook-piece does not possess intrinsically rookish qualities, but is a rook by virtue of its differentiation from other pieces. Thus there is an arbitrary relationship between the signifieds (pieces' functions) and the signifiers (pieces).

The arbitrariness of the signifier–signified relationship is offset, however, by the relative stability of external relationships among signs as elements in a system. In Laclau's words, "the totality of language is involved in each act of signification."[73] This external or systemic relationship, in turn, has two properties. First it is totalizing. Were there no totality, no game of chess, then it would be meaningless to identify this or that piece of plastic as a chessman. Were there no totality, no language, then the identification of this or that sound as an English word (for instance) would be absurd. Second, the rules and conventions that create a systemic totality also limit arbitrariness. Although any object can serve as a rook, rookitude itself is precise because chess' rules are precise. The rook-piece cannot move any which way. To slide a rook on the diagonal is to play a game other than chess. Indeed, every legitimate move must be defined before the white pawn can make the first move, for it is only in relation to that totality of possible moves that we can determine whether any particular move is legal vis-à-vis the game. Again Laclau, "the totality is essentially required—if the differences did not constitute a system, no signification at all would be possible."[74] Or again, "the systematicity of the system is a direct result of the exclusionary limit."[75] And this brings us, finally, to the empty signifier: the signifier that functions as an exclusionary limit because it signifies systemic totality rather than any particular meaning.

God, dharma, freedom, rationality, truth, enlightenment—all function as empty signifiers insofar as they seem to be bursting with significance while simultaneously seeming to be irreducible to temporally determinate meanings. Although they have the formal properties of a Saussurian signifier, they represent no particular signified. Rather, meaningful*ness* is their meaning. They have the meta-linguistic function of marking a subject as universally significant.

Consider Voltaire's definition of *theist* from his *Philosophical Dictionary*:[76]

> The theist is a man firmly persuaded of the existence of a Supreme Being, as good as He is powerful, who has formed all beings with extension, vegetating, sentient and reflecting; who perpetuates their species, who punishes crimes without cruelty, and rewards virtuous actions with kindness.

For Voltaire, mere belief in the existence of a good, just, and powerful deity "is the most ancient and the most widespread" of religions. Voltaire's theist propounds only these common notions, and nothing more. He avers no further metaphysical knowledge concerning the supreme *theos'* attributes or plans. "The theist does not know how God punishes, how he protects, how he pardons, for he is not reckless enough to flatter himself that he knows how God acts, but he knows that God acts and that He is just." And because the theist affirms god's good existence but advances no theories about god's actions and plans, the theist "does not embrace any of the sects, all of which contradict each other." Sectarianism develops when particular, contingent dogmas become the bases for social identity. The theist, by contrast, is "reconciled in this principle with the rest of the universe," because he holds only universal, necessary beliefs. Thus, the theist "speaks a language that all peoples understand" and "counts all wise men as his brethren."

Following Saussure, one might call the theist's elemental religiosity a systemic convention. Laclau would explain it as an "exclusionary limit," a basis for articulating both equivalence and difference. This theology establishes a logic of equivalence: the proponents of a good and powerful *theos* who stay within the bounds of Voltaire's definition, whether ancients or moderns, whether residents of Peking or Cayenne, all are equal *as theists*. "The systematicity of the system is a direct result of the exclusionary limit."[77] The empty signifier, *theist*, takes on social force only to the extent that nominal Muslims, Christians, and Hindus willingly compromise their individuating dogmas in favor of a single shared belief. A Muslim, a Christian, or a Vaiṣṇava who mandates the acceptance of a superordinate theological proposition—*theos'* final revelation was spoken to Muhammad in Arabic; *theos* became his own son, and freed humanity from the taint of original sin; *theos* loves his every disciple as Rādhā, with whom he dances in the forest on autumn evenings—is not a theist. As the condition of possibility for the system, this exclusionary limit is the locus of hegemony, for to control this limit is to control systemic identity.

Voltaire's *theist* provides an apt example of an empty signifier, though not a particularly charged one. So let us take another, Max Müller's use of *Christian*, which is more fraught and less neat. On the one hand, Müller willingly admits that Christian Churches can be as corrupt as any other temporal organization. Like Buddhism, Islam, and every other religion, institutionalized Christianity must be reformed and purified on occasion. Yet, on the other hand, *Christian* is Müller's name for "that religion which is the root of all religions, and of which every historical religion is but an imperfect expression."[78] Here, *as if* emptied of all determinate content, "Christian" becomes a signifier for pure religious positivity. Thus Müller found Justin Martyr's equation of Christianity with rationality so important that he added it to the second edition of *Chips from a German Workshop* (see, page 6).[79]

Likewise, for much of his adult life Müller attempted to convince the leaders of India's Brahmo Samaj to accept the name of Christian.[80] Founded by Ram Mohun Roy in 1828, Brahmo Samaj was a movement for religious and social reform, best remembered for its campaigns against image worship, polytheism, casteism, sati, child marriage, and female infanticide. Roy acknowledged Jesus as a teacher of timeless wisdom and representative of spiritual perfection, but would not accept him as uniquely wise or uniquely perfect, the Son of the Trinity. This rejection of Trinitarian theology was seconded by later Brahmo Samaj leaders. Thus when Müller entreated Keshab Chandra Sen to accept Christ in 1881, Sen answered, "I have always disclaimed the Christian name, and will not identify myself with the Christian Church, for I have set my face completely against the popular doctrine of Christ's divinity." To which Müller replied, "If you had lived in the first century, you would have been a disciple of Christ."[81] Or again, Müller lectured Sen's successor, Pratap Majumdar, "If you accept His teachings as they are recorded, you are a Christian."[82] This, despite the fact that Majumdar expressed his personal distaste for the name of Christian. For Müller these two statements were correlative: "There never was a false god, nor was there ever a false religion," and simultaneously, "The whole history of the world" is an "unconscious progress towards Christianity, its true and sacred character."[83] The pure Christianity of Christ, in addition to being sacred and true, is also the place of *logos* and the Infinite. As an empty signifier, *Christian* delimits and concretizes Müller's values, but in so doing it also excludes. Müller thus framed his once and future pure Christianity in discursive opposition to those phenomena he would keep out: dogmatism, mythology, vain symbols, and ceremonies, as well as other particular religions. This pattern of inclusions and exclusions "fills" Müller's empty signifier. Per Laclau, "to hegemonize something is exactly to carry out this filling function.... The strategies of this filling is what politics is about."[84]

The underlying point is simple enough: a game, a religion, a society, a system will have an identity to the extent that a barrier delimits the inside from outside. The barrier itself is hardly as simple. It provides an identity only insofar as it creates an equivalence among everything on the inside, but excludes, devalues, and thus makes a potential antagonist of everything that does not participate in that order. Thus abstract bases for identity, like *theist*, *Christian*, and *enlightened* mark intrinsic claims of normativity.

This structure helps to clarify the normalization of the modern secular subject as a religious subject, discussed in the previous section. A principle of internal religiosity, be it called faith or spirituality or enlightenment, is presented as natural to *all* reasonable human beings. Indeed, even a principled atheism must be a crypto-theology. As "rules" for being human, enlightenment and spirituality are totalizing. Any specific delimitation of their significance by reference to a positive content will forestall that infinitude. Thus for an abstraction to limit, exclude, and yet identify, it must serve solely, in Laclau's words, as a "simple principle of positivity—pure being."[85] Recall the god of Voltaire's theist: good, just, existent, and nothing more because that is sufficient. As a principle of pure positivity, Voltaire's god can subsume other gods without number into its circle of equivalence. For a theist, Allah and buddha are two names among the *theos'* infinite names. Muslims and Buddhists are brothers as theists insofar as they are willing to empty their divinities of overt, specific, and historically determined characteristics. Max Müller locates all other religions within the pure positivity of Jesus' simple Christian truths in precisely the same way. And yet, of course, *theist* and *Christian* always already are specific and historically delimited—they remain signifiers, even when treated as empty. So too *enlightenment*.

Thus the pernicious politics of hegemony: We call those people zealots who mistake the logic of infinitude for necessity, and then act on that imagined necessity as a moral imperative: *Everybody who can be brought into the order, must be! For their own good!* This is why Laclau has proposed that hegemony "defines the very terrain in which a political relation is actually constrained."[86]

The term *hegemony* is most closely associated with the lexicon of Antonio Gramsci, who, over long hours in prison, turned his attention to the question of why international socialism had failed. Marx had predicted that working men and women would recognize that their common interests oppose those of their employers, understand that they are a numerical majority, and unite in revolution. Why did they not rise up, and what lessons could be taken from this failure? The logic of hegemony was the key. Hegemony names the pivot-point of subordination/ domination, whereby the politically weak accept the values and goals of their dominators as their own. If the proletariat did not revolt, it was not because their passions were quelled by a fear of bullets, but because they did not think of themselves as less than free. They did not feel, and perhaps could not even imagine, a division between their bosses' welfare and their own. In Gramsci's words, hegemony is seen where "the great masses of the population" give their " 'spontaneous' consent ... to the general direction imposed on social life by the dominant fundamental group."[87] Spontaneous, here, is metonymic with natural, commonsensical, and legitimate—the fact that Gramsci ironizes it between quotes is crucial. In a sense, *Beyond Enlightenment* is an extended meditation on those quotation marks.

As a category of analysis, hegemony highlights the mutuality of epistemology, social identity, and power. The systematic totality of intellectual forces that function to create and enforce the consensual acceptance of a particular status quo itself creates a group of people who conceive of themselves as members of a unified community or class because they share that consensus. The category of hegemony thus subverts the expectation that there are natural classes of people, whose individual members all naturally share identity and goals by virtue of shared custom, nationality, history, tradition, belief, biology, or socioeconomic status. Identity is an effect, not a cause, of politics. This needs to be remembered every time we think that black Republican and gay Mormon are oxymorons, like college girls who disdain "feminazis" even as they expect that the corporate world offers equal pay for equal work.

The empty signifiers discussed so far have appeared relatively benign vis-à-vis twenty-first century North America. But let us be clear: Christianity as "filled" by Tom DeLay is structurally equivalent to Voltaire's theism and Müller's Christianity. Indeed, in all world history there may be no example of hegemonic filling to rival a speech made on April 12, 2002 by DeLay (at the time, the third ranking Republican member of the United States House of Representatives):

> Christianity offers the only viable, reasonable, definitive answer to the questions of "Where did I come from?" "Why am I here?" "Where am I going?" "Does life have any meaningful purpose?" ... Only Christianity offers a comprehensive worldview that covers all areas of life and thought, every aspect of creation. Only Christianity offers a way to live in response to the realities that we find in this world—only Christianity.[88]

DeLay would fill all the world with Christianity and nought else. Elsewhere in this speech, DeLay explains why he actively crusaded to impeach President William Jefferson Clinton in the 1990s. Namely, Clinton "was undermining everything that I believe in and everything that I have been working for. And he was standing for the wrong worldview." DeLay's speech was given at "Worldview Weekend," a rally convened to encourage evangelical Christians "to get involved in politics and not to segregate their religious worldview from their daily lives."[89] DeLay himself complained that "[believers] are told, 'You can go in the church...and stay in it, but if you stick your head out and you say anything that reflects your worldview, we're gonna knock your head off.' "[90] Strangely, DeLay's neck still ends at his head though he exercises "secular" political power openly to advance the hegemony of "a biblical worldview."

Here is the quintessence of hegemony: "A class or group is considered to be hegemonic when it...presents itself as realizing the broader aims either of emancipating or ensuring order for wider masses of the population."[91] Hegemonic relations are those in which universals, whose content is the terrain for ideological antagonisms, have their significance fixed, with acceptance of that resolution then providing a criterion for structuring society.

The potential for hegemonic struggle is structural to signifying systems. There is no society without hegemonic articulations, just as there is no communication without shared linguistic conventions. Limits are necessary. Limits order through exclusion. And exclusion is always a potential source of antagonism. It is not a fault unique to religious hegemonies that they posit a transcendental origin for their exclusions, thereby denying the historicity of their universalized particulars as well as of the process of universalization itself; nor it is a unique fault that religious hegemonies devalue the differences that make up the panoply of humanity in favor of a single, arbitrary principle of unification, treated as necessary; or that they sacrifice human diversity on the altar of transhuman unity and posit this sacrifice as the price of salvation. But there is a fault when those who would oppose religious hegemonies imagine that they can accomplish this aim through a strategy of deferential containment. What do we learn from Congressman DeLay? In the USA (at least) only secularists talk seriously about the separation of politics from religion because only secularists have blind faith in the ideal of a religiosity that is constitutively pre-political and therefore functionally apolitical.

No one who watched the World Trade Center fall on September 11 can ever simply believe in belief. No amount of respect can validate the believer's claim that his or her religious institutions, as institutions, exist *only and essentially* to promote peace. No public apology can be accepted that makes a blanket distinction between the "good" faithful and the "bad," with the further excuse that the strident evangelism or fanaticism of the "bad" renders them marginal, corrupt representatives for religion as a whole. Indeed, it is the fatuousness of words like peace, liberty, faith, heart, and home, that renders them such effective markers of ultimate value: it is possible to kill for these words since one can fill each with exactly the set of values for which one is willing to die. Seventeenth- and eighteenth-century Enlightenment thinkers had hoped to make the world safe from religious sectarian strife. But some were led by a strategic pragmatism, others by faith, to expect that religiosity in a highly personalized form, segregated from public power, could nevertheless foster the collective good. The terrible irony is that the lingering force of their analyses now only mystifies the public imagination and fosters apologetic discourse by those very people who should be most committed to criticism. This is the discursive power of enlightenment.

The social construction of enlightenment

This benign introduction to the politics of enlightenment has reached the midway point. Now let us transit from the foregoing broad inquiry towards the particular substance of the book. My concerns require tempering and greater specification. I have exploded a diffuse nebula of theories. To what end? The answer requires several steps. The first enters into a consideration of enlightenment as the *contingent* condition of possibility for Buddhism. That leads to the second step, where Buddhism is presented as a *nominal* phenomenon whose identity belongs to the context of nineteenth-century colonialism. The third step then approaches India's Ajanta caves, a fifth-century CE monastic site that seems to preserve *stable* evidence for the organic interdependence of enlightenment and Buddhism. My reasons for italicizing "contingent," "nominal," and "stable" should become evident shortly.

Ian Hacking's *The Social Construction of What?* presents a lucid critique of the kind of poststructuralist discourse analysis I have employed in the foregoing pages. In Hacking's view, poststructuralists use the phrase "social construction" too often and too loosely. His book begins with a mocking list of recent monographs: *The Social Construction of Authorship, The Social Construction of Emotions, Constructing Quarks, The Social Construction of Serial Homicide, The Construction of Zulu Nationalism.*[92] What kind of analytic value can social-construction language possess if it is applied willy-nilly to subjects ranging from authors to Zulus? Presumably, one might add religiosity, enlightenment, and Buddhism to the list. In Hacking's view, this is a mess. To fix it, he proposes strictly limiting the set of subjects construed as socially constructed. Properly, the phrase should be applied *only* to those phenomena that are conceived— incorrectly conceived—as being natural or inevitable, and therefore as *not* historically determinate, *not* socially constructed. In Hacking's words,

> Social construction work is critical of the status quo. Social construc-
> tionists about X tend to hold that: X need not have existed, or need not
> be at all as it is. X, or X as it is at present, is not determined by the nature
> of things; it is not inevitable.[93]

Accordingly, if a given X is not generally viewed as natural or inevitable, then there is no reason to explicitly denominate X as socially constructed.

As a critic (albeit, a congenial one) of poststructuralist discourse, Hacking pays particular attention to points of linguistic usage that provide "the basis of genuine and fundamental disagreement" between constructionists and their foes.[94] He counts three such "sticking points." When a constructionist proposes, X need not exist, he is attributing three values to X. The first sticking point is *contingency*.

A contingent X is produced through social and/or environmental forces within a natural history that is not guided by the hand of providence, by another divine power, or by strict dictates of logic. The second sticking point is *nominalism*. A nominal X is constituted through the act of naming; its facticity belongs to acts of observation and representation rather than to an intrinsic nature, structure, or reality. The third sticking point is *stabilizing factors*. To the degree that X is perceived as having a stable identity, the constructionist attributes that stability to factors *external* (rather than internal) to X. In sum, X is not an autonomous phenomenon.

As a crude example, the speed of light is 299,792,458 meters/second. For the strong constructionist this is a fact, not because light really moves at that speed (an internal factor), but for complex human reasons: because scientists developed the technological means for measuring light's speed; because they needed tangible results in order to justify the cost of developing that technology; because they hoped to win personal satisfaction and professional prestige; because they had the curiosity to know. The speed of light, on this view, is *contingent* on technology; *nominal* in the sense that it is identified only after deliberate acts of observation; and *stabilized* by the *external* politics of big science.

Indeed, it is clear why Saussurian structuralism, which builds its system of meanings out of the tension between interior and exterior, the arbitrary and the natural, gave rise to social-construction discourse. At ground zero, the link between a signifier and signified is contingent, nominal, and internally unstable. Why do chess sets have a piece that represents a castle? Why does the castle-piece move only in a straight line, horizontally and vertically? There can be no imaginable extra-social reason. For this reason, Hacking would argue that no book should ever be entitled, *The Social Construction of Chess*. Nevertheless, when the rules for moving rooks are considered in relation to the total system of possible rules, the diachronic conditions that arbitrarily produced its conventions are irrelevant and forgotten. In synchrony, those conventions are treated as *de facto* natural.

The study of social construction begins with the recognition that there is often a slippage of value, whereby the *de facto* naturalness of a signified is displaced onto the total sign. Social-construction language reminds us that the precise and invariant rules that define "rookitude" are *also* arbitrary. Hacking is doubtless correct when he indicts scholars for being overzealous, and sometimes imprecise, in their thought about this slippage. Yet, Hacking also observes, and we must remember, that constructionists themselves are often less concerned with the precision of their metaphor than with the anti-hegemonic agenda the metaphor encodes.

This now brings us to enlightenment and Buddhism. Let us consider, for instance, *The Buddhist Religion: A Historical Introduction* (BR), a popular textbook first published in 1970, now in its fourth edition. The introduction to this edition begins with a definition of Buddhism:

> *Buddhism*—as a term to denote the vast array of social and cultural phenomena that have clustered in the course of time around the teaching of a figure called the Buddha, the Awakened One—is a recent invention.

It comes from the thinkers of the eighteenth century European Enlightenment and their quest to subsume religion under comparative sociology and secular history. Only recently have Asian Buddhists come to adopt the term and the concept behind it.[95]

In light of Hacking's analysis, BR's constructionism is patent. Let $X = Buddhism$. Buddhism need not have existed, or need not be at all as it is. Buddhism is not determined by the nature of things; it is not inevitable. Rather, Buddhism is *contingent* upon the eighteenth-century European Enlightenment as well as Asian societies and cultures. Buddhism is also *nominal*. The word "Buddhism" is not merely a new English word for a phenomenon that existed prior to the eighteenth century. Rather, Buddhism is a recent invention, created when the term, as a signifier for the concept behind it, was created.

Finally, there is the issue of *stability*. Buddhism seems to be relatively stable. This is not to say that Buddhism is unvarying. Obviously it is not, given the diversity of national Buddhisms. But BR elsewhere clearly describes Buddhism as the sort of thing that can change in form without changing substance; that can move from India to China; that can be greatly influenced by Confucianism and Daoism, but not be transformed thereby into something other than Buddhism. Is this stability attributable to factors *outside of* Buddhism, or *internal to* it? Will Buddhism exist for only as long as people subsume religion under the intellectual practices of comparative sociology and secular history? Or, rather, is it stabilized by some sort of internal constituent?

The answer turns on the citation's second word, *as*, in the phrase "Buddhism— as a term to denote." In fact, BR validates both forms of stability. The specification *as* allows that Buddhism is contingent and nominal, but only within a well-defined discursive context, namely the context in which the concept behind the term is meaningful. In other words, were people to no longer think about Buddhism as one religion in a panoply of world religions, then that concept, that is, Buddhism as explained by scholars, would disappear. In this way, Buddhism's stability may be attributed to external factors.

But this is not the end of the *as*. With the specification *as* BR hints that the term "Buddhism" might also have a significance altogether different than the one given to it by post-Enlightenment scholars. There might be a second Buddhism; one that is not a term to denote a vast array of social and cultural phenomena. Like the first Buddhism, this second one might be contingent and even nominal. But unlike the first, its stability will be attributable to a factor *intrinsic to Buddhism itself*.

BR's introduction tells us, "Buddhism...is a recent invention." That is one Buddhism. Later, in the first chapter, BR describes the second Buddhism:

Buddhism began with the Awakening of the Buddha...an event that took place in the fifth or sixth century BCE at Bodhgaya, in the Ganges River plain of northeastern India. For Buddhists, the truths to which the

Buddha awakened transcend the conditions of space and time; however there is no denying that the social and cultural context in which he lived influenced the way he expressed his teachings and the way his contemporaries understood him.[96]

Here the origin of Buddhism shifts from the eighteenth century CE to the fifth or sixth BCE. The site of that origin shifts from Europe to India. And the wellspring of that origin shifts from social scientific analysis to an "event" called awakening. (Although BR uses the etymologically correct *awakening*, for the sake of consistency I will substitute *enlightenment*.) Buddhism, here, is no mere concept stabilized by a word. Now it is a determinate *thing* that began at a specific event in the life of a unique individual. Here an experiential event is Buddhism's real source—enlightenment provides a factor internal to Buddhism that serves as a stabilizing factor. Indeed, pay attention to that "however" at the crux of the second sentence. If it is *however* the case that expressions of enlightened truth are mediate and contingent, do we not infer that the enlightenment event, as the condition of possibility for those mediated expressions, may have been *actually* immediate and unconditioned?

BR has no qualms about describing the *signifier*—expressions of truth— as socially and culturally conditioned. But the passage's prose occults the *signified's*—truths realized in an enlightenment event—equal contingency and constructedness. Let X = enlightenment. Can BR allow that X need not have existed; X is not inevitable? Not just for Śākyamuni, for anybody? The *idea of Buddhism* produced by post-Enlightenment social scientists might well be contingent, nominal, and externally stabilized. But BR suggests that the *religion of Buddhism* produced in the enlightenment event might be just the opposite.

By representing enlightenment as an *event*—not contingent, not nominal, internally stable—BR naturalizes as *fact* that a man conceived certain truths in the fifth or sixth century BCE at Bodh Gayā, and that he taught what he (rightly or wrongly) considered to be timeless truth, albeit in historically conditioned forms. Here we observe the displacement of internal stability from signified to sign, from enlightenment to Buddhism, and from generic natural religiosity to religion in history. BR leaves no scope for rumormongers and conspiracy theorists to allege, however unpleasantly, that the enlightenment was a sham; Śākyamuni, a charlatan; and his contemporaries, patsies. Rather, BR offers a scholarly apologetic for Buddhism that doubles as a crypto-apologetic for religion in general. By designating enlightenment as a category definitive of the Other—thus distancing it—while at the same time treating it, unironically, as if it has a real historical efficacy—thus making it exemplary of a class of similar "religious" experiences—BR makes Buddhism into a taxonomic object that can be narrated as part of a history of error, while it simultaneously resists any attempt to make it part of an anthropology of deception.[97] BR thus recapitulates a paradigm of natural religiosity that can be traced right to Max Müller, and before.[98]

The social construction of Buddhism

BR provides one example of the kind of discursive use of *enlightenment* against which this book is working. There are two Buddhisms: one began in Europe as a recent invention; one began in India with an enlightenment event. I would like to consider these two Buddhisms further, in a second example that will also conduct us towards a discussion of the later chapters. In this case, let us look at a point of contention between two scholars, Philip Almond—author of *The British Discovery of Buddhism*—and Jonathan Silk—author of a substantial critique of Almond's work.[99] I will consider Almond's project before turning to Silk.

The British Discovery of Buddhism takes up the Saidean challenge to investigate Orientalism as a factor in the construction of European sensibilities about, and representations of, Asia. Philip Almond's thesis: Buddhism was created by scholars in the first half of nineteenth century. The title's use of *Discovery* is somewhat misleading, for Almond proposes a strong constructionism, not a mere nominalism. Almond does not want, in his words, to give "the impression that Buddhism existed prior to the end of the eighteenth century: that it was waiting in the wings...to be discovered; that it was floating in some aethereal Oriental limbo expecting its objective embodiment."[100] To the contrary,

> it was the Victorians who developed the discourse within which Buddhism was circumscribed, who deemed it a worthy focus of Western attention; it was they who brought forth the network of texts within which Buddhism was located. And it was they who determined the framework in which Buddhism was imaginatively constructed, not only for themselves, but also in the final analysis for the East itself.[101]

In short, Almond treats Buddhism as a "discursive object" in Foucault's now-classical sense of the phrase. Prior to the nineteenth century, neither Europeans nor Asians themselves had a conceptual category equivalent to the neologism *Buddhism*. Why was this category invented, Almond asks, and with what social ramifications? Once a culture was classified as Buddhist, how was that denomination "presented by the West, in the West, and primarily for the West"?[102]

This invented artifact, Buddhism, served Europeans in a variety of ways. As a basis for defining, delimiting, and classifying cultural artifacts from all of Asia, Buddhism provided a pan-Asian Other against which Europeans could view, imagine, and articulate their own superiority. Moreover, Almond proposes that "Buddhist scholarship was not only the cause but also the effect of that which it brought into being—Buddhism."[103] Scholars found in Buddhism a fresh arena within which to pursue a Christian polemic. Thus some lauded Śākyamuni Buddha as an Indian Luther, and Buddhism as a sober retort to the Catholic exuberance of Hindu iconophilia. Others used Buddhism to justify vigorous colonialism. They found proof in the doctrine of nirvāṇa that Buddhists are languid, exhausted people, weak from the tropics' long heat. Philip Almond is not a classicist, reading back and forth between the ancient sources and contemporary interpretations. He does not ask whether Orientalist representations of Asian cultures were accurate or fair. It does not matter to him whether Śākyamuni really did play a role in Indian history comparable to that of Luther in Europe, or whether the British really were more industrious than the Sri Lankans. Whatever values were attached to this entity, Buddhism, whatever the use to which it was put, according to Almond: "Victorian interpretations of Buddhism, whether of its founder, its doctrines, its ethics, its social practices, or its truth and value, in constructing Buddhism, reveal the world in which such constructing took place."[104]

Almond's work is superb when it delineates the political contexts within which Victorians mobilized the category *Buddhism*. But his constructionism remains only half-articulated. As a historian, Almond looks only at British values and British agendas. With few exceptions, his sources are in English, dating to the eighteenth, and especially the nineteenth, centuries. Asian beliefs and practices do not interest him, except as products of Orientalist representation. The question, *if Buddhism did not exist then what did?*, has no currency for him. Where BR gives us two Buddhisms with two origins—one modern, one ancient—Almond gives us only one. He denies the existence of the second, but offers no positive proof of its non-existence. In short, the "discovery" of Buddhism provides a context within which to analyze the articulation of British power, but considerations of hermeneutics and historicism, requiring attention to cognitive and temporal difference, remain outside Almond's purview.

On its own terms, this is not necessarily a problem. Still, Almond's redescription of Buddhism as a modern artifact is both radical in its claim and far-reaching in its implications. This alone makes it a ready target for criticism. The fact that the thesis is only half-articulated makes it vulnerable as well. And the fact that Almond's prose is not always adequate to his thesis does not help matters. Claims to the contrary, Almond often writes as if Buddhism *was* something there in Asia, waiting for the British to find and name, rather than a discursive object determined by the orderings, correlations, positions, functionings, and transformations of nineteenth-century Orientalism. The book's title, *Discovery*, suggests prior objective existence—King Tut's tomb and $E = mc^2$ are conventional objects of discovery—while his chapters prefer words like construction, creation, and imagination. Or again, the status of Buddhism in a sentence cited above— "Victorian interpretations of Buddhism, whether of its founder, it doctrines, its ethics, its social practices, or its truth and value, in constructing Buddhism, reveal the world in which such constructing took place"—is unclear. In the first clause, Buddhism seems to have an ontic reality, in the second, it is epistemic.

Like Almond, I think it problematic to posit the autonomous existence of a singular Buddhism or even multiple Buddhisms prior to the nineteenth century. Given this agreement, I choose to overlook Almond's textual infelicities as artifacts of long linguistic habit, reminding myself of Nietzsche's questions in

27

Beyond Good and Evil (#34):

> Shouldn't philosophers be permitted to rise above faith in grammar? All due respect to governesses—but hasn't the time come for philosophy to renounce the faith of governesses?

Not all readers are thus inclined. Consider, for instance, Jonathan Silk's critique, or rather one of his many critical notes. Silk is especially perturbed by the fact that Almond's examination of Buddhism as an object of discourse does not consider the objective truth-value of that discourse. As Silk writes, "there must be a Buddhism which some people and some works of scholarship are able to reflect more accurately, honestly and directly than are others."[105] By denying this *must*, Almond threatens to undercut the disciplinary basis for Silk's own field, Buddhist Studies. If Buddhist Studies traffics in hyperreal signs of signs, if Buddhism appears to be a coherent object of analysis only because scholars have disciplined themselves into a pseudo-systematicity of representation, then Buddhist Studies' pretension to being a legitimate branch of the human sciences is largely invalid. Buddhist Studies would be a bootstrap operation, pure discourse.

With so much at stake, inconsistencies in Almond's language provide a ready platform from which to attack his category-politics. Silk reads inconsistent statements as signs of a fatal flaw in Almond's scholarly program. He wonders, "Is it really so that Buddhist scholarship 'brought [Buddhism] into being?' " And for an answer, Silk presents a long quote from Almond's book, to which he then responds. First, Almond,

> I, like [Edward] Said, am concerned with the internal logic, the structure of views about Buddhism apart from the question of how Buddhism *'really'* was. That is to say, I am not concerned with the extent to which Victorian interpretations of Buddhism correctly or incorrectly perceived, selected, reflected on, and interpreted the congeries of texts, persons, events and phenomena in various cultures that it classified as Buddhist.[106]

Then Silk,

> There is a subtle fallacy here that may reveal something of the theoretical underpinnings of Almond's discussions. Almond claims not to be interested in the relationship between the objective truth of Buddhism's existence and situation and the Victorian interpretation of that existence. He is interested in how the texts, persons and so forth in Buddhist cultures were presented, in other words interpreted in the West. Unless I have missed something, this does not make sense.[107]

In the movement from quote to critique one finds that Silk did miss something: namely, his own blanching of Almond's constructionism. Almond does not assert an interest in "Buddhist cultures," how they were presented or how they were interpreted. Silk's "Buddhist cultures" is a reductive transposition of Almond's phrase, "cultures classified as Buddhist." The excision of this act of initial classification is itself the *objective* basis for the academic discipline of Buddhist Studies.

Silk has a point, though to make it he reproduces the very writing-out against which Almond writes. Silk demonstrates that for Buddhism to appear to be an independent object *for* scholarship, marked with an ancient provenance, its scholars must forget that the act of classification has an perlocutionary force, like other knowledge-creating operations. Buddhist Studies as field of knowledge exists (in part) to bridge the temporal and psychic distance between ancient Asians and modern communities of interest. Silk's maneuver exemplifies how its practitioners structure that distance in the first place. Almond's analysis calls attention to the hegemonic implication of this discursive operation, but that is not enough. Silk is correct: a thoroughgoing redescription of Buddhism must also inquire into "how Buddhism '*really*' was," the question that Almond eschews. Hermeneutics and historicism, as well as hegemony, are implied by the discursive creation of Buddhism. How else might we determine all the ways in which the academic study of phenomena identified as ancient Buddhism serves contemporary interests?

Granted, I would hesitate to posit an autonomous entity, Buddhism (or Buddhisms), as existing before the nineteenth century. This fact need not obviate other, seemingly competing, givens. To wit, there is no reason to doubt that the man we call Śākyamuni Buddha lived in the fourth or fifth century BCE; that he had followers in his own day; that after his death, people still paid attention to suffering just as texts attributed to him said they should; that others sought happiness for themselves, again following the putative teachings of this deceased buddha; that still others fantasized about freedom, or pledged not to steal or tell lies, or sought to assuage guilt and express love toward a parent, or laid claim to political power and justified the use of force, all by appeal to the words of the buddha, or to an agent whose authority was based in some way upon the buddha. In short, long before Christian mariners plied *gentoo* seas, Asian peoples revered Śākyamuni Buddha as a figure of authority. They bowed before his image; memorized his recollected sayings; left their wives, sons, and parents just as he was supposed to have; and gave material support to such renunciants. When speaking of our contemporaries, we would not hesitate to call such people *Buddhists*. Buddhist is now a fully attested index of identity. Why not use this same name for their premodern brethren? What is gained by investing, intellectually and emotionally, in the term Buddhism? Why should Almond, or I, want to prevent the growth of that intellectual and emotional capital? Reading cultures across history, we misuse and mistranslate foreign concepts all the time; anachronisms are common. Why pay such attention to the anachronistic currency of Buddhism?

If this book is the long answer, then here is the brief one: Strong constructionism threatens more than the sinecure of a few dozen scholars in a marginal academic discipline. The deconstruction of Buddhism raises doubts about the value and values of the taxonomic structure that houses it. Is religion any less constructed than

Buddhism? Religion too is a byproduct of observation and classification at the edges of intercultural contact. Religion too has become so deeply woven into the institutional fabric of the contemporary world that its facticity now seems beyond question. Indeed, religion more so than Buddhism, since religiosity has become stereotyped as a universally human trait—even definitive of humanity—while membership in a specific religion is only ever an accident of time and place.

Were religion a neutral construction it might not warrant such attention. But as a construction, religion is charged, and charged with a positive polarity. The Dalai Lama was speaking mere common sense when he told an audience in 1996: "there is every reason to appreciate and respect all forms of spiritual practice" since "the purpose of religion . . . is to cultivate positive human qualities such as tolerance, generosity, and love."[108] Yes, the Dalai Lama is well-respected beyond his native constituency. That does not make his hegemonic discourse, pro religion, any less disturbing than Tom DeLay's pro-Christian words. No one asks us to appreciate and respect all forms of intellectual practice, economic practice, sexual practice, or political practice. How can we reasonably privilege religion over other social institutions, if we lack objective, systematic criteria for distinguishing the "purpose of religion" and "spiritual practices" from the purposes or practices of science, aesthetics, erotics, commerce, and politics?

In our modernity, the fool is the person who says that religion and/or spirituality are not essentially good; that they are not necessarily desirable presences in the world; that their beliefs, practices, and institutions deserve no special privilege beyond those accorded to other beliefs, practices, and institutions. This is why it is important to pay attention to the anachronistic currency of Buddhism. Buddhism would seem to be a simple thing, but, as a modern artifact, it is not. Its complex epistemological status makes it a valuable point from which to upset the easy quiddity granted to enlightened religiosity in the contemporary world.

Ajanta, a place that's good to think

Ian Hacking's critique of poststructuralism organizes its discourse around three sticking points. We have seen how enlightenment provides one such point, dividing those who would characterize it as a contingent experience (at the extreme, there was no such event, just an incredibly successful charlatan) from those who hold that it derives from the direct nonconceptual intuition of reality as it is, of *dharma* (with the admission that expressions thereof *are* contingent). And we have seen that Philip Almond's nominalism vis-à-vis Buddhism is a sticking point that separates him from Jonathan Silk, whom I treated as a representative for the field of Buddhist Studies. In Hacking's scheme, stabilizing factors provide the third sticking point. More than contingency, more than nominalism—this last is a central focus of *Beyond Enlightenment*. How do we use artifacts from the past to stabilize, naturalize, and hegemonize the present and future?

Buddhism-in-general and Western imaginings about pan-Asian phenomena are not the issues here. For its primary evidence, *Beyond Enlightenment* focuses upon

India or, rather more narrowly, upon the discursive production of Buddhism at Ajanta. Ajanta is a western Indian archaeological site almost universally described as Buddhist in scholarly and popular literature since the nineteenth century. There are more than 30 man-made caves at Ajanta, first carved into a sheer 250-foot high wall of rock between the first century BCE and the sixth century CE. In addition to their excavated architectures, these caves contain a rich archive of artifacts, including inscriptions, paintings, and sculptures.

Ajanta provides a well-circumscribed set of objects about which to theorize; so well-circumscribed, in fact, that the art historian Walter Spink has called Ajanta "by all counts, the most minutely, as well as the most totally, analyzable site ... in the world."[109] Spink alludes here to his own project of interweaving *in situ* epigraphs with an analysis of the site's motifs to reconstruct the social and political history of the place. Spink's highflown phrases are not unique. Writers almost stumble in their rush to aestheticize what Spink elsewhere suggests "may well be mankind's most remarkable creative achievement."[110] These others revel in observations, such as, "It is the Faërie which, ultimately, lingers in memory after a visit to the Ajaṇṭā caves," and "The heart discovers [at Ajanta] its strength, its unfathomed powers. It dares stand free and unashamed."[111]

Certainly Ajanta is beautiful. Perhaps the best preserved site from ancient India, Ajanta hints at treasures sadly lost. But as should be clear, my approach to Ajanta's archive is neither that of a traditional microhistorian focused on the curiosities of a unique ancient place; nor that of an intellectual historian who unpacks local ideologies in relation to translocal norms; nor even that of an aesthete whose heart is freed from shame. One might categorize *Beyond Enlightenment* as a postmodern microhistory. Ajanta provides a body of evidence that allows me to place contemporary processes and predicates of identity creation, constructing Buddhism, in sharp relief. As a place made of stone and paint, shaped by the natural environment as well as human intentionality and carelessness, Ajanta's objective existence is not a matter for dispute. This materiality allows me to take the necessary step beyond Almond, who explicitly denies that Buddhism had a prior objective existence (like a piece of stone waiting to be discovered) but whose prose is fuzzy on the lines separating discovery from invention from interpretation. Caves are not at all like cultures or religions in this regard. With caves, the distinction between discovery and interpretation can be clearly, if not absolutely, delimited. As a material construction, *Ajanta doubles for Indian Buddhism*, an ideological construction. In turn, the uncritical ease with which one apprehends Ajanta as Buddhist might correlate with the uncritical ease with which one accepts religiosity as a fixture in the human world.

Ajanta is good to think for a variety of reasons, the most important of which is chronological. The preponderance of Ajanta's excavations, paintings, and sculptures were paid for by wealthy donors during India's so-called classical age. This premodern patronage had two phases, the first from approximately 100 BCE to 100 CE, the second, circa 462 to 480 CE. Following the fifth century, major excavatory and decorative work stopped, suggesting that the caves were no longer actively used, either as monastic homes or as shrines for pilgrimage.[112] This is why Ajanta is so much better preserved than all other contemporaneous sites. Remote from major population centers, Ajanta was abandoned and neglected almost immediately after it was created. Still, Ajanta was not forgotten. The seventh-century Chinese explorer Xuanzang discusses the site in his *Journey to the West*, and he may even have visited it. But Xuanzang says nothing that suggests Ajanta was a functioning monastery in his day.[113] Other travelers from the seventh and eighth centuries left graffiti, after which no humans made their mark on Ajanta for more than one millennium. Then on April 28, 1819, a British officer named John Smith scratched his name over a painted image, initiating a new era of interest by conservators, scholars, tourists, and tradesmen.[114]

Ajanta was all but abandoned in the fifth century and reoccupied, albeit as an object for study and tourism, in the nineteenth. This 1,400-year caesura makes Ajanta a material double for that contested institution, Indian Buddhism. For even those who look upon Indian Buddhism as a promontory in the social terrain of premodern India acknowledge that it was razed and forgotten. Indian Buddhism differs from other forms of Buddhism, let alone other religious systems, in at least this one significant regard. Even the first time a sixteenth-century Christian ship weighed anchor in a foreign harbor, local Hindus or Muslims, Theravāda *bhikkhus* or Zen bonzes, were there to act as native informants and subjects of ethnographic observation. By contrast, the phenomenon classified as Buddhism had no living representatives in India after the fourteenth century. No native Indian Buddhist ever greeted a European missionary, merchant, or scholar in colonial Calcutta or Bombay.[115] Like Ajanta, the phenomenon classified as Indian Buddhism has a constitutive temporal discontinuity between its premodernity and its modernity, a gap spanned by scholarly constructions. One can agree with Almond and claim that this scholarly bridge is precarious, since it has only one solid footing, on the near edge of modernity. Or one can agree with Silk and argue that the bridge connects solid ground in both eras. Either way, the gap is there. Either way, for Ajanta to have been categorized as Buddhist in the nineteenth century required a synthesis, conjoining ancient Indian material remains with the abstraction of data gained from contemporary informants (albeit, native to Sri Lanka, Nepal, Thailand, China, etc.), with a scholarly praxis influenced by religious, colonial, and mercantile agendas, as well as Enlightenment epistemologies and ideals. Ajanta's artifacts are thus intertexts within two radically separate, yet interdependent, discursive fields. Its images and discursive records can be interpreted within the fullness of the codes available to ancient patrons and inhabitants; and they can be read in relation to the corpus of post-Enlightenment representations of India, of Buddhism, and of religion. At Ajanta we might see how "taking the buddha as an authority" in premodern India was *not* equivalent—intellectually, institutionally, politically, or indeed, categorically and linguistically—to "being a Buddhist" in the contemporary world.

If Ajanta was not a Buddhist site, then what was it?

Walter Spink tells us that after 480 "not a painting, not a piece of sculpture, not a cave, or a cell, or a cistern, nor a single donative inscription" was added to Ajanta.[116] If the people who abandoned Ajanta in that year were not Buddhists, by what name might they be designated? As I noted earlier, my answer will nuance Almond's redescription of Buddhism as a product of the Victorian imagination. For the denial of Indian Buddhism's premodern existence must nevertheless take account of Śākyamuni Buddha's wide-ranging social and cultural currency in fifth-century India. In lieu of Buddhist and Buddhism, this book will characterize Ajanta (the place as well as its affiliated community) with the terms *Śākya* and *bauddha*. I will use these two terms interchangeably. Fifth-century Ajanta was a bauddha/Śākya place populated by bauddha/Śākyas.

My reasons for using the term *Śākya* are patent. Ajanta boasts a total of ninety-seven inscriptions, painted and incised.[117] Of these, sixty record information on fifth-century donors; unfortunately twenty-one of the donative inscriptions are damaged beyond use, leaving thirty-nine as a basis for information about the local community. If we describe a "ratio" of epigraphic material to elapsed time within which that material was created as a measure of "social density," then Ajanta is among the socially densest sites for data on early medieval India. It is a place at which a statistical sampling can yield meaningful results. Of thirty-nine complete donative inscriptions from the fifth century, twenty-eight identify their donor using an epithet that begins with the name Śākya. Most of these twenty-eight are Śākyabhikṣus (renunciant Śākyas); some are Śākya-upāsakas (lay-devotee Śākyas). If we know anything distinctive about the people who made donations at Ajanta, we know that nearly 3 of every 4 identified himself as a Śākya. Elsewhere I have proposed that these Śākya epithets at Ajanta were informed by a socio-spiritual polemic, in which donors adopted Śākyamuni Buddha's family name to assert their legitimacy as his heirs, both institutionally and ideologically.[118] To take the name of Śākya was to define oneself by one's affiliation with the buddha, somewhat like calling oneself a Buddhist today.[119]

The other term I will use to characterize Ajanta is *bauddha*, a secondary derivative of *buddha*, in which the vowel's lengthening indicates connection or relation. Things that are *bauddha* pertain to the buddha, just as things-Śaiva relate to Śiva and things-Vaiṣṇava belong to Viṣṇu. One can read a Śaiva text, visit a Śaiva temple, or take tea in a Śaiva home. Likewise, bauddha can be both adjectival and nominal; it can be used for doctrines spoken by the buddha, objects enjoyed by him, texts attributed to him, as well as individuals, communities, and societies that offer him reverence or accept ideologies certified through his name.

Strictly speaking, Śākya is preferable to bauddha since the latter is not attested at Ajanta. In fact, as a collective noun, bauddha is an outsider's term. The bauddha did not call themselves this in India, though they sometimes did use the word adjectivally (e.g., as a possessive, the buddha's).[120] Despite the lack of a fifth-century precedent for applying bauddha to Ajanta, I will do so for several reasons. First, bauddha means much the same thing as Śākya. Both terms represent this social group as followers of the "same" man, one by reference to his family name, the other by reference to his spiritual title. Second, having another alternative for Buddhist will help forestall the monotony of prose that repeats one single word too often. Finally, bauddha not only sounds like Buddhist, but is sometimes used as such in modern scholarship, as when James Burgess published his *Notes on the Bauddha Rock-Temples of Ajanta*.[121] Indeed, by a happy coincidence, the first description of buddha as "the enlightened" in English (1835) notes, it is because the buddha was enlightened that "his followers have been termed Bauddhas, or Buddhists."[122] The dissonance created by the questions—Why were the rock-temples of Ajanta bauddha but not Buddhist? How was bauddha ideology not Buddhist doctrine?—would seem less dissonant if posed in terms of Śākya.

We require these alternates for the words Buddhist and Buddhism, not because Buddhism is a construction of the nineteenth-century West, but because, as Silk's critique of Almond demonstrates, we must pay as much attention to the materials out of which Buddhism was fabricated, as we do to the builder's plans, their techniques, and the finished edifice. In the fifth century, Ajanta *really* was a Śākya place populated by bauddha. How were those bauddha unlike the people now called Buddhists? And why does that difference matter so? The answers bring us back to the matter of religion, and the fact that this book assumes a series of substitutions, whereby the search for Buddhism at Ajanta is a surrogate for the search for religiosity as a human universal.

2

A PLACE OF EXCEPTIONAL UNIVERSAL VALUE

A world heritage monument

AJANTA CAVES have been inscribed on the World Heritage List of the Convention concerning the Protection of the World Cultural and Natural Heritage. Inscription on this List confirms the exceptional universal value of a cultural or natural site which deserves protection for the benefit of all humanity (Figure 2.1).

Most tourists come to Ajanta for only a day. Their mornings begin in Aurangabad, 100 kilometers south on Maharashtra State Highway No. 8, or at the Jalgaon railhead, 50 kilometers to the north. The two roads are so different that the longer drive sometimes makes for the quicker trip. But no matter whether tourists arrive at Ajanta in air-conditioned calm or sore from constant potholes, upon arrival all are greeted by a swarm of boys hawking geodes and beads and crystals and postcards and color-guides and refreshingly cold drinks, electricity permitting.

Having first gone to Ajanta in December 1982, and spent the better part of a year there in 1992, I returned in July 2000 to interview tourists and workers. Their unpremeditated words describe an Ajanta that sates and frustrates, coexisting uneasily with the humans that impinge upon it. Bill, a 25 year old lawyer from Australia, traveled to Ajanta on the recommendation that it was "something more special...I suppose in terms of a cultural site rather than just a physical landscape or a cityscape." But his experience was mixed. Regulations on tourist flow at the site, barriers and queues, made it "like Disney World," though they also kept "hawkers away from the entrances of every cave." Bill's awkward ambivalence about Ajanta was shared by Trin—a 19-year-old Tibetan living in southern India—but with a difference. Trin found Ajanta "quite dirty." He hypothesized, "If Buddhists lived here they would make it clean, and peaceful. They would make it much cleaner than it is now. (laughing) I think Buddhists should live here." By contrast, Suresh from Calcutta found Ajanta "very beautiful" and "of historical importance...because thousands of years ago Indian civilization was here." This pride of place was shared by Venketeshwar, who was visiting for the first time as an adult, though he had made many school trips when a boy. B.C. Dhaky, from

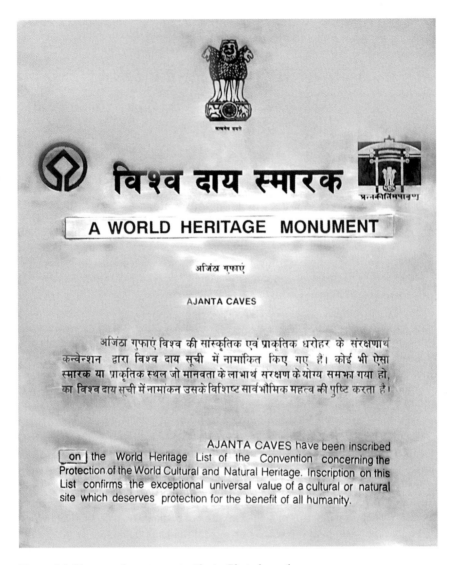

विश्व दाय स्मारक

A WORLD HERITAGE MONUMENT

अजिंठा गुफाएं

AJANTA CAVES

अजंठा गुफाएं विश्व की सांस्कृतिक एवं प्राकृतिक धरोहर के संरक्षणार्थ कन्वेन्शन द्वारा विश्व दाय सूची में नामांकित किए गए है। कोई भी ऐसा स्मारक या प्राकृतिक स्थल जो मानवता के लाभार्थ संरक्षण के योग्य समझा गया हो, का विश्व दाय सूची में नामांकन उसके विशिष्ट सार्वभौमिक महत्व की पुष्टि करता है।

AJANTA CAVES have been inscribed on the World Heritage List of the Convention concerning the Protection of the World Cultural and Natural Heritage. Inscription on this List confirms the exceptional universal value of a cultural or natural site which deserves protection for the benefit of all humanity.

Figure 2.1 Plaque at the entrance to Ajanta. Photo by author.

Golegaon, about twenty kilometers away, had still different reasons for being a frequent visitor: "We like to come here often because it is beautiful in this season, and we have a good time climbing the mountain and swimming under the waterfall." Doubtless because of daytrippers like Mr Dhaky, the *Lonely Planet* guide warns travelers to "avoid, if at all possible, coming here at weekends or on public holidays. On those days, Ajanta seems to attract half the population of India and it's bedlam. The Calcutta rush hour has nothing on this place at those times—hardly the contemplative atmosphere which the monks and builders had in mind!"[1]

Where is Ajanta? Does it exist in the intentions of those monks and builders? In the romantic *!* of the *Lonely Planet's* imagined contemplative past? In the hills comprised of "horizontally bedded alternate flows of massive and amygdular lava" located at Latitude 20 ° 32' North and Longitude 75 ° 45' East?[2] In the lungs of the man who ran into one cave, shouted *Oṃ Namo Śivāya*, and then ran on to the next? In the picnic baskets toted by the Venketeshwar and Dhaky families, or their children's kohl-traced eyes? In the cultural traces analyzed by scholars and appreciated by antiquarians? In the prostrations of Tibetan refugee monks? In the processions of Japanese pilgrims, with their drums and their priests and their flowers? In the words of its builders and inhabitants, preserved in the many inscriptions, painted and incised? In the authority of the scholar who reports on all this? In the labor of the Archaeological Survey of India's Chemical Branch workers, and Physical Branch workers, and guards? In the bus drivers and taxi drivers, hotel workers and food vendors, who serve half the population of India on any given Saturday? In the brass plate next to the site's entrance, on which is inscribed the United Nations Educational, Scientific and Cultural Organization's certainty: Ajanta possesses exceptional universal value; Ajanta contributes to the good of all humanity?

UNESCO has a longtime partner in ICOMOS, the International Council on Monuments and Sites, whose publications include a handbook for the managers of World Heritage cultural sites. Readers of the ICOMOS manual would find nothing remarkable about the range of interests I encountered at Ajanta in 2000. The handbook advises site managers to anticipate the needs of many types of visitors, from the scholar to the student, from the general pleasure-seeker to the reluctant package-tourist, who is "often more interested in the amenities—where to get something to drink, where the toilets are, where to sit down and where the gift shop is," than in the site itself.[3] ICOMOS recommends that World Heritage site managers envision the tourist's itinerary as a trail of needs, in which comfort (or lack thereof) pulls against curiosity, and prestige competes with cost.

As for cost, Ajanta is a case in point. In 1982, everybody paid 2 rupees to enter. One decade later the fee had been raised to Rs 5. But after the Archaeological Survey of India (ASI) recognized the value of the World Heritage brand it initiated a sliding scale, keying the rate for foreigners to United States' currency ($5 or Rs 250), and doubling the Indian rate to Rs 10. After the place became a matter of concern for *all humanity* the cost of entry became a marker of difference, for the ASI understood that money functions to objectify an otherwise ambiguous hierarchy of desires—aesthetic, symbolic, intellectual. Heritage sites possessing exceptional universal value satisfy higher desires than do other historic or cultural sites, and thus, objectively, they command a higher entry fee. Indeed, one might calculate an individual's or community's inherent value by counting tourist flow: How many Rajasthani farmers on pilgrimage through Maharashtra, traveling from Ganesh temple to Ganesh temple, stop at Ajanta, even though Rs 10 represents a significant expense? How many Germans, Italians, Canadians, Sri Lankans, and so on, drop Ajanta from their itinerary when they learn of the exceptional demand the ASI places on their foreign wallets?

Money provides an autonomous field within which to gauge the transvaluation of the archaic and bygone, the outmoded and defunct, the dead and gone, into contemporary social and cultural capital. But this chapter is not about money. The ASI introduced its dual fee structure only after UNESCO had transvalued Ajanta, from an interesting place to an exceptional place, from an Indian place to a global place. That transvaluation is the focus here. What had to be done to transvalue this place, ignored for more than a millennium, into a locus of exceptional universal value whose protection benefits all humanity?

To address this question, the chapter begins by laying out the basis for UNESCO's rhetoric within Enlightenment humanism. Namely, all good men in all ages share a set of core values; these universal values are logically prior to ethnic and national interests; these universal values express the essence of what it is to be human. By naming Ajanta a World Heritage monument, UNESCO offers it as a place at which to encounter humanity at its essential best.

Ostensibly World Heritage status is oriented toward one pragmatic end: the conservation of exceptional places. The instructional literature addressed to site managers, however, sounds a second theme. In the act of valorizing World Heritage monuments, this literature just as strongly emphasizes the value of the World Heritage designation itself as an exceptional brand. In line with this dual message, the chapter will also shift focus, from the value of objects to the value of branding objects. Branding is crucial for the smooth operation of a market economy: brands add value to objects, giving them stable identities that mark the objects as reliable and safe. Why is the World Heritage brand so powerful and so eagerly consumed? The chapter ends by questioning the representation of Enlightenment as the consummation of desire. For a brand to be successful it must identify itself with liberation in some way, with a vision of a future in which consumers are freer and happier for having bought the brand. Freedom, the Enlightenment's ultimate goal, is branding's horizon as well.

An Enlightened view of Ajanta

The plaque outside the ticket booth was made possible in 1983, the year in which the seventh UNESCO Convention Concerning the Protection of the World Cultural and Natural Heritage placed Ajanta on its World Heritage List. This UNESCO Convention itself was established in 1972 with a mandate to "provide for the protection of those cultural and natural properties deemed to be of outstanding universal value."[4] The Convention's List was not intended as a novelty, a roster of sanctioned tourist venues, or a modern reworking of the Seven Wonders. Rather, this designation was expressly aimed at one pragmatic end: conservation. The ICOMOS handbook asserts with pride: "The Convention provides, for the first time, a permanent legal, administrative, and financial framework for international cooperation in safeguarding humankind's cultural and natural heritage. It introduces the specific concept of a 'world heritage' whose importance transcends all political and geographic boundaries."[5] While a gamut of perils, from earthquakes and fires to war to urban sprawl to corrosive carbon emissions to the dirt of tourism itself, threaten every cultural artifact, UNESCO has made a hard choice. It has articulated a set of criteria for determining which artifacts deserve every human being's protection. These World Heritage monuments serve, variously, as destinations for international tourism, symbols of national identity, and fragile archives of scholarly data. They are prized resources that demand rational administration. Thus a site manager's primary responsibility is to identify the particular "values of the site" basic to its global import, and then to protect those values through "the development and implementation of a management philosophy."[6]

Even though the List has grown long—as of July 2005, 137 countries supported 628 cultural sites—according to the Convention's operational guidelines, "it is not intended to provide for the protection of all properties of great interest, importance or value, but only for a select list of the most outstanding of these from an international viewpoint."[7] From this viewpoint, Ajanta had much to recommend it. In order to distinguish places possessing exceptional universal significance from ho-hum pufferies of local color, UNESCO articulated seven criteria, only one of which was required for nomination. Thus in 1983, the Taj Mahal, India's premier symbolic monument, entered the list solely on the basis of its being "a masterpiece of human creative genius." Ajanta, also a masterpiece of human creative genius, satisfied three further UNESCO benchmarks. Ajanta:

- exhibit[s] an important interchange of human values, over a span of time or within a cultural area of the world, on developments in architecture or technology, monumental arts, town-planning or landscape design;
- [bears] a unique or at least exceptional testimony to a cultural tradition or to a civilization which is living or which has disappeared; . . .
- [is] directly or tangibly associated with events or living traditions, with ideas, or with beliefs, with artistic and literary works of outstanding universal significance (the Committee considers that this criterion should justify inclusion in the List only in exceptional circumstances and in conjunction with other criteria cultural or natural).[8]

As a World Heritage monument, Ajanta is thus a bona fide repository of value and values, the universally human, culture, civilization, tradition, belief, art, meaning, and genius. Its importance transcends all political boundaries. In a word, Ajanta is *Enlightened*. The World Heritage Convention articulates how to recognize the Enlightenment embedded in such places and how to protect it for the future.

Before we investigate just how Ajanta fulfills these many roles, let us look closer at the underpinnings of the World Heritage Convention, its conceptual genesis in a European Enlightenment humanism. The eighteenth-century's philosophical anthropology began with twin assumptions. First, human nature is singular and uniform: the essential characteristics of *Homo sapiens* vary neither with time nor place, neither economic status nor nationality. In David Hume's classic formulation:

> It is universally acknowledged that there is a great uniformity among the actions of men, in all nations and ages, and that human nature remains still the same, in its principles and operations. The same motives always produce the same actions: the same events follow from the same causes.[9]

Lacking such regularity, the science of humanity would fail, just as physics would fail if apples fell up to the clouds in China and down from the clouds in Japan. Indeed biology, physics, even mathematics, had a stake in this human uniformity, for Hume took the science of man to be "the only solid foundation for the other sciences."[10] If human beings' sensory and mental faculties were not predictably uniform then we could know nothing about nature's own regularities, since natural laws are mere inductions from empirical observation.

Enlightenment anthropology's second assumption held that human beings are objects that possess universal value, and simultaneously are subjects whose actions can express universal values. In this regard, the Declaration of Independence presents an easy example, where self-evident rights are the natural corollary of humanity's uniform equality. Still more notable is the conclusion to the *Critique of Practical Reason*, where Immanuel Kant wrote: "Two things fill the mind with ever new and increasing admiration and reverence, the more often and more steadily one reflects on them: *the starry heavens above me and the moral law within me*."[11] As Kant saw it, the outer and the inner worlds both exhibit lawful behavior; both are unbounded in scope. But while Kant felt personally dwarfed before the cosmological infinite, the moral law "infinitely raises my worth."[12] Innate rationality granted Kant, as it does all humans, the capacity for moral perfection "independent of all animality." It should be said that while the conception of a uniform nature, and the concern for the moral quality of that nature, were typical of the Enlightenment, not all Kant's contemporaries shared his optimism. Claude-Adrien Helvétius' diatribe against a doctrine of innate goodness—"the child kills flies, beats his dog, and strangles his sparrow"—found its precursor in Augustine of Hippo's earlier observation that, "if babies are innocent, it is not for lack of will to do harm, but for lack of strength."[13]

Conceived thus, Enlightenment humanism remained continuous with Christian anthropology. For Christianity a moral imperative placed human beings above the world of dumb nature. Created by god for Adam's sake, the cattle, birds, and all the beasts were not caught in humanity's double bind, where the expectation of moral perfection was rendered unattainable by the weight of Adam's disobedience. Jesus' sacrifice provided the only possible resolution of this dilemma; saintly martyrs, both of flesh and spirit, showed the way. But Kant, like his Enlightenment brethren, held that although "morals began with the noblest property of human nature . . . it ended—in enthusiasm or in superstition," sectarian Christianity.[14] In this, Enlightenment humanists were responding (no less than Reformation preachers) to existential hierarchies of the kind outlined by the fourteenth-century natural philosopher, Henry of Langenstein: "Just as the Lord gave human beings dominion and care over the animals, so he placed superior and more perfect people above the inferior and more imperfect people."[15] For these later thinkers, human nature was one; the Company of the Saints was just so much mythology; Jesus Christ was neither Alpha nor Omega. Instead, Thomas Paine would describe Jesus' "real character" thus: "a virtuous and amiable man . . . of the most benevolent kind."[16] To the extent that Paine or Voltaire invoked Jesus' name it was to represent him as preaching Enlightened values, worthy, not because they were divine writ, but because they increased human happiness and freedom. Jesus belonged to that company of "good men in all ages" who preach "similar systems of morality."[17]

The World Heritage Convention proceeds from the same moral phenomenology. Its documents assume the existence of a set of core values shared by good men in all ages. These values are logically prior to every particularity of nation, ethnos, or culture. They close all temporal and geographical distance. They are binding on humanity in general. Moreover, the Convention holds that since these values are the common property of the human psychic self, cultural productions that represent them in ways that transcend borders and local passions are the common property of the human social self. Certainly UNESCO is not unique in its embrace of these principles. They are norms for the relatively new academic field of Cultural Resource Management as well, as we read in this statement from William Lipe's influential article, "Value and Meaning in Cultural Resources":

> To the extent that we can travel in the past, we can escape the bounds of competing nations and interest groups as no present-day traveller can. We *must* then view the evidence of the past as a record of *human*, rather than *national*, accomplishment. Hence, if we wish to foster an awareness of the degree to which the fortunes of all human groups are intertwined, and to gain a broad and even dispassionate perspective of the various ethnocentric and nationalist claims of today, there can be no better road to recommend than one that leads back in time.[18]

For what purpose have the Ajanta caves been transvalued from ignored relics of ancient provenance into a locus of exceptional universal value? Ajanta provides a place at which to imagine the fulfillment of an Enlightenment fantasy, in which present political multiplicities (sometimes divisive) resolve into a future apolitical unity (always harmonious).

Lipe's recommendations have not been fully adopted by UNESCO, or by the ASI. They cannot have been. For although World Heritage sites belong to all people *de jure*, *de facto* they are controlled by particular states. The Convention asserts, "Inclusion of a property on the World Heritage List requires the consent of the State concerned."[19] And this too plays back into Enlightenment debates, which reveal a delicate tension between the idealization of the autonomous, agentive individual and the conviction that humankind will, as a collective whole, progress toward "true perfection."[20] For the Marquis de Condorcet, this balance was met through the expectation that the abolition of inequalities—among people and among nations—will be followed by a correlative increase in equality. He imagines that once "a close accord had been established between all [E]nlightened men, from then onwards all will be the friends of humanity, all will work together for its perfection and happiness."[21] Surely Lipe can be imagined a member of Condorcet's fraternity. But Adam Smith offers quite a different model for this progress, with his famous prediction that so-called Enlightened self-interest will have a welcome outcome: If every man works to produce what is for himself "the greatest value," seeking selfishly "only his own gain," he will be "led by an invisible hand to promote an end which is no part of his intention," namely the common good.[22]

The UNESCO document falls within the penumbra cast by Condorcet and Smith. Every state signatory to the Convention agrees "to ensure that effective and active measures are taken for the protection, conservation, and presentation of the cultural…heritage situated on its territory" through a "comprehensive planning programme" that includes "an appropriate staff…scientific and technical studies and research…the appropriate legal, scientific, technical administrative and financial measures."[23] As a dividend for participation in the Convention, every state is then assured "collective assistance" in case it suffers from "insufficient economic, scientific, and technological resources" of its own.[24] Economic inequalities give way to mutual support in these united nations' mutual self-interested dedication to conserving extraordinary material evidence of universal human values.

The heroic present

I began with the question of how Ajanta, as a World Heritage monument, might provide a repository of value and values, culture, civilization, tradition, belief, art, meaning, and genius. What does it mean, in a word, for Ajanta to be an Enlightened monument in our global age? At least the rudiments of an answer are now in place, though of course they raise new problems, the most important being that of time. The Enlightenment's philosophical anthropology harbors a theory of time, presupposing a correlation between positive value and transtemporality. That theory is evident in the earlier citation from William Lipe, in which the road to future harmony "leads back in time." For Lipe, the past is a place in which the contemporary strife of competing nations and interest groups has no place; the preferred present is one not like now. So too the plated brass inscription at Ajanta's entrance presses the site's past into the service of humanity's future. The very fact that Ajanta's presence can be displaced from the present without loss of value is what allows it to be a World Heritage monument. Still, what of the present? Is there an Enlightened present? Might a place like Ajanta exist, not *for* time, but *in* time? The World Heritage Convention articulates criteria for recognizing Enlightenment embedded in such places and offers a means through which to preserve it for the future. How do present actions accomplish that Enlightened aim?

This shift from the question of values and universalism to that of time is inspired by Michel Foucault, whose essay, "What is Enlightenment?," gives us a way to think through temporality as implied by the World Heritage Convention's protocols.[25] Foucault wrote this piece for a conference to be held at Berkeley in 1984, the bicentennial anniversary of Kant's *Was ist Aufklärung?* (The conference was canceled on account of Foucault's death and the article was published posthumously.) Foucault finds novelty in Kant's own "little text" insofar as it presents the philosopher's task as a temporal task because it is a moral task.[26] That is, Kant's *Was ist Aufklärung?* does not pose the philosopher's questions—"what can be known, what must be done, and what may be hoped for"—as abstract matters for epistemology and ethics.[27] It shows, to the contrary, "how, at this very moment, each individual is responsible in a certain way for that overall process" of Enlightenment. Enlightenment is a puzzle of the present. Where presentness is often marked by the perception of an essential cohesive property (thus we are told this is the Information Age), or by its place in an eschatological or teleological framework (as evidenced by Lipe and the World Heritage Convention), Foucault finds in Kant the chrysalis of a novel approach to an Enlightened present: namely, as a process "defined by a modification of the preexisting relation linking will, authority, and the use of reason."[28] Enlightenment is a matter of living one's life *now* in a critical engagement with the past, whenever one's *now* so happens to be. Accordingly, although Foucault's article begins with Kant, it quickly shifts focus to modernity as an existential mode. The question, What is Enlightenment?, becomes, How is one *modern*? Foucault is noteworthy here, not only because he is the preeminent critic of Enlightenment universalism, but for my purposes because representations of Ajanta at all levels of interest—international, national, state, and regional—manifest what Foucault calls the ethos of modernity, a "will to 'heroize' the present."[29] What might this mean?

As a concrete point of departure, consider an advertisement from a campaign produced in 2001 by the Ogilvy and Mather agency for the Maharashtra Tourist Development Corporation (MTDC). These ads were featured in Indian travel magazines and hung as posters in the nation's airports. The one that interests me in particular begins with the headline—"A century ago, you could get much better souvenirs at Ajanta"—and ends with the tag—*The Ajanta Experience* (Figure 2.2). In between, the text reads,

> After Ajanta was rediscovered in the 19th century, a certain Narayan Ekenath was appointed the curator of the caves. Ekenath's specialty was obliging tourists with actual pieces of Ajanta art as souvenirs. Amongst these was a group of five male heads which were auctioned at Sotheby's of London in 1922. They now reside in the Boston Museum of Fine Arts.

Figure 2.2 Advertisement from the MTDC campaign, "The Ajanta Experience." Image graciously supplied by Ogilvy and Mather, Mumbai.

> Tourists today have to settle for far less valuable souvenirs. But they can come back with the satisfaction of knowing that their children, and their children's children, will be able to enjoy the wonders of Ajanta as well.

Foucault describes modernity as an attitude, a choice, a way of acting and behaving, a task, all of which add up to a single word: "heroization."[30] The MTDC's poster, likewise, sells Ajanta as a place at which to play hero. Capitalizing upon the short-sighted greed of yesteryear, *The Ajanta Experience* promises the twenty-first century tourist still greater satisfaction if he fashions himself as an Enlightened hero, whose understanding of the long-term costs of vandalism fosters moral restraint redounding to his own private benefit and the public good.

At first, this might look a page out of Rousseau's *Social Contract*: "The strongest man is never strong enough to always be master, unless he transforms his power into right, and obedience into duty."[31] But the poster's reference to public corruption is unremarkable. Its implicit premise: things have not changed so far from the nineteenth century of Ekenath Narayan. Public office in contemporary India remains a badge of power, but not of trust. One should, again citing Rousseau, "obey the powers that be" (or at least consider doing so).[32] Yet, we know how often those powers do not respect their own oaths of office. When that happens, only personal responsibility matched by personal self-discipline provides a reliable guide for action. It is this jaundice about the limits of public trust that transfigures this MTDC poster's audience from being Rousseau's heirs, "forced to be free," to being Foucault's modernist heroes, who make a "voluntary choice" to invent themselves in contradistinction to the many Narayan Ekenaths who still populate their world.[33]

The heroism of the MTDC's Ajanta experience is a banal heroism, to be sure. But that fact alone should not deprive it of highflown hermeneutics. To explain his conception of modernity Foucault looks to Charles Baudelaire, whose "consciousness of modernity is widely recognized as one of the most acute in the nineteenth century."[34] Baudelaire, in turn, named the painter Constantin Guys as a paragon of modernity, for Guys' paintings "transfigure[d] the world."[35] This is not to say that Guys somehow negated his present reality, or sought an eternal reality behind or beyond the present moment. Such transcendentalism is anathema to the modernist. Quite the contrary, Guys' acts of transfiguration multiplied realities. Guys made "natural" things "more than natural" and made "beautiful" things "more than beautiful." Modernity, for Baudelaire and thus for Foucault, was an accretive exercise, a way of living, in which one was at liberty to choose one's desired reality; in which one mindfully produced that reality, all the while, paradoxically, maintaining an "extreme attention to what is real."

The tourist's heroics, like that of Constantin Guys, lies in negotiating this "difficult interplay between the truth of what is real and the exercise of freedom."[36] Here is the truth of what is real. The MTDC advertisement makes reference to a group of five male heads auctioned at Sotheby's in 1922. Sotheby's received £1000 for this fragment.[37] Here again is the real truth: in 2002 the per capita income in Maharashtra was approximately Rs 24,000.[38] Now let us translate these two truths into 2002 US dollars. The fragment from Ajanta earned $21,500 at auction (doubtless this would have been a significantly higher figure had it really gone to auction in 2002), while Maharashtrians earn about $500 per year on average. In 2002, there was no electronic security at Ajanta; no network of cameras watched the caves. Guards are more or less vigilant in the popular caves, but at 3:00 pm in the hot month of May, really, anything goes. On a whim, or with preplanned stealth, another fragment could easily be stolen for a wealthy collector.

Modernity, Foucault notes, is not just a relationship with time. It is not just the ability to envision one's children and grandchildren visiting this ancient place, and thus to prefer preservation over quick profit. Modernity is also a mode of relationship with oneself. The willingness to forgo such "souvenirs" exemplifies an inner asceticism that Foucault describes as "indispensable" to "the deliberate attitude of modernity."[39] Driving to Ajanta, paying custom at the ticket booth, remaining on the concrete walkways, waiting patiently in lines, neither spitting nor shitting in the less popular caves even though the nearest bathroom is one-third of a mile away, not stealing paintings or carving names into them, in short reconciling one's desires to the authority of governmental reason, are the ritual acts of modernity that transfigure individuals into heroic citizens and respectful tourists, transfigure an experience of Ajanta into *The Ajanta Experience*, transfigure a place into a viable World Heritage monument, and transfigure a nation into a valued participant in an international Convention.

Ajanta then

The MTDC's tourist hero is a thoroughly modern Manu who, in obeying posted rules and uniformed guards, obeys himself as well. In Kantian terms, he is a moral being insofar as he freely submits his will to reason's dictates, expecting no satisfaction or reward for his obedience. And yet Kant recognizes that moral perfection is unattainable. As embodied beings we are never free of irrational drives and desires. No man can follow the moral law *gladly*, no matter what privations it demands.[40] Thus we should not judge the MTDC's tourist hero too harshly if he buys *The Ajanta Experience*, in part, because it promises that doing his duty will yield still greater satisfactions.

The tourist's heroic modernity emerges within a universe of collective possibilities and impossibilities, liberties accepted and liberties rejected. The Enlightened rejection of unEnlightened freedoms, in turn, plays upon a prurient interest in those older, now-shunned freedoms that the site's earliest visitors enjoyed. The former curator, Ekenath Narayan, is an object of scorn, but also of fascination. That prurience allows *The Ajanta Experience's* bourgeois heroism to play a "compensatory function" akin to that described in Janice Radway's ethnographic study of women who read romance novels. Avid readers of "bodice rippers" tend to be women unfulfilled by the "routinized, regimented, and minimally challenging" roles of suburban America housewifery—chauffeur, maid, cook—and alienated from husbands who regard such domestic chores as little more than structured indolence.[41] These women find a missing satisfaction and reason for optimism in romance novels. For our purposes the noteworthy point is that these women also feel abashed at this personal indulgence, which seems to them "hedonistic." Romances are a *guilty* pleasure, forcing these women to "work out a complex rationalization...that not only asserts their equal right to pleasure but also legitimates the books by linking them with values more widely approved within American culture."[42] So too *The Ajanta Experience* poster electrifies the site with a dirty charge through its evocation of Ajanta's wild past, while disavowing that pleasure in favor of other enjoyments marked as suitably modern.

To better grasp Ajanta's modernity—as an ideal present chosen in conscious tension with both an imagined past as well as an actual present—we need to know more about Ajanta's re-creation over the past two centuries. Let us consider the era of Ekenath Narayan, seeking those now-forbidden freedoms for which *The Ajanta Experience* compensates. The following section will then turn to twentieth-century labors that have transfigured Ajanta into a World Heritage site proper.

For rough romance, there is no leading-man to surpass Lieutenant James Edward Alexander, Sixteenth Lancers, of the Order of the Lion and Sun. In February 1824, Alexander was traveling through Maharashtra's countryside when

46

he decided to investigate the little-known caves near the Ajanta pass.[43] The danger was palpable as Alexander arrayed himself in Muselmani costume, and strapped on sabres, pistols, and hunting spears before leaving the caravanserai at Ajanta village. When he passed through the town gate, a native soldier warned: " '*La illah illilah!* (There is but one God) you will never return: for if you escape the tigers, these stony-hearted robbers, the Bheels, will destroy you.' " Indeed, a nearby cairn marked "where unfortunate travellers had been destroyed by tigers." But Alexander remained undaunted, winding along the course of the Waghora River, ever deeper into a glen "remarkable for its picturesque beauty," secreted in the "wild and romantic" hills.

What did Lieutenant Alexander find in the heart of that glen? As an able naturalist, he noted neem trees, mimosas, and *ficus religiosa* lining the way. But then he reached a 250-foot high wall of rock, hanging sheerly above the Waghora's torrent bed, sweeping around in a semicircle, and terminating in a series of waterfalls. The caves loomed high, ranging between 50 and 100 feet above the stream. Alexander ascended. Clambering into the first, and then several others, he found: a

> fetid smell, arising from numerous bats...the remains of a recent fire...the entire skeleton of a man...prints of the feet of tigers, jackals, bears, monkeys, peacocks, &c....impressed upon the dust, formed by the plaster of the fresco paintings which had fallen from the ceilings.[44]

But Alexander also discovered a nice spot to smoke a *chilum*, and in the end he broke out in Horace's ode, "Quae non imber edax non aquilo impotens...," before returning to town.[45] (Figures 2.3 and 2.4.)

If early visitors made a pilgrimage to Ajanta to behold "imperishable monuments of antiquity," as Alexander described it, they did so no less than for the wild adventure.[46] After coming by cart or foot along the riverbed, they would then pick their ways up the rock face, or scramble along ancient stairs, to reach the caves, each suspended in the reaches of the sheer wall; some caves remained inaccessible except by rope. Even in 1828 one complained, "these caves are becoming daily more difficult of access. You pass along narrow goat paths with a chasm of 50 or 80 feet below, the footing not nine inches broad, with scarce any thing to cling to."[47]

From the 1820s to the 1920s, visitors braved many hazards, not to mention the random effects of water, time, and humanity. Lieutenant Blake, who visited in 1839, described the caves as "daily suffering from lying choked in mud," and the Europeans as suffering from the cupidity of the local headman, "a rude jungly individual."[48] Blake also mentioned wasps and bats, which can still strike fear today. Other early tourists loved to complain about the Bhīls, the local aborigines. In 1824, Alexander observed that, had his party lacked firearms, the Bhīls would have slain them to a man. Within a decade, the Bhīls were deprived of their deadly bows, but retained the power to confute European sensibilities. The Bhīls believed that the gods had created Ajanta and that a number of divine beings—some tribal, some Hindu—continued to live therein. These caves were homes for

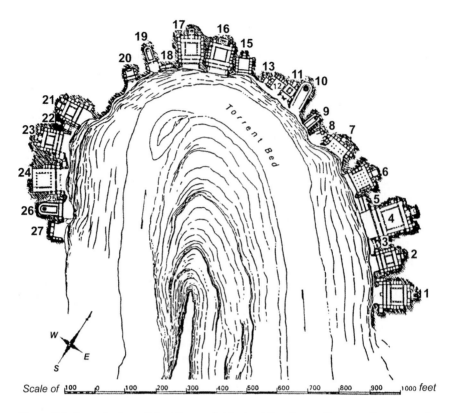

Figure 2.3 General plan of the Caves of Ajanta. After James Burgess, *Report on the Buddhist Cave Temples*, plate XIV.

Figure 2.4 A view of Ajanta, from Cave Sixteen to Cave Twenty Six (from left to right). Photo by author.

Śiva, Pārvatī, and Indra, as well as Gattu Darj, Jagarnath, Kokan Nath, and Jelandar Nath, among others.[49] The Bhīls named individual caves for their indwelling divinities. This confused the Europeans, not least because even the Bhīls themselves held no consensus as to which god inhabited which cave. In the 1840s, James Fergusson brought solid scientific order to the site by numbering each cave, 1 to 29 from East to West. The old Bhīl names are now not used and almost wholly forgotten.

Still other visitors, well before Narayan Ekenath, sought souvenirs but received censure. The MTDC advertisement notwithstanding, one century ago you could *not* get much better souvenirs at Ajanta than you can now, simply because most would disintegrate upon removal. The painted fragment mentioned in that advertisement is the only known surviving plunder.[50] The friable nature of these artifacts was obvious. In 1828 several adventurers found themselves at Ajanta simultaneously, including one Mr Ralph and one Dr Bird. A transcript of the encounter between these two tells us that Dr Bird sought to bring a bit of Ajanta back to Bombay with him. Mr Ralph warned, "as for carrying away the paintings, you can do so *in powder*. I have ascertained that they will not quit the wall in laminae, but crumble under touch."[51] The reporter of this conversation described Dr Bird as "an intelligent young Medical man from Bombay." But we might have reason to question that judgment. For "notwithstanding protestations about defacing monuments, this visitor [Dr Bird] contrived to peel off four painted figures."[52] Those four figures crumbled into powder.

Ajanta now

That is not the last we hear of Dr James Bird. In 1847 he published *Historical Researches on the Origin and Principles of the Bauddha and Jain Religions*, capitalizing upon on his visit to Ajanta two decades earlier. Twenty years had brought about a notable change of heart. For whereas the James Bird of 1828 defaced Ajanta notwithstanding protest, his own book spoke of "the duty imposed on us, as a nation, to preserve these relics of ancient art."[53] Bird was not concerned solely with the caves as memorials to India's past. Rather, presaging the World Heritage Convention's criterion that its monuments must possess exceptional universal value, Bird imagined India's cave temples to be synecdoches for its populace's state of grace. "It is scarcely comprehensible," he scolded at the beginning of his preface, "how our government could have so long neglected monuments of such historical importance, associated as they are with the former state of India, and with the moral and religious condition of its people."[54] He completed his thought at the preface's end: "Those anxious for the welfare and happiness of a heathen people" would find in his book evidence that "Brahmanical prejudices and Hindu customs are not of that unchangeable character so long and erroneously ascribed to them."[55] Attention paid to the reconstruction of historical monuments anticipated a more profound reconstruction, rebuilding India on the foundation of "true religion."[56]

Bird's changed attitude concerning archaeological practice might be tied to a plea made four years before his book's publication by James Fergusson, the leading archaeologist of the day, who indicted Bird in full hearing of the Royal Asiatic Society of Great Britain and Ireland:

> It is sad to think that after standing so many years and exposure to so destructive a climate, after escaping the bigotry of the Moslem and the rough usage of the robber Bheel, they [Ajanta's paintings] should be fast perishing from the meddling curiosity of the Europeans who now visit them. But such is unfortunately the case; for few come away without picking off one or two of the heads he thinks most beautiful or interesting, and as most of them are reduced to powder before they reach their destination, they are lost to the world for ever. The only instance of this I can refer to in print is...where it is stated, that Dr. Bird peeled four figures off the Zodiac in cave No. 17.[57]

Inspired by Fergusson, the Royal Asiatic Society issued a Memorial to the East India Company, soliciting "their interposition to preserve the Caves from all such causes of injury and decay as may be obviated by means within the authority of our Indian government," and requesting that it employ accomplished artists to copy the Ajanta's paintings, "before it was too late."[58] Within a year, the colonial government authorized money for repairs, and hired Captain Robert Gill of the Madras Army, "who was at that period probably one of the best artists in India."[59]

The modern history of Ajanta is a tale of fighting time and losing. Captain Gill arrived at Ajanta in 1844 with fanfare, bodyguards, and his own elephant. For more than twenty years he carefully copied the paintings, sending his reproductions by bullock cart to Bombay, and thence to London. In 1866, all but five of his canvases were placed on display at the Crystal Palace Exhibition, not long before a fire swept through the exhibition in December, destroying twenty-years' work. Six years later John Griffiths, Principal of the Bombay School of Arts, began annual excursions with his students to pick up after Gill's loss. Read the hope in this description of Griffiths' project, published in 1884:

> Mr. Griffiths and his staff have been at work for five or six seasons, and the results of their labours are sent to England as soon as completed, and placed in the India Museum. A good deal yet remains to be done, but there is every reason to believe that, before long, copies of the whole of the fragments...of these truly wonderful frescoes will have been executed.[60]

On June 12, 1885 the majority of Griffiths' 125 paintings, each canvas between 20 and 30 feet square, were lost to a noon-time fire that swept through the museum's storage area.

These mishaps were followed, naturally, by more. John Cumming's history of archaeological conservation in India tells us that Griffiths and his students, joined by other well-intentioned artists, slathered cheap varnish on the paintings to bring out the colors. Not long thereafter, the temporary fix "not only made the brush-work more indistinct, but in some cases where the dirt had not been removed beforehand from the fresco, converted the entire painting into a dingy patch."[61] In the early 1920s, the Nizam of Hyderabad, in whose territory Ajanta lay until independence, appointed two Italian experts in art restoration, at the royal sum of £400 per month, plus expenses, to resolve this solution and preserve the art. At the time, the Nizam's Director of Archaeology said of Professor Lorenzo Cecconi and Count Orsini's labors that "the repairs to the caves and the cleaning and conservation of the frescoes have been carried out on such sound principles and in such a scientific manner that these matchless monuments have found a fresh lease of life for at least a couple of centuries."[62] As the decades have passed, the return on the Nizam's investment in the future has been less than anticipated.

Nevertheless, the Nizam was the man most responsible for transforming Ajanta, from the difficult preserve of committed and intrepid travelers to a destination ready for tourists. He built roads and bridges, enabling cars to drive directly to the caves. He built a rest house for the weary in easy walking distance of the site. He cut a walkway into the hillside, making it possible for visitors to walk from one cave to the next without having to descend to the torrent bed. In short, the Nizam was the initial architect of what the MTDC later advertised as *The Ajanta Experience*.

This experience is becoming increasingly regularized and (re)constructed. Local workers, whose great-grandparents served early visitors by carrying packs and lanterns, scaring away swarms of bees and bats, or clearing the caves of mud and debris, are now watched by overseers brought from Nepal, who have no local ties and for that reason are presumed to be free of the small kindnesses that lead to petty corruption. Now the ASI rebuilds crumbled walls and patches icons so that a casual glance does not perceive the decay brought about by centuries of rain, mud, bees, and parrots. Now the ASI cleans paintings. But in the act of wiping away the soot that covers and protects Ajanta's paintings, restorers also remove the color washes and fine lines that define their subtle grace. Indeed, this last fact has led the art historian Walter Spink to publically campaign against the ASI's efforts. For Spink, the ASI's chemical branch might well be second only to Ekenath Narayan as a named agent of permanent damage.[63] Still work progresses apace.

There is even a plan to build a museum near the site. As a repository for artifacts found near the caves it will be like any other archaeological site museum. But at Ajanta there will also be a special section, recreating Caves Sixteen, Seventeen, and Twenty One.[64] This last addition is said to be in response to tourists' complaints that, because they are now permitted in the caves for only fifteen minutes at a stretch, they lack sufficient time "to soak in the beauty of the frescoes." For this reason, the "artificial caves will be created, lighting them brightly and projecting photographic images on the walls to enable art aficionados and scholars to study the paintings at leisure."[65]

From values to value

My purpose for reproducing this brief, already out-of-date timeline for Ajanta's modern production is not to mock early visitors, the Nizam, or the ASI, which now administers the site. Rather, my purpose is to destabilize the equation between contemporary valuation of Ajanta as an exceptional and universal place, on the one hand, and contemporary expectations that it is a locus of *authenticity*, on the other. To continue that destabilization, the chapter now takes a major turn. We have a sense of the Enlightenment universalism implicit in UNESCO's naming a site to the World Heritage List; and a sense of Ajanta's exceptional placement within a range of physical, social, and imaginal landscapes. That is to say, we have a sense of World Heritage *values*. Now it is time to talk about World Heritage's *value*.

To begin, let us take an insight from Dean MacCannell's *The Tourist*, a work foundational to the field of Tourism Studies. MacCannell places tourism at the cusp of the secular and the religious, the modern and the primitive. It is an "inescapable conclusion," he writes, "that tourist attractions...provide direct access to the modern consciousness or 'world view,' that tourist attractions are precisely analogous to the religious symbolism of primitive people."[66] There is much to criticize in these words, from MacCannell's pairing of "primitive" and "modern" as antipodes, to his predication of modernity as a time in which the religious is sublated into the secular. Still, let us pursue the analogy: tourist travel is the secular equivalent for religious pilgrimage. Why? What links the two? In a word, authenticity. Like the literal-minded Christian or Jew who travels to the Holy Land to see what Jesus saw and tread where Moses trod, tourists traverse the globe in search of an *authenticity* their own lives lack. Whereas the religious person unselfconsciously inhabits his authentic self, the modern secular person inhabits his workaday life as a charade of shifting values and incomplete selves, inauthentic, detached from deep wellsprings of heritage and meaning. To recapture the substance of reality, the tourist looks for authenticity in "the souvenirs of destroyed cultures and dead epochs."[67] The tourist actively seeks out other nows, untouched by his own everyday today.

MacCannell's model of tourism has obvious resonances in Foucault, for whom modernity is a relationship of self-fashioning, in which one enacts a reality of one's choice while paying exquisite attention to the real. Given MacCannell's religious metaphors, however, Jonathan Z. Smith's treatment of *ritual* provides a still better fit. For Smith, ritual too is a means for negotiating temporal existence. Where MacCannell's tourist is "condemned to look elsewhere, everywhere, for his authenticity," Smith's ritual "represents the creation of a controlled environment where the variables (accidents) of ordinary life may be displaced precisely because they are felt to be so overwhelmingly present and powerful....Ritual gains force where incongruity is perceived and thought about."[68] Where MacCannell's middle American travels in order to escape a daily routine that has "turned [him] against himself, fundamentally dividing his existence," Smith's ritual creates "a relationship of difference between 'nows' " in which participants perform "the way things ought to be in conscious tension to the way things are."[69]

Smith's ritualism, like Foucault's modernity, recreates the world while leaving the world intact. Dean MacCannell's theorization of tourism fits this pattern, albeit with at least one crucial difference. Unlike Foucault's modernist and Smith's ritualist, MacCannell's tourist always fails to bridge the gap between the actualized and the actual. Seeking authenticity, tourists only ever find "staged authenticity."

> A mere experience may be mystified, but a touristic experience is always mystified. The lie contained in the touristic experience, moreover, presents itself as a truthful revelation, as the vehicle that carries the onlooker behind false fronts into reality. The idea here is that a false back is more insidious and dangerous than a false front, or an inauthentic demystification of social life is not merely a lie but a superlie, the kind that drips with sincerity.[70]

When one goes to Ajanta today one stands sincerely in slow-moving queues and stares sincerely at retouched paintings behind glass. These authentic experiences share little with Lieutenant Alexander's wild and romantic Ajanta, or the wholly unstaged truth revealed to Dr Bird, who carefully lifted paintings off the wall only to see them become dust. But if Ajanta is now a stage, the staging—the creation of what McCannell calls a "false back"—is itself an acknowledged dimension of the "real front." At a World Heritage monument like Ajanta, staging is an *authentic* experience in its own right. One goes to Ajanta to enjoy one's own Enlightenment, apart from the Alexanders, Birds, and Ekenath Narayans of yesteryear. Indeed, the World Heritage Convention's *raison d'etre* is to promote and facilitate staging in the name of conservation; to take Ajanta out of the temporal flow, making it a modern place at which the past becomes a resource for the future.

The Mahābodhi Temple (the site of the buddha's enlightenment) in Bodh Gayā provides cognate example of "staging." This temple's nomination to World Heritage status in 2002 came with a proviso: UNESCO demanded the creation of a "buffer zone." All buildings located within one kilometer of the temple had to be razed—all shops, hotels, offices, even Buddhist monasteries.[71] To be an authentic bearer of exceptional universal value, Bodh Gayā's temple has to be segregated from everything that might stigmatize it by association with the contemporary world. Consumer culture, global capitalism, and transnational movements of peoples and goods thrive on the commodification of certain civilizational remains as possessing World Heritage value. Local economies and political structures at all levels benefit from that commodification, though the hoteliers and shopkeepers in Bodh Gayā who lose their livelihood might disagree. As scholars of cultural resource management never cease repeating, in this economy the past is a precious resource.

Given the cliché of religion as a source for answers to life's unknowns, it makes sense for MacCannell to pair tourism with religious pilgrimage. Both involve a journey beyond the seeker's own well-trodden world in search of a pure ground, a spectacle of ultimacy. In both cases, proponents would deny that they are principally oriented toward the consumption of manufactured goods (material, experiential, even spiritual). And yet despite that disclaimer, both are patent instances of consumerism: futile, for their authenticities are ever only "staged." We pity someone who imagines that package-tour villages and rebuilt caves, let alone museum pieces, show him mother India as she *really* is/was; who does not recognize authentic staging as local reality; who does not understand his own modernity enough to see that although nostalgia for the premodern seems to be a form of esteem, it is in fact just the opposite: staged authenticity valorizes neither the past nor tradition, but the modern's dominion over both.

The postmodern winks at ersatz realities and enjoys the game of seeing through games. That attitude is not in evidence at UNESCO, or in the ASI's stagings at Ajanta. Operational guidelines for implementing the World Heritage Convention require a "test of authenticity" to ensure that nothing present at a site is inconsistent with the World Heritage value of that site.[72] Passing this test is a necessary condition for World Heritage status. The guidelines do not detail the test's exact parameters, yet authenticity is so serious an archaeological value that UNESCO requires even the means for adjudging authenticity be "authentic." In this spirit, consider the following statement from Myra Shackley's textbook, *Visitor Management: Case Studies from World Heritage Sites*. This book's introduction begins with the usual platitudes—every World Heritage site is unique; all are humanity's common inheritance—leading to Shackley's observation: "World Heritage is a fragile non-renewable resource which has to be safeguarded both to maintain its authenticity and to preserve it for future generations."[73] Note, "resource" does *not* refer to sites or their artifacts. Here, without irony, Shackley names the *World Heritage* designation itself as that pearl of great price.

What can it mean for World Heritage to be authentic or a non-renewable resource? We can readily understand how Ajanta's paintings are non-renewable, whether their irrevocable loss is at the hand of an expert restorer or a stealthy thief. But World Heritage is not a physical object, the remains of a defunct culture transvalued through advertisements, transportation networks, and history books. World Heritage is a contemporary phenomenon, a modern consensus about the past. As an object, the World Heritage designation belongs in the company of the Rolls Royce badge, the yellow label on a bottle of Veuve Clicquot, or Chanel's linked c's. It is a luxury brand whose coveted trademark guarantees the presence of *exceptional universal value*. If "A Diamond Is Forever," so should be a World Heritage monument. But while De Beers markets eternal love through the strength of carbon's covalent bonds, UNESCO sells its universal value as a rarity preserved in the oxymoron of evanescent stone.

Lasting love need cost only three months' salary, but the price of universal value is the present itself. For World Heritage is a non-renewable resource whose universal value can now be consumed only at monuments bearing the UNESCO mark. To build brand equity, the Convention devalues the present. Its criteria stipulate that tangible association with a living tradition is not a basis for inclusion on the World Heritage List, except in a few extraordinary cases.[74] Shackley's textbook, likewise, can be read for its marketing potential:

> The List contains universally recognized sites, like the Pyramids or the Great Wall of China, but it also includes smaller, less well-known properties and monuments whose significance is universal and which transcend existing cultural values.[75]

"...and which transcend existing cultural values." Why is Shackley condescending toward the *cultural*, insinuating synonyms such as small-scale, parochial, narrow, self-interested, and of course, insignificant? Does she understand that her characterization of those lesser cultural values as *existing* distributes opprobrium to the people who live by them now?

Myra Shackley commits a classic parapraxis when she names World Heritage as a non-renewable resource in need of protection: out slips UNESCO's fantasy. However, the wish expressed here is not the Enlightenment's overt desire for all humans to unite within a single great moral project (in this case, to preserve the human past). Rather, the wish is latent: All people should buy *World Heritage* as a definitive source of Enlightenment in the modern world. The appearance of authenticity must be preserved at Ajanta, for Enlightenment is nothing other than that *appearance* sold as something universally valuable to all human beings.

Strategic brand management

One does not have to be a semiotician to evaluate the broad significance of brands in the contemporary world, nor be a sibyl to augur that branding is a key to the heritage industry. Package tours find their direct ancestor in package goods. As a cure for monumental woes, the World Heritage designation is an avatar of patent medicine. Thomas Hine has traced the modern practices of packaging and labeling to seventeenth-century London, where Mr Stoughton manufactured Drops, Mr Turlington packaged the Original Balsam, and Mr Daffy sold an Elixir. One can count many reasons that such consumables began to circulate at this time, including cheap glass production, burgeoning literacy, the Reformation's granting of sovereignty to the individual conscience, and even the fact that the abstemious could find a legitimate high within a patent medicine's liquors.[76] But while these factors all contributed to the genesis of our consumer economy, marketing experts point more generally to the personalization of market goods as the solution for the dark spot at the core of a market economy. The market is a risky place, requiring consumers to transact business without adequate information. We do not know who makes the things we buy, or when the things were made, or where, or under what conditions. Commodities are risky. Packing, and later branding, are the market solutions to that risk.

Given that commercial transactions transpire at a great social, temporal, and geographical remove from their objects' place of manufacture, the circumstances of the transaction itself must erase any doubt that an object will serve its intended purpose without unforseen consequences. To encourage widespread distribution, manufacturers placed patent medicines in uniquely shaped packages bearing personal names as a guarantee of safety and consistency. The package created a trusted identity with which a buyer could have a relationship, what we now call a brand. As Hine puts it, "even those medicine sellers who were honest and who believed their product benefitted mankind recognized that it was more important to sell an idea, a feeling, a reassuring package, than it was to sell the contents."[77]

If this nostrum for consumer anxiety was formulated by eighteenth-century hucksters, it took until the 1980s for Madison Avenue to guess the secret ingredient. Indeed, although Dr Brown, and Uncle Ben, and Aunt Jemima sold their goods beginning in the last century, it was only in this latter decade that a "Copernican revolution" occurred in how brands were conceived and valued.[78] Jean-Noël Kapferer describes this revolution:

> Prior to 1980, companies wished to buy a producer of chocolate or pasta: after 1980, they wanted to buy KitKat or Buitoni. ... The vision has changed from one where only tangible assets had value to one where companies now believe that their most important asset is their brands, which are intangible and immaterial.[79]

One can scare up any number of academic bugaboos to analyze this transformation—the culture industry, manufactured consent, commodity fetishism, late capitalism, hyperreality—but that is not necessary. For critical theory has met its match in the business press, which not only recognizes the phenomenon, but also, at least in the case of marketing guru Tom Peters, exclaims the point with great force if little subtlety: "Brand! Brand!! Brand!!!"[80] Lacking context, who could know that, "Just say no to COMMODITY. Say yes to WOW!" does not protest a World Trade Organization cabal, but flings the shit of a white-collar revolution.[81] Yet who now could fail to anticipate that this same writer sells WOW! as a commodity?[82] We inhabit a time when marketing, not manufacturing, is the CEO's priority; when companies compete, ostensibly, not for the consumer's dollar, but for his mind; when a company's brand might be valued at a much higher multiple than its tangible assets; when the statement, "everything and everyone is capable of becoming a brand," is not a lament but an eager promise;[83] when branding can have Twenty Two Immutable Laws and Ten Commandments; and when an uncanny parallelism exists between branding's Tenth Commandment—"The purpose of a brand is to be a vehicle for transferring both value and values"[84]—and the agenda of an Enlightened convention on World Heritage.

In sum, marketers have theorized that the most successful capitalists will be those who emphasize the second clause, not the first, in Brillat-Savarin's, "tell me what you eat, and I'll tell you what you are." You *are* what you buy. Creating meanings and forming identities, commodity consumption is now how we are human. Brands, which began as a means for alleviating worries due to the distant origin of consumer goods, and then became a way to distinguish between otherwise identical commodities, now combine these functions. Brands allow people to be secure in their individual identities.

World Heritage fits the bill. Shackley's textbook speaks plainly: "The term 'World Heritage Site' is instantly recognized as designating something very special, in tourism terms a definite 'must see.' "[85] One can easily guess at a range of explanations for this must-see attitude, from fascination with the exotic through the raising of social capital by consuming special, rare goods. Dean MacCannell would add at least one more explanation: No matter where tourists go, no matter how rare or special the place, they seek authenticity. UNESCO's own stipulation of authenticity as an attribute of all World Heritage sites would confirm MacCannell's insight. Yet reflection on the work of branding suggests that even if MacCannell is correct about the tourist's tragedy—the authenticity he finds is staged—MacCannell is also wrong. The World Heritage brand guarantees that by visiting World Heritage sites, tourists are themselves authenticated. By concerning themselves with monuments of exceptional universal value, tourists find their own values to be exceptional and universal. By acting to preserve the world's heritage, they themselves become worthy of all humanity's protection. If the World Heritage Convention has its conceptual genesis in Enlightenment humanism, then consumers of listed sites may consider themselves Enlightened. Enlightenment is nothing other than the ability to recognize, and act appropriately in relation to, sources of exceptional universal value. One can just imagine Tom Peters' incitement to Enlightened action: Buy! Buy!! Buy!!!

On utility and appearance

This chapter began by inquiring how caves created in the first half of the first millennium CE, then ignored for close to 1,500 years, have been transvalued into objects possessing the highest possible worth. In exploring this question, I took a cue from William Lipe's introduction to resource management, a field that studies cultural artifacts' "use and benefit—in the present and future."[86] Thus, the chapter has explored several uses to which Ajanta has been put. In the nineteenth century, the site offered colonial explorers an object of fascination: its exotic location—remote even for India—so strikingly at odds with the high culture found in its frescoes. Those paintings' preservation, in turn, presented the British with an opportunity to expand their colonization from the military sphere to the cultural, as well as to adjudicate personal animosities, as we see in James Fergusson's public indictment of James Bird. Likewise, when the aboriginal Bhīls worked for the British as guides, they used the occasion to offer a meek resistance through subtle mockery. During the twentieth century, the Nizam of Hyderabad built roads, making the caves easier of access and speeding their deterioration. Simultaneously he began a process of museumification in the name of preservation. After independence, the Nizam's stewardship was replaced by that of the ASI. More recently, the MTDC has initiated plans to complete the Nizam's work by making Ajanta fully a museum. It will build a duplicate Ajanta controlled by its own organization: a new Ajanta at which visitors are not discomfited by having to climb a steep slope or swelter in the open sun. On the museum's walls, all might view projected slides to their hearts' content.

Finally, the chapter explored a complex of ideological uses for these caves. Their preservation makes India a valued member in the family of nations. People who act to foster their preservation are valued as citizens and as human beings. The caves are thus useful as a place at which to observe the pageant of modernity unfold. This is a *ritual* function in Jonathan Z. Smith's terms, because it permits one to conceive multiple *nows*, and to act in such a way as to produce the desired *then*. To expand the metaphor: By granting or withholding World Heritage status, UNESCO plays the role of high priest; a charismatic institution, its mysteries transubstantiate once-mere stone into an extraordinary source of universal value. UNESCO's transforming utterances know no divinity, just the Enlightenment's sacred optimism that when human beings (re)discover their nature in full they will produce a society of unbroken peace and unfettered freedom.

For resource managers, a society's forward progress can be judged by how it uses the past, how it cares. But even Kant recognized that human beings are incapable of full dedication to present morality unless they receive some hope of future recompense. Duty too requires marketing. Hence, for Kant, morality requires religion, which repackages the imperative toward the highest good as a divine command, branding it Salvation. Duty—appropriate utility—can be represented as a source of transcendental value, but only by being sold as something other than utility, by appearing to be more than merely useful.

The relationship between appearance and utility can be explained with greater precision through the Marxian distinction between the *use-value* of a commodity—its power to fulfill natural needs—and the *exchange-value*—its power to command a price in the marketplace. Writing on commodity aesthetics, Wolfgang Haug aligns these two dimensions of value with the two parties in a commercial transaction. Buyers are anxious about use-value; sellers about exchange-value. Successful sellers thus ensure that their goods *appear* useful to buyers.

> In all commodity production a double reality is produced: first the use-value; second, and more importantly, the *appearance* of use-value. For, until the sale is completed (and the exchange-value has been realized), use-value figures only in as much as the buyer promises him- or herself the use-value of the commodity. From the seller's (i.e., exchange-value) position, until the sale is effected, the commodity's promise of use-value is all that counts. Right from the start, therefore, because of its economic function, the emphasis is on what the use-value *appears* to be.... The commodity's aesthetic promise of use-value thus becomes an instrument in accumulating money.... Whoever controls the product's appearance can control the fascinated public by appealing to them sensually.[87]

This is why you pay more for Gold Medal Flour than the no-name generic. Both make the same cookies, but you expect Gold Medal to be diligent about keeping rat feces out of its product, and do not expect the same level of care from a generic mill. Your fears are Gold Medal's bounty.

World Heritage sites would seem to differ from flour in at least one respect. Namely, these places do not need to manage the appearance of utility. The reason is simple: World Heritage sites have no exchange-value since, possessed of exceptional universal value, they always already belong to all humanity. They can never become objects for exchange in a marketplace. Who has the right to sell them? Who could afford to buy one? So, if World Heritage sites appear useful, it must be because they really are authentically useful.

Is this correct? Are World Heritage sites essentially uncommodifiable? In light of the previous section's analysis of branding, one is rightfully suspicious of that conceit. It may be the case, rather, that the characterization of World Heritage sites as bearers of pure use-value is pure ideology. Per Haug, in capitalist systems—this holds as true for social or cultural economies, as for monetary—use-value enciphers exchange-value. The *appearance* of utility makes an object worthy of exchange. The greater the glamour attached to that appearance of use, the greater the potential price. What is more attractive, more useful, more worthy, than something having universal worth? And what is more in need of encoding within the cryptogram of *universality* than an object that, while being perfectly useless, must be accepted as perfectly useful: an object like a painting, like a musical score, like an ancient neglected cave, or (to recall Kant) like religion? Perhaps the value added to World Heritage sites is the perception that they belong to all, that they deserve every rupee they receive, and that a will toward the preservation of their ancient authenticity makes one truly modern.

In this way, World Heritage sites might be sold in much the same way that Sprite soft-drink has been sold. In the late 1990s Sprite ran a series of commercials that capitalized upon the unreality of the standard soft-drink fantasies. By drinking Sprite, the boys in these ads did *not* become he-man hunks, or suave Romeos, or skillful athletes. The boys did not change at all, and the ads admitted that Sprite offers nothing to consumers who expect to enhance their social standing through consumption. The commercials ended with a series of slogans: Image is Nothing. Thirst is Everything. Obey Your Thirst. Thus, these commercials artfully disclosed the common ploys for enhancing a commodity's exchange-value—the extra charge that makes *this* thing more desirable than *that*—while valorizing, in turn, the salience of genuine utility. These commercials presented Sprite as an honest solution to the problem of a universal, innate, transcultural, transtemporal, human need—thirst—completely untainted by commercial ideology. But who was fooled? Sprite's no-image was itself an image; the appearance of mere utility added value.

The earlier, pre-1990s, ideal of branding was *a posteriori* universality. This was achieved by personal items like Kleenex, Band-Aid, and Q-Tips when their names became synonymous with entire categories of products. Sprite's engagement with thirst went deeper. Had its advertisements been fully successful, the thought, "I'm thirsty," would no longer be formed, only, "I need Sprite," even as one reached for water. It is not that "water" would have become a form of Sprite, but that the need-for-Sprite would have named a biological need. In that advertisement, the *image* in "image is nothing" was synecdochic for all desires manufactured in a sociocultural matrix. By subordinating the sociocultural to the biological, the ad naturalized its message as an element of will: Obey Your Thirst strove to be the voice of conscience.

To my knowledge, Sprite did not achieve that success in its gambit for *a priori* universality. Nor has Nike appropriated *élan vital* with the phrase, *Just Do It*; nor has Home Box Office become the new standard for calendrical time with its words, *Sunday is HBO*. Douglas Holt and Juliet Schor describe these slogans' objective:

> Marketing learned . . . people must experience consumption as a volitional site of personal development, achievement, and self-creation, not as a place in which they are simply mapping their lives on some advertiser's template. . . . Thus, monopolizing the public channels of meaning creation is becoming more important than monopolizing *particular* meanings.[88]

In this light, the complex of symbolic gestures through which UNESCO naturalizes its hegemony over international tourism, indeed over planetary geography, is patent, brilliant, and at the cutting edge of commercial representation. What more effective way to monopolize the creation of meaning than to control channels of access to legitimate sources of meaningfulness? This is what the World Heritage designation seeks to accomplish. UNESCO's jurisdiction over judgments of transnational and transtemporal value places it at the juncture of time, space, creativity, and human nature. The far edge of this monopolization is demarcated by Myra Shackley's statement in page 54: "World Heritage is a fragile non-renewable resource which has to be safeguarded both to maintain its authenticity and to preserve it for future generations."[89] Here, all material, psycho-social, and symbolic values and fears attached to human locales—the Taj, the Great Wall, Machu Picchu, Ajanta—are transferred to the UNESCO Convention. Places that had once been forgotten, defunct, or simply of local interest are transvalued into places at which to enjoy extraordinary spectacles of the authentic and universally human. Their unlimited worth becomes that of UNESCO itself.

Cutting through spiritual materialism

Why the sarcasm? Why condemn UNESCO? Do you want to see the Coliseum corrode or the stūpa of Barabudur collapse down upon itself? Maybe UNESCO does mobilize an Enlightenment ideology of universal humanity in order to naturalize its own political authority and power. Always everywhere institutions have done the same. At least in this case the benefits are indisputable: conservation and preservation. As ciphers for authenticity and universality, World Heritage and Obey Your Thirst materialize a kindred spirit. So what? Even if the representations of these things as merely useful does hide the fact that consumers are being sold upon *appearances*? We do need to drink liquids. We do need to know where to go on vacation.

Finally, unable to restrain himself any longer, James Twitchell chimes in, "Commercialism *is* our better judgement. Not only are we willing to consume, and not only does consuming make us happy, 'getting and spending' is what gives our lives order and purpose."[90]

Such dissenting voices remind us how easy it is for targeted critique to slip over into carping when a deception, even one with a seemingly benign outcome, fills one's vision. This is the case in this present instance, especially insofar as the criticism of UNESCO belongs to a broader critical tradition aimed at capitalism's depredations. Where should we look for the genesis of that tradition if not in Marx's depiction of the bourgeois everyman in the *Economic and Philosophic Manuscripts*: a moralistic rant about a human being so besotted by "inhuman, sophisticated, unnatural and imaginary appetites" that he willingly signs a Mephistophelian pact, selling his own life-force (in the alienated form of money) for the satiation of "depraved fancies" and "morbid appetites."[91] Disgust at bourgeois humanity continues to the present day though, of course, critics now have no necessary allegiance to Marx. Even Tom Peters, the best selling business-author of all time, calls commoditization a blight, and clamors for Revolution.[92] Clearly, Marxist politics has lost the power of its native tongue. Still, there is no shortage of critics to point out that the language of consumerism includes only empty signs. Unalloyed consumerism has been blamed for effects as varied as cultural fragmentation, the decline of participation in public life, the abominations of shoppertainment and entertailing, the failure of the nuclear family, spiritual malaise, conformity, bad taste, boredom, and a surfeit of beige.[93] We might wonder whether these same critics would be openly skeptical about the way in which UNESCO sells the world on itself by selling Enlightenment in the place of World Heritage monuments. Is the valorization of exceptional universal value a symptom of this same social disease? And how might a critique of consumerism redound to the representation of Ajanta as an authentic repository of Enlightenment values, a locale within which to conceptualize an Enlightened future?

Toward addressing these questions, let us consider a new form of counter cultural expression that has arisen to liberate a society of consumers whose lives are dominated by market forces. This group, the *culture jammers*, is an urban street movement in which people alter public billboards or posters to subvert their messages and highlight the disjunction between corporations' and consumers' interests. According to Kalle Lasn, a semi-spokesman for culture jamming's "very diverse tribe," such activism is crucial, for "a continuous product message has woven itself into the very fabric of our existence.... *We ourselves have been branded*."[94] If advertisers monopolize the public channels of meaning creation, then this species of resistance may be the most effective way to create new and revolutionary meanings. Two academics with evident sympathy for the culture jammers, Douglas Holt and Juliet Schor, add to Lasn's lament: "Little remains sacred, and separate from the world of the commodity. As a result people become ever more desperate to sacralize the profane consumer world around them, worshiping celebrities, collections, and brand logos."[95] Though the arch-conservative jurist, Robert Bork, belongs at the other edge of the political spectrum, he expresses a similar view: "Affluence brings with it boredom. Of itself, it offers little but the ability to consume, and a life centered on consumption will appear, and be, devoid of meaning."[96]

Beneath these positions, both Left and Right, both anti- and pro- materialist, we find a common ground for all parties: the valorization of meaningfulness. Rampant materialism plays a "liberating role" in Twitchell's world, while it makes Lasn's (and Bork's) a "horror of disconnection and anomie."[97] Despite their divergent evaluations, however, Twitchell and Lasn share a common field of discourse. Both speak in abstract about meaningfulness, even if their meanings are at antipodes. They struggle to hegemonize *authenticity* as the source and ground of meaningfulness. In this case, as in the UNESCO Convention, authenticity finds its conceptual genesis in the Enlightenment's philosophical anthropology: the conception of human nature, uniform and invariable, as the subject of a grand narrative of progress toward perfection. Kant's 1784 answer to the question, "What is Enlightenment?" speaks of human nature as having an "original vocation" that lies in its movement toward a state in which each human being individually, and humanity collectively, dares to think for itself.[98] Twitchell and Lasn share this vision of Enlightenment, even if they bitterly disagree over what the Enlightened think about. For Twitchell, people like to think about material objects—this is an authentic act that gives life meaning—while Lasn holds that people cannot think freely as long as media and cultural networks force them to be preoccupied with mere stuff—materialism is indexical of an inauthentic life, that is, one that lacks meaning.

The matter of existential meaning, of course, is not easily extricated from that of religion. As we saw near the beginning of this chapter, Enlightenment humanism is suspended in a Christian semiotic solution. Indeed, although the Enlightenment is famed for its trenchant critique of sectarianism, and known for its few "out" atheists, this was also a creative period for constructive theology. Writing in 1624, Edward Herbert expresses the basic predicate of the Enlightenment's religious humanism: "religion is the ultimate difference of man."[99] To be human is to be religious; the capacity for religion makes one human. As part of this same discussion, Herbert mentions a traveler's report about an obscure tribe without religious practices; he rejects this report outright, and says of the purported atheists, "in reality they are not atheists." But Herbert is only a father to the age of reason. Enlightenment thinkers in general (Hume being a noted exception) considered humanity's uniform and invariable nature to be intrinsically religious. Indeed, natural religiosity was the x-factor that guaranteed uniformity and invariability. And humanity's natural religiosity found its most providential expression in the exercise of reason. From Voltaire's *Philosophical Dictionary* we learn, "This is the character of truth; it is of all time; it is for all men; it has only to show itself to be recognized; one cannot argue against it."[100] Likewise, Kant's *Religion Within the Boundaries of Mere Reason* teaches that "there is only *one* (true) *religion*; but there can be several kinds of *faith*."[101] Lately the terms have changed somewhat: now a singular haze of universal *spirituality* contrasts with the doctrinaire distinctions between *religions*. But contemporary oxymorons like the science-of-spirituality and Buddhism-without-beliefs can be traced to this Enlightenment troika: religiosity, human nature, and reason. During the Enlightenment, religiosity came to be represented as a pure use-value within the economy of a universal human nature—it gives meaning. Of course we should be suspicious that this pure value has only the *appearance* of use—meaning is not really worth it.

The legacy of the Enlightenment's religious humanism is immediately obvious when we look deeper into the writings of Twitchell and Lasn. Both resort to religious terminologies at crucial points in their arguments. Both use religion to express the high stakes: the very definition of humanity. Both are overtly interested in *salvation*. In this, James Twitchell's title, *Lead Us Into Temptation*, could not be clearer. The full Biblical verse reads, of course, "lead us not into temptation, but deliver us from evil" (Matthew 6:13). With his inversion, Twitchell recasts the world of human desires as a new Jerusalem in the making. If Adam's sinful consumption caused the Fall, then paying a glutton's heed to the injunction, Obey Your Thirst, will usher in the millennium. Nobody who looks at the book's cover-art could miss the point. Based on Jan Brueghel the Elder and Peter Paul Rubens' "The Garden of Eden with the Fall of Man" (1615), the cover shows us Adam and Eve tempted by the serpent. But where Genesis' Adam and Eve were lured by a luscious fruit, here the Tree of the Knowledge of Good and Evil is fecund with watches and furniture and appliances and all the stuff of modern living. Behold the exaltation of the consumer's post-Lapsarian Eden of stuff! Thus Twitchell posits that the language of things is the language of meaning. If "we have always been desirous of things" then no act is more authentic than *buying*.[102] In facilitating this universal human value, advertising and religion are "part of the same meaning-making process. They attempt to breach the gap between us and objects by providing a systematic order *and* a promise of salvation."[103] The chime of a cash register is as much an indicator of angelic translation in this wonderful life as the ringing bell of a Christmas tree.

While Douglas Holt and Juliet Schor also frame consumerism in religious terms, their outlook is quite different. Holt and Schor include religion and spirituality within a list of the "deepest connections that are increasingly dominated by market transactions," alongside motherhood, DNA patterns, and sexuality.[104] Indeed, they would agree with Twitchell that celebrity spokesmen are our new saints, and brand logos are contemporary icons on the altar of commerce. But Holt and Schor see this as a merely strategic sacralization of "the profane consumer world." They use the categories sacred and profane as if these bespeak objective essences—the commodity being essentially and unambiguously profane. Thus they interpret consumers' metaphorical sacralization of commodities as a "desperate" attempt to find authentic, even spiritual, meaning within a world in which "little remains sacred, and separate from the world of the commodity."[105]

Culture jammer Kalle Lasn's work is also replete with metaphors that capitalize upon a rhetoric of religious essentialism. Sometimes he borrows from Christianity, as when he portrays himself as working toward a "millennial moment of truth" or alludes to cognitively jarring experiences after which "things can never be the same again."[106] Lasn has a lucky buddha on his keyring, however, so it is no surprise that his metaphors of choice derive from Zen Buddhism. Lasn compares the impulse to engage in culture jamming to the ascetic regimen required of Zen monks; he likens the culture jammer's desired result to the end sought by a Zen master, when he "may suddenly throw you a wildly cryptic, inappropriate, even obscene answer to your harmless query"; and he advises culture jammers to look to the buddha's life for lessons.[107] To describe his overall project, Lasn brings together terminologies borrowed from both Christianity's and Zen's lexicons: "Only a chain of spontaneous acts will lead to salvation."[108] Lasn has a clear conception of salvation: the ability to act authentically, spontaneously, and freely, unburdened by the manipulations of commercial culture.

Lasn might not be aware, however, that insofar as Zen Buddhism informs his value-system, he has himself become a consumer "manipulated in the most insidious way."[109] Since the early 1990s, academic historians have literally re-presented Zen-spontaneity, redescribing it as a rhetoric of spontaneity, an ideology of spontaneity, serving nativist, nationalist, militarist, and sectarian purposes.[110] Indeed, Lasn (no more than Twitchell) seems not to recognize *religion's* discursive function: religiosity as a fact of language. Lasn allows his vision to be conditioned by the lingering traces of the Enlightenment's singular natural religion as the expression of the human core, on the one hand, and, on the other, by a received image of Zen that one historian calls "not only conceptually incoherent but also a woeful misreading of traditional Zen doctrine, altogether controverted by the lived contingencies of Zen monastic practice."[111] Lasn is the unwitting tool of eighteenth-century European intellectuals and medieval Japanese media-moguls just as certainly as the kid who thinks that he is merely obeying his thirst when he buys a Sprite.

Zen-spontaneity is Zen ideology. I wonder whether, upon investigating the veracity of this assertion, Lasn would continue to find Zen to be the epitome of a pure utility, having no value beyond the spontaneity for which it calls. Is Lasn so influenced by the Enlightenment's religious humanism that even this deception would not shake what he calls his "faith in the true spiritual nature of the human being"?[112] But I do not mean to pick on Lasn here. In terms of the political differential between Lasn's and Twitchell's positions, I lean toward the former in my ideals and the latter in my practices, and thus, after death, am destined to be chased by bees screaming outside the door to Hell. Indeed, it might seem obvious that Twitchell's celebration of consuming things is far more obnoxious than Lasn's innocent and well-intentioned appropriation of a pernicious foreign rhetoric. I am not so sure. When Lasn translates Zen ideology into transhuman fact he is consuming enlightenment. Holt and Schor eat the same diet, albeit strongly spiced with a Christian pepper, when they essentialize sacrality and profanity into a world of spirit and things. But the long-term environmental consequences of this spiritual materialism, this creative consumption of the sacred, might be just as dire, if not as obvious, as those predicted for the overconsumption of material goods. Juliet Schor has a book, *Do Americans Buy Too Much?* Do Americans (and not just Americans) buy too much into the truly spiritual nature of the human being?

If a Tibetan teacher, Chögyam Trungpa, had not devised the phrase *spiritual materialism*, I might have, albeit with an almost opposite meaning. For Trungpa, spiritual materialism is an impediment that must be "cut through" in order to achieve authentic spirituality. The simile Trungpa uses to describe this odd materialism is timely. Spiritual seekers are like shoppers who buy many beautiful antiques from all over the world. So many hours are devoted to buying, however, that these people never find time to appreciate their purchases' beauty. Collecting the wisdom of the Sufis and the wisdom of the saints, spiritual aspirants never realize the intrinsic spirit that makes the wisdom valuable: "Proper shopping does not entail collecting a lot of information or beauty, but it involves appreciating each individual object."[113] Buddhists describe the path to enlightenment as having eight dimensions, from proper livelihood through proper understanding. Trungpa adds a ninth: proper shopping.

This is not how I use the phrase. Rather, in my lexicon spiritual materialism is materialism tainted by a desire for spirit. Taking the desire for "meaning" to be the desire for the satisfaction of desires, I use *spiritual materialism* to describe an approach to materiality that forecloses the possibility that material objects can be directly "meaningful," and thus that the true value of an object is always, somehow, factored in its semiotic relationship to an indwelling spirit. This is the attitude that things cannot make us happy; or if things do seem to satisfy a desire for happiness it is only because they signify some pure essence, existing beyond their material forms. This is spirit as the ultimate brand, for its role is to alleviate all material anxieties except one, the anxiety over its own unseen presence. Spiritual materialism in this sense comes through clearly when Holt and Schor represent the world of the sacred and the world of things bought-and-sold as incommensurable. Given these scholars' presuppositions, that is, sacrality exists and commodities have no part in it, the adulation of Princess Diana and the hunt for the perfect Jimmy Choo shoe would naturally reflect a desperation for some greater meaning. We can also think back to MacCannell's tourist who, like the religious person on pilgrimage, seeks authenticity, but unlike the religious person, finds only staged authenticity. The World Heritage designation "sacralizes" that staging.

If, however, the sacred too is a name-brand, a quite different system of values accrues. The sacred is "profane." Or rather, sacred and profane no longer function as evaluative terms for desirable and undesirable meanings. Meaningfulness itself becomes a suspect value.

Lasn speaks of a "deeply felt sense of betrayal" when brands, which sell dreams, do not deliver the goods. No brand is more pernicious in this way than America, which promises democracy and freedom, but only delivers corporate greed.[114] But to respond to this fact about America with a sense of betrayal is to be a spiritual materialist. It is as if one only had a late epiphany that Sprite's slogan, Image is Nothing, is carefully crafted to create an image and sell soft drinks. It is as if one expects authenticity and spontaneity to be waiting, just on the other side of branding and commoditization. This is a species of fetishism: the imputation of spirit to matter and the subsequent adulation of that matter as an occult dwelling for the spirit. For Chögyam Trungpa, people become spiritual materialists when, by constantly shopping for spiritual wisdom, they imbricate genuine spirituality within a materialist ethos. I would say, rather, that such shopping taints perfectly good stuff with the stain of spirit.

Kalle Lasn also describes how *not* to be a spiritual materialist. A revelatory anecdote: Lasn's local supermarket charges patrons a quarter to use its shopping carts. One day, angry at himself for supporting this greedy corporation, Lasn jammed a big bent coin into the slot where he would normally put his quarter, hammering it tight with his lucky buddha. He then left the store, going instead to a little fruit and vegetable stand down the road. Lasn ends the story, "I felt more alive than I had in months."[115] Where did this good feeling come from? Was it the act of armed (albeit with a buddha) resistance against sterile corporate tomatoes? Or did Lasn feel good about shopping at the smaller, more personal store? If the aesthetics of the shopping experience itself turned him on, then he might be Twitchell's man more than he would like.

Twitchell's analysis of American materialism is useful here because he offers a way to understand how and why, contra Trungpa, the worth of the things can be had in the act of shopping itself: they are valuable *because* they can be bought. For Twitchell, the fact that they are commodities can serve as a pure use-value, inspiring the apothegm: "consumption has become production."[116] This inversion may not be *fully* true for things like cars and beer, though these commodities receive furious marketing. But it is fully true for spirit. And for meaning. And for e/Enlightenment. And for the designation, World Heritage Monument, as a promise of exceptional universal value.

One of the principal complaints that Kalle Lasn and other critics levy against consumerism is that it manufactures desires, displacing sources of life's meaning away from genuine and universally human engagement with family, friendship, spirituality, community, ongoing self-improvement, or indulging a reverence for nature. One of the principal complaints that James Twitchell and others levy against those critics is that in our day, in our world, consumerist desires are meaningful because they genuinely express the human essence. Both, of course, are right. Most desires are manufactured, none more so than the desire for *meaning*. The list of genuine biological *needs* is rather short. One can satisfy them easily at Ajanta by sleeping in the caves; drinking water from the cisterns; and eating the locally available fruits. But insofar as "consumption is production," the desire for meaningfulness creates the expectation that a real meaning exists. Thus theologians reject the possibility of genuine atheism, or characterize atheism as itself a source of religious meaning. And thus anomie and meaninglessness are the inevitable concomitants of religion. The perfect life as comprehended by terms such as enlightenment, authenticity, immediacy, spontaneity, genuineness, and freedom, is a life lived in pursuit of the ultimate brand. The only way to satisfy this desire fully is to stop buying the brand.

Branding Ajanta, branding Enlightenment

Let us now return to Ajanta:

> There is a growing awareness among the enlightened new generations of world peoples, that the great works of art of mankind are part of human heritage and not only of one country or another. This happy realisation is partly the result of the faster means of communication and accessibility of the monuments of the world. And this augurs for the emergence of one world culture. Then men and women will begin to roam over the globe in search of psycho-social phenomena to confirm their own feelings, hunches, and revelations about the meaning of life and they may find therein the works of great artists rendered up through the creative imaginations of the past. Self-education of the people's sensibilities may become universal.[117]

This passage is found in a booklet produced by MTDC in the mid-1970s, several years before Ajanta achieved World Heritage status. An expensive publication, its cover was vibrantly colored card-stock, embossed and painted with gold; its pages were heavy rag. Indeed, this was a suitable medium within which to express so ambitious a vision. For here we find Ajanta at the epicenter of a golden age that has been three centuries in the making, at least since the Marquis de Condorcet described his vision of the "eternal chain of human destiny."[118] Through Ajanta we can imagine a world whose transportation and communication networks are so advanced, and its people so wealthy, that all are able to traverse the planet at will. Peace begets peace, for these travelers discover that culture is a matter of humanity not of nations. Thus all respect the past and share concern for their united future. Peace also begets harmony, for people fill their extra hours with imaginative or intellectual pursuits, but harbor no jealousy at one another's genius. Though born in different lands with diverse tongues, all speak the language of the human heart. They share a single spiritual vision of life's ultimate meaning.

Smile if you will. But the pamphlet cautions against cynicism: "This is not a Utopian dream. Already there is evidence of this emergence among the millions of tourists who go in search of the past."[119]

Smile if you will, or don't if the spirit doesn't move you. For the final question raised by this true dream, as by the World Heritage Convention which shares its values if not its purple prose, is: How do we respond to the sales pitch? French advertising executive Jean-Marie Dru has proposed that for a brand to be successful it must identify itself with liberation in some way, with a vision of a future in which people are freer and happier for having bought the brand.[120] This makes sense, for if shopping creates identity, what personal traits are more alluring than freedom and happiness? Think what you will of consumer society, proponents and critics alike agree that freedom, e/Enlightenment's *summum bonum*, is branding's horizon as well.

3

A TALE OF TWO HISTORIES

It depends upon what the meaning of the word "is" is.
(President William Jefferson Clinton,
grand jury testimony, August 17, 1998)

The postcolonial past

One of the principal aims of postcolonial scholarship is to theorize a means by which the colonized or subaltern can find himself in time, a retroactive witness to his own exclusion. This critical intervention into history's telling begins with the politics of authorship. Thus a certain kind of reader might mistrust the previous chapter's treatment of Ajanta, given that it privileges accounts written by the British and by anglicized Indians. Does history change depending upon whether an author is a citizen of the United Kingdom or of India? An ethnic Bhīl or caste brahmin? A Buddhist? A historian by profession, or a licensed tour guide? Or a young man romancing his girl by telling mock-serious stories as they stroll among the caves? This is the question of authority writ large, suggestive of a multiplicity of possible histories, mostly untold.

There is, however, another way of accounting for Ajanta's temporality, more intimate and more profound, that does not tabulate the number of alternative histories but instead assays viable alternatives *to* history. This latter pursuit goes to the value of academic history itself as a normative discourse through which to represent collective memory. Both meanings of "value" are in play here: What *good* is history? Is history *good*?

One critic to interrogate the value of academic history in these latter terms, Ashis Nandy, answers both questions in the negative. A political psychologist, Nandy looks beyond the pain of the colonial condition toward a postcolonial therapeutic of psychological resistance. He writes on behalf of what he calls "traditional India," an ideal India whose peoples' sensibilities and rhythms of life remain unalloyed by a European intellectual or economic presence. In Nandy's reckoning, "the Enlightenment's concept of history" was unknown to traditional India. Indeed, he doubts that traditional India would accept the academy's "objective, hard history" as "a reliable, ethical, or reasonable way of constructing the past."[1] Nandy frames this split in terms of both object and outcome. Professional historians value comprehensive and unambiguous collocations of data. They aim "at nothing less than to bare the past completely"; to leave no memory unremembered; to banish all forgetfulness.[2] The academic historian's primary responsibility is to the past itself, while he is secondarily responsible to generalized principles, such as accuracy and objectivity. A concern for the contemporary effects of his objective analyses may be tertiary at best, a nice supplement to his practice as historian. By contrast, "traditional Indian constructions of the past are primarily responsible to the present and secondarily to the future."[3] In Nandy's terms, they care more for ethical effects than for objective truths. They do not value the past in its own right. To the contrary, such constructions rely upon a principled forgetfulness "that seems directed against the heart of the enterprise called history."[4] According to Nandy, it is "important *not* to remember the past, objectively, clearly, or in its entirety."[5] Only a past that has been structured through "principled forgetfulness and silences," as well as memories, offers traditional India a means for "expanding human options by reconfiguring the past and transcending it through creative improvisations."[6]

The translation of Nandy's views from the realm of theory to that of policy would have far-ranging implications for the contemporary treatment of Ajanta. Nandy admits as much when he volunteers that traditional India's constructions of the past "are meant neither for the archivist nor for the archaeologist."[7] I doubt that Nandy's India would have supported Ajanta's elevation to World Heritage status, since "hard" historical documentation was critical to that bureaucratic process. When nominating Ajanta, the Indian government was required to submit "on the appropriate form . . . a brief analysis of references in world literature (e.g., reference works such as general or specialized encyclopedias, histories of art or architecture, records of voyages and explorations, scientific reports, guidebooks, etc.) along with a comprehensive bibliography."[8] UNESCO demanded that the Indian government implement Enlightenment evidentiary protocols, while Ashis Nandy decries that obligation's epistemological burden upon the Indians themselves.

To borrow a word from Chapter 2, Nandy is asking why there must be only one set of criteria for adjudicating Ajanta's *authenticity*. Let traditional Indians enjoy their own alternate, but no less authentic, Ajanta experiences. Let them pay no heed to the wants or needs of academic historians, connoisseurs, antiquarians, and anybody else who thinks that the past is necessarily better off being left just as it was!

For me, the possibilities and limits of Nandy's historiographical imperative became clear on a warm July evening, as I ate dinner with an officer in the Archaeological Survey of India (ASI) who had been posted to Ajanta several years earlier. First, a matter of context: just because Ajanta is an import cultural monument, requiring the delicate care of skilled technicians, does not mean that Ajanta is a desirable place to work. Imagine an urbane New Yorker who somehow finds himself posted to the deep Ozarks. My dinner companion admitted that he had been exiled to Ajanta as punishment for a professional misstep that he did not care to discuss. Yet, by imagining Ajanta's apotheosis, he found solace. Here are his words, recollected and transcribed soon after the meal: "If one treats Ajanta with complete devotion and complete love, it will grant every desire. This is why I take my work so seriously, and try to do such a good job here. This is why I will stay at Ajanta for three more years, or maybe five: whatever I ask for, I will receive." Later in the evening, he also referred to Ajanta as *bhagavān*, the name of god.

The direct, non-symbolic, identification of a terrestrial feature as a living divinity is not uncommon in India. The Ganges River is a goddess in her own right, while Mount Govardhan is Kṛṣṇa in the lithic flesh. But this story turns on my surprise at hearing an archaeologist, a man with an advanced degree and scientific training, speak of Ajanta in these same terms: calling it *bhagavān* and expecting it to act with the prerogatives of divine grace. At the time, the word that came to me unbidden was *fetishism*, as I had recently read a series of masterful articles by William Pietz on the subject. Pietz shows that the category *fetish* arose from the ethnographic musings of early-modern European merchants to describe their African trading partners' unaccountable practice of valuing trifles of "obviously" little worth. Fetishes were material objects—sticks and stones—whose material itself was treated as if possessed of subjectivity and intrinsic value.[9] When Charles de Brosses published the first theory of *fetishism* in 1760, the merchants' disdain for their trading partners was reformulated as a general critique of religion: to attribute subjective intelligence or innate power to (what Europeans considered) an inanimate object, and then to submit before that object's imagined will, is religion's most primitive form, definitively unEnlightened. Thus I found my dinner companion's statement odd on two accounts. In general, here was a professional scientist articulating the nonsense of fetishism. In particular, here was a man, employed to preserve Ajanta's past, articulating a private fantasy that fetishized a historically Buddhist place as a Hindu *bhagavān*. If he was going to infuse Ajanta with spirit, he should at least have chosen the correct spirit! To return to Nandy's language, this ASI officer's job required him to think through the alternative histories of objective data, yet in other moments the same man exhibited a principled forgetfulness when he saw that same stuff in a manner that had nothing to do with its hard historical past and everything to do with his own pained present.

Upon further reflection I have decided that *fetishism* is the wrong term here. As objects of desire, fetishes are structurally interesting, for they are imbricated within multiple and competing systems of value. "The discourse of the fetish has always been a critical discourse about the false objective values of a culture from which the speaker is personally distanced," in Pietz's words.[10] If a man controlled by his fantasies is called a fetishist, then the analysis of the fetish begins with the analyst's delimitation of baseline reality. Fetishes materialize a swirling subterranean flow of valuation, in which differentiated desires function as ciphers for the discursive control of normality. What *should* you want to own: beads or gold? What *should* bring you to orgasm: feet or fucking? How *should* we view Ajanta: the body of a living god or a repository of objects possessing exceptional universal value that transcend their local culture? The category *fetish* mystifies through its promise of demystification. It reveals much about the analyst while obscuring the analysand behind a flash-powder effect that only seems to grant full exposure.

Ashis Nandy was right to distrust the ethics of demystification, to suspect scholarly motives and objectives. My rush to judgment that evening was doubly dubious, given the curious overlap between the words *fetish* and *fact*. Both are derived from the Latin root, *facere*, to make. "Fact" is a direct formation from the past participle, *factum*, that which is made, either naturally or through human agency. "Fetish" derives from *facticius*, "formed by joining the past participle stem *fact-* to the adjectival suffix of condition, quality, or state, *-icius*."[11] In the Roman world, Pietz observes, *factitius* always connoted human manufacture and allowed for the sense of the English factitious or fraudulent.[12] In short, both facts and fetishes are constructed and therefore historical. They differ in that the human element in the creation of a fetish allows for deception. Fetishes have an appearance of use-value but they lack the substance that would make them *truly* useful. They seem to have real value, but are real only as fantasies. With facts, by contrast, what you see is what you get. That is not to say that facts are unconstructed: No one would deny that the formula $E = mc^2$ is a linguistic construct, historical. But as a fact, it is understood to possess integrity and substance independent of the context of its "discovery" or expression. Mass–energy conversion transpires naturally, whether or not its formula is known.

Of course, the force of poststructural analysis has been to destabilize all such appeals to naturalness and objectivity, even in relation to the hardest of hard science. Thus Bruno Latour and Steve Woolgar's modern classic in the sociology of science, *Laboratory Life*, argues that scientific facts are neither natural nor objective. Scientific facts are manufactured in laboratories, in which *nature* and *objectivity*—the very preconditions for facticity—are the most crucial creations. " 'Out-there-ness' is the *consequence* of scientific work rather than its *cause*."[13] Though we naively consider office politics, economic incentives, personal beliefs, interpersonal rivalries to be epiphenomenal to the "hard and solid world of facts," these social factors are intrinsic to a manufacturing process whereby linguistic statements are made into representatives of objective reality.[14] If this manufacturing process is successful, the result should be that "the *construction* of a fact . . . appears unconstructed by anyone."[15]

To call the archaeologist at Ajanta a fetishist, therefore, I would also have had to entertain the possibility that his representation of Ajanta as bhagavān was in fact true. Instead of fetish, therefore, I have come to think of the archaeologist's confession as an instance of what literary critic A.K. Ramanujan calls "an Indian way of thinking."[16] Like Nandy, Ramanujan explains the Indian through the negation of a European caricature. In this case, European epistemologies prefer context-free universals as the sources of truth and value. Ramanujan cites an easy example, Immanuel Kant's ethical imperative: "Act as if the maxim of your action were to become through your will a Universal Law of Nature."[17] For Kant, one must not lie even one time unless one desires all people to be authorized to lie always. Even benevolent motives do not mitigate this imperative: were a man to come to your door threatening to kill your friend hiding inside, *you may not lie* to protect your friend.[18] Native Indian epistemologies, by contrast, favor context-sensitive rules and interpretations. Thus the classic brahmanical social order described in the *Laws of Manu*, in Ramanujan's words, "seems to have no clear notion of a universal *human* nature" and "no unitary law of all men."[19] It is necessary for the brahmin-human to recite the *gāyatrī* mantra every day, while the śūdra-human is proscribed from ever hearing the *gāyatrī*; the kṣatriya-human will be fully disgraced if he is caught cheating at dice, while the vaiśya-human will be shamefaced if he would go bankrupt rather than cheat his customers. Moving from the normative to the descriptive, Ramanujan's own reflection on the question of an Indian way of thinking began with inconsistencies he recognized in his own father, who was both an academic astronomer and a folk-wise astrologer. Ramanujan would have found nothing amiss in the divergence between the ASI officer's book-knowledge that Ajanta was first created by Buddhist devotees of the buddhas and his own affective response to it as his Hindu bhagavān.

Ramanujan notes that "both Englishmen and 'modern' Indians are dismayed by this kind of inconsistency" represented by his father and the archaeologist.[20] This chapter is an expression of dismay at that dismay, beginning, in particular, with my own embarrassing dismay at the ASI officer's multiplication of religious identities for Ajanta; my own initial impulse to condemn him as a fetishist; and thus my own fetishizing of historical fact. In short, this chapter proposes that a history of Ajanta that reconstructs the site's religious provenance from its artifacts can never be true. Histories based upon the assumed facticity of religious identity are particularly vexing. We see this in the ongoing uses to which "traditional India" puts Ajanta, whether that India is represented by nineteenth-century peasants or a twenty-first century archaeologist. How does Ajanta exist in history as an object? What is true of Ajanta if the statement, "Ajanta is Buddhist," does not represent the agreement of a historical cognition with its historical object, that is, is not a context-free fact?[21] Thus this chapter's epigraph: sensitive to the modalities of time, President Clinton reminds us that, here, not even the meaning of "is" should be granted and presupposed as context-free.

A brief excursus on graffiti in Caves Twenty Two and Ten

Like Ashis Nandy, Dipesh Chakrabarty of the Subaltern Studies collective also wonders about academic history's worth and, by extension, about the careful treatment of artifacts privileged for conservation. Chakrabarty asks,

> Why is history a compulsory part of education of the modern person in all countries today?...Why should children all over the world today have to come to terms with a subject called "history" when we know that this compulsion is neither natural nor ancient?[22]

Though Chakrabarty plays at provocation, his appeal to naturalness and antiquity as indices of value blunts his point. Nevertheless, the tension implicit in Chakrabarty's questions arises from what he perceives as the role historical discourse plays in splitting human beings into two discontinuous selves. On the one hand, there is the "interiorized private self" whose personal stories "often themselves bespeak an antihistorical consciousness."[23] On the other hand, there is the public person who has "inherited" from colonizing Europe an abstract discourse of universal rationality, freedom, equality, and rights, against which to measure his social self-representation. The two hands do not carry selves of equal weight. The burden of a westernized modernity is that the public selves it proffers—State-citizen, wage-earner, commodity-consumer—overwhelm the interiorized private self to such a degree that people come to trivialize or even forget their own discontinuous plurality of odd other moments. And Chakrabarty lays the blame for this loss of playfulness, in part, on those whose job it is to bureaucratize the past—historians.

> So long as one operates within the discourse of "history" produced at the institutional site of the university, it is not possible simply to walk out of the deep collusion between "history" and the modernizing narrative(s) of citizenship, bourgeois public and private, and the nation state.[24]

As for people, so too for caves. Ajanta also has multiple selves. There is the public Ajanta. This is a place for historians who mold data into facts, and facts into a cohesive story about change and context, actors and intentions. This Ajanta's rock cubbies and plaster walls are identified with times past, even as they persist into the present. This Ajanta is the subject of general or specialized encyclopedias, histories of art or architecture, records of voyages and explorations, scientific reports, and guidebooks, just as UNESCO requires.

There are other Ajantas. They receive little recognition. Comprehensive bibliographies do not note them, for their data is disordered. They collude neither with history as produced in academic institutions, nor with modernizing narratives. To consider them scientifically, we might line them up along a continuum. In one part of spectrum we find the Ajanta of soaring platitudes: Mukul Dey's "shrine of Religion and Art"; Richard Lannoy's Ajanta, which "surpasses the oneiric and reaches an authentic psychedelic intensity;" Anna Pavlova's ballet *Ajanta's Frescoes*, staged to great acclaim in 1923 London.[25] In another spectral region we find the ASI officer's response, whereby Ajanta becomes bhagavān. Dedicated to

Figure 3.1 Caves Twenty One, Twenty Two, and Twenty Three (from left to right). Photo by author.

the preservation of Ajanta's physical remains, he imaginatively transfigures the site, leaving no outward trace of this inner art. And still elsewhere on the continuum are the Ajantas of visitors who have not been so kind. Let us consider two private Ajantas whose transfigurations have been less than delicate. What might one say about those Ajantas?

Enter Cave Twenty Two (Figure 3.1). This tiny cave's cells are barely roughed-out pits. It does not have a major cult image. Its paintings offer some details of interest to specialists in bauddha iconography, but nothing for the casual visitor. Cave Twenty Two is also inconvenient. To reach it, tourists must climb a length of narrow uneven steps, up from the main walkway. Yet that inconvenience gave Cave Twenty Two a second life—as a toilet. Although the Ajanta scarp is one-third of a mile long, there are no dedicated toilet facilities near its eastern end. Go to Ajanta often enough and you will smell tourist urine almost everywhere. But until the door was padlocked in the 1980s, Cave Twenty Two was special. Insignificant; ignored by its *chowkidar*; situated near the far end of the scarp, where tired men, women, and children are not eager to climb more steps for no good reason: Cave Twenty Two became *the* cave in which to shit, to gain rough relief.

What mystical tie connects toilets with graffiti? For when Cave Twenty Two was still unlocked, many who made the climb also added their names and initials to its blank canvas. Well, almost blank: most of this graffiti was scratched in a rear chamber, onto a painting of seven buddhas plus the bodhisattva Maitreya seated in a line beneath their personal bodhi trees, symbolic of enlightenment. In addition to this human activity, water and burrowing insects have long damaged this painting, creating gaps which the ASI then filleted with cement to prevent further breakage. Graffiteers alight upon the cement as well (Figure 3.2).

A cultural historian might wonder about the symbolic dimension of these appropriations through which diverse individuals present themselves to our attention. Why, for instance, did G.S.S. scratch his initials into the cement rather than the painting? Can this be read as a sign of respect for the buddha? Or does it show G.S.S.'s faith in the longevity of this medium? In the ritual space of Cave Twenty Two did he thus take communion in modernity? Or, possibly, did G.S.S. score the cement as an act of defiance against the flat featureless void of commodified experience? Was he inspired by a hatred for all sociopolitical institutions that would fix his own alienation within a cement of platitudes? Was he a culture jamming comrade of Kalle Lasn?

How about विजय शर्मा (Vijay Sharma), whose name in Devanagari script is scratched only on the painting itself? Was this an act of antiquarian bravado; a vote of confidence in the sticking power of ancient plaster and a rejection of modernity's matrix? Or did विजय शर्मा have a sectarian agenda: to express his personal disrespect for the buddha? A verse painted beneath these buddhas during the fifth century reads, "Someone who commissions an image of buddha will enjoy good looks and good luck in this life."[26] Had विजय शर्मा known this, would

Figure 3.2 Detail from a painting in the rear of Cave Twenty Two. Photo by author.

he have taken the same action? Or would he have feared becoming ugly and ill-fortuned upon his act of defacement? Will G.S.S. escape विजय शर्मा 's possible fate because his initials stay on the cement?

The heady liquor of postmodern analytics mixed with the intoxicant of postcolonial critique can make any act of violence seem a potable solution for the headaches of modernity. Thus, we might imagine a drunkards' debate. On the one side, advocating a traditional India that finds the Enlightenment's predicates and purposes unethical, Ashis Nandy is the obvious partisan of Ajanta's graffiti artists. Nandy might redescribe G.S.S. and विजय शर्मा as crusaders against the *ferenghee* universals contained in the UNESCO Convention and its network of advocates; as freethinkers who refuse to buy the hollow Westernized commodity that is the MTDC's *Ajanta Experience*; as people who, seeing themselves as more than consumers of so-called Enlightened values, creatively express their own enlightened selves.

On the other side of the debate stands the MTDC, whose condemnation of Narayan Ekenath (see page 43) is clearly transferable to G.S.S. and विजय शर्मा . To satisfy momentary whims, these men (one assumes that both are men) destroy others' potential for enjoying the past. Another partisan on this side is Alan Moorehead, whose 1954 article in *The New Yorker* is unequivocal, if understated, in its condemnation of native tourists who cut their names into Ajanta's frescoes: "One can't help feeling that a vandal with a fine hand for Hindi script is just as bad as any other."[27] One might speculate about Nandy's retort in support of विजय शर्मा . But let's face it, this side includes all right-thinking people, unable to accept any justification for a vandal's momentary act of self-expression when compared to the cultural treasure lost.

We do not know much about G.S.S. and विजय शर्मा : perhaps they are made of straw. The debate takes on greater interest when we consider that these two were not the only men in the modern era to have scratched their names with a sharp object over an ancient buddha. For instance, one finds the following graffito scratched onto the robe of a standing buddha, 7' 5" above ground level in Cave Ten:

John Smith 28 Cavalry
28 April 1819[28]

Whereas evidence for G.S.S.'s and विजय शर्मा 's presence is now secreted behind a locked door, John Smith's name has been widely published since its discovery in the 1960s. In the words of its epigrapher, M.K. Dhavalikar, "though of a recent date, this is an extremely interesting inscription."

One need not strain to grasp why G.S.S. and विजय शर्मा were not received with the same forbearance as that granted to John Smith. Namely, the latter's graffito provides objective, hard data that a European visited Ajanta in the year 1819. This date, conjoined with John Smith's notation of his military service, confirms published accounts as well as local legends about the caves' re-entry into history, leading Dhavalikar to suggest that "it would not be farfetched if we take him to be the discoverer of Ajaṇṭā."[29] Presently, John Smith's tale begins every guided tour. After a group gathers at the entrance, it is instructed: Turn around. Look up across the river bed, at the distant plateau above the hill, upon the place from which John Smith first espied the caves while seeking tigers. Mukul Dey's *My Pilgrimages to Ajanta & Bagh* continues the tale with particular verve (published in 1925, it does not know the British officer's name):

> In the year 1819 a British officer, retired from the Madras Army, was out alone in the jungle close to Ajanta village, hunting round for tigers. Unsuccessful, he wound his way on and on through the wild stony tracks. Having pursued for some time his haphazardous course, and imagining himself far enough from all human beings, he was surprised to hear but a little way off a boy's shrill voice. Hastening his steps, the captain soon came up to a young herdsman talking to his herd of half-wild buffaloes in the middle of the jungle.
>
> The boy, seeing a sahib, and consequently thinking to earn a little tip if he should show him the actual home of the tigers, led him a little way off from where he was standing and, pointing above the trees, said: "Look, sahib." Following eagerly with his eyes the boy's extended arm, he saw through the thick green foliage a little golden-red color peering between a few mauve carved pillars or columns.
>
> The captain, intensely excited, feeling himself about to make an important archaeological discovery, sent immediately to the village for men to come with torches and drums, with axes and spears, to hew down the tangled clusters that throttled up the entrance to the caves. Thus a clearing was made in the jungle, and a passage forced into these long-forgotten city temples.[30]

In fact, John Smith's graffito is also the focus for a second advertisement in the MTDC's *Ajanta Experience* series. As discussed in the previous chapter, this advertising campaign operates out of a will to represent the contemporary tourist to himself as, like the god of Exodus, a being who consumes without destroying. Thus, the MTDC disparages tourists from seeking the kinds of souvenirs once sold by Narayan Ekenath, who cut painted figures from Ajanta's walls in gross violation of his job as caretaker. Responsible tourists are satisfied with less "authentic" keepsakes. Similarly, this second advertisement censures Smith for his nineteenth-century addition, but places such acts of graffiti completely in the past. The copy reads:

> Almost two centuries ago, a certain Mr. Smith defaced a painting of the Buddha on a pillar in the tenth cave of Ajanta.... The only purpose Smith's act of vandalism served was to tell us the date when Ajanta was rediscovered in the modern age. Thankfully, such acts have been totally stopped.[31]

78

Despite the MTDC's rebuke, its advertisement acknowledges that John Smith's vandalism still serves at least one legitimate purpose. By contrast, G.S.S.'s and विजय शर्मा 's names in Cave Twenty Two would seem to offer nothing of interest to historians or tourists (Figure 3.3).

Of course, such acts have not totally stopped. And, of course, despite the flimsiness of my earlier semiological musings about G.S.S. and विजय शर्मा , their names can serve a scholarly hermeneutic as well. Cave Twenty Two is not like other toilet stalls: its graffiti is plain boring. Indeed, the fact that the graffiti in Cave Twenty Two is so cursory, so laconic, and uncommunicative, might give Nandy his best argument vis-à-vis the psychic drain of Enlightened modernity; or Chakrabarty his, vis-à-vis the loss of the playful private within the bourgeois public. No graffiteer took a stand in this cave except, perhaps, to urinate. In ancient Rome, one could find the scurrilous, "Scummy Ready-for-Anything gives it to her lovers all the time," as well as the salutary, "Crap well," scribbled along the cloaca. We all have our favorite bathroom humor. But over the past century, Cave Twenty Two has failed to incite even gutter jocularity, let alone libel.

If the act of scratching graffiti recreates an artwork as a palimpsest of layered values, then Cave Twenty Two's buddha image has been recreated in two almost completely disjoined layers. The symbolic value of the ancient layer's buddhas seems to lack any power to incite contemporary visitors into exposing their own symbolic selves. What might be read as iconoclasm seems not to be iconoclasm,

Figure 3.3 A sign inside Cave Ten. The paintings along this cave's aisles are probably the most graffiti-damaged at Ajanta. Photo by author.

but disregard. What might inflame as desecration seems not to be desecration, but disinterest. This graffiti communicates nothing except the erstwhile presence of the graffiteer. It neither possesses meaning, nor strains after meaning. Yet is this not in keeping with the value given Ajanta by the World Heritage Convention: an extraordinary place at which to encounter universal values, such as Antiquity and Culture? Indeed, what place offers the contemporary graffiteer a better chance for immortality than the surface of a protected ancient painting? (Note that conservators have scratched several names off the concrete, while leaving intact all names on the paint.) Cave Twenty Two's names demonstrate that, in our world, an ancient cultural artifact can provide a context within which to enjoy the anticipation of meaningfulness without its having to offer any meaning in particular. Granted, G.S.S. and विजय शर्मा left out their dates. Nevertheless, is not the history lesson they teach at least as valuable as that provided by John Smith?

Ajanta in history

The padlock on Cave Twenty Two opens a door onto Ajanta here and now as a place abstracted from time: World Heritage Monument, MTDC *Experience*, cultural patrimony, Saturday afternoon jaunt, place to make one's mark (no longer). The graffiti in Cave Ten, by contrast, remains a visible witness to history-proper in the making. M.K. Dhavalikar describes John Smith as "one of the earliest visitors to the caves after they fell into disuse sometime in the eighth century and were consequently consigned to oblivion."[32] Let me fill out the details of Ajanta's schoolbook history, the short version.

During an efflorescence of support for bauddha renunciants in the first century BCE, donors sponsored the excavation of several residences and shrines into the sheer wall of a hidden ravine. Though far from cosmopolitan centers, these caves were easily visited as a day trip by merchants, wanderers, and armies, because they were just two miles away from a strategic pass on a well-traveled road connecting north and south India. After the first century CE work stopped, probably due to the fall of the Śātavāhana dynasty, which had made the region safe for travel and trade. We have no positive knowledge about the next few centuries' inhabitants. If Śākya monks, renunciants from other sects, highwaymen, soldiers, or refugees did make a home there, they left no recognizable clues.

In the last half of the fifth century CE, however, this place was reborn when courtiers of the Vākāṭaka overlord, Hariṣeṇa, began to excavate anew. Vākāṭaka patrons considered theirs an exalted undertaking. One described his donation as "almost measureless" and bragged that small men could not even imagine what he had made; another named his cave *Śrī Vaijayanta*, eponymous with the palace of Indra, king of the Vedic gods.[33] As a heaven on earth, this grand project was closely associated with Hariṣeṇa's reign. It began soon after Hariṣeṇa's ascension (*c*.460), a public display of the Vākāṭakas' power, wealth, piety, and strategic interests.

Before Walter Spink, the dominant chronological sequence for the Vākāṭaka caves had been fixed by James Fergusson and James Burgess "between the years 500 and 650, with a very little margin either way before or after these dates."[34] To arrive at his considerably earlier dates and shorter span—462 to 480 CE— Spink employed a type of motival analysis, which fathoms the site's artistic and architectural material in their own depths before setting them within a historical context based upon epigraphic and textual gleanings. His own preferred metaphor is archaeological. Spink envisions Ajanta as a "dig" that "breaks into a number of distinct levels or strata, reflecting the way that its patronage was affected by political, economic and other factors."[35]

Levels One and Two (c.462–471). A Vākāṭaka ruler named Hariṣeṇa inherited his father's throne in approximately 460. Almost immediately thereafter "a consortium of the emperor's richest and most powerful courtiers" hired architects and artisans to realize this great project.[36] These courtiers included Varāhadeva, one of Hariṣeṇa's minsters; Buddhabhadra, a noble become monk, who tells us that he was "bound in friendship with a minister of the mighty King of Aśmaka over the course of many lifetimes"; and an unnamed feudatory *rāja* subordinate to Hariṣeṇa. Further, Spink has argued that one of Ajanta's caves was the dedication of Hariṣeṇa himself, while another may have been patronized by a close relative, perhaps one of the ruler's wives.

Ajanta's first two Vākāṭaka levels are characterized by an exuberance of creative activity, during which the vast majority of caves were begun and several nearly finished. In terms of patronage, Spink's reading of the site has each cave funded individually by a single donor, a pattern that stands in stark contrast to the collective patronage found at the earlier places dedicated to the buddha, such as Sāñcī or Bhārhut, where individuals, religious-associations, and whole towns severally donated capital to be applied toward programmatic structural elements.[37] This new pattern of patronage is indeed suggested by the site's epigraphic evidence: every inscription recording the donation of a full cave presents its donor in the singular. But something happened to the Vākāṭaka realm, either economically or politically, for the end of this period of efflorescence is marked by rushed and expedient work site-wide, followed by a general cessation of all activity at Ajanta, with a few short-lived exceptions.[38]

Hiatus (c.472–474). Following this general interruption, the site seems to have gone into complete remission for several years. In line with his emphasis on the singularity of patronage and the presence of an overarching bureaucracy regulating the site, Spink observes:

> Not a single image of any type whatsoever was added to any of the caves at the site during the Hiatus. This does not so much suggest the site's abandonment during this period—except of course by the craftsmen, who could find no work there—as it does its continued occupation and preservation of the insistent exclusiveness that had characterized the site's patronage from the start.[39]

Levels Three and Four (*c*.475–478). Following the hiatus, work started up again at Ajanta in earnest. After several years, however, the site seems to have suffered another sharp blow, for once again there is a period of rushed activity, culminating in the abandonment of most caves in an incomplete state.

Level Five (*c*.479–480). Finally, after the abrupt halt of Ajanta's programmatic phase, there began a "period of disruption." By then Ajanta was renowned for its grand, palace-like excavations, which Spink identifies with the first four levels. But the walls of numerous caves were also covered by minor iconic figures—single buddhas or group displays of buddhas and bodhisattvas; several of the minor icons were also inscribed with the names of donors and, sometimes, the reasons for the act of patronage. In Spink's reckoning, the disorderly placement of these images bespeaks the demise of the bureaucratic structure that formerly had protected the individual donors' "private property" with such vigilance. Then, abruptly, after two years, this haphazard chaos also came to an end. The site was abandoned, inhabitants and artisans leaving for points unknown. After 480, "not a painting, not a piece of sculpture, not a cave, or a cell, or a cistern, nor a single donative inscription" was added to Ajanta.[40]

Ajanta was not completely ignored after the Vākāṭakas. Scattered graffiti and a traveler's report teach us that Ajanta's caves remained known and were even visited in the seventh century, though they probably did not house a stable bauddha community.

Then all is silence until the brink of the seventeenth century, when the Mughal author Abū al-Fazl's *A'in-I-Ākbari* (1598) reveals local knowledge of the site: "In the sides of the hills twenty-four temples have been cut, each containing remarkable idols."[41] Abū al-Fazl notwithstanding, scholars typically focus on 1819, the year in which Ajanta was "discovered" by one or several British officers. If the *A'in-I-Ākbari* provides the earliest second-millennium notice of Ajanta, then John Smith's graffito preserves the oldest distinct evidence for humans at the site in our era. The first reference to this site in European scholarship comes from William Erskine, who read a paper to the Literary Society of Bombay in 1821 and published it in 1823.[42] Since then, an ever growing number of people have sought the Ajanta experience: to behold the artifacts of an extraordinary lost classical civilization secreted within a romantic, savage wilderness.

This linear tale punctuated with distinct periods—creation, abandonment, creation, abandonment, forgetting, decay, rediscovery, and conservation—receives the institutional imprimatur, *history*. Its narrative stream flows in easy confluence with other stories that burble their source in Enlightenment ideals. One such story is that told by art historian Walter Spink, whose historiographic imagination hearkens back to Thomas Carlyle's conception of history as the biography of great men. For Spink, Ajanta "ranks as one of the world's most startling achievements, created at the very apogee of India's Golden Age."[43] And Spink reads this artistic magnificence as a sign of the Vākāṭaka monarch Hariṣeṇa's political supremacy. How could Ajanta be *Ajanta* unless "Hariṣeṇa...was surely the greatest king in India and possibly in all the world, at this time"?[44]

This certainty about Hariṣeṇa's personal greatness, in turn, becomes the bedrock for Spink's reconstructions of fifth-century Vākāṭaka politics. Linear temporality likewise enables Alan Moorehead, writing in the decade after Indian independence, to conceive a "beguiling dream" in which India is more than a new nation-state—it is a civilization reborn. As inspiration for this dream, Ajanta demonstrates "that there had once existed a composed and steady civilization in India under native rule, with a native art of its own and a religion that was part of everybody's life."[45] Thus the memory of one golden age begets the promise of another.

Most crucially for our purposes, this linear history also sustains the long-held contention that Ajanta is a Buddhist place. Such was the 1821 hypothesis of William Erskine, based upon hearsay evidence. Eyewitnesses in the mid-nineteenth century confirmed Erskine's guess. Still more recently, Hans Bakker's political history of the Vākāṭaka dynasty observed that Ajanta's

> caves belong to the Buddhist, not the Hindu tradition. That this should be so is already remarkable in itself. By all we know of Hariṣeṇa he was a Hindu; nevertheless, the material remains of his reign that we possess are almost all directly linked to the Buddhist faith.[46]

Indeed, I earned my PhD in the field of Buddhist Studies with a dissertation that called Ajanta "a living memorial to Buddhism in India, a matrix from which that ancient religion is excavated...daily."[47]

Perhaps the most extended set of statements along these lines belongs to Sheila Weiner's *Ajanta: Its Place in Buddhist Art*. I cite this book, not because it has had broad influence upon the study of Ajanta, but rather for its clear expression of a certain common sense about the site, one that also vigorously informed my own initial approach. This common sense begins with a recognition of Ajanta's singularity. Ajanta "occupies a unique position in the history of Indian art because it is the only extant site of such grandeur which combines painting, sculpture, and architecture."[48] No other body of *in situ* artifacts, Buddhist or Hindu, is so well preserved from the ancient period. And because Ajanta is so comprehensive, it provides "a kind of document which visually traces the development of Buddhist thought and evolution from early monumental inceptions through the proto-*Mahāyāna* and *Mahāyāna* periods."[49] The investigator of Buddhism at Ajanta must still control for ambient historical noise. That is, dynastic changes and military events during the first five centuries CE played a role in delimiting the movements of monks, artists, and pilgrims across the Indian social landscape; the flow of resources; the circulation of ideas. But in the end, iconographic innovations and stylistic changes at Ajanta can be explained by reference to Buddhist materials alone (scriptural, architectural, artistic, and epigraphic), "irrespective of speculation regarding the effects of political vicissitudes upon Buddhist centers."[50] Thus, the kind of surprise that Hans Bakker evinces—Hariṣeṇa, a Hindu king, is known almost exclusively for Buddhist material remains—might be taken as confirmation for Weiner's point that although fifth-century Ajanta "is referred to as a Vākāṭaka or Vākāṭaka-Gupta site, these terms tend to confuse rather than clarify the historical and religious position of Ajaṇṭā vis-à-vis the development of Buddhism in India."[51] And, finally, Ajanta's lessons about Buddhism in India have a distinct terminus. "There is little at Ajaṇṭā to suggest the future course of Buddhist thought and practices. As such, it is perhaps the last of the extant *Mahāyāna* sites devoid of Esoteric influences."[52] To learn Ajanta's lessons, a scholar should be backward-looking. He certainly does not need to look forward beyond the fifth century, except for a brief glance at Xuanzang in the seventh. With Xuanzang, Ajanta's history effectively comes to an end.

Weiner's guiding assumption, "above all Ajaṇṭā is a Buddhist site," repeated at the beginning of her book and at its end, is not unique to her. Nevertheless, these words will serve this chapter as a dictum to be resisted and sentence to be parsed. One might ask: What is included in the "all" over which *Buddhism* is superordinate? What is Ajanta *not* because it *is* "Buddhist"? But above all I am concerned with the timing of Weiner's word, "is."

When *is* history?

Admiring Ajanta, Alan Moorehead imagined India's future as an ancient civilization reborn, while Weiner looked back to see Mahāyāna Buddhism still-born there. But why do we tell Ajanta's tale from the beginning? Something happened in this place during the tenth century. Can that something be historical, even in its silence? Does it merit the historian's attention without any reference to Buddhist thought or Vākāṭaka politics? How about Ajanta in the seventeenth-century? Abū al-Fazl mentions Ajanta in a gazetteer of the provinces in Akbar's Mughal empire, its administrative divisions, and revenues. We learn that these caves were located in the Baitalwādi district, in the neighborhood of Batialah, "a fort of considerable strength."[53] (The fort, now called Vetalwadi, is now in ruins.) We also learn that this territory had two major landowners, both Rājputs, named Medni Rāo and Kāmdeo, with 300 cavalrymen and 2,000 foot soldiers between them. Did Medni Rāo and Kāmdeo go to the caves then to worship sadhus, who might have squatted therein and painted the signs of Śiva on the walls? Did these Rājputs track the tigers who preyed on their people to Ajanta's lairs? In 1824, Lieutenant James Edward Alexander, Sixteenth Lancers, of the Order of the Lion and Sun, found a skeleton in one cave's dark corner. Was it left there by Medni Rāo or Kāmdeo? By a tiger?

Abū al-Fazl's *A'in-I-Ākbari* is a well-known text whose translations into English and French numbered among the first works of eighteenth-century Oriental scholarship. Nevertheless, no European scholar of Ajanta has heretofore noted this work. That may be due to ignorance of the source, or it may be due to a perception that the *A'in-I-Ākbari's* mention of Ajanta is insignificant since the Mughal document said nothing about the site's creation, abandonment, or entrance into modern global consciousness. The *A'in-I-Ākbari* also named *bauddha* as a native Indian doctrinal system, but did not connect that philosophy to these caves.[54] Although ignored, the *A'in-I-Ākbari* nevertheless owns a place in Ajanta's linear history, albeit the history of its forgetting. For a place to be legitimated as having a history, for it to receive the discursive imprimatur of the term *history*, is for it to be located within a naturalized temporal flow that is singular, comprehensive, and regular. We expect that all events are related in time along an objective axis. The non-reception of the *A'in-I-Ākbari*—like the padlock on Cave Twenty Two—reminds us that location, or rather localizability, on this axis is also synecdochic of value. Insofar as the historian expects that *"everything* can be historicized," in Chakrabarty's phrase, history becomes "the site where the struggle goes on to appropriate, on behalf of the modern, these other collocations of memory."[55] If this chapter explores a broad issue, the value of the past as a repository of the present, then its more specific questions ask: Do the intentions of past actors—whether founded in the niceties of Buddhist doctrine or the necessities of Vākātaka power—provide an adequate horizon against which to gauge present identity?

Certainly one might look to Ajanta for history, but receive, Rashomon style, perspectival shadowgraphs of reality. There will be a Buddhist history as well as a bauddha history. And a Muslim history, albeit one of relative disinterest. And a Hindu history too, in which the stone "buddhas" are worshiped as gods other than buddha. A Vākātaka history. A Sātavāhana history. Even a European history, whose perspective is that its account alone offers exceptional universal value because it alone organizes all those other histories into a cohesive framework, enabling historians to judge each, both on its own limited merits and in relation to the totality. This hegemonic appropriation of the local and the particular for the universal is what led Nandy to declare his disinterest in alternative histories. Nandy asked for alternatives *to* Enlightenment history. How might we think about that distinction?

Enlightenment history (EH) is ideally linear. Alternatives to Enlightenment history (-EHs) do not idealize linearity.

EH proceeds forward as a procession of names and dates, events and causes.
-EHs are found in adventitious happenings that come to pass, occasionally, here and now.

EH's narrators presuppose that human beings act from conscious, presumably reasonable, motives, thus allowing R.G. Collingwood's words to become a methodological dictum: "The cause of [an] event, for [historians], means the thought in the mind of the person by whose agency the event came about.... The historian is looking for these processes of thought. All history is the history of thought."[56]
-EHs find their norm in deviance, diversity, and dissent. Their narrators suspect that human beings are like unhappy families, each one human in his own way.

85

EH circulates the Enlightenment currency of universality, in which all local systems of value and contending sources of coercive power are rationalized into a shared morality and stable civilization.

-EHs are minted in private economies of pleasure, and have no systematic political program. This is not to say that they are apolitical, just anarchic.

EH is expressed in terms useful for the morphological and genealogical comparison of ideologies—terms like religion and politics, Buddhism and Hinduism, Mahāyāna and Hīnayāna, Vākāṭaka and Raj.

-EHs are neither articulate nor consistent. They are best known by their messes, not their meanings.

EH's narrators seek to reconstruct the past by decoding archaeological artifacts or physical debris as material cryptograms of past motivations and values.

-EHs begin with the premise, stated by Nandy, that "all times exist only in present times and can be decoded only in terms of the contemporaneous."[57] Thus their narrators use the stuff of other material cultures to negotiate their own presents.

EH is framed in the language of authorial intent, asking: Who made Ajanta and why?

-EHs are a matter of response. To understand them one asks: How have people reacted to the stuff already there? Creation is already an instance of response.

Jamais vu

The mutuality of EH and -EHs can be clarified by Christopher Nolan's film, *Memento*, which earned critical acclaim in 2001.[58] *Memento* recounts several days in the fictional life of Leonard Shelby, an ex-insurance investigator suffering from a special form of amnesia. A blow to Leonard's head as he attempted to thwart his wife's rape and murder rendered him unable to make new memories. He remembers that cataclysmic event as well as his happy life before it. Leonard knows that he lost everything on that night, and fills his present with fantasies of revenge. Indeed, Leonard even knows his enemy's name: John G. The search for rough justice is hampered, however, by the fact that no experience or datum remains active in Leonard's brain for more than a few minutes. Only the systematic creation of physical data—notes, photographs, and for particularly important information, tattoos—enables Leonard to maintain a semblance of temporal continuity. For our purposes the most crucial detail may be that Leonard places unwavering faith in the facticity of the written word. Whether these words are inscribed on paper or skin, he never doubts their one-to-one correspondence with the truth. At one point Leonard complains, "[My wife's] gone. And the present is trivia which I scribble down as fuckin' notes." Yet, apart from that trivia Leonard would have no present at all (or if there is a difference, he would have only a present).

The film's first image is that of a left hand holding the Polaroid of a bloody corpse—there's been a murder—the hand shakes the photo, and its picture becomes duller, less distinct—*Memento's* time is moving backward as ours moves forward—we watch Leonard's past fade before our eyes—our future is his loss of memory, the past he no longer has. This disorientation structures the film. For *Memento* works, not as a flashback that collapses the finish into the start, but by slipping serially, scene by scene, backwards through abstract time. When Leonard is asked what it is like to have no memory, he answers, "It's like waking. It's like you just woke up." Leonard's life is a series of awakenings. He is constantly "waking up" to find himself in the midst of a chase or to find a man tied up in his closet or to find a dead body at his feet and a Polaroid in his hand. Thus the audience too wakes up to find that human behavior is not easily generalized or regularized or universalized.

Immanuel Kant has been called the inventor of the modern subject, an invention predicated upon an equally modern conception of time.[59] For Kant's human, time is one and many, infinite and infinitely segmented. Time is the medium of human experience; neither the outer world, nor the inner, can be experienced as atemporal.[60] Moreover, this experience is constrained by a logic in which temporal order is an *a priori* order that moves in one direction only: "*B* can only follow *A* in apprehension, but the perception *A* cannot follow but only precede *B*."[61] Granted, this irreversible chain of cause-and-effect is not necessarily a truth about the real order of noumena. Still, it is apodictic for the cognitive reception of that noumenal order, and the fashioning of a phenomenal order of things by the human mind. In fact Kant identifies three "Analogies of Experience"—three rules "in accordance with which unity of experience is to arise from perceptions"— corresponding to three modes of time.[62] Insofar as time has the quality of duration, things are perceived as having an enduring substance. Insofar as temporal moments are successive, things are perceived as changing in a sequence of causes and effects. Insofar as there is the simultaneity of diverse substances, things are perceived as having reciprocal, mutual interactions. In a Kantian world, all experiences are necessarily patterned as substantial, causal, and contextual. Human beings cannot make objective judgments about temporal events within a single temporal system unless they experience the world in just these ways. Lacking these three Analogies, we cannot have objective, hard history. Lacking these three, valid subjectivity, the recognition of one's own actual place in the world, is also impossible.

This is where *Memento* becomes interesting. Leonard's search for revenge goes awry insofar as he *expects* that enduring substantiality, causality, and contextuality condition his experience, while we in the audience see that they do not. For Leonard causality is inverted: effects always precede their cause. He lacks the ability to contextualize experience: the world is always just as it is. Historicity, not history, is Leonard's problem of high moment. This is the insight Nandy finds lacking in European Enlightenment conceptions of history. Historians, he complains, "have sought to historicize everything, but never the idea of history itself."[63] Nandy would like this film.

Although Leonard has no ability to learn, he is nevertheless confident about his knowledge. "You know, you know who you are, and you know kind of all about yourself. It's just for day to day stuff notes are really useful." Leonard remembers the details of his life before his memory loss. This certainty about his own past obviates doubts concerning his present. Unable to experience linear time, Leonard nevertheless presumes that his identity is continuous within it. He negotiates time without entering time. Indeed, the deceptions of linearity are crucial, both for Leonard and for *Memento* as allegory. History, in Enlightenment terms, involves the study of intentions in context. As matters of free volition, historically significant actions carry a moral and juridical charge. Likewise, for Leonard's vendetta against John G. to be just, he must believe that his actions are contextually appropriate gestures expressing a righteous motivation.

To ensure justice, accordingly, Leonard must take special care that the facts on which he acts are correct and fair, for he is ever aware that his life could become a series of inappropriate responses to mistaken incitements. Thus Leonard takes a doctrinaire position on the relative value of physical evidence over narrative (personal or collective):

> Memory's not perfect. It's not even that good. Ask the police. Eyewitness testimony is unreliable. The cops don't capture a killer by sitting around remembering stuff. They collect facts; they make notes; and they draw conclusions. Facts, not memories. That's how you investigate.

Were he unable to trust the systematic veracity of his photographs, notes, and tattoos, Leonard would lose access to the transcendental self that grounds his moral certainty. To borrow a line from Nandy, Leonard has an "uncritical acceptance of the idea of history."[64] Nandy further warns that uncritical acceptance of this sort can result in "violence and cruelty." *Memento* would agree if the definition of violence and cruelty includes the "wrong" man being killed for what are materially established as the "right" reasons.

For the Kantian subject, truth is "the agreement of a cognition with its object."[65] In this light, Leonard's truths are moments of ignorance cloaked in a verisimilitude of truth. Leonard possesses only objects; faith alone enables him to translate those objects into sources of knowledge. However, Leonard's faith in his system of fact-keeping constantly leads him astray. He acts with purpose and moral clarity because his long-term memories allow him to be certain regarding his identity and mission. For the movie's audience, by contrast, an inverse relationship obtains between increasing knowledge of Leonard's activities and decreasing approval for his motivations. Leonard's self-conception is askew. He has become a serial killer. His lack of awareness about who he is *at present*—the fact that for him actions have no present context and no present concern; that everything he does is evaluated only by reference to the hallowed past—enables others to use Leonard to do their dirty work. Leonard's world is filled with opportunists who know his infirmity and take advantage of it. A motel owner, for instance, tricks Leonard into renting multiple rooms. Others manipulate him into murder, by transfiguring their diverse enemies into his one personal demon.

Leonard is certain that John G. killed his wife and destroyed his memory. His chest bears the tattooed injunction:

JOHN G. RAPED AND MURDERED MY WIFE. FIND HIM AND KILL HIM

But the facticity of bodily inscription is not a guarantee of fact. At the film's beginning (which, recall, is its historical end) we also read a tattoo on Leonard's leg, bearing John G.'s license plate number, SG137IU. There are many John G.'s. The singularity of this datum, SG137IU, becomes the objective, hard fact Leonard needs to know that he has identified the true John G. once and for all. As the film unfolds into the past, however, what at first is received as an infallible truth transmogrifies into a fabulous lie. *Leonard had this license number tattooed onto his leg as an intentional act of self-deception.* Another man named John G., not the real killer, angered Leonard. Aroused by that moment of hatred, Leonard wrote a note to himself containing the license plate number. Leonard knew that he would forget his short-term motivation. Leonard knew that he would "wake up" to discover that he had finally identified the true John G. Leonard lucidly forced himself to see the wrong John G. as the actual villain filling his eternal present.

In the end, *Memento* shows us time as a progression of moments of response woven together through the agency of a dangerous self-deception: the existence of a transcendental identity provides a fixed locus for moral authority. Stripped of this transcendent context, each moment of response becomes discontinuous, ambiguous, indeterminate. Linear time: maybe we cannot live without it, but certainly we ought not trust it.

A mountain's lifetime of graffiti

Leonard's life goes awry insofar as expects that enduring substantiality, causality, and contextuality still condition his experience even after his trauma. Leonard becomes a monster, not because he is an amnesiac, but because he holds onto his faith in Enlightenment subjectivity as the normative ground of moral action even after he is no longer biologically capable of being *that* subject. This is where post-colonial critique comes in, with Nandy's proposition that the western Enlightenment's hegemony over discourse on the past is unfortunate if not unethical, and Chakrabarty's call for "a history that deliberately makes visible, within the structure of its own narrative forms, its own repressive strategies and practices."[66] Both Nandy and Chakrabarty imagine a meandering ahistory in which personal time is not devalued in favor of the totalizing constraints of Kantian temporality.

For the purposes of this chapter, however, *Memento* offers more than a pop-culture exemplum of the moral ambiguities inherent in Enlightenment theories of time. The film also suggests a conceptual structure through which to consider the two narrative modes within which Ajanta figures: the EH narrative of intentions and the -EHs narrative(s) of receptions. In *Memento*, Leonard's tattoos provide the most important data for his participation in temporal flow. He receives them as true facts even when (from the audience's perspective) they lie. Whenever Leonard, shirtless, looks in the mirror, tattooed words tell him: "John G. raped and murdered my wife. Find him and kill him." Until a laser removes this directive from Leonard's chest, it will delimit his identity. His present and future can have no purpose except service to the hallowed past.

Ajanta's inscriptions can be likened to Leonard's tattoos in this regard. Both species of text are uniquely, materially, located in space and time. Both rely upon wider webs of signification for their canons, ideas, and formulae. Both offer the cultural historian determinate points of entry into specific intertextual moments. And like tattoos, which can be divided into multiple sub-genres, Ajanta possesses several types of inscription: long *praśastis* that celebrate noble families and patrons; donative records of varying length (some simply name the donor, others also express a desire to share spiritual merit created by the donation with others); painted labels that name figures painted on the walls; didactic verses from a literary work, Ārya Śūra's *Jātakamālā*. Finally, there is graffiti.

Ajanta boasts a mountain's lifetime of graffiti, unauthorized scratches, gouges, and daubs. The remainder of this chapter looks to that graffiti as a source for "other collocations of memory," to recall Chakrabarty's phrase. It takes little effort to recognize the former presence of Śākyas at Ajanta, given that Cave Sixteen's *praśasti* dedicates it to the Three Jewels—buddha, dharma, and saṅgha—and Cave Twenty Six's donor likens his patronage to the act of an affluent and influential bodhisattva. But it does require casual inattention to miss the Śaivite tridents on Cave Eleven, or the uncaring defacement of ancient paintings in Caves Ten and Twenty Two, or the many symbols scribbled on the walls of One, Ten, Sixteen, Seventeen, and Twenty One. And it requires a still deeper ideological commitment to argue, as does Sheila Weiner, that historians who would "recognize [Ajanta] for what it is" must see it as "a Buddhist site, part of the mainstream, in its time, of Buddhist art and thought, which existed and prospered in an essentially Brāhmanical world."[67] *In its time Ajanta was part of the Buddhist mainstream, and thus, now, it should be recognized for what it is— Buddhist.* This is Leonard-logic. How do we delimit *its* time? If Weiner directs historians to "disregard the various dynastic appellations which have been appended to Ajaṇṭā," certainly other, more contemporary, markers of social and cultural significance have even less claim upon the historians' time. If Ajanta *is* Buddhist, then "graffiti" denotes that which, being non-Buddhist, deserves no place at Ajanta, and thus may be overlooked even as it exists right there before one's eyes.

In relation to Ajanta, at least, graffiti belongs to the intersection of the two historical modes, EH intention and -EHs receptions. Based upon inscriptions, art, and architectural patterns, we consider that place to have an intended meaning as Śākya monasteries and Śākya shrines. When G.S.S. and विजय शर्मा scratched their names into Cave Twenty Two they violated that intention, yet their presence and its impact cannot be denied. Graffiti appropriates culturally significant space and time for the present. The vandalism that conservators try to stop by padlocking doors simultaneously provides data for the study of contemporary reception. Graffiti reveals how people make places their own, how they mark presence, how they assert themselves in opposition to dominant powers. Yet, we can recognize "graffiti" as such only insofar as we consider certain graphemes to be misplaced in their places. Thus a consideration of graffiti points to the utility of Enlightenment history while simultaneously denying its ultimate privilege. As a physical presence graffiti marks temporal transition since it overwrites something already there, yet in so doing it also forces one to notice the ideological dimension of institutional privilege given to origins and essences. A graffito abhorred in one temporal moment can become a later moment's prized "datum" or "artifact," even "inscription." John Smith's 1819 addition to Cave Ten is received with such ambivalence. Who can say whether G.S.S.'s and विजय शर्मा 's names will transform, discursively, from "graffiti" to "inscription" one day?

Ajanta's history can be told as a history of graffiti. Such a telling does not deny the significance of intention as one force shaping the site. Rather, it attends to what intention leaves out. Leonard was perfectly certain of his righteous vengeance when he shot John G. at the beginning/end of *Memento*. He knew the truth: so lucid was his motivation and so obvious the agreement between inner sense and outer fact. Of course, Leonard was wrong. The corpse at Leonard's feet had not killed his wife. Leonard's murder of *that* John G. was not a holy expression of the call to vengeance tattooed on his chest. Leonard strategized that his own forgetful ignorance would guarantee his righteous conviction. What is "forgotten" by those who desire to recognize Ajanta for what it is, *is* now in the present—Buddhist? How can one narrate Ajanta's history, not as a tale of causes, events, and actions, but as one of reactions and appropriations?

Cave eleven: the Śaivite years

Let us consider a set of Śaivite tridents painted on the pillars and walls of Cave Eleven. Most guidebooks ignore this cave, or like the *Lonely Planet* pass it off as "not of great interest," unaware that its verandah is a fine spot for an afternoon snooze.[68] Perhaps such anonymity has protected Cave Eleven's Śaivite graffiti from the chemicals of well-intentioned curators. In Śaivite iconography, the trident holds a variety of symbolic associations. Its most basic function as a weapon is to destroy evil and restore cosmic order. But the icon's three tines and flowing banners also serve as mnemonics for diverse doctrinal trinities: three divisions of time, three parts of the cosmic cycle, three primordial qualities, three worlds, three chains of bondage, three states of consciousness, three aspects of consciousness, among others. Presently, we have no way of knowing whether Cave Eleven's tridents are doctrinally elite, or merely the humble markings of an unsophisticated devotee. Further, unless the ASI analyzes the paint, there is little prospect of dating them with precision. One of the few published notices of these tridents belongs to John Griffiths in 1896. The fact that they lie above the thick soot that blankets Cave Eleven's walls suggests that the tridents were painted not too long before this date.[69] The possibility of a nineteenth-century provenance is further advanced by Griffiths' description of witnessing the Makara Sakrant festival at Ajanta. This mid-January celebration of the sun's transit from the Tropic of Cancer to the Tropic of Capricorn initiates six months of longer, warmer days. During the festival, a Śaiva renunciant would sometimes lead a procession from cave to cave at Ajanta, "jingling hawkbells to ward off wild beasts, snakes and evil spirits...marking his trail by smears of red paint on the largest boulders that lie in his path."[70] (Figure 3.4.)

We do not know the year in which Cave Eleven's tridents were painted. Nevertheless, when considered in the context of Makara Sakrant as described by Griffiths and other nineteenth-century observers, they provide hard evidence that Ajanta enjoyed a post-1819 cultural renaissance. After so many centuries' hiatus, Ajanta offered local villagers a place at which to gather and celebrate. Such was not Griffiths' interpretation, since for him the tridents belonged to an hour of decline. We might see Griffiths as a kindred spirit to Myra Shackley, introduced in the previous chapter. Shackley's textbook on tourist management tells us that World Heritage monuments "transcend existing cultural values."[71] The tridents earned Griffiths' contempt, in part, precisely because they *expressed* existing cultural values. Griffiths claimed, "To those who know modern India where Buddhism has been dead and done for centuries, it is unnecessary to dwell on the pathetic fact that these painted halls have now no interest for the people."[72] Of course, the tridents' relatively new paint was evidence that people *did* remain interested in Ajanta's halls: they were the wrong people, however, having the wrong interests.

Griffiths' distaste for the culture existing at 1890's Ajanta becomes clear in a set of hierarchical oppositions through which he contrasted the site's hallowed past with its grievous present. First he imagined Ajanta's split temporality in terms of the split between the sacred and the profane. "Traditions of...sacred character must have long existed" in this place.[73] However, now that "nothing in the subjects or in the art of the pictures has any connection in the peasant's mind with any article of faith," those sacred traditions have been supplanted by "periodic pleasure fairs," like Makara Sakrant, in which thousands of people "hold high carnival, bathing in the river, feasting on sweetmeats, buying toys and nick-nacks, firing guns and crackers." Second, Griffiths contrasted the holy life of Ajanta's original inhabitants with the unholy lives of those who dwelt there in his day. For the first, he approvingly cited an earlier article, which described the caves' authentic inhabitants as "venerated *bhikshus*" who "alone with nature...devote[d] their time to contemplation and self-restraint."[74] Griffiths lamented these Buddhist monks' absence and condemned their contemporary substitutes: matt-haired, ash-smeared devotees of "the *bhang*-besotted *jogi*-god," who "during their often protracted stay disfigure the pictures and sculptures with the smoke of their cooking fires and rudely daubed red tridents in honor of Śiva."

Figure 3.4 Two tridents painted on a pillar inside Cave Eleven. This same pillar is visible in Figure 3.6. Photo by author.

The third contrast elevated the Enlightened British above everybody else. Griffiths proudly asserted, "the preservation of monuments of ancient art is a purely modern idea."[75] In fact, preservationist values were special to a British modernity in particular, for in Griffiths' view they were "scarcely yet accepted in Europe" in 1896. Given that even the Continentals could not see antiquities' continuing worth, Griffiths held no hope for Ajanta's local "peasants"—one century later, Nandy will call these same people "traditional Indians"—since preservation was "entirely unknown in the East." Rather, the peasants regarded Ajanta's sculptural and pictorial masterpieces "with indifference; or, at best, as mysterious and

93

dangerous shades, fit only for owls and bats and the unclean spirits of modern Hindu demonology."

Griffiths desired Ajanta to preserve changelessly a native culture proper to its locale, as a pure reminder of Buddhism's ancient genius. Thus he looked askance at contemporary uses of the site, including the Śaivite markings on Cave Eleven's walls. To recall my earlier symbology, Griffiths was an ambassador to Ajanta from the land of EH, Enlightenment history.

How might an ambassador from the land of -EH have received those tridents? For an answer, let us transport *Memento's* Leonard back to the nineteenth century. Leonard will become the companion of one Lieutenant Blake, who visited Ajanta in 1839 and published an account of his trip in the *Bombay Courier*.[76] Leonard "wakes up" in 1839 knowing nothing of his present circumstances apart from the horse beneath him and the military man at his side. Where am I; how did I get here; with whom; why—such questions shoot impotently through Leonard's head. Yet, Leonard can observe the hubbub all around. Indeed, Lieutenant Blake and Leonard have arrived at Ajanta on the day of the Makara Sakrant festival. The villagers are prostrating before the monolithic sculptures and rubbing the stones with oil. Curious, Leonard asks Blake to explain the villagers' actions. Blake responds by disparaging the Indians as confused in their worship. "They have no knowledge of their own mythology: the blind adoration of the villagers around... is the mere oozing out of ignorance which requires *some* outlet."[77] They worship the god *Jelandar Nath* in this cave, while in that one they worship *Machandarnath*. But these local names are incorrect. For "the whole of these caves are undoubtedly Buddhist; the curly-headed figures, the contemplative postures, the associations, and the plans of the excavations are... incontestible proofs."[78] Leonard nods politely. But he has no idea what Blake is talking about, since Leonard is no less ignorant than the foolish natives about the "true" identity of these curly-headed figures. Leonard cannot see the transcendental value of a past "Buddhism" because he sees no present-day "Buddhists." Thus Leonard also lacks the capacity to snigger knowingly when Blake tells him,

> [The natives do not] suppose these caves are the work of men: they declare that their gods dug them out one long dark night. I have heard a native assert that their gods scratched out the stone with their hands and then ate it! On asking him why he supposed this, he replied, that as there was no vestige of the excavated stone in the vicinity, their gods must have eaten it. Q.E.D.: verily, the digestion of these architects and their credulous disciples are pretty much on par.[79]

The natives' legend is certainly unpalatable, but Blake's own tale of an ancient group of Buddhists is not so easily swallowed either. Blake seems sure of his conclusions about Ajanta's religious provenance. But they hardly satisfy Leonard's stomach for long-term knowledge, since there is no living morsel of "Indian Buddhism" on which to chew. That name, Buddhism, lodges solely in Leonard's short-term memory, though it takes on the fleeting appearance of being antique fact by the fact of the stones' own solidity.

In *Memento*, Leonard tattooed SG137IU on his leg, knowing that he would soon forget: "This is not the license plate of the man who killed my wife but of a man *I want dead*." Later, Leonard murdered John G. with the facile faith that his vengeance was just. The conceit in this little exercise has been that Leonard has not yet willed himself to know that Ajanta is Buddhist because he does not yet know that he should desire that knowledge. Now imagine that "Ajanta is Buddhist" has been tattooed on Leonard's left foot. In that case, he would certainly shake his head in ready agreement every time Blake mocked the villagers' non-Buddhist worship. But Leonard cannot know, indeed Leonard can never think to ask why he tattooed "Ajanta is Buddhist" on his foot in the first place. For Leonard, his foot is tattooed thus for no better reason than because these words remind him of a truth. Leonard will not accept that what he takes to be incontrovertible fact also has a history; that his fact bears the traces of now-forgotten desires; that what he takes to be the original cause of Ajanta—Buddhist piety—may be the effect of his own contemporary interest.

This same game can be played again and again. Now Leonard "awakens" in 1896 as John Griffiths' companion. Again, Leonard observes all sorts of activity at Ajanta. Again, he does not conceptualize that activity in relation to Buddhism because he sees no self-described Buddhists. Now, John Griffiths' equivocations make little sense. Leonard hears Griffiths disparage contemporary Hindu festivals at the caves. Griffiths teaches Leonard that Ajanta is Buddhist, and "the first essential of the saintly life of Buddhism" is "seclusion from the world and the active business of life."[80] When Leonard inspects Ajanta's paintings, however, he is puzzled that so many seem to celebrate the active business of life. Griffiths has a ready solution: Yes, Ajanta's art shares "to the full that joy in life which is a marked feature of early Hindū poetry."[81] And yes, "those who think of Buddhism as the austere creed of a recluse, repressing human sympathies, and moulded on the life of and teachings of Shākya-Muni himself, may perceive some incongruity between the vivid humanity, and gaiety of these representations, and the ascetic purpose of the halls they adorn." But this perception of incongruity merely reveals the observer's ignorance. There is no real incongruity here, for in point of fact "the Buddhists of Western India—nay, the Lord Buddha himself—was, after all, a Hindū." Sensing Leonard's continuing confusion, Griffiths elaborates. Perhaps the "modern spirit…sees a paradox in this natural development" by which the buddha, "who came to abolish gods ended by adding more divinities to that mighty host." Still and all, "scholars…may be left to trace in these pictures evidences of the harmony or fusion of creeds which we are in the habit of regarding as in perpetual conflict."

Huh? Griffiths describes Buddhism as dedicated to withdrawal from the world, but Buddhists as full of joy in life? Buddhists make caves with an ascetic purpose, but decorate them gaily? The buddha was an iconoclast against Hindu gods, but he was a Hindu? Buddhists too are Hindus, but scholars consider them the

Hindus' enemies? In sum, Buddhists are fun-loving ascetic Hindu-hating Hindus? Leonard has lost his time, not his mind. How is Leonard's understanding of Ajanta's paintings enhanced by Griffiths' equivocations from hard history? If truth is found in the correspondence of cognition and object, what kind of object must Ajanta *be* for the crazy people Griffiths describes to have been its creators? How mad are we to think that we can divine which actual insanity drove them to cut, sculpt, and paint holes in the sheer side of a ravine?

Maybe you too are dumbfounded. This much is clear: Nineteenth-century villagers celebrated Makara Sakrant at Ajanta. Buddhas, Buddhists, and Buddhism were nowhere visible as they worshiped the gods living at Ajanta: *Machandarnath, Yeknath, Goraknath, Raja Indar, Raja Bhat, Harri Itul Bal Gopal Walla, and Jelandar Nath*. The local people were enjoying Ajanta; they were not Buddhists; they did not care.

A brief summary

This chapter began with Ashis Nandy, A.K. Ramanujan, and Dipesh Chakrabarty's critical assessments of Enlightenment universalism in relation to the particularities of Indian life. In a sense, all three focused our attention on strategies of forgetfulness. Nandy was the most explicit, with his claim that traditional India's engagement with time includes "a principle of principled forgetting," whose ethical imperative is violated by the Enlightenment will toward a totalization of memory. Traditionally, Indians have remembered to forget. Chakrabarty did not use these same terms, though he also located the "connection between violence and idealism" in history understood as global progress toward a uniform modernity.[82] The politically engaged historian recollects the victims of this violence—that is, people who do not see universalist rationality as self-evidently reasonable—in order that the world may "once again be imagined as radically heterogeneous."[83] Europeans often forget to remember such people. And Ramanujan described memory in terms of an epistemological grammar: traditional Indian mentalities never forget that all knowledge and all action is structured within particular socio-material contexts.

The chapter first engaged with this range of critiques by introducing an officer in the ASI an archaeologist, historian, and bureaucrat who has not allowed his professional training to take full reign over his imagination. For him, Ajanta is a Hindu bhagavān, whom he serves through his duties as preserver of its ancient artifacts. Lacking the guidance of Nandy, Ramanujan, and Chakrabarty, my first impulse was to dismiss this ASI officer as a fetishist, unable or unwilling to recognize the unliving materiality of Ajanta's matter. With their assistance I came to see this, not as a question of fetishism, but facticity. As a historian, I have long treated "Ajanta is Buddhist" as a given truth, a harmony of object and cognition, form and name. Thus, the ASI officer seemed doubly ignorant. But I read Nandy, Ramanujan, and Chakrabarty as countering that this harmonization is problematic, not because Ajanta's objects (paintings, inscriptions, sculptures, even walls) actually reflect multiple ideological and institutional sources, but because I am not even certain how many people I must ignore or belittle in order to convince myself that my observations about Ajanta's "actuality" are context-neutral. In the statement, "Ajanta is Buddhist," the copula "is" is not a mere artifact of linguistic practice, but a hegemonic bid to appropriate all temporality for the universal time of the academic historian. The fantasy of objective, universal time is itself a fetish object. The scholar who asserts "Ajanta is Buddhist" treats its stones as if they preserve a living, innate intelligence. He has forgotten the Enlightenment's first lesson: matter is dumb.

Cave Eleven: square to an English inch

Let us now return to Cave Eleven. In this case, we will look at several descriptions of this cave written over a four decade period by James Fergusson, arguably the most influential nineteenth-century scholar of the western Indian caves. Before Fergusson, Ajanta's caves were identified by a hodgepodge of local god-names, Machandarnath, Jelandarnath, and so on. Fergusson instituted the well-ordered system of number-names still employed today. Fergusson put the spirit of science into the study of Indian cave architectures, but it was a poltergeist who took up residence.

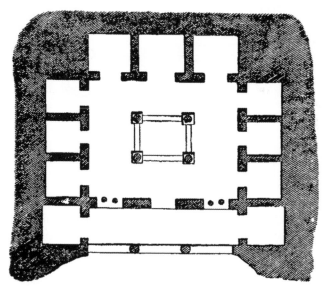

PLAN OF VIHARA NO. II.

SCALE 50 FEET TO 1 INCH.

Figure 3.5 James Fergusson's 1863 plan of Cave Eleven. From *Rock-Cut Temples of India*, page 12.

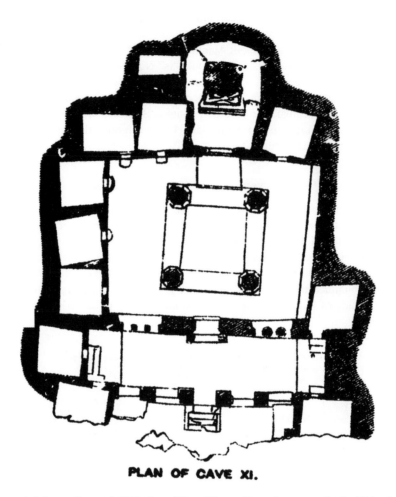

PLAN OF CAVE XI.

Figure 3.6 James Burgess' 1882 plan of Cave Eleven. From *Report on the Buddhist Cave Temples*, plate XXVIII, no. 2.

Consider two ground plans for Cave Eleven (Figures 3.5 and 3.6). The first was published by James Fergusson in 1863, the second by James Burgess in 1883. The earlier plan shows a cave that would be any architect's pride. The angles are right; the walls are straight and probably plumb; cells have equal sizes and are evenly spaced; proportions are harmonious; symmetry reigns. Indeed, even the scale fits an English inch. Twenty years later Cave Eleven is envisioned anew, in haphazard asymmetry. Now the rear wall has four cells, one of which contains a half-carved statue of buddha, while the right wall contains no cells at all, just a long bench. (Cave Eleven's right wall could not have held cells: they would have broken through into the already-present Cave Ten.) Corners are no longer right.

All harmonies are lost. It goes without saying that the 1883 plan is more accurate. Still, if we allow that Fergusson was a careful draftsman and honest observer, we might wonder why he published this idealized plan in lieu of one that disclosed Cave Eleven's messy reality. Was it a matter of drawing from memory due to lost notes? Was it a matter of audience: Fergusson's plan was included in a book of photographs aimed at a popular audience back in England, while Burgess' is found in a volume directed at professional scholars?

Both responses are possible, neither will do. An answer that does suffice will begin with James Fergusson's own place in the history of Ajanta's historicization.

India's rock-cut temples have been known to Europe at least since J.H. van Linschoten's 1579 *Discours of Voyages* described Elephanta, near Mumbai. Continuing commercial and colonial transactions, the Portugese and Dutch followed by the French and British, opened so many hundred more similar excavations to European eyes that, almost three centuries later, James Fergusson was able to address the Royal Asiatic Society with these words, "There are few objects of antiquarian research that have attracted more attention from the learned in Europe, than the history and purposes of Cave Temples in India."[84] However, Fergusson saw no cause for triumph in this broad interest. His paper, beginning on so expectant a note, soon became a lament: "the subject of Indian antiquities" lies in a "state of hopeless neglect."[85]

In fact, Fergusson's 1843 paper stands as a watershed in the study of India's cave temples. These excavations had long captured the colonists' popular imagination. A dilettante troop of doctors, lawyers, and lieutenants devoted their holidays to scrabbling in the rough in order to add to a genre of scholarly writing that married descriptions of local color to archaeological description and historical conjecture. These reports still amuse. But when it came to science, Fergusson found them to contain "so little that is satisfactory ... and such discordant opinions" that he considered it crucial to remake and professionalize the field.[86] For this task, James Fergusson presented himself as an authority bar none:

> There are few buildings or cities of importance in India which I have not at one time or other been able to visit and examine. I had besides the advantage, that as all my journies were undertaken for the sole purpose of antiquarian research, I was enabled to devote my whole and undivided attention to the subject, and all my notes and sketches were made with only one object in view, that of ascertaining the age and object of these hitherto mysterious structures.[87]

Thus Fergusson set out to articulate definite criteria for categorizing cave temples, for comparing their significant features, for dating them individually, and for tracking their evolution across the millennia. In the long run he expected, as would Walter Spink more than one century later, that "the history of the times depends upon the evidence of the caves just as much as the history of the caves depends upon that of the times."[88]

James Fergusson is not important for us because he developed novel investigative techniques. An architect by training, he presents himself as a skilled observer who had the time and opportunity to survey caves and compare them to structural remains whose dates were more certain. Rather Fergusson holds pride of place as a historian of architectural India because he first enunciated the categories that art historians still use to describe places like Ajanta. And crucially for us, Fergusson grounded his taxonomy in the spread of religions. With understated exactitude, Fergusson asserted that all India's cave temples can be classified, first by reference to a specific religious order—Brahmanical, Buddhist, or Jain—and then according to function. As for Buddhist caves, there are only two functions. Either they can be monasteries (*vihāra*) or they can be temples (*caitya*). Since 1843, Fergusson's assertion that "these two classes comprehend all the Buddhist caves in India" has become a methodological given.[89]

Fergusson placed Ajanta at the head of his survey, as "the most perfect and complete series of Buddhist caves in India...[and] in some respects the most interesting."[90] Ajanta was not given the pride of place because it is the largest cave site in South Asia. That privilege is held by Junnār, where the number of individual excavations tops 150. Nor is Ajanta the most ancient site. In the third century BCE, two centuries before Ajanta's putative start, a Sri Lankan princess had already dedicated several caves "for the welfare and happiness of beings in the boundless universe."[91] Rather, Fergusson placed Ajanta at the head of his survey for two reasons. First, he regarded Ajanta as "without any admixture of Brahmanism," a "purely a Buddhist series."[92] Given his surmise that India's religions were unique species, possessing distinct morphologies and divergent genealogies, Ajanta served as touchstone for the classification of other cave sites, enabling him to distinguish Buddhist from Jain from Brahmanical. Second, Fergusson held that "almost every change in cave architecture can be traced in them [Ajanta's caves] during a period of about one thousand or twelve hundred years." Thus, Fergusson treated Ajanta as "a sort of chronometric scale" for all India's Buddhist excavations.[93] Ajanta was Fergusson's key.

In London, Fergusson presented himself to the Royal Asiatic Society as the man most able to use this key, to unlock mysteries of Indian history that had been secreted behind a wall of scholarly inconsistencies and fallacies. He asserted his authority based, in part, upon the breadth of his first-hand knowledge of India's ancient architectures, and in part upon the fact that archaeology was not a secondary passion for him but his chief vocation. In this light, we can now return to the two ground plans for Ajanta's Cave Eleven. For clearly, the bluster of Fergusson's discourse is not supported by the verity of his art. The 1863 plan does not map lithic reality. What spirit of otherworldly matter is Fergusson mapping? Truth being the agreement of cognition with its object, Fergusson's plan tells a truth that has only a secondary relation to the material facts of Cave Eleven. So, if Fergusson's "notes and sketches were made with only one object in view, that of ascertaining the age and object of these hitherto mysterious structures," then what object does correspond to the plan he published?[94] If Ajanta is the key to the history of Indian Buddhist architecture, how precisely is Cave Eleven Buddhist?

Here is the shortest answer: Cave Eleven's central buddha sculpture is large-scale graffiti (Figure 3.7). The cave's original authors had not planned for this figure. Because the buddha was sculpted at a later date by a later hand, Fergusson felt he could leave it out of his representation of the cave, and indeed that he could restore the plan to its pristine, pre-graffiti state.

Here is a slightly longer explanation. Fergusson discusses this cave 3 times over 40 yeras, and in all 3 instances he notes the same problem. Namely, Cave Eleven's pillars and buddha figure belong to different times and intentions. Let us observe how Fergusson changed his presentation of, and solution for, this perceived inconsistency. In 1843, Fergusson placed Cave Eleven near the beginning of the first period of creative activity. This *vihāra's* antiquity was established for him by its proximity in space and form to Cave Twelve, which he considered the site's earliest. Whereas he prioritized Cave Twelve because of its plain simplicity—it is "entirely without pillars, and there is no sanctuary or image, nor apparently, any visible object of worship"—Cave Eleven appeared slightly more advanced because it uses internal pillars to delimit a central pavilion.[95] Furthermore, according to the 1843 paper, the buddha shrine "seems to have been an afterthought," but nevertheless was roughly coeval with the remainder of the cave.[96]

Figure 3.7 Cave Eleven's central buddha. Note the tridents painted on both pillars. Photo by author.

In 1863, twenty years later, Fergusson again placed Cave Eleven near the beginning of Ajanta's first period, as the second oldest *vihāra*. Again, he corroborated this chronological rank by reference to the excavation's simple pillar forms and small size. But unlike the earlier publication, the 1863 text did not mention Cave Eleven's buddha image, either to call it an afterthought or intrusion. Instead, Fergusson made the blanket observation that, "in ancient times, no sculpture or images were introduced into the Viharas."[97] "Ancient times," here, means the first period of creative activity (*c*.BCE 100–100 CE). Writing in 1863, Fergusson dated all buddha figures to Ajanta's second phase. To suit this progressive understanding of Indian art history, Fergusson rendered Cave Eleven's buddha invisible, despite its overt presence. The 1863 ground plan showed Cave Eleven as Fergusson imagined it "in ancient times." His book included neither a token nor a sign that this was not how the cave looked in 863, let alone 1863.

Recalling the previous chapter, we might guess that Fergusson used this representation of Cave Eleven for its *appearance* of utility: the appearance of veracity was what his book required. Rather than label the plan "a Buddhist vihara" or "a typical vihara," he specified, "Plan of Vihara No. 11," as a prop to sustain that appearance. The plan was rationalized and neat because unaesthetic details would distract from that appearance. Yes, the plan was a cartoon, not altogether inappropriate for a picture book on a Victorian coffee table. But the plan was also an archetype—ideology in graphic form—in support of a myth—ideology in narrative form—of Indian Buddhism as a historical subject.

Of what is this plan an archetype? What myth about Indian Buddhism does it support? The Fergusson of 1863 answered with silence. In 1880, he found the missing words in the language of bauddha polemic:

> It depends wholly on whether the age of Cave XI is to be determined from its architecture or from its sculpture to know whether it is to be classed among those of the first or Hināyāna [*sic*] division, or to belong to the second or Mahāyāna class of caves. Its architecture certainly looks old ... but there is an image of Buddha, unfinished, in the sanctuary, and *bassi relievi* at either end of the verandah containing images of Buddha.... The probability is that this cave ... was remodelled [*sic*] at some period long subsequent to its original excavation, and that all its sculptures belong to a much later date than its architecture.[98]

No longer was it the case that India's Buddhists carved *vihāras* for monks and shrines for the buddha "in ancient times," only to do so again later, in times slightly less ancient. In 1880, Ajanta documented a progression of Buddhist institutions, Hīnayāna giving way to Mahāyāna. Fergusson was laconic in 1843—the architectural forms are clearly early and the image, an "afterthought"—and he was actively evasive in 1863. In 1880 neither discursive strategy was necessary, for in *The Cave Temples of India* Fergusson made an easy analogy between Ajanta's artifacts and Indian Buddhism's institutional history. A simple, superficial test allowed scholars to assign cultural productions to the appropriate *yāna*: a cave that is "generally plain in style, and devoid of images of Buddha for worship" must belong to Hīnayāna Buddhist patronage, while the "multiplications of images of Buddha... is most characteristic of caves of the Mahāyāna sect."[99] Indeed, this *yānic* distinction lent further nuance to Fergusson's original 1843 taxonomy, when he founded the history of India archaeology upon distinctions between the Buddhist, Jain, and Brahmanical religions.

To recall the strategic "brand management" attempted by Sheila Weiner, whose book on Ajanta was published almost one century after *Cave Temples*, we see Fergusson's continuing influence. Weiner demands that every interpretation of Ajanta begin with the fact it is a *Buddhist* site. Thus she still presents Ajanta as "a kind of document which visually traces the development of Buddhist thought." She still distinguishes an "early *Hīnayāna* aniconic phase" from a "*Mahāyāna* period characterized by the introduction of cult images." And she still finds it worthwhile to describe a "mainstream of Buddhist thought and art" fully distinct from, albeit resident within, "a tolerant, but nevertheless essentially Brāhmanical, world."[100]

Now we can solve the puzzle of the 1863 plan. Of what is it an archetype? What myth about Indian Buddhism does it support? In Fergusson's world, Hīnayāna and Mahāyāna were more than mere denominations of Buddhists whose contentions over doctrine ramified to their ritual practices and iconological sensibilities. The Orientalists who taught Fergusson terms like *Hīnayāna* and *Mahāyāna* also taught him that these *yānas* fell into a hierarchy of value fixed by their successive dates. The later *yāna* represented a corruption of the buddha's original teachings and the ruination of his religion's formative spirit. Thus, for instance, *The Cave Temples of India's* index contains these two entries: "Hīnayāna, the followers of the 'lesser vehicle,' the purer sect of Buddhists," and "Mahāyāna, the sect of 'the greater vehicle,' a later and corrupt form of Buddhism."[101] These editorial comments fit a pattern that Philip Almond, writing on the "discovery" of Buddhism in nineteenth-century Britain, describes as "the obsession throughout the middle and latter part of the nineteenth century with the quest for origins—biologically, geologically, and historically."[102] In this case, original, essential Buddhism involved only "the practice of morality and a few simple ceremonial observances."[103] Analogously, the "original or Puritan Buddhists" needed only spartan architectures; members of the Hīnayāna were "content to live by themselves, or with only one or two companions in rude caves."[104] The 1863 plan showed Cave Eleven as a Hīnayāna monastery restored to its ideal modesty and orderliness; it mapped a Buddhism restored to initial purity. Indeed, Fergusson's contempt for the Mahāyāna was unabashed: "Mahāyāna monks congregated into large and magnificent monasteries, richly adorned... replete with every comfort, it may almost be said, with every luxury."[105] Is it any wonder, therefore, that they also introduced "a whole system of idolatry... at total variance with the simpler form of faith that characterized the earlier caves"? To remove the taint of the degenerate Mahāyāna ethos, Fergusson had to displace its latter-day cult image. Cave Eleven became a space within which to observe Buddhism's decline and to correct history's errors.

The MacGuffin

Graffiti is ineluctably temporal. Thus it might seem that Fergusson's 1880 strategy—that is, using native bauddha terms like Hīnayāna and Mahāyāna in order to historicize Cave Eleven's buddha as a kind of degenerate graffiti—is the antithesis of his earlier unhistorical erasure of this figure. That impression would be wrong. The 1863 plan also has a place in time, while the 1880 description also has an ahistorical dimension. That is to say, the 1863 plan was useful for Fergusson insofar as it appeared true to his readers. For us, it remains useful/true as a map of Fergusson's ideological position, if not of Ajanta's physical space. Likewise, terms like Buddhism, Hīnayāna, and Mahāyāna remain current, not because they necessarily increase the accuracy of theories about fifth-century Indian history, but because they make those theories appear more precise, and therefore more "saleable" within an intellectual economy that prizes hard data and objectivity. These are value-added words. Knowledge of them gives one what seems to be a straight map to historical verities and neat plan for historical research: *Hīnayāna* and *Mahāyāna* inform us about the history of Buddhism; *Buddhism* informs us about the history of religion; *religion* informs us about human social history; *history* informs us about how people negotiate their present. Recall the prior chapter, where Douglas Holt and Juliet Schor said of advertising: "monopolizing the public channels of meaning creation is becoming more important than monopolizing *particular* meanings."[106] The same may be said for scholarship. The value of Buddhism, religion, etc., inheres in the fact that these terms foster and shape acts of scholarly communication, as much as in any specific information they impart.

Buddhism, religion, etc., dominate the market for knowledge insofar as the value-added qualities that these terms appear to bestow, for example, hardness and objectivity, enjoy sanction in the modern university. It is easy to forget, however, that such words quickly become scholars' close intimates; professional identities hinge on the labor exerted to delimit their meanings. Sharp insights bring knowledge, yes, but also food on the table, personal satisfaction, and a sense of well-being. A total institutional focus on the hardness of hard data thus accomplishes something like an illusionist's misdirection, forcing attention away from the human factors in knowledge-production. This is why *Memento* is so resonant as an allegory of the historian's craft: here we observe what happens when a man ignores his lived present out of a single-minded fixation on hard facts about matters long past. Of course Leonard is a caricature. He is physically unable to form short-term memories, and therefore has no point of contact with the present other than the past he remembers. Leonard's obsession to find the man who murdered his wife really is all he possesses; without it, he would have no impetus to take the notes and ink the tattoos that document his present. Nevertheless, one can still imagine Fergusson nodding in agreement as Leonard affirms the efficacy of his investigative techniques, and their institutional sanction: "The cops don't capture a killer by sitting around remembering stuff. They collect facts; they make notes; and they draw conclusions. Facts, not memories. That's how you investigate." And one can imagine a sanctimonious parody: "Historians don't capture Ajanta by sitting around watching yogis paint tridents on Cave Eleven's pillars. They collect facts about *yānas*; they make notes about inscriptions; and they draw conclusions about Buddhism."

Although Leonard makes good methodological sense, we also know that his fidelity to these same principles allows him, in all innocence, to live a life of wanton criminality. Murder is an improbable outcome of Fergusson's 1863 deception regarding Cave Eleven—that is not the point. We historians are people who negotiate the present by forming narratives about the past. How swiftly and how completely must we forget the fictions of our truths to preserve self-respect while doing our work? What crimes or misdemeanors might we commit because we have forgotten that we, no less than Ashis Nandy's traditional Indians, practice principled forgetfulness? Fergusson's 1843 paper began by making several points: Before him, the study of Indian cave architectures was a haphazard mishmash of opinions; he would be the first man to create a science of this subject; his science was founded upon the long-attested distinction between India's three religions, Buddhism, Brahmanism, and Jainism. How much did Fergusson have to "forget" about religious identity in India to be so certain of himself and his science in 1843? Is 1863 just the year in which Fergusson got sloppy, so we caught his crime? Is 1880 the year in which he explained why the 1863 plan really was not criminal at all, that is, the plan showed the cave in its original conception, and therefore its higher truth?

For the historian, Leonard is interesting because Leonard does not care about the present. He lives for the past and for the future, while absent from the present. His present is vivid with danger, sex, money, drugs, and violence, yet he does not recognize its influence. He drives a Porsche and wears a couture suit, but never wonders how an ex-insurance investigator on disability could afford such items. The search for the killer drives Leonard. It seems of vital importance. But it has little direct bearing upon what actually happens day-to-day. It is a very busy lot of nothing. Alfred Hitchcock has a useful term to talk about such a lot of nothing: MacGuffin. What is a MacGuffin? When François Truffaut asked, Hitchcock replied:

> It might be a Scottish name, taken from a story about two men in a train. One man says, "What's that package up there in the baggage rack?" And the other answers, "Oh, that's a MacGuffin." The first one asks, "What's a MacGuffin?" "Well," the other man says, "it's an apparatus for trapping lions in the Scottish Highlands." The first man says, "But there are no lions in the Scottish Highlands," and the other one answers, "Well then, that's no MacGuffin!" So you see that a MacGuffin is actually nothing at all.[107]

Not quite nothing. The MacGuffin provides a rationale for action, quieting questions about intentionality. In Hitchcock's world, to know why Janet Leigh, driving late into the evening, ends up at the Bates Motel, explains little or nothing about *Psycho's* cinematic power. Or *Notorious*: Claude Raines plays a Nazi who smuggles uranium, of vital interest to American agents Cary Grant and Ingrid Bergman. But for Hitchcock the uranium, the MacGuffin, is "of no importance whatever," since for him *Notorious* is a love story: "simply the story of a man in love with a girl who, in the course of her official duties, had to go to bed with another man and even had to marry him."[108] *Notorious* is no more about Nazi uranium or the mid-1940's fear of the bomb, than *Psycho* is about Janet Leigh's theft of $40,000 or the justice of her fate, than *Memento* is about a man searching for his wife's killer or the woes of anterograde memory dysfunction, than Ajanta is about Buddhism or a sectarian polemic that severs Mahāyāna from Hīnayāna. The three films listed here, at least, are about the vulnerable alchemy of emotion that catalyzes when people meet in heated circumstances, not what pushes them into the fire.

A film's MacGuffin moves its players, but it is those players' humanity that holds an audience's interest. Indeed, the MacGuffin only moves the players so far: Cary Grant risks his life for Ingrid Bergman even after he learns about the uranium; Janet Leigh resolves to return the $40,000 before she showers, and Anthony Perkins never knows about the cash. So, if the details of a MacGuffin are of no importance whatsoever to an audience, a film's characters gain the viewers' full sympathy when they willingly abjure (or at least turn their attention away from) the MacGuffin despite its transcendental value. Again, *Memento* is an exception. For Leonard, the pursuit of his wife's killer is all-consuming, while from the audience's perspective it is completely pointless. Leonard is told that his quarry has been dead for months, yet he never gives up the search. Hitchcock describes the "purest expression" of the MacGuffin as "nothing at all!"[109] What is more like "nothing" than the desire to kill a dead man whom one has already killed? But Leonard will not stop fashioning that nothing into something. Thus he is not Cary Grant, nor Janet Leigh, not a hero, nor even human. He makes a fetish of a MacGuffin and makes himself a monster: a caution to the professional historian.

The pursuit of mysteries from the past also involves MacGuffins. To see them as such, a historian should be sensitive to the line between actor and audience. Sometimes he will find only relative differences between the value that ancient actors place on ideas and objects and his own system of valuation. Sometimes he will have to judge: although ancient actors grant their presuppositions an ultimate status those people are wrong, even self-deluding. Sometimes it is easy for a historian to account for the gap that divides the emic perspective from the etic, insider from outsider, the ancient from the modern. Sometimes it is not.

Take Ajanta, for instance. Academic protocols require modern analysts to anchor etic interpretations of the site in a knowledge of how people at Ajanta conceptualized their lives. This concedes the gap between audience and actors, but until that gap is acknowledged it cannot be bridged. *Buddhism, Buddhist* and *religion*, of course, have no ancient Indian provenance; *Hīnayāna* and *Mahāyāna* are native to India, but not attested at Ajanta. Nevertheless, there still might be value here, since all of these words can facilitate the comprehension of other words, words that were used at the site. So, when we use *these* words to explain artifacts at Ajanta, we take on a role akin to that of a film's Director: we create MacGuffins that sate curiosity about intentionality, enabling our own readers to enter into the mystery of the place. But these terms are not the story. Though words like Buddhism, religion, etc., can be exceptionally valuable, they have no *necessary* place in Ajanta's interpretation. Their place is circumscribed, and sometimes it is reasonable just to ignore them, as when Cary Grant turns his attention away from uranium, and Janet Leigh from the cash. It is when scholars can not relinquish the terms of their analysis that they create monstrosities. Weiner's dictum, "above all Ajaṇṭā is a Buddhist site," and Fergusson's 1863 plan, have an ideological kinship with *Memento's* Leonard, who lies to himself in the present in order to create a past that will be the proper precursor to a future of his liking—all of this occurring, of course, in time out-of-time.

4

THE ANTHROPOLOGY OF
ENLIGHTENMENT

Life is change. How it differs from the rocks.
(Jefferson Airplane, "Crown of Creation")

The buffalo and the cow

To put this better, let me borrow a favored word from Henry David Thoreau: extravagance. Near the end of *Walden* Thoreau writes: "*Extra-vagance!* it depends on how you are yarded. The migrating buffalo which seeks new pastures in another latitude, is not extravagant like the cow which kicks over the pail, leaps the cowyard fence, and runs after her calf, in milking time."[1] Thoreau's -*vagance!* shares its Latin root, *vagus*, with vagrancy and vague. These words bespeak an indeterminacy that has no place in the field of academic history, and a wanderlust that receives no ready welcome there either. Thoreau's image of mad mother cow adds yet another element—danger. Fences provide security; leaping them is perilous in any field.

There is no doubt that Indian history prompts a certain kind of scholar to extravagant expression. Some would stay close to the names, dates, and events that fill their earnest ruminations. But, in truth, those fence-posts are not so high; nor are they quite so sturdy as they seem. And beyond stretches an open vista, its horizon vague. Among the fence-posts that pen the cows of history-proper apart from their wild sisters, none have a firmer footing than the standards of religious identity. Even when personal names, regnal dates, and the details of events are tentative, there seems to be clear certainty that the inhabitants of India can be distinguished, one from the other, by means of religion. If one cannot specify the year in which an event transpired, one can at least identify the religious affiliations of the actors involved. So too for Ajanta. We can place the site within a variety of contexts by means of historical records that require ginger attention, both to their subtleties and their hyperboles. But however loud scholars may shout in debate over chronology or relationships among the principal figures responsible for Ajanta's creation, they speak with one voice when they say that Ajanta is Buddhist. The site's religious provenance has long fixed the parameters of its historical possibilities.

Of course, there have been occasional extravagances. In 1843, James Fergusson described Ajanta as purely Buddhist, without Hindu admixture. Almost forty years later he repeated this claim.[2] Yet, while Fergusson was certain about the purity of Ajanta's identity, he presented Buddhism itself in rather fuzzy terms. In Śākyamuni's own day, Fergusson observed in 1843, Buddhism and Brahmanism "could not have differed much... as we find the kings and people changing backwards and forwards, from one to the other, without difficulty or excitement."[3] Forty years later, Fergusson's view had not altered: "Springing as it did from Brahmanism, of which it might be regarded as only a modification, or one of its many sects or schools, Buddhism did not at first separate from the older religion."[4] Fergusson seems caught between two truths. Or take his opinion that Ajanta's Cave Twenty Six contains "figures so comical and extravagant in design, as prove too clearly that the religion of Sakya Muni no longer existed in its original purity when the cave was undertaken."[5] This expectation that Śākyamuni's religion possessed an "original purity" does not readily coordinate with the model of Buddhist identities as melded with Brahmanic, and Buddhism as a quasi-sect of Brahmanism. Is it true that Buddhism as found at its source, Śākyamuni, possessed an original purity? Or is it true that the difference between Buddhism and Brahmanism was tenuous in the beginning, and only became a fixed fact after centuries of change? Where is that original purity from which Cave Twenty Six's comical and extravagant figures diverge?

For nearly forty years Fergusson held to the proposition that Ajanta is purely Buddhist. Yet, strangely, his works also recorded the presence of non-Buddhist elements at the site. One such anomaly was the form taken by pillar-brackets inside Cave Twenty Six: four-armed "fat figures with judges' wigs."[6] This multiplication of arms was notable, in Fergusson's view, as "the only instance I am aware of in these or any other Buddhist caves, of such a piece of Hinduism." By 1863, Fergusson discovered a second instance, though once again he called it unique in this regard. This image is located on a wall near the entrance to Cave Nineteen (Figure 4.1):

> Opposite to the Choultrie last described is an alto-relievo of a considerably more modern date than the Chaitya to which it is attached, and probably the only thing that can be ascribed to the Brahmans at Ajunta. It represents Vishnu sitting under the canopy of the seven-headed snake—a very common Brahmanical arrangement—with Sareswati by his side. On the other side stands an attendant with a chowrie in his hand.[7]

For us now, Fergusson's remarks demonstrate an unfamiliarity with common iconography rather than an overt Brahmanical presence. Cave Twenty Six's four-armed brackets may be unique at Ajanta, but are not Hindu for that reason. Similarly, *The Cave Temples of India* later re-identifies Vishnu and Sareswati as a nāga king and his anguine bride.[8] But my question here has little to do with the details of Fergusson's observations, and even less to do with lacunae in his

Figure 4.1 A nāga and nāginī at the entrance to Cave Nineteen. Photo by author.

knowledge of iconography. The puzzle, rather, is why Fergusson made extravagant claims about Ajanta's singular religious provenance—claims that "kick over the pail, [and] leap the cowyard fence" of his own determinations vis-à-vis the site's material remains.

Fergusson was not alone in his extravagance. Chapter 3 introduced Sheila Weiner's more recent demand that historians view Ajanta as a mainstream Buddhist site in a Brahmanical world. And we can also look back to 1821, the year in which William Erskine first brought Ajanta to public attention in his paper, "Observations on the Remains of the Bouddhists in India." Erskine was a product of the Scottish Enlightenment, whose approach to history, following the lead of Adam Smith and William Robertson, was decidedly "philosophical." Jane Rendall describes the Scots' historiography thus: It was "concerned to apply to the study of man and society methods of enquiry comparable to those of the natural sciences...involv[ing] the formulation of general laws on the basis of observation, and the available evidence about the history, economy, culture, and political institutions of different societies."[9] Of course, while close attention to social forms is now expected of all historical inquiry, this philosophy's evolutionary model, in which civilizations progress through stages according to regular laws, is no longer an operational norm.

The question of progress was of concern to Erskine in 1821, however, when he addressed a regular meeting of the Literary Society of Bombay. Erskine sought to identify the grounds of Indian civilization. Given this agenda, Erskine's presuppositions, the things he accepted as matters of common sense, are all the more striking. "It is well known," Erskine asserted near the beginning of his paper, "that all of the countries included under the general name of India have, from very remote times, been divided between three great religions, the Brahminical, the Bouddhist, and the Jain."[10] Given such divisions along religious lines, he proposed that "it would obviously much facilitate and extend the means of accurate information, if some simple tests were generally known, by which certain classes of antiquities could instantly be referred to the religion to which they belong."[11] Erskine's grand aim was thus "to fix, if possible, some obvious criteria by which even a transient observer may discriminate the Bouddhist from the Brahminical temples."[12]

Note Erskine's language. He required accuracy but he also desired transparency. Erskine expected that criteria for distinguishing monuments, Buddhist from Hindu from Jain, could be "simple," "obvious," "instantaneous," and suitable even for "transient observers." In a word, Erskine wanted to give casual tourists the spontaneous ability to recognize the religious affiliation of the places they visited. Such spontaneity would be impossible without there also being fixed, even objective, bases for religious identity. For a transient observer to immediately but accurately distinguish Hindu from Buddhist remains, the distinction between these two religions would have to be substantial, not contingent on perspective or phronetic strategy. Erskine's scientific archaeology required both Buddhism and Hinduism to be the kinds of things that could be discovered, described, and duly categorized. Their substantive differences would be marked by morphological indices which, while visible on an artifact's surface, would also reflect divergent genealogies. And it is for this reason that Erskine concluded that archaeological forms, properly comprehended, would enable scholars "to infer the existence of the Bouddhist religion in situations where we do not learn from history that it ever prevailed."[13]

This is the discursive fence in which scholars of Ajanta have been "yarded," to recall another of Henry David Thoreau's words. Buddhism and Brahmanism (or Hinduism) demarcate what seem to be natural limits to our knowledge of India's past. Even if we acknowledge that the sources allow only imperfect reconstructions of that history, it is Buddhism and Hinduism that we seem to be reconstructing, however imperfectly. To pursue Thoreau's metaphor to its end, extravagance requires us to attempt an escape from the yard of fixed religious identity, at least to test how sturdy its fence really is. Richard Davis has suggested that "the challenging, borrowing, contradicting, polemicizing, appropriating, and modifying that goes on across religious boundaries, and even the constructing and subverting of those boundaries, are ongoing dynamic processes that give both form and content to the religious history of India."[14] This is a crucial insight so far as it goes. But to give Thoreau the next-to-last word—"I fear chiefly lest my expression may not be *extra-vagant* enough, may not wander far enough beyond the narrow limits of my daily experience"[15]—the specified boundary of a "religious history of India" may need to be leaped over as well.

The primacy of matter

One dilemma faced by educators in many fields, especially at the introductory level, is choosing a textbook. A teacher will want a certain perspective on the field and breadth of coverage, but he will also want an interpretation with which he can agree. Compromise is inevitable. Certainly this is the case with Richard Gombrich's *Theravāda Buddhism*, a textbook I excerpt when teaching introduction to Buddhism. *Theravāda Buddhism* emphasizes social history, much to my delight. But I still find myself struggling with the details. The work defines Buddhists as those people who take refuge in the Three Jewels—the buddha, the dharma, and the sangha—and then defines the Jewels as three facets of enlightenment. The buddha is the man who "attained [e]nlightenment by realizing the Truth." The dharma is the truth realized, the substance of enlightenment. The sangha, third, "not only consists of those who have decided to devote their lives to striving for [e]nlightenment; it also preserves the memory of the Buddha's Teaching," that is, his expressions of enlightenment.[16] Enlightenment thus serves as a nodal point at which Gombrich's scholarly analyses of Buddhism intersect with native bauddha discourses. Things are "Buddhist" insofar as we can follow a chain of significance back to enlightenment itself (for the bauddha), or a discourse thereon (for the scholar). One Ajanta inscription declares, "He is called 'buddha' because he attained enlightenment spontaneously."[17] In the face of such a material association with enlightenment, it seems inconceivable not to call Ajanta a Buddhist place.

But I chose the phrase, nodal point, with care. It is taken from *The Interpretation of Dreams*, where Freud uses it to characterize an element in a dream in which "a great number of dream-thoughts converge."[18] Freud's premise is that every event or element in a dream bears meaning, but invariably meanings are distorted. To interpret a dream one must first identify the elements that are repeated in diverse ways throughout the dreamscape. These are *overdetermined* nodal points around which the dream's meanings coalesce. That is to say, these dream-elements have multiple (potentially) contradictory, simultaneous, determinants;

they cannot be resolved into a single identity or meaning or truth. Because of overdetermination, even though dreams *can* be interpreted, they "regularly have more than one meaning."[19] By characterizing enlightenment as a nodal point, I am allowing that every doctrine, practice, social form, etc. that scholars call "Buddhist," however diverse or mutually contradictory, can be associated with a comprehensive structure by reference to enlightenment. This word/concept functions to fix the range of values that scholars will impute to Buddhism. But due to overdetermination, there is no way to reduce out the labor required for the determination of meaning. Enlightenment does not possess a natural or objective value that makes it the necessary and universal nexus of historical reality. Rather, the very act of unification—the stipulation "Buddhist"—gives enlightenment its meaningfulness after the fact. Out of this paradox, Freud's poststructuralist interpreters, Ernesto Laclau and Chantal Mouffe, have formulated a general "logic of overdetermination" that enables "the critique of every type of fixity, through an affirmation of the incomplete, open and politically negotiable character of every identity."[20] The spontaneous or commonsensical determination, in which Ajanta is Buddhist because one can follow a chain of associations from its artifacts to enlightenment, has a history with distinct political causes and effects.

It should be clear that when I characterize enlightenment as overdetermined, I am not speaking of enlightenment as a matter of "religious experience." Whether anybody has ever been fully and perfectly enlightened as described in bauddha doctrinal treatises is fully beside the point; likewise, the question of whether such enlightenment is even possible. But scepticism is no more proper here than credulousness. The only matter that matters is the material form in which enlightenment forms an intersubjective object. How is enlightenment a solidly material thing—either as a matter of fact or matter of discourse? The question of materiality is primary. Without it, we have nothing to say about enlightenment at all.

What is more material than stone, or more solidly intersubjective than a large mural sculpted out of stone? The next section thus begins to investigate the materiality of enlightenment by introducing a sculpture of events related to Śākyamuni's enlightenment. Anybody fluent in the buddha's life-story can simply, obviously, and instantaneously identify the sculpture's subject matter, just as Erskine had hoped would be possible for Indian artifacts in general. However, that success itself raises new concerns. For it is not equally obvious why we halt our investigation with this clear and reasonable interpretation. Other interpretations are possible. Why not pursue them? The answer comes in the chapter's second half, where I introduce an anthropological model—the *scriptural human*. Within this anthropology, human beings are like scriptures, for the significance of their actions and ideas can be determined by reference to an unknown, even unknowable, but nevertheless real, transcendental absolute. In fashioning the Buddhist human as a scriptural human—thereby circumventing the multiplicity entailed in overdetermination—scholars of Buddhism have had to disregard the primary materiality of enlightenment. They have dared to treat enlightenment as a spiritual truth.

The conquest of Māra

Where better to begin the search for enlightenment at Ajanta than on a wall sculpted with the tale of the buddha's enlightenment?

The battle took place in Bodh Gayā, India, when Śākyamuni was 35 years old. But its antecedents encompass a history reaching back uncountable aeons. To keep the story short, the bodhisattva first learned about human frailties only six years before the battle. On a day seemingly like any other, he set out for an afternoon's diversion in a country garden. Though there was no hint of wind or rain, Śākyamuni did not reach the garden. For on the road the prince saw something new: a man broken with age. At 29, Śākyamuni had been raised in such delicate circumstances that he had no prior experience of old age; nobody had ever told him that people wither with senescence. He returned home to ponder the dull eyes and sagging muscles of that man, with terrible foreboding. The following day, a second trip to the garden was interrupted when the bodhisattva saw a bloated man and learned of sickness. Then a third journey on a third day failed due to his first sight of a stiffened corpse. Śākyamuni's father, who had sought only the best for his son, now feared the worst. For on the fourth day the prince met a renunciant, who, though head shaven and dressed in ragged robes, was serene and self-possessed. Soon the prince left his kingdom, his position, his wife and father, to seek that same tranquility for himself: to be free from every fear of old age, disease, and death.

Six years passed without bearing their desired fruit. Śākyamuni learned to concentrate his mind and climb through psychic trances like rungs on a ladder. He starved himself, and patiently endured the cruel play of local villagers, who poked his ears with twigs. Still, he did not know himself to be free from the relentless repetitions of old age, disease, and death. So he resolved to change his approach. Rather than concentrate on the exhaustion of his self through rigid bodily and mental discipline, he would attempt to examine that self and that body to intuit their mystery. He matched his resolve with action, shifting over to a new seat, the *vajrāsana*, the diamond seat at the base of the Bodhi tree, where he declared: "I will not unfold my legs until I have stopped up the torrent of defilements."[21] Māra, the Evil One, could not ignore this challenge. As sovereign lord over the Realm of Desire, Māra held his subjects fast through their own mental and moral filth. By not yielding his seat beneath the tree, the bodhisattva threatened Māra's own in heaven.

Six years of striving climaxed in a final night, at the end of which bodhisattva became buddha. That evening's combat, pitting prince against god, became a popular subject for bauddha literary and visual arts. Some of the finest examples of the latter are found at Ajanta. In Caves One and Six, once-lively paintings of the battle cover a large wall near the monolithic icon of a buddha. Both paintings have been damaged by rain, insects, and souvenir hunters. But what remains illustrates Māra's army, 360 million strong, with the delight of macabre whimsy. His cavalry is staffed by wild hybrids, dwarves transmogrified into boars, inauspicious owls, and all manner of demons with red bulging eyes; his infantry held a phalanx of snake-breathing discus-throwing blemyes. Though stone places restrictions on the artist's imagination, it is also permanent. As one donor at Ajanta observed: "[Because] a man will enjoy [himself] in heaven for as long as his memory remains on earth, one should create a memorial that lasts as long as the sun and moon in the mountains."[22] Indeed, a 11' tall by 10' wide mural cut into Ajanta's mountain, depicting Śākyamuni triumphant over Māra, can lead us through the story, though its individual figures are poor compared with those in the paintings (Figures 4.2 and 4.3).

Figure 4.2 Cave Twenty Six's Māravijaya mural (note, the bottom left corner is cut). Photo by author.

Figure 4.3 A line illustration of the Māravijaya. From John Griffiths, *The Paintings in the Buddhist Cave-Temples of Ajanta* (London, 1896), 1:24.

Cave Twenty Six's bas-relief can be read starting at the bottom left, where Māra, crowned and shielded by the umbrella of royalty, enters the scene to displace the bodhisattva from the *vajrāsana*.[23] At first the Evil One tried sly subterfuge, weaving a tale that involved Śākyamuni's ne'er-do-well cousin Devadatta, a palace coup, and harm to the prince's family. Māra urged him to leave this place and dutifully rescue his kin from Devadatta. Though this story did shake the bodhisattva with unsettled angers and desires, he quickly saw through the trick and calmed himself.

As a god, Māra next challenged the bodhisattva's right to the *vajrāsana* through a contest of karmic authority:

"Why are you sitting here?"
"To attain supreme knowledge."
"Prince, where will your supreme knowledge come from?"
"You became sovereign over the Desire Realm, Evil One, by performing just one sacrificial rite. Over the course of three countless aeons, I made innumerable trillions and trillions of sacrifices, giving away my head and hands and feet and eyes and flesh and blood, my sons and daughters, my gold and silver, all with the express purpose of attaining supreme knowledge. Really now, how could somebody like myself suppose that he will *not* attain supreme knowledge?"

But Māra was not deterred: "You yourself admit that I hold dominion over the Desire Realm, proving the efficacy of my action. Where's the proof of your grand claims?" Looking now at the image, we see the bodhisattva's right hand point toward the ground, an iconographic gesture called "touching the earth," for the earth goddess herself had been an eyewitness to all the bodhisattva's acts of personal sacrifice. At Ajanta, the goddess climbs out of the earth to the right of center; one knee is bent, the other straight; her left hand holds a billowing scarf, while her right hand at her mouth calls all to hear the truth: "Evil one, it is just as the Blessed One says!"[24]

Despondent at Śākyamuni's solid victories, Māra pondered how else he might harm the bodhisattva. But Māra was not alone in his quest. At the bottom right of the mural, Māra's three young and enticing daughters—Desire, Pleasure, and Lust—offer their support. They would gladly dance and sing their way into the handsome prince's heart. But the cymbals did not move him, nor the drums, nor the calls to erotic play. The bodhisattva's silent composure can be read in this mural by the shift of visual focus from its lower register to its upper. In Ajanta's stone, Māra's daughters remember the still promise of ecstasies forestalled forever. For them it was a cruel fact that, in Sanskrit, *smāra* means both memory and love.

Māra was not able to best the bodhisattva by appeal to his affection for his family, his libidinal urges, let alone the magnitude of his sacrificial deeds. The only avenue of attack left was violent force. Hence, the upper left shows an army of ugly demons as frighteningly angry as Māra's daughters were appealing. Again, the bodhisattva countered the assault. Ironically, it was emotion that saved him. By filling his mind with benevolence, the bodhisattva transformed every missile and arrow into a flower, which then fell softly to the ground. Marveling at their failure, Māra's soldiers are shown in active retreat. Clasped hands display obeisance as they pass off the wall in the upper right.

Finally, in the top center, the gods beat the kettledrum of victory. Tonight a buddha will be born!

Māra attacked Śākyamuni in the evening. The lifetimes of hard practice that had prepared the bodhisattva to withstand that onslaught found their fruition over the course of a single night. This was not a swift moment of blinding intuition, but a nine-hour marathon of mental gymnastics. Once Māra was dispatched, the bodhisattva entered into a series of progressively deeper meditations until he reached what Śākya scholastics call the Fourth Trance. In this cognitive state, he could still perceive and contemplate materiality, while remaining wholly untouched by matter. The first thing the bodhisattva did then was to develop several superpowers, the psychic effluvia of this trance. Now he could fly, walk on water, or swim through the earth, and even hear human and inhuman cries no matter how far away. These powers would come in handy.

Next the bodhisattva decided to investigate why Māra's troupes had become so malign. With his new psychic abilities, the bodhisattva read their minds, which he found to be perverse and poisoned and prejudiced. These investigations gave him a detailed knowledge of the many different states of mind. Śākyamuni could tell the impassioned from the disciplined, the confused from the clear, and so on. He began to wonder who among the horde had been his kin in former lives and who his enemy. For the answer, the bodhisattva surveyed his own thread of past existences. He saw the countless times he had been born and died, learning the details of every single life. Then Śākyamuni's divine eye shifted from himself to other beings. He ascertained that all beings are like himself. All die and are reborn into high castes or low castes, wealth or poverty, heaven or hell, based upon whether they do good or bad deeds, support or contemn holy men, hold correct views or believe in lies.

About six hours had passed when the bodhisattva finally discerned a pattern within all this frenzied busyness: living beings are caught in the eddy of saṃsāra by currents of desire, birth, and ignorance. Three hours till dawn, but now Śākyamuni could dry out these floods of evil inclinations, saṃsāra's subterranean source. Thus he focused his attention on the four truths that transform one into spiritual nobility. He realized in precise terms, "This is the noble truth of suffering. This is the noble truth of suffering's origin. This is the noble truth of suffering's end. This is the noble truth of the path that leads to the end of suffering." Once the bodhisattva had perceived these four truths directly and fully, his mind was released from the flood of desires, rebirth, and ignorance. Free, he became aware of his freedom.

> My birth is finished!
> My effort is consummated!
> What had to be done is done!
> I will never be born again!

Now a buddha, he had realized perfect enlightenment, and lit up like a ball of living flame just as the sun began its daily ascent.

Reading and rationality

Ajanta's stone relief—100 square-feet of Śākyamuni triumphing over Māra—would have remained suggestively inchoate without the appropriate texts to identify its forms. In the early nineteenth century, when Europeans first visited the Ajanta caves, they had no literary precedents through which to determine what they saw. Thus they saw very little beyond hunting scenes, domestic scenes, seraglio scenes, Welsh wigs, Hampton court beauties, elephants and horses, an Abyssinian black prince, shields and spears, and statues that they called "buddha" because of the curly hair.[25]

Early visitors to Ajanta described what they knew, saw what they thought they knew, and ignored the rest. In this, those intrepid travelers were hardly alone. Indeed in the eighteenth century, as colonists increasingly found it necessary to understand India, early Orientalists asserted their intellectual mastery of the subcontinent squarely upon their ability to read its texts. Before the study of India's languages had begun in earnest, tradesmen, adventurers, and missionaries relied upon native informants for lay ethnographic data. In the 1767 opinion of John Zephaniah Holwell (best known for his contemporaneous report on the Black Hole of Calcutta), however, this lay reportage was not especially valuable. At best a native informant could tell the British that "such and such a people . . . worship this stock, or that stone, or monstrous idol."[26] Think back to Lieutenant Blake from the prior chapter, who ridiculed his Bhīl informants' belief that Ajanta had been created by the gods in a single night, and that the caves were inhabited by gods whose names Blake had never heard before or since. Blake *knew* Ajanta as Buddhist: this is Holwell's legacy. For Holwell's generation of Orientalists introduced the principle that a hard-won reading knowledge of native languages was the only path by which Europeans would reach the rational pith of India's people:

> A mere description of the exterior manners and religion of a people, will no more give us a true idea of them; than a geographical description of a country can convey a just conception of their laws and government. The traveller must sink deeper in his researches, would he feast the mind of an understanding reader. . . . [W]as he skilled in the language of the people he describes, sufficiently to trace the etymology of their words and phrases, and capable of diving into the mysteries of their theology; he would probably be able to evince us, that such seemingly preposterous worship, had the most sublime rational source and foundation.[27]

As for the living, so too for the rocks. The earliest British to visit Ajanta suspected that the caves were Buddhist. The first European report on the caves, William Erskine's 1821 address to the Literary Society of Bombay, made this judgment largely because the site contains "sitting figures with curled wigs."[28] (This same detail inspired Lieutenant Alexander to hypothesize that Buddhists were originally "crisp-haired aborigines . . . who were driven from India to Ceylon after the introduction of Brahmanism." That hypothesis, in turn, led him to "conceive the age of the caves of Adjunta to be nearer three than two thousand years."[29]) Erskine's 1821 address is balanced by an interesting account concerning Dr James Bird's visit to Ajanta in 1828:

> A Dr. Bird from *Sattarah* . . . comes with a design to draw up some account of the caves, dismounts from his horse at 8 a.m. Mutual greetings. In three minutes my new acquaintance praises Mr. Erskine of Bombay; quotes him and *swears by him*, and tells me these are Jain cave temples.[30]

And twenty years later, James Bird's own monograph called Ajanta *bauddha* overall, but identified several of the site's monolithic sculptures as *jaina*, either because of emblems on their thrones or because he saw them as naked.[31] Perhaps two visitors in 1828, Mr Ralph and Captain Gresley, put it best as they bantered back and forth, ignorant yet enthralled. Gresley warned Ralph, "The fewer theories you form, the fewer blunders you will make," to which Ralph responded with Thoreauvian extravagance, "We *must* form theories—we cannot remain awake and not do so."[32]

Whether one agrees with Ralph or with Gresley, one thing is certain: scenes like that of the bodhisattva and Māra were left in stony silence during the first half-century of reportage on Ajanta. Such figures were just too exotic. Though an eye educated in Greek steles and the art of medieval Christian miracles might have decoded this mural's method for spatializing time—repeating Māra in each quadrant—the zigzag from bottom left to top right would not have been obvious, and the nature of the battle or its ultimate outcome even less so.

Writing in the mid-eighteenth century, J.Z. Holwell called Indians' worship "preposterous," yet he also expected that their religion sprang from a rational source. I trust that Holwell would approve of the above interpretation of Ajanta's narrative relief, based as it is upon an appropriate text, the *Mūlasarvāstivāda vinaya* (MSV). By genre, the MSV is a compendium of disciplinary rules for Śākya renunciants; it also contains a trove of narratives, folklore, descriptions of practice, and doctrines. The absolute date of this text is uncertain, though we can be confident that some form of it was current at Ajanta, and that the site's painters and sculptors often used it as a direct inspiration for their compositions. Nevertheless, Dieter Schlingloff, who has completed the greatest amount of work toward identifying specific literary antecedents for Ajanta's narrative art, also observes that these murals cannot be reduced to mere illustrations of literary precedents: "Although the artists were bound fairly closely by the literary tradition of a particular school, which can usually be identified, they nevertheless retained a certain degree of freedom to pursue their own iconographic tradition, or to use their own imagination."[33] This mural both subtracts from the text (the MSV's description of Māra's army includes many more types of figures than are actually shown; in the MSV, when Māra's daughters ply their womanly charms the bodhisattva turns them into wizened crones), and adds to the text (in the bottom right, Māra is shown drawing on the ground with a stick, a detail without precedent in the MSV).

Holwell had predicted that knowledge of native languages would give colonists a new, more sympathetic understanding of native practices. This certainly comes true in application of the MSV to Ajanta's wall. Not only does the text permit the identification of the mural's many figures, it even enables the discernment of a coherent logic in its plan. This latter intuition is in keeping with the British Orientalists' expectation that the knowledge of native languages would be a prelude to comprehending the lost heart of native theologies and rituals, in which reposes a universal rationality and wisdom.

Determinism, from Laplace's demon to Luther's god

Interpreted through the MSV, Cave Twenty Six shows us more than a coherent narrative. It reveals Ajanta's fifth-century Śākyas to have been Enlightened and modern after their own fashion. Recall, Chapter 2 touched upon the link between modernity and Enlightenment. If *Enlightenment* is a mode of living critically engaged with one's own present world, then *modernity* is an attitude or ethos that emerges out of a universe of possibilities and impossibilities, freedoms accepted and rejected. According to Kant's "What is Enlightenment?" an Age of Enlightenment will be one in which reasonable explanations, developed through the analysis of regular patterns in nature, supercede intellectually puerile explanations that invoke god's plan or god's inscrutable purpose. In this Kantian light, Śākyamuni's enlightenment provides an allegory of modernity's heroic progress. A celebration of rational perfectability, Ajanta's wall tells a timeless tale.

The MSV permits us to determine figures, to determine meanings, even to determine rationality. It satisfies (in part) Erskine's desire for simple and obvious criteria through which to determine an answer to the question, Are these artifacts Buddhist? Moreover, it allows me to determine the first element of the anthropology of e/Enlightenment: e/Enlightenment is possible insofar human beings are rational beings. This is not a blinding insight, true, but it does provide a ground for further analysis. As foreshadowed on page 113, my full exposition of the anthropology of e/Enlightenment will focus upon the so-called scriptural human. "Scripture," here, bespeaks a curious union of rationality and religiosity, whereby every human being carries within himself everything necessary for knowing that which is worth knowing about every other human being. To get from here to there, we might ask why Erskine expected that criteria for determining an artifact's identity would provide a sufficient basis for fixing that artifact's identity. What would he have understood to be the intellectual force of the act of *determination*? This question leads to "the scriptural" in two steps, as we trace the naturalistic determinism of Enlightenment science back to the religious determinism of faith in the Word, articulated in the Protestant Reformation.

As always, Kant is a prime spokesman for the Enlightenment ethos. He concludes the *Critique of Practical Reason* with the following meditation:

> Two things fill the mind with ever new and increasing admiration and reverence, the more often and more steadily one reflects on them: *the starry heavens above me and the moral law within me* ....The first begins from the place I occupy in the external world of sense and extends the connection in which I stand into an unbounded magnitude....The second begins from my invisible self, my personality, and presents me in a world which has true infinity but which can only be discovered by the understanding.[34]

Dwarfed beneath the heavens, so vast and regular, Kant found within himself a moral universe of equal rationality and grandeur. The brilliance of Boyle and Newton encouraged Kant to fancy that human choices and actions might also be brought into conformity with regular, irrevocable, and (in the ideal) fully articulable laws. In the examples of chemistry, physics, and mathematics, he found reason to recommend "that we take the same path in treating of the moral predispositions of our nature and can give us hope of a similarly good outcome."[35] When it comes to knowing both the inner and outer worlds, Kant held "science (critically sought and methodically directed) [to be] the narrow gate that leads to the *doctrine of wisdom*."[36]

Of course, the expectation that scientific method could be brought to bear on humanity hardly originated with Kant. No better example is available, perhaps, than the way in which the name of Isaac Newton became an epithet for scientific genius in the human sciences. Christopher Berry's study of the Scottish Enlightenment tells of Newton's transfiguration into a trope. Isaac Newton was "*the* hero of the Enlightenment," and thus Adam Smith was called the Newton of political economy; Jean-Jacques Rousseau became the Newton of the moral world; and David Hume, the Newton of the human sciences.[37] The historian who first mentioned Ajanta in 1821, William Erskine, himself a child of the Scottish Enlightenment, sought "simple," "obvious," and "instantaneous" criteria for determining whether a monument is Buddhist, Hindu, or Jain. Erskine did not express an ambition to be the Newton of Indian archaeology, though he certainly would have understood the title, and welcomed it. To earn this honor, a man had to translate Newton's scientific determinism into his own respective sphere of human inquiry.

In the Enlightenment ideal, deterministic explanations à la Newton would be brought to bear on all dimensions of human social and psychic life. Despite the will toward a positive science of humanity, however, the most coherent expressions of determinism continued to come from the natural sciences. In the *Principia Mathematica*, Newton described his "wish" to derive all natural phenomena "by reasoning from mechanical principles." Yet, it was not Newton, but the

Marquis de Laplace, who gave us a vision of determinism in its most perfect form:

> We ought then to regard the present state of the universe as the effect of
> its anterior state and as the cause of the one which is to follow. Given for
> one instant an intelligence which could comprehend all the forces by
> which nature is animated and the respective situation of the beings who
> compose it—an intelligence sufficiently vast to submit these data to
> analysis—it would embrace in the same formula the movements of the
> greatest bodies of the universe and those of the lightest atom; for it,
> nothing would be uncertain and the future, as the past, would be present
> to its eyes.[38]

Later physicists christened this intelligent being, "Laplace's demon." Possessing
full knowledge of the universe at one moment, and knowing all the rules govern-
ing celestial mechanics, Laplace's demon is able to calculate the past as well as
the future with absolute precision. Probabilities and indeterminacies have no
place in this demon's universe, for his supernal intelligence resolves multiple
visions into a single omniscient gaze. In order to update this deterministic vision
for a modern audience, Karl Popper likens the Laplacian cosmos to a motion-
picture reel. Like a film, "the future co-exists with the past; and the future is
fixed, in exactly the same sense as the past."[39]

We are heirs to this Enlightenment determinism. This legacy is shown by our
"faith" in the value of linguistic knowledge, inherited from colonial Orientalists.
But even more crucially it is seen in our status as beneficiaries of determinism's
metaphysical assumptions. This metaphysics conditions how we receive Ajanta's
mural. We see Māra reduplicated into every corner and thus measure a linear temporality. Māra defines the limns of this visual world through his distributed presence: we follow Māra to follow the story's progress. Once we know the narrative,
it seems self-evident that the mural should be read as a narrative. The MSV gives
us simple and obvious criteria that a literate observer, even if transient, can apply
instantaneously. In this way, we make ourselves over into Laplace's demon, at the
pinnacle of a hierarchy of rationalities. We scan back and forth, from the inchoate
mural, to the Sanskrit book, now again to the mural. We expect that if our intellects
were vast enough, and possessed the full surfeit of data, then nothing here would
be uncertain. We gauge the difference between the variety of data about the buddha's life and the MSV's representation of that life. We gauge the difference
between the MSV and other literary accounts. We gauge the difference between the
MSV and Ajanta's sculptural relief. We comprehend all of this with an Enlightened
mind that presupposes (as did John Zephaniah Holwell) that all worship has a
rational source, even if it appears preposterous at first glance. We thereby take on
the mantle of conservators of religious normativity and judges of religious action.
We expect that by resolving indeterminacy we might comprehend Ajanta's Śākyas
within a single omniscient gaze, just as we comprehend this mural.

In this practice, we are the faithful heirs of Roger Bacon, Isaac Newton, and other founders of Western science, whose ambitions Roger Hausheer describes in the clearest terms:

> They sought all-embracing schemas, universal unifying frameworks, within which everything that exists could be shown to be systematically— i.e., logically or causally—interconnected, vast structures in which there should be no gaps left open for spontaneous, unattended developments, where everything that occurs should be, at least in principle, wholly explicable in terms of immutable general laws.[40]

If this describes Laplace too, it also speaks to the humanists who investigated people and social formations in anticipation of equally robust results, scholars of Buddhism included.

There is still another connection to be made between the scientists of physical nature and of human nature. As the story goes, Napoleon Bonaparte once asked Laplace why he did not mention god in his work on celestial mechanics. At the time, the Marquis' answer, "Sire, I have no need of that hypothesis," might have seemed the height of wit. Now, it bespeaks the Marquis' naivete. For it has become an historical *idée reçu* that the epistemological context within which modern science arose was highly inflected by the sixteenth and seventeenth centuries' diverse theologies. Belief in the existence of all-embracing schemas and universal frameworks, complemented by faith in the human mind's ability to comprehend that totality, has a "religious origin," connected by Karl Popper "with ideas of divine omnipotence...and of divine omniscience."[41] I prefer the word "theological" in lieu of Popper's "religious" here. Still, why would not the same be true for the human sciences, which so modeled themselves on the physical? If the anthropology of e/Enlightenment is a scriptural anthropology, it is because the Enlightenment's anthropological universalism has a theological genus.

Popper names Martin Luther and Jean Calvin in particular as the godfathers of scientific determinism. Indeed, to meet the eternal forebearer of Laplace's demon one can open Luther's *The Bondage of the Will* (hailed by its translators as "the greatest piece of theological writing that ever came from Luther's pen") virtually at random.[42] Neither Laplace's demon, nor the Protestant god leaves anything to chance:

> Natural reason herself is forced to confess that the living and true God must be One who by His own liberty imposes necessity on us. He would be a ludicrous Deity...if His foreknowledge of the future were unreliable and could be falsified by events.... He would be equally ludicrous if He could not and did not do all things, or if anything were done without Him.... Seeing that He foreknew that we should be what we are, and now makes us such, and moves and governs us as such, how, pray, can it be pretended that it is open to us to become something other than that which

He foreknew and is now bringing about?...Either God makes mistakes in His foreknowledge, and errors in his action (which is impossible), or else we act, and are caused to act, according to His foreknowledge and action....This omnipotence and foreknowledge of God, I repeat, utterly destroy the doctrine of "free will."[43]

For Luther, divine attention, knowledge, will, and action are coequal. Indeed, because the universe expresses god's will in everything, even damnation is just: "The highest degree of faith is to believe that He is merciful, though He saves so few and damns so many; to believe that He is just, though of His own will He makes us perforce proper subjects for damnation."[44] Just as later scientists expected to discover nature's laws through reasoned induction based upon empirical observation, so Luther deduced that "on reason's own testimony, there can be no 'free will' in man, or angel, or in any creature."[45]

Determining Buddhism

Luther's god was an ancestor of Laplace's demon, yet one cannot overestimate the importance of the shift from religious determinism to scientific determinism. Laplace described his demon as omniscient but not omnipotent, since for him nature is moved by laws that express no will beyond their own lawfulness. (The disenchantment of nature will make possible a theory of fetishism as fallacious re-enchantment.) This caveat noted, however, one also cannot ignore Peter Gay's amusing reminder: "All the men of the Enlightenment were cuckoos in the Christian nest."[46] Laplace did not honor his theory's relation to god. We should not be equally unfilial. If the previous section introduced the Protestant genus of scientific determinism, this one turns to that god's role in determining the identities of sculpted figures at Ajanta. Is there some way in which, by reading the Cave Twenty Six mural through the MSV, we are apprehending it with "Protestant" eyes?

Granted, it seems mere common sense for historians to use the MSV as the interpretive key for Cave Twenty Six's mural. The appeal to a textual precedent is normal behavior, sequenced right into a historian's DNA. But I am not the first to interrogate this practice. Gregory Schopen does just that in a celebrated article from 1991, "Archaeology and Protestant Presuppositions in the Study of Indian Buddhism." Schopen is an ingenious scholar of Buddhism; his fresh ideas express a historiographical vision sensitive to the limitations and problems of the available sources. This 1991 article is a case in point. In it, Schopen calls attention to an odd theological gene twisted into the helix of Buddhist Studies' genome. Determinism in the academic study of Buddhism is a bastard child of religious determinism, for according to Schopen a specifically Protestant attitude toward scripture has served as the primary determinant of Buddhist Studies' evidentiary focus and intellectual agenda.

"Archaeology and Protestant Presuppositions" begins with an expression of surprise at Buddhist Studies' "decidedly peculiar" history. In the eighteenth and nineteenth centuries two bodies of data became available to European scholars, the archaeological and the literary. Why, Schopen wonders, was "overriding primacy [given] to textual sources"?[47] Why did historians choose to reconstruct Indian Buddhism through texts that "may not even have been known to the vast majority of practicing Buddhists," rather than relying on material artifacts "that record and reflect at least a part of what Buddhists...actually believed and practiced"?[48] Schopen's answer, briefly stated, is that those early scholars were guided less by Enlightenment epistemology than by Protestant soteriology: "The methodological position frequently taken by modern Buddhist scholars, archaeologists, and historians of religion looks...uncannily like the position taken by a variety of early Protestant reformers," such as Luther, for whom "true religion" was located solely in the scriptural Word.[49] In Schopen's view, Buddhist studies' genetic Protestantism predisposes it to ascribe primary authority to literary sources. "Textuality overrides actuality. And actuality—as expressed by epigraphical and archaeological material—is denied independent validity as a witness."[50]

If you doubt Schopen's insight, just recall John Zephaniah Holwell's 1767 directive to fellow colonists: Do not attend to India's exterior manners and religion but to the etymologies of its words and the mysteries of its literate theology. Or read Erskine in 1823, for whom archaeological remains are not sources of "authentic history" because "the external symbols of these religions depend, as might be expected, on the doctrines and mythology which they teach" in their literature.[51] Instead, sacred books and "chief religious works" are the essential media through which to determine "the peculiar tenets and practices of the Bouddhists that are likely to affect their religious edifices."[52] Erskine allows scholars to use archaeology to indicate the otherwise lost presence of Buddhists on the Indian religious landscape, but only books will tell us what those Buddhists were *really* about.

Which sources are contingent, and which necessary, for the proper study of Buddhist history? By shifting the contingency/necessity line between texts and artifacts, Schopen makes it impossible to accept unconditionally the earlier interpretation of Cave Twenty Six's wall. Granted, the artifact does correspond to the text. But is this correspondence a sufficient basis for closing off further inquiry into the mural's primary significance? Or is the identification of the mural as Śākyamuni's triumph over Māra itself contingent upon our treating Ajanta's Śākyas as if they were like Protestants, for whom texts determine total meaning? We acknowledge that Cave Twenty Six's sculptors were innovative in their use of literary precedent. Should we not be still more willing to imagine that the cave's diverse visitors saw this wall with diverse eyes—and that such diversity also matters? The heart of Schopen's critique is his concern that the singular privileging of literary sources "effectively excludes what practicing Buddhists did and believed from the history of their own religion."[53] When texts alone determine what we see, "our picture of Indian Buddhism may reflect more of our own religious history and values than the history and values of Indian Buddhism."[54]

Schopen's cautions are serious. However, the trajectory of this chapter—skittering from Fergusson to Erksine to Holwell to Kant to Laplace to Luther—forces the question: Are Schopen's cautions serious enough? Most scholarship, in his view, "does not even consider the possibility that the texts we are to study to arrive at a knowledge of 'Buddhism' may not even have been known to the vast majority of practicing Buddhists."[55] But why does Schopen ironize only *Buddhism* here? If Ajanta's Śākyas would not recognize the scholars' Buddhism, why assume they would recognize themselves as the scholars' *Buddhists*? Must there have been Buddhists or Buddhism in ancient India, institutional identities that are structurally parallel with Protestant and Christianity? If we eschew the primacy of texts for the writing of history, should we not also be willing to relinquish a model of social order abstracted from those texts, when that model also expresses "Protestant presuppositions"? And how about our conception of human beings and human nature? John Zephaniah Holwell proffered linguistics as grounding a hermeneutical recovery of India's original rationality, with language as the avenue to theology. What are the stakes in his correlation of the rational with the religious?

These questions lead in two directions. The first is somewhat fanciful. Schopen does not renounce the use of all literary sources. Texts "that could be shown to have been actually known or read at a given place at a given time, or to have shaped the kind of religious behavior that had left traces on the ground" are suitably archaeological.[56] The MSV meets these criteria when applied to Ajanta. But does that mean the MSV necessarily *must* be used? What might we apprehend in Cave Twenty Six if we interpret its sculpture without direct reference to a Śākya literary precedent? The next section will take this question seriously: a thought experiment to open our eyes, if you will, to the limits of Schopen's reworked necessity/contingency line. For beyond privileging literary texts over artifacts, the field's anthropology has Protestant presuppositions as well.

When the Enlightenment disentangled omniscience from omnipotence, it became increasingly easy to see that the praxes of knowledge themselves are sites of power; our knowledge, our naming, creates the objects that we study. Thus after the thought experiment is concluded, we will return to a discussion of theological traces in Buddhist Studies' practice. This second iteration will not ask how Protestant presuppositions determine the sources we use to reconstruct the past, but rather how they determine our conception of the people who created, used, and still use our "sources." It seems inconceivable to study the religion of past humans without due consideration of the history within which *humanity* and *religiosity* were constituted as objects of scientific knowledge (even if only in the human sciences). Enough preaching, now for some fun.

Other readings. Other rationalities?
A counterfactual interlude

Historical and disciplinary assumptions predispose scholars of Buddhism to expect that the most accurate and valid way to interpret an archaeological artifact is to determine its relation to a scriptural text. Nevertheless, eyes released from that assumption might still read meaningful patterns on Cave Twenty Six's wall, inconsistent with those derived from the MSV. Occam's razor is a sharp tool with a slippery handle. Granted, the principle that plurality should not be assumed unnecessarily provides a cornerstone of the modern academy. But *necessity* is a social judgment, not a matter of *a priori* logic. The proposition that Luther is an Enlightenment forefather makes it "necessary" to imagine alternate readings of the Ajanta relief. Will these other readings be better than the one we already have, based upon the MSV? Already the game has begun: better in what context? better for whom? For now, let us simply pursue these alternate theories for alterity's sake. Let us be extravagant.

The first alternate approach to this mural will ignore the plot, forget the temporal dimension, and shift attention away from the relief's outer quadrants toward its central axis. Without that outlying visual noise, the remaining elements line up neatly. On center, reading from top to bottom, we see flying dwarves beating a drum, the canopy of a *Ficus religiosus* hanging over a throne on which there sits a man who gestures toward a woman dancing, accompanied by musicians. How can we make something of this tableau? Well, if the earlier appeal to the MSV was informed by a theory of time, then let us now try one of space: Mircea Eliade's exposition of *sacred space*.

Sacred space is useful here because Eliade presents its universe as the polar opposite of the cosmology envisioned by the Marquis de Laplace. "For religious man," Eliade begins, "space is not homogeneous; he experiences interruptions, breaks in it; some parts of space are qualitatively different from others."[57] The antithesis of such religiously inflected space is Laplace's "geometrical" profane space, whose extent is "homogeneous and neutral; no break qualitatively differentiates the various parts of its mass."[58] The former is subjective, the latter objective. The profane sphere gives "no orientation . . . by virtue of its inherent structure."[59] The sacred, by contrast, "allows the world to be constituted, because it reveals the fixed point, the central axis for all future orientation."[60] For Eliade, *Homo religiosus* is defined, in the first place, by his fixation upon this center. "It seems an inescapable conclusion that the true world is always in the middle, at the Center."[61] And this center is a privileged place, not only because it orients existence, but also because it marks "a break in plane and hence communication among the three cosmic zones," heaven, earth, and underworld.[62] *Homo religiosus* knows where he is, where he wants to go, and how to get there.

To read the relief as a narrative through the MSV is to arrive at the ironic conclusion that Māra is the story's hero (albeit a tragic hero) whose actions unify the plot.[63] It is perhaps fitting, therefore, that this reading relies upon a model of space as *profane*, for it requires that every place on the wall possesses equal value vis-à-vis the overall significance. Certainly an emotional chiaroscuro grades the space in shadow and light. But the shades balance fully. Māra and bodhisattva need each other for this story to work: Māra has no place apart from his interest in moving Śākyamuni from the tree; Śākyamuni has no narrative identity except through his reciprocal relation (we know *which* moment this is in the bodhisattva's life through the presence of Māra).

Sacred space, too, can be located in the relief. Sacred space is oriented space. Its full dimensionality is not the product of skillful manipulations of light and dark on a two-dimensional plane, but rather of the inability to be kept in plane, snapping the lines that separate heaven, earth, and underworld. The supermundane reach of this axis is well-represented in the sculpture at Ajanta, where heaven is the drum-beating dwarves; earth is the tree, throne, and man; and the realm of death is the dancer. By means of that tree, this regal man will be able to renounce the girl in order to ascend into the sky. He will attain divine status when he forsakes death's cacophonous troupe for the syncopations of eternal life. Thus told, the mural is paradigmatic, not narrative. One can eschew text-derived identities, names like Śākyamuni or Māra, and still retain meaning. The activity in each of the four quadrants is equally peripheral to the ultimate significance, for it is all equally not central to the spatial composition.

For Eliade, *sacred* and *profane* are not strategic categories, derived from observation, used to organize a body of data. To the contrary, he treats these as elemental categories that structure consciousness *a priori*. This is why the Eliadean interpretation can, on its own terms, find a rationality sculpted on Ajanta's wall without direct reference to textual sources, whether bauddha or otherwise. The meaning, essentially, is in the archetype which is able to teach the viewer by its visible structure alone, no words needed. The following commentary is quite in sympathy with Eliade's view: "There is nothing intellectual about the Ajanṭā frescoes. Everything of importance is perceived by direct apprehension."[64]

There is a moment of puzzlement here. If Eliade's archetype locates the center as an axis linking heaven, earth, and underworld, on what grounds does the dancer represent death's nether region? Flying dwarves may be self-evidently celestial; trees, thrones, and human beings, terrestrial. But in whose phenomenology do dancing girls manifestly belong to the underworld? To answer this, one might point to a pandemic misogyny that has included the bauddha among its historical vectors. However, the delineation of sacred space should require no such stigmatization of a textual tradition. Might we make this equation, instead, oriented by the model of sacred space itself, based upon the appearance of three registers stacked on a central axis? Is there an elemental algebra to this space, in which an *axis mundi* + heaven + earth requires the deduction of an underworld for its solution? In short, without reference to a bauddha narrative, ought we nevertheless associate the dancer with death because human beings are "hardwired" to see, and sculpt, the sacred oriented along the center in just this way?

A historian of Zen and Buddhist visual practice, Bernard Faure, denies this possibility. Faure's criticism is directed, not at Eliade, but against a tradition of art criticism that considers the visual act to be precognitive:

"Seeing comes before words," John Berger argues. Yet our gaze is always already informed by words, discourse.... As the conscious gaze...is always already mediated by discourse, apparently no primacy of perception exists. Although words can never replace seeing, seeing is already informed through knowledge, discourse, and words.[65]

Following Faure, let us contemplate Ajanta's dancer once more. Overt visual information from an unstudied glance provides no cue that she is a fatal attraction. Her hips are heavy with promise, her breasts ample. What in this mural warns one away from her enticements? Indeed, an eye lightly educated in traditional Indian dance would become still more desirous. Her right hand holds a position known as *kapittha*, used to narrate acts such as offering flowers, applying kohl, or milking cows, as well as iconographically used to indicate the goddesses of prosperity and learning, Lakṣmī and Sarasvatī. In short, if one assesses this sculpture's central axis without presupposing the Eliadean scheme, but also without resorting to bauddha narratives, one will see an auspicious performer before a royal seer; maybe even Lakṣmī dancing for beloved Viṣṇu, her time marked in the skies as well as on the ground. The army in the upper corners? It belongs to a failed suitor. We skip from the MSV's tragedy to Eliade's allegory to a possible romance or comedy.

To find death in this dancer we must still look outside the picture-plane to "knowledge, discourse, words." Interestingly, Eliade's schematization of sacred space coordinates with the MSV. The name *Māra* itself translates as *death*; our discursively conditioned gaze watches death's daughter. Eliade's spatial archetype and bauddha texts lead to parallel readings of the relief: the mundane sphere is transcended by renouncing deadly passions embodied in the female form. Still despite this coincidence, the Eliadean reading cannot fully support its own self-authorizing claims without appealing to an intertextual network of possibilities. Granted, an Eliadean might approach the relief with texts other than those used by the Buddhologist—perhaps texts that are less overtly tied to the intentionalities of this place—but the necessity for a discursive guide remains. If death is definite here it is only because, as Faure reminds us, we know bauddha names. The Eliadean reading may be no more ideological than that based upon the MSV, but ideology becomes ever more evident as it becomes less hegemonic.

It seems that this little exercise in producing an alternate reading for alterity's sake confirms the early Orientalists' prediction: fluency in ancient languages is key to recognizing India's native rationalities. This encounter with Eliade was not a complete loss, however. If nothing else Eliade reminds us, first, eyes comprehend multiple grammars; and second, pay attention to the center as the axis of presence. In fact, these two lessons might suggest that we have been reading this image all wrong. Eliade's crypto-theological vocabulary cannot stand on its own. But does the MSV provide the right vocabulary? Does it speak the language of this mural? For although Ajanta's artists did not slavishly adhere to texts, if we lock our gaze in an even tighter focus—it has moved from a total view, involving tension between center and periphery, to the central axis, now look to the sculpture's central point—we see an iconographic innovation that borders on a transgression. There is one more language to bring to bear on this sculpture: a formal language of gesture.

Drawing from the model of dance drama, Indian iconography developed a vocabulary of symbolic hand gestures (*mudrā*). Several of these *mudrās*—for instance those indicating generosity, meditation, and fearlessness—were part of a pan-Indian gestural vernacular. One *mudrā*, however, was exclusively bauddha; it was used only to mark the moment at which Śākyamuni bodhisattva called upon the earth goddess during his battle with Māra. In bauddha art this gesture, the *bhūmisparśa mudrā* (literally, gesture of touching the earth), often is found alone, the sole iconographic marker for the grand array of events spelled out on Ajanta's wall. When describing the relief (see page 116), I reported that the bodhisattva's right hand is in the *bhūmisparśa mudrā*, in keeping with that convention. In fact, I lied. The *bhūmisparśa* is formed by the fingers pointing straight downward and the palm facing toward the bodhisattva's knee. At Ajanta, the hand is lightly cupped, its palm facing outward toward the viewer. This is the *varada mudrā*, the gesture of giving a *vara* (literally, a "chosen," and hence something desired, a boon) (See Figure 4.4).

When one reads along the center axis it does seem that the bodhisattva, on the cusp of enlightenment, is making a gift that somehow directly involves the lithe

Figure 4.4 Two standing buddhas, their right hands in *varada mudrā*, from the facade of Cave Nineteen. Photo by author.

girl toward whom his hand appears directed. The certainties here are few, the possibilities multiple. The use of the *varada mudrā* suggests that this bodhisattva, whose image cut into Ajanta's mountain will last as long as the sun and the moon, perpetually fulfills desires. Whose desires? Desires for what? Is the bodhisattva rewarding the girl for her dance? Is she now guaranteed buddhahood in some future life because she has offered her body thus? Is the bodhisattva rewarding those people who paid for the creation of this relief? There are the small kneeling figures at the image's lower corners, outside the main picture-plane. Will those patrons become buddhas? Will they be reborn in heaven, there to enjoy the ecstasies of celestial nymphs? Is she a gift? Or again, is the gift being given to viewers, you and I? The bodhisattva's right hand is six feet from the floor; his finger tips graze our heads as we walk past. Will we become buddhas? Will we enjoy heaven? The girl is just our same size, and looking right at us. Is she ours to enjoy? Are we implied by the scene as well? These many questions share no one answer. But we do know that after the battle with Māra the bodhisattva became an enlightened buddha infinitely capable of satisfying every being's every desire.[66]

A brief note on hegemony

The moment of extravagance has passed. Where before there was one interpretation of the Cave Twenty Six image, now there are three. Each corresponds to a distinct way of gazing at the figure, and thus to a distinct construction of space. For the first interpretation—the mural as Māravijaya—every point on the wall is more or less essential to the construction of meaning since every point is equally necessary for a complete reconstruction of the sculptor's intentions. Those intentions, in turn, are identified by reference to a literary source, the MSV. Here, linguistic knowledge, granting primary access to bauddha doctrine and myth, is the sine qua non of significance. The mural's second interpretation—the Eliadean—does not require specialized linguistic knowledge. In the Eliadean gaze, the configuration and location of an artifact in space mark its meaningfulness. Look to the central axis! *Homo religiosus* recognizes this significance naturally, without training; secular scholars require the technique of phenomenological comparison to rediscover these universal structures of meaning. Finally, our third view of the Ajanta relief is gained through eyes focused on a single point: the main figure's gesture of generosity. This gaze has such a tight focus, however, and the boon offered is so particular in nature, that we cannot see what the *vara* is, to whom it is being given, or why exactly it is being sought.

This much is obvious: only the interpretation substantiated by a Sanskrit text holds consensus amongst professional scholars of Buddhism. The other two are speculative; they over-interpret the evidence; they make for fancy rhetoric, but little knowledge; they are tendentious, and show their agendas a little too openly. Śākya texts offer the most accurate basis for interpreting Cave Twenty Six's mural and for Ajanta in general. But it is this appearance of indisputability, this going without saying, that interests me; just as the second chapter was interested in

UNESCO's naming Ajanta a World Heritage monument possessed of exceptional universal value; just as Chapter 3 was interested in the differentiation of inscriptions from graffiti as sources for history. I do not know if anyone has ever been moved by the spirit to see the dancer in Cave Twenty Six's relief as Lakṣmī rather than as Māra's daughter. Nor can I calculate how many are offended by the proposal that Śākyamuni is offering a dancing girl for orgasmic pleasure to his devotees, instead of calling the earth goddess to witness his aeons of self-sacrifice. This is not a numbers game. I do know, however, that the considered acknowledgment of the potential for such alternate views transforms a seemingly value-free observation into the articulation of a historically situated institutional discourse.

Still, the point of this exercise is not to champion an eisegetical *anything goes!* in the interpretation of Ajanta's artifacts. As Ernesto Laclau observes, "to say that everything is contingent... would only make sense for an inhabitant of Mars."[67] Allow me to continue Laclau's thought:

> It is true that in the *final instance* no objectivity can be referred back to an absolute ground; but no important conclusion can be drawn from this, since the social agents never act in that final instance. They are therefore never in the position of the absolute chooser who, faced with the contingency of all possible courses of action, would have no reason to choose. On the contrary, what we always find is a limited given situation in which objectivity is *partially* constituted and also *partially* threatened; and in which the boundaries between the contingent and the necessary are constantly displaced.

There are no groundless interpretations of Cave Twenty Six's wall. But now this can be translated into the understanding that there are no apolitical interpretations of Cave Twenty Six either. If hegemony is marked by the "spontaneous" experience of the contingent as if necessary, or of the political as if apolitical, then the purpose of the previous section's extravagant fancies was to shift our eyes back to those quotation marks around *spontaneous*. The "spontaneous" acceptance of an interpretation as apolitical indexes hegemony achieved; strident assertions of apoliticality index a will to hegemony still unrealized.

Schopen redux: true religion

This long aside began in response to the critique of Buddhist Studies articulated in Gregory Schopen's "Archaeology and Protestant Presuppositions." The problem is twofold. First, in Schopen's words, scholars of Indian Buddhism "uncannily," "remarkably," and "strikingly" resemble sixteenth-century Protestant reformers, for they locate "true religion" in written documents, in the word.[68] Second, insofar as scholars look for Buddhism in texts rather than artifacts, in the study of ideologies rather than that of embodied practices, their reconstructions of religion must reflect Western religious history and values as much as (if not more than) those of Indian Buddhists themselves. The field's *contingent* textualism subverts its *necessary* positivism: this is Schopen's critique. Schopen writes against the Protestant presupposition that texts trump things, but for him it still goes without saying that there exists an historical entity, Indian Buddhism, that historians should represent on its own terms with the greatest possible precision.

Moving forward, it is noteworthy how Schopen expresses his positive agenda. The final few pages of the article speak repeatedly about the *location* of religion. And indeed, the concluding sentences suggest that Schopen might himself be on a crusade to relocate "religion" to his side:

> It is possible, finally, that the old and ongoing debate between archaeology and textual studies is not—as is frequently assumed—a debate about sources. It may rather be a debate about where religion as an object of investigation is to be located. It is possible, perhaps, that the Reformation is not over after all.[69]

But I am not interested in the Christian tussle so much as in the fact that Schopen does not interrogate the positive object of his analysis, by asking whether there is *a* religion, or religion-in-general, to be (re)located. For him, the question always is of place: "*where* religion is actually located."[70] Thus although Schopen recognizes and acknowledges that his archaeological imperative remains entangled in a theological skein, he does not move to cut the knot. Like the scholars whom he critiques, Schopen would follow the thread of evidence to religion's true or actual location. And that is why, although I find his scholarly voice refreshingly punchy, I also find him to be still too "Protestant." Let me explain.

Schopen cites Karlstadt, Zwingli, and Calvin as authorities, but Martin Luther's doctrine of *sola scriptura* fits this same pattern. Luther, like his sixteenth-century brethren, positively embraces scripture while repudiating other sources of knowledge. Recall from an earlier discussion, Luther propounds an ideal of perfect determinism. Given that god's attention, knowledge, will, and action are simultaneous, Luther demands "reason's own testimony" deduce that neither men nor angels have free will. However, although god determines everything, human beings have only limited comprehension of this all-pervading will. The Word alone tells us what god wants us to know, and therefore what we ourselves should desire to know. The attempt to discern god's nature and majesty and plan through any source other than scriptural Word is sinful and wrong. Thus Luther even repudiates reason when it treats nature as a book to be read theologically. Reason engaged in natural theology or in the theology of nature is "the devil's bride... the lovely whore... the foremost whore the devil has."[71] One cannot pull aside the curtain of transcendence by force of logic, but in the scriptural Word one might catch a glimpse of that beyond.

Although Schopen is a singularly innovative and exciting scholar of Buddhism, he is also frustratingly conservative. For when Schopen encourages Buddhist Studies to think beyond its Protestant presuppositions, he addresses only half of

Luther's legacy. The doctrine of *sola scriptura* is not easily disentangled from Luther's theological distinction between "God Himself" and "the Word of God," that is, total reality versus what human beings are given to know of reality.[72] (This is just a preliminary foray into Luther's theology and view of scripture. Both receive fuller treatment in page 142.) Schopen critiques the Protestant's exclusive attention to the scriptural Word, saying that there is more to know than the stuff of books, but he never questions the determinist ideal that underlies it. That is, Schopen advises scholars to give up the History of Religions, "which was and is essentially text bound."[73] He urges them to pursue an Archaeology of Religions, "primarily occupied with three kinds of things then: religious constructions and architectures, inscriptions, and art historical remains," for these things directly reveal "what religious people actually did."[74] But this archaeological practice, like the textual practice of "Protestant" Buddhist Studies, keeps faith with the recoverability of the genuine, the original, the pure, and the actual.

This faith makes Luther's shade laugh! Luther too insists that scripture is adequate to reality, since the Bible "can have no more than one simplest sense, which we call the scriptural or literal meaning."[75] In this case, adequacy is guaranteed by the fact that the Holy Spirit is both scripture's author and its best interpreter. The apparatus of scientific philology—expertise in original languages, in grammar, in the historical conditions of authorship, and so on—contributes to eliciting scripture's literal significance. But in the end, for Luther, scriptural reality must be accepted on its own terms, "no matter how absurd those things which God says in his Word may appear to reason."[76] Likewise, archaeological artifacts are adequate reflections of historical reality only if they are scriptural after this fashion. Schopen expects the sources for an Archaeology of Religions will legislate their own closed and, in the ideal, perfectly determinate network for interpretation that one must accept—even if it violates every preconception about Indian Buddhism that has been derived from books. In sum, Schopen argues over which objects deserve to be treated as scriptural, but does not ask whether the very fact that he raises this argument might itself mark *scripturality* as an abstract property open to further interrogation.

Where we've been and where we're going

This chapter began with puzzlement at James Fergusson's observations about Ajanta's religious provenance. On the one hand, he consistently calls the site Buddhist. On the other hand, he identifies two minor images which contradict this point; and he suggests that Buddhists themselves did not have an exclusivist religious identity—one could be Buddhist almost as a matter of daily fashion. Buddhism, for Fergusson, seems to possess a pure core which is not affected by the practices or beliefs of living people, but which does provide a basis for categorizing expressions of personal religiosity. William Erskine is less complex. But he too writes as if *Buddhism* is a substantive, self-evidently meaningful category, of primary value for the reconstruction of Indian history.

Neither Fergusson nor Erskine names Buddhism's essence, but several introductory textbooks do. If Buddhism is the sort of thing that can be simply, obviously, and instantaneously identified, then *enlightenment* is the reason why. Śākyamuni's enlightenment is Buddhism's historical condition of possibility. I supposed, accordingly, that if Ajanta is Buddhist, enlightenment will be writ large upon its walls. I gave myself an easy task. The walls are painted with sexy queens and dwarfs and elephant processions, all of which might have been more difficult to link to enlightenment than the chosen relief. My search for enlightenment involved a determinist chain of inferences, leading from inchoate stone, to assumptions about a universal human rationality, to the MSV, and then back to a recognition of the enlightenment-event itself right there in Cave Twenty Six. This hermeneutic strategy, I proposed, would be obvious and immediately acceptable to most practitioners of Buddhist Studies. Gregory Schopen might be an exception, insofar as he problematizes the field's valorization of literary sources: this bias expresses Protestant presuppositions, and it results in inaccurate representations of Indian Buddhist values and religiosity. Inspired by Schopen, I imagined alternative interpretations of Cave Twenty Six that putatively did not rely on Sanskrit texts, or enlightenment, or even the buddha. Rather, these readings treated the wall as "scripture" in its own right: as an object that reveals actual religiosity, conveying the key to its true and proper interpretation. My point in that exercise was not to propose better or more viable interpretations of the mural than that provided by the MSV, but to suggest that Protestantism is more than a source for Buddhist Studies' presuppositions about the wellspring of true religion. It is the field's *élan vital*. Schopen himself is working within a "Protestant" predication of the human being as a historical actor when he imagines that there is true religion, or true religiosity, to be recovered through the scholarly analysis of archaeological artifacts. Artifacts can be scriptural only as a displacement of the human beings who created those material remains. Only a scriptural being can author scripture, as when the Word revealed the Word.

If that is where we have been, then the Enlightenment anthropology that conjoins scripture with reason is where we are going. As overdetermined nodal points, *religiosity* and *human nature* have been sites of fierce ideological conflict for the past half-millennium. The history within which European intellectuals came to believe in an unchanging, uniform human nature, explicable in terms of general laws, is a political history. Just as the concept "law of nature" mediates the encounter between human rationality and the physical world, so religiosity has come to serve the same purpose for the psycho-social world.

Let me clarify this point with a ready example. David Hume's essay, "Of Miracles," famously begins with the definition of a miracle as a violation of natural law, and just as famously concludes with the maxim that "no human testimony can have such force as to prove a miracle."[77] Were Almighty God Himself to perform a miracle, no reasonable man could accept it as such. For the laws of nature discovered through regular empirical observation are sufficient to explain all terrestrial events; any personal experience or second-hand testimony that might seem to substantiate a violation of nature's laws can itself be explained-away in naturalistic terms. Hume's argument can be translated into our terms thus: Natural phenomena are not, and can never be, overdetermined. In the reworking of Protestant theology by Enlightenment rationalism, religiosity came to play a parallel role for the human world broadly construed. There is a genealogy of *religion* such that the assumption of a natural, universal—even rational—religiosity has become the means of regulating—even denying—the overdetermined, multiple possibilities for being human.

Rational human beings are religious beings has become a determinant law of human nature, and thus the predicate of a unitary humanity. Just read the following words of Peter Berger, a leading sociologist. Berger's essay seeks to explain why secularization theory—the theory that economic and political modernization would bring about a decline in religion—failed, and why religion so dominates contemporary world affairs:

> Cardinal Ratzinger and the Dalai Lama will be troubled by different aspects of contemporary secular culture. What both will agree upon, however, is the shallowness of a culture that tries to get along without any transcendent points of reference. And they will have good reasons to support this view. The religious impulse, the quest for meaning that transcends the restricted space of empirical existence in this world, has been a perennial feature of humanity. (This is not a theological statement but an anthropological one—an agnostic or even an atheist philosopher may well agree with it.) It would require something close to a mutation of the species to extinguish this impulse for good.[78]

Even granted that Berger's book is published by Eerdmans, a Christian press, his rhetoric is striking.[79] For Berger, religion is concerned with transcendence. And religion thus gives life meaning. And humanity, as a biological species, has always been religious. And this impulse to transcend the human world is self-evidently good. And not even atheists should deny the foregoing description because it rationally belongs to the secular discourse of anthropology. And secularists who deny these points are small-minded and anti-human, bothersome to both an arch-reactionary, Cardinal Ratzinger (now Pope Benedict XVI), and arch-modernizer, the Dalai Lama.

We can see here how Berger overdetermines secularization theory's failure: so numerous are the reasons that "genuine" secularism is impossible. At one level, Berger acknowledges a distinction between the theological and anthropological as discursive spheres. A science of humanity need not incorporate one of divinity. But how is a statement that equates the will toward god with the will for good not, at least, *crypto*-theological? Eliding the two, Berger (re)produces a science of humanity that I call a *scriptural anthropology*. Berger's discursive sleight-of-hand is not unique. It also informs Schopen's faith that archaeological artifacts can be revelatory of actual Buddhist religiosity. Likewise, we are guided by a scriptural anthropology when we treat Cave Twenty Six's mural as something whose identity can be substantially fixed by reference to an ancient bauddha text.

The scriptural human 1: the human component

In 1808, J.D. Paterson found "striking proof" that Hinduism "was founded on pure Deism."[80] Twenty years earlier, Sir William Jones allowed that Indians had seen by the light of natural religion until they "deviated, as they did too early deviate, from the rational adoration of the only true God."[81] And still one-half generation before that, John Zephaniah Holwell claimed that

> howsoever mankind, either of *Europe, Asia, Africa* or *America*, may differ in the exterior modes of worship offered to the Deity, according to their various genius; yet... there are some *fundamental points* of every system, wherein they *agree* and profess unanimous faith; as may be gathered, either from their *express doctrines*, or evidently implied, from their modes, or ceremonials of worship, howsoever differing in manner and form, from each other.[82]

Holwell then enumerated fourteen such fundamental points. Indeed, we might follow the Orientalists' discursive entanglement of human nature with rationality, with belief in divinity, still further, back through another century, back to Edward Herbert, Lord of Cherbury (1582–1648). Writing in 1757, John Leland called Edward Herbert the first, most eminent, and best of Deist philosophers. For our purposes now, he is the most useful. Herbert sought (in Leland's words) "to overturn all revealed, or as he calls it, particular religion, and to establish that natural and universal religion...as that which alone ought to be acknowledged and embraced as true and divine."[83]

Edward Herbert lived in a Europe agitated by the Thirty Years War, and an England enduring a Civil War. He was a soldier and diplomat; a self-professed Citizen of the World in a world sundered by sectarian animosities—schisms among Protestants, as well as the mutual hatred of reformers and Catholics. As a social theorist, hoping to convince fractious sects to unite into "a true Catholic or universal Church," Herbert was a laughable failure.[84] As a theorist of religion, Herbert's importance, noted by John Leland in the eighteenth century, remains noteworthy today. When Peter Berger uses biology to justify religion as universal and good he echoes Edward Herbert's assertion that if we deny the somatic foundation of religiosity we "strip ourselves of all humanity."[85] For Herbert, religion determines humanity's unity as a species. "Religion is the ultimate difference of man."[86]

As an epistemologist, Herbert began his chief work, *On Truth*, with a series of axioms, the first of which reads, simply, "Truth Exists."[87] For Herbert, truth is eternal, omnipresent, self-revealing, differentiated, measured to human capacities, and intellectual.[88] For all this, however, truth is not a transcendental substance; it is not the sort of thing that can be the special property of ecclesiastical authorities or mystical visionaries. Truth, rather, is comprised of the clear certainties that "all men of normal mind believe," and thus is imminent in human relations.[89] Indeed, Ronald Bedford describes Herbert as "obsessed" with "the problems of sectarian persecution, the claims of individual Churches to possession of an exclusive route to salvation, and the abuse of religious instinct by 'authority.' "[90] Herbert sought the facts about humanity and its world that receive universal acceptance, without resort to institutional authority. For as he repeated throughout the work, "whatever is believed by universal consent must be true"; "universal consent... is in the last resort the sole test of truth."[91] Epistemological universality offered Herbert the most assured ground for imagining a Europe in which people recognize their common humanity, unite politically, and live together in peace.

The ground of Herbert's epistemological universality is a creature I call "the scriptural human." This phrase will remain suggestively obscure until the end of this section. And while it might seem that its elucidation should begin with Herbert's theory of knowledge, it begins in fact with Calvinist theology. For Calvinism dominated the England of Herbert's day, and he dedicated *On Truth* "to every sane and unprejudiced Reader," in order that they might reject the faults of Calvinist exclusivism in favor of religious universalism.[92] In particular, Herbert assailed the Calvinist understanding of Providence: how god expresses his will in-and-through creation. Earlier I cited several passages from Luther's *The Bondage of the Will*, attesting to a vision of god as an absolute sovereign whose knowledge, will, and action are coequal. Calvin concurs in this view of divine majesty, taking it to a logical extreme. Whereas Luther's god is an inscrutable judge who is righteous though he makes us damnable, Calvin preached that even before creation god had already determined whom he would save and whom he would damn.[93] This principle, which Calvin himself called god's "dreadful decree," was restated at the international Synod of Dordrecht (1618–19), convened five years before *On Truth's* publication:

> That some receive the gift of faith from God, and others do not receive it proceeds from God's eternal decree.... Election is the unchangeable purpose of God, whereby, before the foundation of the world, he has out of mere grace, according to the sovereign good pleasure of his own will, chosen, from the whole human race... a certain number of persons to redemption in Christ.... This elect number, though by nature neither better nor more deserving than others, but with them involved in one common misery, God has decreed to give to Christ, to be saved by him.... The good pleasure of God is the sole cause of this gracious election; which does not consist herein, that out of all possible qualities and actions of men God has chosen some as a condition of salvation; but that he was pleased out of the common mass of sinners to adopt some certain persons as a peculiar people to himself.[94]

Some men are foreordained for everlasting life, and some for neverending torment; damnation, no less than salvation, being given gratuitously, totally irrespective of an individual's merits.

This understanding of Providence provides an entry into Herbert's theory of knowledge, for he deemed its vision of humanity as wholly in thrall to the caprice of a gloomy god to "blasphem[e] against Nature."[95] In lieu of Calvin's

Providence, entangled with "so many dispensations, secret decrees, and doctrines of predestination," Herbert presented Providence as threefold. The first, "Supreme Providence," that is, god's ultimate wisdom, expresses itself in the human world in two lower forms: as *nature*, which Herbert called "universal Providence," and as *grace*, which he called "particular Providence."[96] By attributing all positive value to god's will alone, Calvin sundered natural processes from divine grace. By setting grace and nature on an equal plane, Herbert hoped to show that human beings could contribute to their own salvation. And *truth* was the means for accomplishing that end. The very existence of truth presupposed a god who created human beings with minds capable of knowing truth, and who fashioned nature such that knowledge of it could result in saving grace. "Our mind," in Herbert's words, "is the best image and specimen of divinity."[97]

Supreme Providence created human beings in god's image by inscribing us with what Herbert calls *Natural Instinct*. This Instinct is "not the mind or soul itself."[98] Rather, it is a faculty by means of which objects are known, each according to its own specific nature. Herbert, like Kant in Chapter 3, would assent to Thomas Aquinas' definition of knowledge as the "conformity of a thing with the understanding."[99] For Herbert, every object possesses its own inner mark; "every difference ... indicates a principle of individuation which characterizes it and serves to distinguish it from others."[100] For truth to be possible, therefore, the mind must have some structure that recognizes these differences. "Every object corresponds to a reciprocal faculty in us."[101] That faculty is Natural Instinct.

This brings us, finally, to the core of Herbert's epistemology: the *Common Notions*, matters of universal assent without which "it would be impossible to establish any standard of discrimination in revelation or even in religion."[102] Given that Herbert defined Natural Instinct as "whatever appears in the same way in every man," the Common Notions that derive from the exercise of Natural Instinct must also be panhuman.[103] Herbert's translator explains:

> "Common Notions are criteria of truth because there is universal agreement upon them.... Common agreement on points of religion or morality among people of all periods and countries is the sole test of truth. It provides mathematical certainty, and is the first and last word of philosophy and theology. Unanimity of opinion is the surest mark of divine purpose."[104]

Of the many Common Notions Herbert discussed, those concerning religion form the doctrine for which he is now best remembered. Herbert adduced five such Common Notions:

1   There is a supreme deity.
2   This deity ought to be worshiped.
3   Virtue combined with piety is the chief part of divine worship.

4   Men should repent of their sins and turn from them.
5   Reward and punishment follow from the goodness and justice of god, both in this life and after it.[105]

For our purposes, these specific doctrines are not important, but rather the logic whereby these Notions become universal truths. All human beings must be religious, for god created both nature and humanity in such a way that the exercise of Natural Instinct would produce these five Common Notions. By Herbert's logic, if all beings are not religious in just this way, then religion itself cannot be true. Thus he held atheism to be impossible. When Herbert heard of a remote people lacking religious beliefs and practices, he summarily dismissed the report with a claim that its author was "ignorant of the language of that country"; this appeal to language nicely foreshadows J.Z. Holwell and the British Orientalists.[106] Hariṣeṇa ruling over fifth-century India, no less than 1819's officers of the Madras Cavalry, belong to the same single human species by virtue of their identical innate religiosity: "I conceive that our mind is not only created in the image of God or in the copy of that image, but it has, in the Common Notions, some shares in the Divine Universal Providence."[107] Although the Common Notions form a self-authenticating epistemological structure, any remainder of uncertainty can be disregarded due to their ultimate derivation from god.

Herbert's Common Notions fulfill a structural role within his epistemology that is parallel to Holy Writ for Lutheran/Calvinist soteriology. Herbert's anthropology was articulated (in part) in opposition to the Calvinist predication of the human being as debased by sin, wholly alienated from the divine, and saved or damned through god's gratuitous election without any justification through personal merit. But as I suggested in the previous section, the representation of humanity as naturally religious closes off the multiple possibilities for being human, just as the Calvinist doctrine of gratuitous election negates the soteriological efficacy of free will. Herbert determined that human beings cannot determine that there is no god. Luther/Calvin determined that human beings cannot determine their own salvation. Hume determined that even god cannot determine a violation of nature's laws, a miracle. If the logic of overdetermination holds that every identity is incomplete and negotiable, then determinism works through a strategy of stipulating which possible identities must be rejected as impossible. These "impossibilities" thus become the condition for the possibility of social-belonging. One denies atheism and becomes a Herbertian; one denies the soteriological efficacy of works and becomes a Lutheran/Calvinist; one denies the miraculous and becomes a Humean. Look back to Berger. Note the echoes of Herbert in his attribution of the following propositions to even atheists and agnostics: religiosity is a fact of human genetics; religiosity is good. Note his exclusionary strategy: to deny these points is to deny one's own humanity, and even to deny goodness. If the human mind was "created in the image of God," and "shares in the Divine Universal Providence," then the study of humanity's natural religiosity is itself the stairway to heaven.[108] The "secular" religious studies scholar naturally fulfills religion's aims.

The scriptural human 2: the scriptural component

I still have not explained the scriptural human: the human being who, like scripture, is autonomous and self-authenticating insofar as he serves god's will. The discussion of Edward Herbert, Lord of Cherbury, brought us through the *human* half of this discussion. To clarify *scripture*, let us again return to Martin Luther and Jean Calvin. For although Herbert deemed their theology to be "a blasphemy so great that those who indulge in it seek to destroy not merely human goodness, but also the goodness of God," their discourse nevertheless permeates his own.[109] The place to begin is with *The Bondage of the Will*, where Luther resorts to a theological trope, the distinction between "God Himself" and "the Word of God."[110] (I introduced this distinction in a cursory manner in page 135, while discussing Gregory Schopen.) The former, Luther sometimes calls the Hidden God, and instructs, "Wherever God hides Himself, and wills to be unknown to us, there we have no concern."[111] In the abstract this makes good sense. If god is the source of all, one should gratefully accept the little he willingly reveals. But how can the hidden god not be an object of fascinated speculation? This is god himself as the determiner of life and death, as the author of predestination's mysteries. And so again Luther cajoles, since the will of "God in His own nature . . . is inscrutable and incomprehensible," he must "be left alone."[112]

Believers, rather, should shift their gaze toward scripture. Eyes averted from God Himself are directed to the gospel, "for it is by His Word . . . that we must be guided."[113] Peter Steinmetz intimates the novelty of Luther's emphases, by characterizing his approach to scripture as "a Reformation understanding of the gospel."[114] Robert Grant further explains:

> Scripture for the reformers is not one of several pillars which uphold the house of faith; it is the sole foundation . . . . The Church was not to be the arbiter of the meaning of scripture, for scripture, the word of God, was the Church's judge.[115]

Unlike Edward Herbert, a relatively unknown figure, Protestant hermeneutics has been a subject of widespread investigation, so I will try to move through it with unusual dispatch, by making three points.

The first is encompassed by Luther's slogan: *sola scriptura*. Scripture is all we can know of god's will, and that is sufficient. For Luther, "no believing Christian can be forced to recognize any authority beyond the sacred scripture"; and for Calvin, "the Scriptures obtain full authority among believers only when men regard them . . . as if the living words of God."[116] For this reason, Luther and Calvin speak against other avenues to god, such as speculative reason and mystical union. Catholic scholasticism allowed for natural theology, reading god's will in the body of nature. But for Luther and Calvin, despite the fact that all creation expresses divine order, one cannot find god in nature, only in scripture.

The translators of Calvin's *Institutes* explain,

> the revelation of God in creation, for Calvin, would have been the basis of a sound natural theology only "*if* Adam had remained upright." Because of sin no sound theology of this type is possible. Scripture is the only medium of knowing the Creator.[117]

Not the world, but the Word, is the way to know god.

A second dimension of the Reformation's understanding is that scripture is self-authorizing and self-interpreting. Peter Steinmetz speaks of an "exegetical optimism" in early Protestantism, which believed in the possibility of "a theology which was wholly biblical and excluded all philosophical and speculative questions."[118] The basis for such a hermeneutics is to be found in another slogan: scripture interprets scripture. Given that scripture is the only way to know the divine, everything worth knowing has to be enveloped therein. This, in turn, entails a twofold revision of scriptural hermeneutics away from medieval paradigms. First, Luther and Calvin emphasize that scripture is easy to interpret, even for the common man. Per Luther, "Those who deny the perfect clarity and plainness of the Scriptures leaves us nothing but darkness."[119] And one can appreciate the metaphorical irony of a second citation:

> Everywhere we should stick to just the simple, natural meaning of the words, as yielded by the rules of grammar and the habits of speech that God has created among men; for if anyone may devise "implications" and "figures" in Scripture at his own pleasure, what will all Scripture be but a reed shaken with the wind, and a sort of chameleon?"[120]

Calvin concurs: scripture should to be taken at face-value—read literally not figuratively—since "we have an open and naked revelation of God in the word...and it has nothing intricate in it, as the wicked imagine, to hold us in suspense."[121] The only requirement placed on an interpreter by Calvin is "to let his author say what he does, instead of attributing to him what we think he ought to say."[122] Scripture contains the revealed will of god himself; its revelation is overt, on the text's surface. Thus it takes precedence over institutionalized churches and learned schools of interpretation. There is no valid source for scriptural authority or scriptural meaning outside scripture itself.

Almost. After all, even literal readings can disagree. This brings us to the third crucial dimension of Luther and Calvin's engagement with scripture. Only a select few have the capacity to interpret scripture correctly: those who have been enlightened by god. As Calvin writes:

> This bare and external proof of the Word of God should have been amply sufficient to engender faith, did not our blindness and perversity prevent it. But our mind...has such a dulness that it is always blind to the light of God's truth. Accordingly, without the illumination of the Holy Spirit, the Word can do nothing.[123]

143

And there is a spectacular corollary to this enlightenment: faith in scripture indexes election to eternal life through god's saving grace. As Weber's *Protestant Ethic* famously explicates, Protestants were not willing to heed Luther's pleas to "let God be God," and to "only fear and adore" god without any direct concern for their own posthumous fate. But while Weber elaborates the relationship between this anxiety and economic activity, Calvin sticks to the Word. His discussion of predestination begins with the "baffling question" of why "out of the common multitude of men some should be predestined to salvation, others to destruction."[124] Of course, the mystery of why the world was created in this fashion belongs to the hidden god, and cannot be answered. Nevertheless, god does give the elect a sign by which they can recognize his gratuitous call to salvation: "the very nature and dispensation of the call . . . consists not only in the preaching of the Word but also in the illumination of the Spirit."[125] Merely encountering the Word is *not* a sign of election. Those who lack god's favor may also read the gospel; but for them it is "wrapped in enigmas" because god wants to cast them "into greater stupidity."[126] Those whose hearts have been enlightened by the Holy Spirit, by contrast, will receive his Word with proper faith. They will understand the book, accept its authority outright, and not indulge in curious inquiries about eternal election. One who can act so possesses "a trustworthy attestation of the eternal predestination of God."[127] (Figure 4.5)

Figure 4.5 A billboard along I-10 in Beaumont, California, February 2005. Photo (and photoshop) by author.

With this, we can now read the scriptural human. Here I expand the meaning of *scripture* to include the class of objects possessing the following three characteristics: (1) Scriptures are accepted as self-authorizing sources of exceptional universal value. This requires no further comment. (2) Scriptures are accepted as coherent and totalizing texts that carry within themselves the key to their true and proper interpretation—such interpretations are often called "literal." Competing interpretations based upon extrinsic keys are necessarily false. The doctrine that enlightenment through the Holy Spirit is a prerequisite for proper understanding of the Bible is paradigmatic here. This stipulation allows subjective, personal readings of the gospels to be represented as objective and literal, since, after all, when one reads the Bible through the Spirit one is merely allowing Word to interpret Word. (3) Anybody who voices doubt over the naked performativity of points 1 and 2 is threatened. Yes, Luther and Calvin certainly do seem to be engaged in some shady hermeneutics. But do not forget that the Holy Spirit's enlightening touch also leaves the stain of salvation: the only way to be sure one's faith is a genuine gift of grace is to be able to accept, without question, exactly that which most severely violates good common sense, reason, and regular experience. Someone who cannot accept scripture according to points 1 and 2 should not expect to escape an eternity of brimstone.

Mutatis mutandis, the Herbertian scriptural human possesses exceptional universal value because, created in the image of god, his mind is structured through Natural Instinct. Thus he knows the Common Notions, which require no special insight to realize because he has been "hardwired" by Supreme Providence. Moreover, he knows they are true because they receive universal assent, that is, they are self-authorizing and provide their own interpretive key. When one asks why that should be the case, Herbert's rejoinder parallels that of Luther/Calvin. Like reading Word through Spirit, god is both the Common Notions' definitive subject and their ultimate author. A belief in god's Providence is necessary. Without it, Herbert's epistemological system, not to mention his hopes for a world in which sectarian strife is inconceivable, comes to naught. Nevertheless, as with the Luther's and Calvin's shady hermeneutic, there is still room for doubt. John Butler observes, "the weakest part of Herbert's argument is his stress on the argument of *consensus gentium*, believing as he did that it transcended religious, political, philosophical, and ethnic considerations."[128] Again, Luther's and Calvin's discourse is strategic. Like the reformers, Herbert threatens unbelievers. The five truths of natural religion serve the divine judge as criteria for his Final Judgment:

> Every religion, if we consider it comprehensively, is not good; nor can we admit that salvation is open to men in every religion. For how could anyone who believes more than is necessary, but who does less than he ought, be saved?[129]

To misuse the human mind, the best image of divinity, by formulating novel doctrines that divide man from man, is perilous in the extreme.

Herbert's anthropology is Christian prejudice mystified by association with god-given reason and truth, instead of Christian prejudice mystified by association with god-given Spirit, Word, and faith. For Herbert, human beings themselves are scriptures to be read. At the most "literal" level this reading tells us that we are religious beings because we are rational beings, and vice versa.

Overdetermination and the politics of impenetrability

Standing before the Literary Society of Bombay in 1821, William Erskine shared a series of truths with his audience: Religious identities are simple and obvious; they sit on the surface, so that even transient observers might distinguish them immediately; yet surfaces only give material expression to deeper theologies and myths, which themselves are ciphers for the essential core of what it means to be a human being. As for rocks, so too for the living. Now we know something of the anthropological background to this common sense, in which religion conjoined with reason becomes the basis for humanity's unity-in-difference. This is not to say that the men of the Literary Society of Bombay were necessarily Herbertians. Between the seventeenth century and the nineteenth, theorists proposed many different versions of natural religiosity. John Locke, for instance, directly criticized Herbert. Where Herbert disallowed atheism, Locke accepted that whole nations can have no god or religion.[130] And where Herbert's god inscribed human beings with a natural instinct, Locke denied all innate ideas, including that of god: the exercise of reason upon external sense data or the inner workings of the mind, leading from the known to the unknown, was the only avenue to the divine. Yet, Locke did adduce a theory of natural religiosity, for like Herbert he too correlated religiosity with universal rationality. God was "the most natural discovery of human reason."[131] When Locke scratched an atheist, he found a man who had squandered his god-given rationality by not pursuing the thoughts that would lead him to the creator.

Despite their differences, Herbert and Locke were both stakeholders in an economy of human nature for which reason and religion are twin coins of the realm. Let me repeat, Locke was only one among many to nuance the category "natural religion" after Herbert and before Erskine.[132] Though fascinating, I will not survey that company, for all its members work within the determinism of a scriptural anthropology: every human being carries within himself everything that he needs in order to know what is worth knowing about every other human being. But look back to my definition of scripture: there must also be a threat. In this case, the predicates of natural religiosity protect human beings from their own indeterminacy. Thus Kant sermonized to the "friends of the human race and of what is holiest to it" against dangerous libertines who indulge in "an unbelief of reason."[133] Though logic cannot prove god's existence, Kant held that reason nevertheless "*needs* to assume" that divinity really exists.[134] For without god, rationality cannot provide the ultimate touchstone of truth. Rather every man would be able to assert that his own subjective enlightenment is a universal reality, resulting in social anomie.

> If it disputed that reason deserves the right to speak *first* in matters concerning supersensible objects such as the existence of God and the future world, then a wide gate is opened to all enthusiasm, superstition and even to atheism.[135]

Ominously, there would also be "a confusion of language." Likewise, Voltaire called the belief in "a rewarding and revenging God" a "universal, necessary prejudice," and a "very good prejudice" at that.[136] In Herbert's day, in Voltaire's day, in Kant's day, the rational belief in god, or the strategic teaching that morality requires theism, may well have been regarded as effective countermeasures against sectarian fanaticism. In our day, Peter Berger continues their line.

Now if we would give up god, we should be also willing to accept that human beings are like a mountain's ancient mural: overdetermined and often impenetrable. Any *actual* religiosity we find likely belongs to our own economy of desire.

In sum, this chapter explored tensions that arise from the determinist encounter with overdetermined matter—rock and living. The concept of overdetermination was first introduced by Freud, who understood dream-elements to have more than one cause or express more than one wish. And because dream-elements (let alone hysterical symptoms) have multiple antecedents, they legitimately support multiple explanations or interpretations. There is no gainsaying the lithic facticity of Ajanta's wall. However, whether it enters discourse as a "Buddhist" fact or a "Hindu" fact, a "religious" fact or a "political" fact, is not a "fact" of the stone itself, but of the discursive sphere within which the stone is contemplated and identified. Attention to overdetermination acts as a ward against scripturalization, that is, against imagining that an object can contain or determine the singular key to its own *literal* interpretation. As I fantasized about possible readings of the Cave Twenty Six mural, I was interested less in their verisimilitude to truth than in their hermeneutic ramifications. It is possible to tell stories without referring to the MSV or any other bauddha source. The Eliadian can find archetypal Man transiting to The Divine; the Hindu can work up a nice local myth about Viṣṇu and Lakṣmī; the libertine can use the MSV, but end up with a pimp buddha.

Perhaps nobody would ever call such interpretations *Buddhist*. But a historical investigation that presupposes that words like *Buddhist* and *Buddhism* provide simple, obvious, and immediate access to the living—as they are on their surface *and* in their depths—has not yet engaged with the materiality of material artifacts. This is why I chose to focus on a mural depicting Śākyamuni's enlightenment-event. The chain of inferences linking a sculpted image to a tale about Māra's defeat on the eve of enlightenment will not be more complex than the sequence of steps leading from the totality of Ajanta's artifacts to the world religion, Buddhism. In the former instance, the MSV provides the key link, enabling historians to express certainty about the stone's meaning. In the latter, enlightenment fulfills the parallel function. Enlightenment is a nodal point; the definitively "Buddhist" cipher for natural religiosity; the sort of thing that can resolve a human being's true identity. If humanity is determined as a species by its religiosity, then Buddhists throughout the world are those humans whose religiosity is articulated in terms of enlightenment. As a religion, Buddhism begins with the buddha's enlightenment.

But enlightenment becomes enlightenment only in the midst of a hermeneutic process, within a discourse. If enlightenment is not a fact of Indian history but of the discursive sphere within which that history is articulated, can Buddhism be otherwise?

Mainstream Buddhist Studies is an academic discourse *about* Buddhism that analyzes the religious discourse *of* Buddhism. That must change if Buddhism is itself not a determinate thing—not a religion, that is, a historically delimited, institutionalized expression of humanity's innate and constitutive religiosity—but a discourse, ultimately impossibly fixed through an enlightenment which is itself inextricably discursive. Now, if you are worrying—as did Kant—about the slippery slope of indeterminacy, in which communication degenerates into a confusion of tongues and thence to eisegetical libertinism, recall Ernesto Laclau and Chantal Mouffe's logic of overdetermination introduced near the beginning of this chapter. Multiplicability of meaning is the basic post-structuralist insight. But Laclau and Mouffe emphasize that *politics* is a logical entailment of this anti-essentialism. Identities can never be fixed, but the struggle to fix them, however impossible, is how we spend our time! Indeed, when has politics not been constitutive of Buddhist Studies? Gregory Schopen critiques the field for its Protestant politics, which locates true religion in the scriptural Word instead of material artifacts or ritual behaviors. And where Schopen sees a symptom I see a syndrome: Buddhist Studies' discourse assumes a universal religiosity tied to Protestant anthropology; a methodological positivism tied to Protestant theology; a determinist ideology tied to Protestant cosmology; a privileging of texts tied to Protestant soteriology. Thus I criticize Schopen in turn for his politics: for still valuing true religion; for still having a stake in the past existence of Indian Buddhism; for still accepting a discourse within which enlightenment is plainly religious. In turn, how can I not expect that members of an academic field that valorizes determinate meaning will not resist my attempt to deprive its source materials of unique, innate, self-constituting, field-specific criteria for fixing real significance?

By imbricating bauddha enlightenment within the discursive construction of humanity as naturally religious, scholars transform a place containing ancient artifacts, partially inspired by bauddha ideologies, into a *Buddhist Ajanta*. Let me reiterate: my aim in redescribing Buddhism as a discursive formation is to undermine the construction of humanity as a natural class whose values and salvation are uniquely fulfilled by religious institutions (or by engagement in an non-institutional "spirituality"). This is a matter of politics, not ontology. Accordingly, deconstructive claims—"Buddhism did not exist," "Ajanta is not Buddhist"—are only intermediate steps in a longer query into the privileging of abstractions and universals in the imagination of social order.

5

WHAT DO GODS HAVE TO DO WITH ENLIGHTENMENT?

> His illusions were all the imagination he had—a ferocious poverty.
> (Peter Straub, *Koko* (New York: Dutton, 1988), 560)

There are no gods in Buddhism

We live in remarkable times. Today, unsure how to begin this chapter, I decided to order books for my next semester's course, "The Buddhist Imaginary." Then to delay further, I read the reviews posted to amazon.com of my preferred textbook, Rupert Gethin's *The Foundations of Buddhism*.[1] In what earlier era could I have learned instantly the opinion of Todd Martin from Agua Dulce, California:

> ★☆☆☆☆ The WORST book on this subject EVER
> This autor is writing about some other religion. It's the only explanation. Not one thing he says in the first 20 pages is factually correct. I stopped reading shortly after he says "The Gods gathered on the day the Buddha achieved enlightenment as if they knew something important was going to happen." All I could think was, "what gods?," because there are no gods in Buddhism. The very idea of a God or Gods goes against everything the Buddha ever taught.[2]

I know nothing more about Todd Martin. But his review (which 6 of 44 people found helpful) brings us to the heart of this chapter: What do gods have to do with enlightenment? What do India's long-dead bauddha have to do with Buddhism? What does Buddhism have to do with what the buddha taught, the dharma?

What was Todd Martin thinking? To my eye, the passage he cites from Gethin looks benign. Gethin does not grant the gods an instrumental role in Śākyamuni's enlightenment. He does not represent buddhahood as a gift conferred by heavenly grace or as an instrument of divine will. Nor does Gethin magnify gods into omniscient, omnipresent, omnibeneficent beings, who, through their own power, fashion the cosmos *ex nihilo* and determine universal providence. Had Gethin made *those* claims, Martin's voice would probably just echo a chorus of critics rehearsing Buddhist arguments against the theological construction of monotheist creator gods. But Gethin does not say that.

Todd Martin's condemnation is all the more curious in light of Śākya sources, in which divinities (Māra, Indra, Brahmā, Nārāyaṇa, Śiva) are ubiquitous. Śākya books give advice on how to achieve divine status. At Ajanta, heavens and gods are painted on the walls; the desire to be born in their midst is announced in the inscriptions. To get personal about it: If the mere mention of gods is transgressive for a Buddhist, then how should we classify Buddhabhadra, the donor of Cave Twenty Six? Buddhabhadra's bona fides seem beyond reproach. He calls himself a bhikṣu and a learned bodhisattva who hoped to assist all living beings on the path to buddhahood.[3] Yet other words through which Buddhabhadra identifies himself may appear less than enlightened: rich, powerful, desirous of worldly pleasure as well as of liberation. Moreover, Buddhabhadra is a theological triumphalist. His *praśasti* compares the buddha to Śiva and Kṛṣṇa by name. The buddha is superior to those gods because, despite their divine status, both have fallen subject to other's will: Śiva was cursed (on many occasions) and Kṛṣṇa died. Buddhabhadra declares, "gods' victories are reversed, for they are subject to adversity," but nowhere does he problematize divinity itself as an existential state. Indeed, Buddhabhadra desired that his parents and benefactors would enjoy themselves in heaven for as long as a sun and moon hang above the earth. That, in part, is why he commissioned his cave in the mountains.

Given that Todd Martin rates *The Foundations of Buddhism* as the worst-ever book on Buddhism, must Buddhabhadra then be the worst-ever Buddhist? Perhaps Buddhabhadra was not a Buddhist at all. For on amazon.com Martin opposes even the most temperate appeal to divinity. His words are clear. God in the singular, and gods in the plural, have no place in Buddhism. Any positive discourse on divinity is antithetical to the entire corpus of Buddhist teachings.

Todd Martin's frustration with *Foundations* evidences a common, intractable problem for scholars of religion: where to draw the line between what is necessary or essential to a particular tradition and what is contingent. Indeed, Martin's remarks have a long pedigree, for observers and scholars have often expressed uncertainty about the bauddha treatment of divinity. One of the first notices of such puzzlement is found in the 1691 memoire of Simon de La Loubère, an envoy to the Siamese court from France. Loubère reports that the Portugese understand *nirvāṇa* to mean that the soul has become god. In Loubère's opinion, however, the Portugese get it wrong. The Siamese do not understand nirvāṇa to entail any such apotheosis, since for the Siamese nirvāṇa is "a manner of being," not of divinity.[4]

Loubère's account is suggestive. But let us skip centuries, to the nineteenth, when growing knowledge of Asia inspired diverse, contradictory attempts to comprehend Buddhism in theological terms. Common sense held that if most souls living in Burmah, Siam, Laos, Pegu, Cambodia, Thibet, Japan, Tartary, Ceylon, the Loo-Choo, China, Siberia, as well as Swedish Lapland were all established in one religion, with one founder, then all would also adhere to one common theological principle, at least.[5] Yet Buddhism was so varied theologically that scholars could not even be sure what to call it. Was Buddhism "The Protestantism of the East" as was argued in the 1869 *Atlantic Monthly*. Or did the Buddhist religion resemble Roman Catholicism, as was argued in the 1870 *Atlantic Monthly*?[6] Or was Buddhism, "no real religion," per the observation of Oxford's Boden Professor of Sanskrit, whose thought continues: "It has no God, no Supreme Being, no real prayer, no real clergy. It lays no claim to any supernatural revelation."[7] Or was Buddhism better considered "a philosophy rather than a religion" because Buddhists pursue the enlightened goal of universal rationality?[8] Or was the Sinologist, Samuel Beal, correct? Buddhism is "a religious system" in terms of its practices *and* a philosophy "so far as the abstract principles are concerned."[9]

These various citations and authors date to the 1860s through 1890s. One generation earlier, scholars had fewer facts about the bauddha but were no less confused. Frederick Maurice's *The Religions of the World and Their Relations to Christianity* (1847) offers a nice summary of the state of the field in his day:

> What are we to say of a doctrine which is sometimes represented as one of almost perfect Theism; sometimes as direct Atheism; sometimes as having the closest analogy to what in a Greek philosopher, or in a modern philosopher, would be called Pantheism; sometimes as the worship of human saints or heroes; sometimes as altogether symbolical; sometimes as full of the highest abstract speculation; sometimes as vulgar idolatry?[10]

Maurice asks, what are we to say? By the end of this chapter, we will still not have said anything to solve these nineteenth-century problems: Are gods essential to Buddhism? Is the buddha himself a god? Is Buddhism a religion or philosophy? For (a)theological issues are not resolved through enlightenment, theistic or atheistic, but through the analysis of hegemony, that is, of the social force exerted by the assertion and acceptance of a putatively non-speculative, necessary, apolitical truth.

This chapter inquires into the hegemonic function of the disarticulation of gods and enlightenment. What is the social force of the claim that a positive discourse on divinity is antithetical to Buddhism, the religion of enlightenment? For a quick, clear example of ideological disarticulation as social articulation, consider the work of Edward Conze, an important twentieth-century buddhologist. What is Conze doing when he advises, "Much of what has been handed down as 'Buddhism' is due not to the exercise of wisdom, but to the social conditions in which the Buddhist community existed...One must throughout distinguish the exotic curiosities from the essentials of a holy life"?[11] Later in this same work he returns to this point in a comparison of Buddhism and Hinduism: "There is nothing, or almost nothing, in the Buddhist interpretation of spiritual truth which ties it to any soil or any climate, to any race or tribe. Hinduism as compared with it is full of tribal taboos."[12] What is Conze doing?

Each of the chapters in this book has considered hegemony after a fashion: Chapter 2, the hegemony of exceptional universal value over the discursive construction of Ajanta's spatiality; Chapter 3, the hegemony of linear intentionality over the discursive construction of Ajanta's temporality; Chapter 4, the hegemony of a scriptural anthropology over the discursive construction of Ajanta's materiality. In this way, Ajanta provided a basis for exploring how Enlightenment (and by extension, Protestant Christian) ideologies are articulated through the representation of Buddhist enlightenment. By contrast, this chapter will not focus on Ajanta. Instead it will look somewhat more systematically at the work of hegemony. This reflexive moment is appropriate since I, no less than the Protestant or Buddhist, am engaged in a struggle for ideological dominance. This analysis in terms of hegemony asserts my own e/Enlightened perspective, my own ability to recognize, and disclose, contingencies of power that others regard as necessities.

The discussion proceeds in several stages. The first takes a closer look at Todd Martin, whose brief posting on amazon.com provides a basis for reviewing several categories presented in previous chapters: scripturality, hegemony, discursivity. Following that, the discussion turns to two contemporary bauddha theologians, Satya Narayan Goenka and Richard Hayes, for whom Buddhism, when taken on its own terms, is not religion but truth. This section culminates in Hayes' dualist social vision, pitting an ideal Buddhist society modeled on what he calls "the original Sangha" against a foolish society dedicated to what he calls "the mythology of enlightenment." The conclusion then summarizes the chapter's diverse points in a catchphrase: vigorous public polytheism is secular wisdom for the modern age.

Enlightenment in the garbage heap

Why should a historian care what some guy from Agua Dulce, California, thinks about gods and enlightenment? What is the scholarly value of an opinion posted on a bookseller's website? This is just information-age archaeology, like excavating a garbage heap. The workaday charge of ephemera is what makes it interesting. Indeed, one might dig still deeper into the heap, seeking the logic that divides enlightenment from the gods. For Todd Martin that logic is a matter of fact. Thus Martin accuses Gethin: "Not one thing he says in the first 20 pages is factually correct." The most egregious error of fact: Gethin places gods at the buddha's enlightenment. Likewise, Martin denounces Gethin's scholarship as devoid of value because he fails to assert positive facts:

> The writing is dreadful. The author goes on and on giving dates as facts, only to turn around 2 sentences later and explain how those facts are disputed and probably wrong. He spent at least 5 pages talking about events 1500 years before Buddhism that had absolutely nothing to do with Buddhism itself.

> I skimmed ahead and saw page after page after page listing date after date as if any of it was relevant, regardless of the Buddhas teaching about the poison arrow. If you know the Buddhas teaching of the poison arrow you will know what I mean. Those dates are irrelevant at best. The fact that there is no proof they are accurate is dangerous.[13]

Martin uses a discourse of fact and facticity in order to pair secular history and theological belief together as two iterations of a single epistemological error. A concern for historical uncertainties, like a concern for the gods, diverts one's attention toward incorrect facts, irrelevant facts, even dangerous facts, that are only ever matters of debate and speculation. Martin is particularly dismissive of god and gods, I would guess, because divine beings are signifiers for ultimate value(s). To treat a being as absolute when it is not even a positive matter of fact that the being exists—this is a gestural synecdoche for total unenlightenment. Conversely, I would guess, demythologization must be the enlightened gesture par excellence.

As a hermeneute, Todd Martin authorizes his rejection of gods, of academic history, of *The Foundations of Buddhism*—in sum, of unenlightenment—through appeal to a scriptural precedent, "the teaching of the poison arrow," found in "The Shorter Discourse to Māluṅkya." This brief text from the Pāli canon involves a dialogue between Śākyamuni and a monk named Māluṅkyāputta. The latter initiates the conversation by asking the buddha to resolve several metaphysical conundrums: Is the world eternal? Is the world infinite? What is a buddha's existential status after his final nirvāṇa? In fact, Māluṅkyāputta threatens to abandon his robes if the buddha withholds the answers. Śākyamuni's response has two parts. First he interrogates Māluṅkyāputta's expectation. To paraphrase with some dramatic license: "O foolish, foolish man, when I made you a monk did I promise to answer questions such as these? No! So why now do you act as if I did make that promise?" Following that, the buddha speaks in parables in order to explain, not the answers Māluṅkyāputta wants, but why Māluṅkyāputta's questions are themselves inappropriate:

> It is as if there were a man struck by an arrow that was smeared thickly with poison.... And the man might say, "I will not draw out this arrow as long as I do not know whether that man by whom I was struck was a brahmin, a kṣatriya, a vaiśya, or a śūdra....as long as I do not know his name and family....whether he was tall, short or of medium height..."
> That man would not discover these things, but that man would die.[14]

Todd Martin's "poison arrow," in short, is a figure for Buddhism as an anti-speculative pragmatism that focuses on *duḥkha* (suffering; imperfection), *duḥkha's* causes, and the means for bringing *duḥkha* to an end. This purpose delimits the buddha's teaching and discipline. No other knowledge is necessary. Indeed, language found in the *Mūlasarvāstivāda Vinaya* provides additional scriptural backing for Martin's position. Recall, from the preceding chapter, the night of enlightenment. The story ends when Śākyamuni realizes the "correct" facts, the undisputed, unchanging facts about *duḥkha*. But the story begins with Māra, and with Śākyamuni's puzzlement as to why Māra's followers are so nasty. Curious, Śākyamuni uses his psychic abilities to probe those demons' minds, and in so doing develops a taxonomy of mentalities. He distinguishes the impassioned mind from the disciplined, the confused mind from the clear, and so on. Of particular interest here is a phrase the text repeats to describe the cognitive process whereby Śākyamuni pursues this mind-science: *X yathābhūtam prajānāti*, Śākyamuni recognizes *X* for what it is.[15] This Sanskrit phrase connotes epistemic exactitude. Śākyamuni recognizes every mental state and every truth in its own particularity, and then apperceives the dharma, the universal law that establishes an equivalence among all those particulars.

In this light, a properly Buddhist datum must meet two criteria. It must be definite, not speculative; also it must serve the project of enlightenment, which is nothing other than the bare recognition of reality as it is. And there is a third criterion. For one still needs a way to be certain that one is asking the kinds of questions that lead to enlightenment's clarity. Who wants to waste billions upon billions of lifetimes pursuing useless queries? The Shorter Discourse shows the way. At the end of the text, the buddha's last words to Māluṅkyāputta are given in the form of a command: "Accept what I did not explain as 'unexplained.' Accept what I did explain as 'explained.' "[16] The buddha neither affirms nor denies his own occult capabilities. Perhaps he could have satisfied Māluṅkyāputta's metaphysical curiosity, or maybe not. Śākyamuni just articulates a binary structure for knowledge, and redirects Māluṅkyāputta's attention from the wrong pole to the right one. What Todd Martin calls "Buddhism itself" belongs entirely to the right chain of equivalences on Table 5.1. The left column must represent either pseudo-Buddhism or that which is not Buddhism at all.

Todd Martin's review is odd and unsettling. Odd, in part, because his words are so poorly chosen. Unsettling, because Martin's primary linguistic infelicity is to use "Buddhist" and "Buddhism" as if these words *do* adequately name the class of things explained by Śākyamuni; as if these identities are not themselves

Table 5.1 Organization of knowledge based upon "The Shorter Discourse to Māluṅkyāputta"

The "unexplained"	The "explained"
Gods; informational facts about history, especially those that are matters of scholarly debate	Duḥkha; the cause of duḥkha; the cessation of duḥkha; the path leading to the cessation of duḥkha
Speculative	Factually correct matters about which one can be certain
Prolongs saṃsāra	Leads to detachment, quiescence, enlightenment, nirvāṇa

matters of history, speculation, and dispute. Martin writes his criticism of Gethin in the language of fact. Yet, one needs only a quick glance back to the first chapter to recognize the counterfactual burden Martin places on these words. That chapter cited *The Buddhist Religion*, whose first page reports, "*Buddhism*... is a recent invention. It comes from the thinkers of the eighteenth century European Enlightenment and their quest to subsume religion under comparative sociology and secular history."[17] I imagine that Martin's distaste for Gethin's book stems, in part, from the fact it argues for this selfsame point.[18] The point is not simple but simplistic: If Buddhism is of recent provenance, then Buddhism cannot *itself* have been explained by the buddha. If there is no act more unenlightened than placing ultimate value in a god whose existence one cannot assert as a positive matter of fact, then, *mutatis mutandis*, there is no identity more unenlightened than *Buddhist*, for as a historical entity, Buddhism is not a positive matter of fact. Granted, the words Buddhist and Buddhism have become accepted "insider" categories; the sort of people who treat the Shorter Discourse as scripture also use these words for themselves and their religion. Nevertheless it is a matter of unenlightened speculation to project this contemporary usage to a time before the words originated within an "outsider" discourse. The next three sections will consider the structure of that unenlightenment by reviewing three themes introduced in earlier chapters: scripturality, hegemony, and discursivity.

A look back, stage 1: the scriptural

Todd Martin is not a nut. The Shorter Discourse to Māluṅkya is frequently cited in academic introductions to Buddhism, as well as in contemporary publications of a more openly popularizing or apologetic nature. Nor is Martin's mistrust of speculation remarkable. Look back to the prior chapter's discussion of early Protestant theology which, in David Steinmetz's words, sought to be "wholly biblical and exclude all philosophical and speculative questions."[19] Early Protestants shared this Pāli text's anti-speculative stance: only knowledge derived from a literal reading of scripture as revelatory of god's will had value; the ability to read the Bible *literally* held the promise of election. We find the same complex of values expressed in Edward Herbert's statement: "How could anyone who believes more than is necessary.... be saved?"[20] Or recall Gregory Schopen's puzzlement at the fact that scholars have not used solid archaeological matter to reconstruct Indian Buddhism, but rather rely upon texts about which they must speculate concerning their dates and places of authorship as well as their community of interest. All give the same e/Enlightened advice: Attend only to that which is there, right before one's eyes, just as it is; for only by doing so can one achieve something real, lasting, or legitimate. All share an aversion to the speculative, though their stakes vary. For a man poisoned by an arrow, correct knowledge brings the correct antidote. The Protestant becomes confident of his own salvation. Schopen rights an academic field gone awry. And the Buddhist who sees things just as they are inquires into *duḥkha*, becomes detached, attains enlightenment and, finally, nirvāṇa. Speculation, metaphysics, theory, *dṛṣṭi*, violate the e/Enlightened understanding, since they build reality as it is into an architecture of desire.

A nice statement of this principle is found in Diderot and d'Alembert's *Encyclopédie*. The entry dedicated to the *philosophe* teaches that a such a man "knows how to suspend judgement" when he does not possess a "proper basis" for correct judgment.[21] The *Encyclopédie* calls this rationality the philosophe's "most perfect trait." Is it not wise advice? Yet, even such Enlightened wisdom permits Cartesian doubt: How does one know that a proper basis exists, that is, that correct judgment is even possible? Or, granting that such a basis does exist, how does one know that one has found it, and not a deceptive simulacrum conjured by an evil genius? Uncertainties are legion. Would it not make more sense for a philosophe simply to suspend all judgment? Should not a perfect philosophe be a perfect sceptic?

Similar questions were raised in the preceding chapter, which sought a proper basis for identifying a mural in Ajanta's Cave Twenty Six as the Māravijaya, Śākyamuni's victory over Māra. That chapter wound in serpentine fashion to conclude that historical certitude presupposes anthropological determinism. As I wrote in page 137: There is a genealogy of *religion* such that the assumption of a natural, universal—even rational—religiosity has become the means of regulating—even denying—the overdetermined, multiple possibilities for being human. *Rational beings are religious beings* has come to be viewed as a determinant law of human nature, and thus the predicate of a unitary humanity.

Yet that was not the final answer—and for the same reason that the Shorter Discourse to Mālunkya does not simply reject metaphysical speculation and affirm the pragmatics of *duḥkha*. After rejecting and affirming, the Pāli text adds two imperatives: "Accept what I did not explain as 'unexplained.' Accept what I did explain as 'explained.' " This is the last thing the buddha says in this text. *Dhāretha* (accept!), a second-person imperative, is derived from the root, *dhṛ*, to hold, which is commonly used in bauddha literature for meanings that range from actions of the body—carry, bear, and wear—to actions of the mind—remember, memorize, and understand. The translation *accept* bridges these two realms of meaning. One steps onto the straight path to enlightenment when one holds Śākyamuni's words as authoritative. Not only does that act of holding require Mālunkyāputta to relinquish his idle curiosity and metaphysical wonder, he must drop every subject the buddha did not see fit to explain. Without the buddha's guidance Mālunkyāputta would only bring himself pain and more pain, death and redeath, caught in a fantasia of the unknown. The buddha makes no direct threat; he does not bully; he imposes no penalties. But as the image of a poisoned arrow makes clear: this is a dangerous world. Safety lies in wisely accepting the buddha at his word. To stray beyond the buddha's literal word is to expose oneself to limitless suffering.

Enlightened beings are wise beings who identify appropriate authority, accept it, adhere to its dictates as they engage in worldly activity, evade danger, and become assured of their own emancipation. The preceding chapter introduced this complex explanation under the rubric of *the scriptural*—integrating rationality, religiosity, interpretability, certitude, and threat of danger. In more schematic terms, the scriptural is known through three criteria: Scriptures are self-authorizing sources of exceptional universal value. Scriptures are coherent and totalizing texts that carry within themselves the key to their true and proper interpretation; such interpretations are often called "literal." And to doubt a scripture's absolute value or to read it improperly results in limitless suffering.

At stake in the scriptural is the location of authority. Does it lie on the open surface or in the hidden depth? Ostensibly, the scriptural requires that one accept surfaces at face-value, for a scriptural surface does not merely re-present reality; the scriptural surface is literal reality itself. Recall Martin Luther's distinction between the "Word of God," which is revealed, and "God Himself," who remains hidden. A genuine Christian (for Martin Luther) accepts the Word and does not strive to know God Himself; a genuine Buddhist (for Todd Martin) accepts the truths of duḥkha and does not strive to know other truths. But as we proceed now toward a review of the structure of hegemony, it is crucial to recognize that the priorities in this relationship are out of balance. The surface is given pragmatic and epistemological priority, since it is an empirical object; the depth is given logical and ontological priority, even though it is unfathomable. Thus Luther's genuine Christian accepts the Word and does not strive to know God Himself, even though that Christian also does believe there is more to God Himself than the Word. Thus the Buddha deflects Māluṅkyāputta's focus to duḥkha, but does not obviate the things about which Māluṅkyāputta speculates, such as eternity and nirvāṇa. This is the scriptural sleight-of-hand: surfaces are able to sustain the burden of reality because, in fact, they do re-present an occult reality. God is a universal who particularizes himself in scripture. But it is the anticipation of universal excess—the imagination of an incalculable surfeit of divinity—which guarantees that those particulars add up to more than their sum total.

In turn, let us recall how Luther coaxes readers to adhere to the surface of the Word, thereby avoiding a dangerous fascination with the transcendental unknown. He promises that a reader who can accept the literal Word can also know himself to have been accepted by the Holy Spirit. "Nobody who has not the Spirit of God sees a jot of what is in the Scriptures"; "those who deny the perfect clarity and plainness of the Scriptures leave us nothing but darkness."[22] To read the Word literally *is* to read it spiritually. This spiritual/literal reading does not speculate, does not express personal desire, does not calculate or connive, but rather betokens acceptance, grace, salvation. So too Calvin: the ability to take scripture at face-value, without wrapping it in enigmas, is possible only for one illumined by the Spirit. Only the elect can accept that god saves some and damns others gratuitously; only the elect can praise this god as perfectly just, when from a human perspective, he appears cruel, random, and malicious. Or to paraphrase The Shorter Discourse, only a member of the elect can obey the command *dhāretha*: accept the elect as "elect" and accept the unelect as "unelect," even when that means that perfectly "innocent" people must suffer infinite torment.

In fact, it is easy to recognize the unelect. If you think, "aha, the politics of the apolitical," when you read the following phrases, then consider yourself damned: the collapse of the literal into the spiritual; the warning that to seek beneath the surface is unnecessary and dangerous; the derogation of speculation, fantasy, and intellectual whimsy.

A look back, stage 2: hegemony

There is another word that describes the process by which one segment of a society proffers its own desires and ideals as exceptional, universal values bearing on the social whole: hegemony. The damned are damned because they clamor about hegemony, a noise heard most strongly earlier, in this book's first chapter.

Recall, that earlier discussion of hegemony drew heavily upon the work of Ernesto Laclau, for whom *the political*, *the social*, and *hegemony* represent three phases in the contingent expression of power.

> *Politics* is "the ensemble of decisions taken in an undecidable terrain . . . in which power is constitutive."
> *The social* is "the sedimented forms of a power that has blurred its own contingency."
> *Hegemony* is a "theory of the decision taken in an undecidable terrain . . . [This category] emerged in order to think about the political character of social relations."[23]

In short, hegemony is not a fixed, irrevocable state of unequal power. Power is always contingent and one investigates hegemony in order to understand the dynamic struggle to manage and erase traces of that contingency. The successful hegemon controls discourse such that his wants are accepted as proper and necessary by his community. The erasure of contingency, the disavowal of partisanship, the representation of truths as absolute and experiences as spontaneous—unsullied by arbitrary wants or selfish calculations—is the foundational social act. There can be no society as such without hegemony.

In this light, scripture is an especially effective instrument of erasure. For a scriptural community will deem itself good, wise, blessed, saved, elect, because its members are able to see a "spirit" that outsiders do not see. For these insiders, the spirit sits there right on the surface. How dull-witted must those others, those outsiders, be if they do not see it!? As literal-spirit, scripture fosters the coalescence of social wholes. Scripture effectively divides a righteous, rational, illumined, spiritual elect, whose members live peaceful lives in accord with the explained/revealed, from an unelect, whose members, to their peril, dabble in the unexplained/hidden.

There is no need to recapitulate the first chapter's explication of hegemony in full. Let me revisit the points that will become useful as the current chapter progresses. Ferdinand de Saussure's structural linguistics provides a groundwork. Saussure's theory, in turn, is best considered against the background of a correspondence-theory of language. We encountered such a theory in page 154, in the *Mūlasarvāstivāda Vinaya's* use of the phrase *yathābhūtaṃ prājānati* to pair the buddha's cognition of mental states with characterizations of those states. Genesis 2:19–20 provides a still better example:

> So out of the ground the Lord God formed every animal of the field and every bird of the air, and brought them to the man to see what he would call them; and whatever the man called every living creature, that was its name. The man gave names to all cattle, and to the birds of the air, and to every animal of the field.

Here, words are meaningful inasmuch as they match discrete elements of objective reality, that objectivity being guaranteed by the creator's transcendence.

Saussure's innovation was to disentangle the subjectivity of words from the objectivity of things. Linguistic value is not a function of a positive congruence between *this* word and *that* thing, but rather is relational within a total rule-based system of sounds and significances. A word's meaning is relative to its place within a system of linguistic difference, in which the relationship between signifieds and signifiers is arbitrary and conventional. Indeed, it is crucial to remember that Saussure does also limit contingency. Social convention provides an external basis for judging linguistic usage.

Saussure's theory is complex, and one might wonder whether we need it for the language of everyday stuff, beasts and birds. When it comes to abstract entities and foci for ideological contention, however, wonderment ceases. Consider Todd Martin and Rupert Gethin. Martin is fully certain: there are no gods in Buddhism. Yet every account of Śākyamuni's life includes tales of gods; every stratum of the archaeological record includes images of gods; and the people of every Buddhist land worship gods. This discrepancy is easily explained when we recognize that Martin is working with a correspondence-theory of language. For him, "Buddhism" has only one legitimate referent: what the buddha taught. To apply this word to any other subject matter is just plain wrong. Appeal to a correspondence-theory allows Martin to reject conventional usage, for he does not use the word "Buddhism" to communicate, but to indicate reality. By contrast, Rupert Gethin demonstrates Saussure's salubrity when he writes, "As is fashionable to point out these days, 'Buddhism' is something of an intellectual abstraction: in reality there is not one Buddhism but many Buddhisms."[24] By loosening the connection between linguistic meaning and worldly facticity, Saussure provides a ground-work for Gethin's articulated integration of the abstraction, *Buddhism*, with the concrete reality of diverse *Buddhisms*. Some Buddhisms are theistic, others are atheistic; Buddhism is thus both and neither.

Structural linguistics loosens the connection between wordly meanings and worldly objects. Poststructural discourse analysis severs it. In this latter analytic mode, Buddhism is not an intellectual object that bears an abstract, albeit substantive, correspondence to some *thing* in the world, mediated through diverse

Buddhisms. Buddhism, rather, is fully a discursive object in its own right. There is no need to posit a set of Buddhisms as objective antecedents to the abstraction, Buddhism. Both words, "Buddhism" and "Buddhisms," have their own specific values, determined by their differential locations within a system of verbal and intellectual practices. So, if Saussurian structuralism sabotages Todd Martin's attempt to affix "Buddhism" to the objective reality of the buddha's teachings, poststructural analysis sabotages Gethin's attempt to affix reality to the multiplicity of "Buddhisms." That is, we would not even recognize the existence of historically particular Buddhisms were we not already in possession of the translocal, transtemporal abstraction, Buddhism.

To return now to the matter of hegemony: Poststructural linguistic analysis (i.e., deconstruction) and hegemony are complementary, "two sides of the same operation."[25] Indeed, I find Ernesto Laclau useful precisely for his application of this poststructural turn to the formation of social order. Deconstruction addresses the process by which discursive objects come to be accepted as extra-discursive objects. We might even say that deconstruction destroys scripture, for it "*reactivates* the moment of decision that underlies any *sedimented* set of social relations."[26] The analysis of hegemony then addresses the broad consequences of that "moment of decision" within the human world. In our terms, deconstruction problematizes "Buddhism" and "enlightenment," allowing the study of hegemony then to consider how *Buddhism* and *enlightenment* function to create a "Buddhist" identity at both the personal and collective levels.

Laclau writes, "The hegemony of a *particular* social sector depends for its success on presenting its own aims as those realizing the *universal* aims of the community."[27] This sounds sinister, so remember, hegemonic struggle is structural to signifying systems. There is no society without hegemonic articulations, just as there is no communication without shared linguistic conventions, for the very concept of "system" presupposes a closed totality. Structurally, hegemony requires an "exclusionary limit." On one side, the system is fully present; on the other, fully absent. Inside, everything is equivalent to everything else. The "empty signifier" lends its name to this shared identity and is valued as a "simple principle of positivity—pure being."[28] From an insider's perspective, *apolitical* characterizes the equivalential relationship within the system, for it seems to be a relationship in which selfish power has no role. One can trust that the command, *dhāretha*, is issued only for benevolent reasons. Within this same phenomenology, *politics* is what transpires beyond the exclusionary limit. Out there, everybody and everything is not equivalent. Differences of power, of belief, of identity breed fear, anger, want, and strife. Indeed, when difference is itself perceived as a kind of equivalence, then the far side of the limit becomes the locus of pure negativity, the agent of calamity, the genius of damnation, Māra. If the command *dhāretha* comes from out there, one will not follow it, for one does not trust its intent. The crucial point is that the determination of what counts as apolitical and benevolent, distinguished from what counts as political and treacherous, is itself always a political determination.

One speaks of hegemony as a matter of *struggle* since, being propagated through contingent articulations of power, hegemony is never total or complete. The creation of a social identity at any scale—person, community, civilization— separates an "us" from a "them." That boundary, in turn, is contingent, imperfectly drawn, mutable, and always a potential source of contention. For instance, one might define a *Buddhist*, stipulatively, as someone for whom a buddha is an ultimate authority; a Buddhist trusts that, because a buddha is perfectly enlightened, his command *dhāretha* must always lead to beneficial results. Insofar as one is a Buddhist, one's abstract ideals, concrete cosmologies, economic pursuits, clothing and bodily comportment, even diet, can be traced back to one's trust in enlightenment. In this instance, so-called Buddhists might legitimately differ over the details of doctrine, diet, and so on, as long as they concur on this one point: there is a buddha who realized unexcelled and complete *bodhi*. Of course, this unanimity vis-à-vis *bodhi* also necessarily excludes everybody who disagrees from membership in the Buddhists' consensual society. That exclusion is an irreducible ground of social antagonism. Even if there really are Buddhists as I describe, even if there really is synarchy inside their social unit, even if *internally* all antagonisms are allayed, there is no logical solution to the possibility of *external* antagonism, since, by definition, "they" are not members of "our" society. "They" have no necessary stake in "our" peace. Closure—no matter whether it establishes personhood or peoplehood—is the ground—the very bedrock—of the political: it is the condition of possibility for identity and it is the condition for the impossibility of peace.

A look back, stage 3: Buddhism as a discursive object

Todd Martin condemns *The Foundations of Buddhism*. By his count there is not even one factually correct statement about Buddhism in its first twenty pages. After this review of hegemony, Martin's gambit is clear. Martin seeks to deny the implications of the arbitrary, radically historical constitution of the Saussurian sign, taking "Buddhism" as his empty signifier. Martin would fill this signifier's void with the same prudence taught to Māluṅkyāputta. Martin fails, in part, because the word "Buddhism" cannot be adequately emptied. As an English word, "Buddhism" is a nineteenth-century discursive formation that just cannot be disentangled from its modernity.

The first chapter explored that modernity in some detail by reference to Philip Almond's *The British Discovery of Buddhism*. Recall, Almond argues that neither Asians nor Europeans possessed a conceptual category equivalent to Buddhism before the nineteenth century. Buddhism did not exist: not even as an unnamed object "floating in some aethereal Oriental limbo expecting its objective embodiment."[29] That is to say, in the seventeenth and eighteenth centuries, Asians themselves did not exhibit a specific sense of ideological solidarity across nations, such that a so-called Buddhist populace in Thailand would have actively identified the peoples of Tibet, or China, or Japan, as members of their same community. In fact, Almond adduces only a single citation to the contrary, from 1795, in which one Michael Symes reports the "Birmans assert with confidence that the Chinese are Boodhists."[30] Having neither an expectation that natural religiosity is a universal human constant, nor a conception of religion in which god holds first place, Asia's "Buddhists" did not perhaps realize that they must share a corporate identity, determined by their common interest in the buddha. They were not aware that their mutual differences, historical and cultural, differences of worship and dogma and social organization and mores, were subject to reduction, leaving as a remainder what seemed, to Westerners, to be a shared reverence for a single deity. They did not know they were all Buddhists.

If the simple maxim of discourse analysis reads, the word supports the thing, then any dullard will realize that to change a thing he must first change its name. Thus have I attempted to circumvent Buddhism's discursivity, to span a 1,500-year gap, by identifying Ajanta as *Śākya* or *bauddha* when discussing it in a fifth-century CE context, and reserving *Buddhist* for references to the site and other phenomena as manifest (materially or discursively) in the modern age. A majority of Ajanta's inscriptions identify individual patrons as a Śākya-bhikṣu or Śākya-upāsaka; it is a positive fact that *Śākya* was the dominant index of social identity at the site in the fifth century. The designation *bauddha* is attested, not at Ajanta, but in ancient textual sources, as an outsider's name for followers of the buddha. I assert as positive truth: In the fifth century, Ajanta was locale dominated by self-identified Śākyas, and a place at which the people revered buddhas.

This truth creates a new set of problems, of course, for discourse analysis is not just newfangled nominalism. It does not presuppose a correspondence-theory of linguistic value, but a theory derived from Saussure in which linguistic value is an emergent property of arbitrary conventions fluxing through time and power. No objective middle ground exists for translating the sounds we use, or the concepts associated with those sounds, from one linguistic system to another. The cognitive map of a twenty-first-century English speaker simply cannot be isomorphic with that of a fifth-century speaker of Sanskrit; and the precise quantity of lost meaning is incalculable. This is all well known. At one level, it makes the denial of Ajanta's Buddhism a tempest in a teacup, a portentous reiteration of the banal: Sanskrit and English are different languages.

Yet, even if one grants that bauddha and Buddhist have divergent meanings within their native linguistic structures, why not treat them as two names for a single phenomenon? Let me rephrase this questions in terms of two metaphors, corresponding to two approaches to the issue. First, is there no way for a historian to determine the major constellation of practices and doctrines they share in common by blacking out the few odd stars at which they diverge? Second, is there no analytic value in the fact that the two belong on the same family tree, linked through a common ancestor, the enlightened buddha? Let me take up each possibility in turn.

As for the first, a taxonomic tool for stipulating identity-in-difference is ready at hand (Table 5.2). In 1975, Rodney Needham introduced polythetic classification

Table 5.2 Individuals 1, 2, 3, 4 form a polythetic group, while 5 and 6 are monothetic. After Rodney Needham's "Polythetic Classification"

	Individuals					
	1	*2*	*3*	*4*	*5*	*6*
Taxa	α β γ ρ Ω	γ ρ Ω λ	α β ρ Δ π	α β γ Δ π	F G H I	F G H I

into the lexicon of the social sciences and humanities, borrowing this technique from the natural sciences, where taxonomy has been a matter of theoretical interest since Aristotle.[31] Perhaps the best way to describe polythetic classification is by contrasting it with the more obvious monothetic classification. In the latter, all members of a class share one unique taxon (or set of taxa) as a necessary and sufficient condition for class membership. A rigid logic divides monothetic groups. Polythetic classification, by contrast, is more robust since this method organizes taxonomic classes around a gestalt of features. "No single feature is either essential to group membership or is sufficient to make an organism a member of the group."[32] The analyst himself—or rather, the analyst as member of a profession and institution, anticipating a specific outcome, and barraged by an endless stream of niggling distractions—names the classes (e.g., Buddhism; Hinduism) and stipulates the taxa (e.g., accepts the past existence of an enlightened buddha; shaves head; asks reasonable questions after skin is pierced by poisoned arrow). The analyst weighs the relative value of each taxon for indexing class membership; and he assigns the statistical measure of affinity required for class membership. Moreover, because this method entails the logical possibility that characteristics shared by members of taxonomic class may be fewer in absolute number than characteristics not shared, the analyst himself artfully chooses the exact harmonic at which the crisp note of identity sings through a potentially infinite static of difference.

Indeed it should be easy to articulate a matrix of polythetic taxa to classify the fifth-century bauddha and twenty-first-century Buddhist as belonging to the same class. A polythetic approach would unify the bauddha and the Buddhist through their mutual possession of taxa α, β, γ, ρ, while acknowledging that the fifth-century bauddha's taxa Δ and Π are not shared by the modern Western Buddhist, who is uniquely possessed of Ω and λ. As a hermeneutic strategy, polythetic classification bridges the gap of categorical and intellectual difference opened up by Saussurian linguistics. It is a means for asserting identity through the management of difference.

This *management* matters, the fact that anyone can articulate a scheme to rationalize his desires through the management of difference. Remember Jean Calvin—a brilliant man—taught that it is reasonable, indeed necessary, to read the bible as a literal document. The book means just what it says! Somebody who scoffs at this literalism and reads the bible as an allegorical or mystical document is deranged by god. Certainly, no secular historian of Christianity asks himself whether god *truly* prefers one kind of reading or another. The question is non-sense. A historian, rather, will reduce Calvin's god to a logical or psychological or sociological or martial or economic function, asking: What does Calvin *do* with taxa when he differentiates sociological units, the elect from the unelect, by claiming that god has a definite hermeneutic agenda? Likewise, any intelligent student could—as a final exam question, for instance—generate a list of words, texts, doctrines, and rituals shared in common between a fifth-century bauddha and a twenty-first-century Buddhist. But we would not then ask: Are the two *truly* the same, or *truly* different? We would inquire, first, into the student's taxa of choice. What presuppositions and priorities did the student bring to bear on his choice of taxa? How does the student manage the differences? This leads into a second question: Why would a professor ask his students to create a taxonomic system within which commonalities between groups are given discursive priority over differences? By definition, a taxonomic system is a system that emphasizes similarity by hierarchizing difference. Why does the teacher want "Buddhism" to belong to a taxonomic system at all? What does this tell us about the politics of knowledge in his classroom? And third we wonder about broad context. How do identities become quasi-transcendental objects, treated as if they express them-selves *in* history, rather than being emergent products *of* history? These questions are not meant to illuminate reality, theological or historical. They illumine human choices, institutions, hegemony.

The redescription of Buddhism as a discursive object problematizes the utility of Buddhism within the writing of positive history. Polythetic classification represents one method for managing that problem. There is no good reason that scholars should not identify Ajanta's Śākyas and today's Buddhists as members of a shared class. Yet there is also every good reason for them to recognize the artifice involved, and to bear in mind the contingencies of their practice, driven, not by past facts, but by present needs. To study Buddhism is the scholar's right because it is his responsibility.

Polythetic classification provides a synchronic approach to the identity-in-difference between Ajanta's Śākyas and today's Buddhists. New problems and possibilities arise when we inquire into the groups' diachronic relationship as two descendants from a common ancestor, and thus as "blood-kin" in the same family. Donald Lopez' introduction to his anthology of modern Buddhist writings, *A Modern Buddhist Bible*, helps us to think through this case. Lopez, here, is concluding his answer to the question, "What is this form of Buddhism, and in what sense is it modern?"

> Like all religions, Buddhism has evolved over the centuries.... The Buddhism encountered today, both in Asia and the West, is very much the product of this historical evolution. The starting point of that evolution would seem to be with the founder of Buddhism, the Buddha himself.... Yet it is difficult to describe his original teachings, for none of the words traditionally attributed to the Buddha were written down until some four centuries after his death. Over the centuries Buddhists have sought to represent his original teachings and true intentions in an effort to secure the acceptance of a wide variety of developments in Buddhist thought and practice. During the past two centuries, Buddhist thinkers from across Asia and the West began to describe a Buddhism that transcends the concerns of locale and sect. This version of Buddhism...I refer to as modern Buddhism.... [33]

What reader would pause over these sentences? Who would think twice about Lopez' words of choice, so pat and so true, representing Buddhism as a typical religion that began during the life of its remarkable founder. Lopez' statement is nuanced. Carefully, he does not exaggerate the facts and avoids any reference to a transcendental essence that unifies Buddhism's evolving forms. By using the subjunctive, "would seem to be," and noting that teachings attributed to the buddha post-date his death by several centuries, Lopez emphasizes the religion's dynamic historicity. But notice, the sentence beginning "Over the centuries" uses the word "Buddhist" twice: once for people, once for cultural phenomena. Why such inelegant prose from a usually excellent craftsman? The odd repetition suggests that Buddhist thoughts and Buddhist practices exist independently of, even prior to, Buddhist people. Buddhists look to the buddha to authorize thoughts and practices that are, in some way, already "Buddhist." The condition of possibility for Buddhism to have an integral existence as an evolving religion is that Buddhists act as if their thoughts and practices originate with a *specifically Buddhist* buddha.

Recall Laclau's words about the complementarity of deconstruction and hegemony cited in the previous section: "The role of deconstruction is...to *reactivate* the moment of decision that underlies any *sedimented* set of social relations."[34] The image of disturbing sediments well describes the effects of attending to Buddhism as a discursive object. It is a waste of time to draw family trees until after one considers the history within which the thing, Buddhism, is a religion like all other religions; and until after one determines whether this evolutionary metaphor has systematic explanatory value. What *makes* the buddha the ancestral source of all evolved Buddhisms? Is it Śākyamuni's own natural property, that is, his enlightenment? Is this his genetic patrimony? Or is it, as

Lopez hints, the fact that the figure of "the enlightened buddha" has political power within sectarian discourse? In other words, is Lopez suggesting a new monothetic taxonomy whereby Buddhists themselves solve the problem of diachrony for scholars? Namely, a local sect is properly Buddhist—no matter when it existed, or where—if it identifies Śākyamuni Buddha as a spiritual ancestor, and if, based upon that family relationship, it lays ideological claim to the buddha's original teachings and true intentions? If this is the case, however, perhaps we should also reconsider the phenomenon Lopez calls modern Buddhism. Is this not just one more local sect (granted, a very diffuse locality) that has attained nearly absolute hegemony over the figure of the enlightened buddha within the Western academy?

Indeed, before one concludes that Buddhism began with the buddha and evolves like all religions, one must inquire about Śākyamuni Buddha's value in Brahmanical discourse. Beginning in the fifth-century, brahmin texts presented their own gods, usually Viṣṇu, as voicing the buddha's words. Occasionally these bauddha doctrines are treated as weapons in the war between gods and demons; bauddha sūtras are divine misinformation, propaganda hurled against the enemy, as effective as any sword or arrow.[35] By following the buddha, demons rejected the real truth, hastening their own doom. Occasionally bauddha doctrines are treated as seminal *Hindu* articulations of non-violence and universal compassion. Thus the twelfth-century *Gītagovinda* praises Kṛṣṇa for taking the form of the buddha in order to end the ritual slaughter of animals.[36] Occasionally modern Hindus name the buddha as a glorious figure in their own past. Two examples should suffice. In the preface to a collection of essays celebrating the 2500th anniversary of Śākyamuni's nirvāṇa, Sarvepalli Radhakrishnan, then the President of India, wrote: "The Buddha did not feel that he was announcing a new religion. He was born, grew up, and died a Hindu. He was restating with a new emphasis the ancient ideals of the Indo-Aryan civilization."[37] This point is made with even greater verve in a 1925 tract, *Buddha-Mimansa*, which concludes that "the original Religion of the Buddha was . . . part and parcel of the Hindu system based upon the World-old Religion (Sanatana Dharma) of the Vedas."[38] When the buddha's religion is a subspecies of the Hindu, and Śākyamuni is a teacher of Vedic truth (if not Vedic sacrifice), then his words bespeak the historical non-difference, the identity, between "Buddhism" and "Hinduism" so-called, *not* the independent evolution of Buddhism itself.

A premature peroration

Here is the heart of the matter. As scholars, it is hardly our role to be partisans for one faction, or the other, as they struggle to control a shared discourse and, with it, hegemony over a shared social order. When it comes to a place like Ajanta, unoccupied for more than one millennium, this much is certain: no modern Buddhist possesses a prior right to delimit how modern scholars represent its social and intellectual life; no scholar is under any logical obligation to consider modern Buddhist sensibilities when he represents Ajanta. The same holds true vis-à-vis contemporary Hindus. A scholar who expects that today's Buddhists appreciate or understand Ajanta better than he does *because they are Buddhists* treats Buddhism as a coherent and integral entity: an entity whose institutions were founded by Śākyamuni Buddha, and whose doctrines have evolved in time without losing their abstract core. A scholar who expects that today's Buddhists appreciate or understand Ajanta better than he does himself *because they are Buddhists* treats enlightenment as something more than a fact of discourse—as if some people really might become fully enlightened buddhas. For such a scholar, enlightenment plays a systemic role parallel to the role of "God Himself" in Luther's theology. God Himself is the logical ground of Luther's system; this hidden entity is an object for faith, not knowledge. Likewise, no scholar of any repute would claim to have direct access to pure expressions of the enlightened buddha's mind, the foundation of Buddhism itself. Yet, this unknown, unknowable Buddhism is the logical ground for any representation of Buddhist sectarianism that systematically *denies* that sects for whom Śākyamuni is a Hindu god and a teacher of Vedic truths have *as legitimate* a claim on the buddha as those sects for whom he is the foremost critic of Vedic revelation.

Without enlightenment—the "word to which [Buddhist] 'things' themselves refer to recognize themselves in their unity"[39]—it is impossible to identify Ajanta as one Buddhist place in a panoply of Buddhist places. Ajanta *was* a Śākya place, whatever that might mean. The assertion that "Śākya" is just another name for "Buddhist," and thus that Ajanta *is now* Buddhist, makes sense only within a modern phenomenology that treats Buddhist enlightenment as a particular expression of rational, natural religiosity. As scholars, it is not necessarily our job to be collaborationists in the universalization of religion.

In the fifth century CE, Śākya Ajanta was embellished with nāga shrines and yakṣa shrines; with paintings of Indra and Brahmā and other gods walking the earth; with stone panels in which Avalokiteśvara rescues distressed petitioners from thieves, mad elephants, and demons; with super-sized stone buddhas. Whether or not the very idea of god or gods goes against everything the buddha ever taught, gods existed at Ajanta in the past and they continue to live at Ajanta to this day.[40] It matters how we identify Ajanta. Ajanta *was* a Śākya place. To mark the difference between this Śākya Ajanta and a Buddhist Ajanta, we would need to know more about Buddhism as an artifact of modernity. So far, our review of scripturality, hegemony, and discursivity has transformed Todd Martin's assertion, "There are no gods in Buddhism," from an apophatic definition of Buddhism into a cataphatic assertion of hegemony. However, this review also demonstrated that the term *Buddhism* itself is too well-marked by modernity to be an effective instrument of differentiation. The claim that Ajanta's Śākyas were not Buddhists *because* they worshiped gods divests the word "Buddhist" of its conventional significance; the claim that Śākyas were Buddhists *despite* their worship of gods makes a fool of Todd Martin. To move beyond this dilemma we need more sophisticated interlocutors.

Vipassana meditation and the promise of global enlightenment

According to Donald Lopez,

> During the past two centuries, Buddhist thinkers from across Asia and the West began to describe a Buddhism that transcends the concerns of locale and sect. This version of Buddhism, what I refer to as modern Buddhism, although hardly monolithic, has a number of characteristics...that have been widely accepted around the world.[41]

We might draw two conclusions from this. First, if only two centuries have transpired since thinkers began to push beyond the boundaries of locale and sect, then all non-sectarian Buddhism is modern. Either Buddhism did not exist before the nineteenth century, or if it did exist, it never overcame sectarian parochialism. Second, all contemporary appropriations of Śākyamuni Buddha are not modern; even in this day and age there are staunchly sectarian Buddhists. "Contemporary Buddhism" and "modern Buddhism" are not synonymous phrases. To think through the tension between contemporaneity and modernity, the next two sections will consider two modern Buddhist thinkers. How does these modern Buddhists' disarticulation of gods and enlightenment (which they articulate, in part, by critiquing contemporary "sectarian" Buddhists) ground a modern vision of a universal society of free and equal citizens in which power and partisanship play no role?

Philip Almond was not the first scholar to recognize that Buddhism balances on a rickety base. Over a century ago, T.W. Rhys Davids already noted that "the people we now call Buddhists...did not call themselves so"; and, "what we call Buddhism...[is] what the founder of that religion called the Dharma."[42] The two authors whom I will focus on below join Rhys Davids in presenting the word "Buddhism" as an anachronism; both eschew (albeit weakly) personal identification as a Buddhist; both proffer *dharma* (Pāli *dhamma*) as *the* appropriate name for their ideals, values, practices, and goals. The first, Satya Narayan Goenka, is a master of vipassana meditation. An active teacher and organizer since the 1960s, Goenka has established more than fifty Vipassana Meditation Centers throughout Asia, Europe, North America, and Australia. The second writer is Richard Hayes, currently a member of the Philosophy Department at the University of New Mexico. Hayes' website lists his principal research interests as, "The history of Indian Buddhist scholasticism in the context of Indian philosophy; Buddhist logic and epistemology; history of metaphysics in India; Buddhist psychology and Jungian analytic psychology; Sanskrit grammar and Indian philosophies of language."[43] But Hayes is also an important voice outside academia, as author of *Land of No Buddha*, a volume of sermons and reflections on Buddhism in contemporary North America.

At sunrise on October 26, 1997, Satya Narayan Goenka performed the groundbreaking ceremony for the Grand Vipassana Pagoda.[44] Currently under construction in north-east Mumbai, this pagoda will be the largest domed-structure in the world, 85 meters wide at the base and 96 meters high. To mark the occasion, Goenka issued a dedicatory plaque, from which we learn that Goenka, his wife, and "their vast global Dhamma family" hoped that the Grand Pagoda would "spread the munificent wisdom of Vipassana as truly expounded by the Buddha Gotama for the benefit, happiness and liberation of many." For outsiders, these words are a quick introduction to the ideals of Goenka's global vipassana movement. But for those in the know, Goenka's words are more resonant still, since they echo a stock passage repeated throughout the Pāli canon, which tells of the buddha sending his monks forth into the world to spread the dharma for the benefit, happiness, and liberation of the entire world.

Two weeks before the dedication ceremony, Goenka published a short article entitled, "Why the Grand Vipassana Pagoda?," in his organization's newsletter.[45] The forceful clarity of Goenka's words testifies to his enthusiasm for this project. Someone who accepts Goenka's authority cannot put down this article without believing that the Grand Pagoda is an excellent idea indeed!

This article reveals Goenka to have been concerned that his dharma-children might not recognize the pagoda's exceptional, universal value. Lacking proper guidance, a novice might easily mistake this enormous golden monument for a shrine, a temple, or some other such place at which the votaries of sectarian religion worship their god. Nothing could be further from reality for Goenka, since Śākyamuni "was neither a god nor an incarnation of any god nor a prophet of any god....He was not a mythological being but a completely historical person." As a figment of history, Śākyamuni's genius lay in his having discovered the "natural laws" of karma, including the law that "meaningless rituals" do not produce favorable results. How terrible the irony, if the Grand Vipassana Pagoda were itself to foster credulous and wayward ritualism. How terrible the irony, if the buddha, who "re-established the ancient true eternal Dhamma in its pristine purity," became an object of prayerful reverence as the mere founder of a religious sect. Goenka calls the pagoda a "bright light-house" that "will again bring to light the ancient eternal universal tradition of Dhamma for the benefit of the world." His *apologia*, "Why the Grand Vipassana Pagoda?," should guarantee that no member of the vast global dharma family will obscure the pagoda's light behind the nescience of organized religion.

Even in the world of marketing, it is an immutable law that a successful company must "own a word" in order to burn its way into the consumers' mind.[46] When one's good is not a manufactured commodity but something that is ancient, true, eternal, universal, and pure, not just any word will do. Goenka's article begins:

> The Buddha did not teach Buddhism. During his lifetime, he did not convert a single person to Buddhism. One will be surprised to hear this and will not want to believe it, because we have been hearing, speaking, reading and writing contrary to this fact for such a long time. But the

historical truth is that the Buddha neither taught Buddhism nor made any person a Buddhist. The Buddha taught Dhamma and made people righteous.... Not only during the lifetime of the Buddha but even in the next few centuries, we do not come across words like "Buddhist" or "Buddhism" anywhere.

These assertions locate Goenka in the discursive middle ground between Philip Almond and Todd Martin. Goenka agrees with Almond: it is anachronistic to treat Buddhism as an ancient phenomenon. Indeed, thanks to CD-ROM technology, Goenka's people scanned "the entire teaching of the Buddha as well as the vast literature of the related commentaries, sub-commentaries, and sub-sub-commentaries"—7,448,248 words—to establish as fact that "the word 'Buddhist' has not been used with regard to his teachings or his followers." Still, this agreement is superficial, since Almond and Goenka hold opposite stakes in the anachronism. Almond disavows any interest in the question "of how Buddhism '*really*' was."[47] For Almond, Buddhism as a past *realia* is an effect of modern discourse; even its pastness is a contemporary effect, endowing Buddhism with an appearance of use-value for a cultural economy in which the exotic past commands a premium charge. For Goenka, by contrast, anachronism is problematic, not because it mystifies a modern discursive formation as an ancient entity, but because, by misidentifying the true nature of Buddhism's ancient existence, it endangers humanity's future.

Indeed, Goenka's shift from Buddhism to dharma betokens his fundamental agreement with Todd Martin. Both want to speak a language of positive fact as their only language. From Goenka we learn, the "universal modern technology" of the CD-ROM offers proof-positive that the buddha did not teach Buddhism. Likewise, exhibition galleries at the Grand Pagoda will remove misconceptions about the man, Gotama himself. Space is limited. Not every incident in Gotama's life can be displayed. So Goenka has one firm criterion for what to include: "whatever is exhibited will prove that the Buddha did not establish any religious sect. He never had any intention of converting anyone and confining them within the bounds of an organised religious sect." Moreover, by bringing "the true nature of the historical superhuman Buddha" to light, these galleries will replace "blind belief in divine miracles" with a new respect for "human effort and valour." Śākyamuni's "true nature" as a "historical superhuman" must be represented with precision. This is where Goenka and Martin part ways. To claim there are no gods in Buddhism is imprecise: there are no gods in dharma.

Or rather, Buddhism is not just an imprecise rendering of Sanskrit dharma or Pāli dhamma. For Goenka, the success of these words, Buddhism and Buddhist, is a direct sign that the buddha's followers "forgot the essence of the true teaching." Buddhism does not just mislabel dharma, fundamentally it misleads *from* dharma. Coined in parallel with terms like Protestantism and Judaism, the word Buddhism bespeaks an institution that evolved in history, and that only a select few have ever encountered. Buddhism represents the social displacement of Śākyamuni Buddha's insight, not the enlightened truth itself. Thus, whereas dharma is universal, for everyone, Buddhism is "limited to those people who called themselves 'Buddhists.' " And whereas dharma has a "universally beneficial nature" that contravenes "all the artificial barriers of caste, race, class and religion," Buddhism is "confined by the narrow bounds of an organised religion" and finds itself "in the shallow row of the different religions of the world." Buddhism demeans dharma.

In terms of the formal structure of hegemony, dharma is Goenka's empty signifier, which he uses to exclude Buddhism-as-religion, -as-sectarian, -as-limited, -as-political from the positivity of "eternal Dhamma in its pristine purity." Indeed, Goenka's answer to "Why the Grand Vipassana Pagoda?" articulates a network of associations within which the pagoda as a source of dharma also becomes a source for enlightenment, universal beneficence, universal compassion, universal love, accurate information about the life and accomplishments of Śākyamuni Buddha, personal satisfaction for pilgrims, spiritual merit, glory for the city of Mumbai, civic peace, and even strengthened relations between the peoples of India and Myanmar.

Finally, at the crux of this system of inclusions and exclusions is the technique of vipassana meditation, which Goenka sometimes calls "universal" and sometimes "beneficial." Universal = beneficial is hegemony's elemental equation. The practice of vipassana is a necessary (though not sufficient) condition for the buddha's enlightenment to dharma and liberation from saṃsāra. The practice of vipassana is a necessary condition for an enlightened society, a dharmic society, in which differences of caste, race, class, and religion have no power to divide. However, in Goenka's historical account, the people of India forgot this practice. And "when the technique of Vipassana was lost, the original teaching of the Buddha was lost." And "because of the loss of Vipassana, most people forgot the universal and eternal importance of the Buddha's teaching pertaining to all countries." The loss of vipassana, in sum, was the proximate cause for the degeneration from the buddha's own community, an egalitarian brotherhood organized around dharma, to what we see today: limited sectarian Buddhisms. Thus, vipassana is the agent of Goenka's apocalypse.

Fortunately because a few wise people in the neighbouring country of Myanmar preserved this universal technique of Vipassana in its pure form for centuries, from generation to generation, it has arisen again. It has returned to India. It has arisen again in the world. In the past nearly three decades through its practice, it has been completely proved that the original teaching of the Buddha is not meant to be confined within the bounds of a religion. It is universal. People of all religions, races, castes and communities of the world can take advantage of this beneficial technique, they are already benefiting from it. One can believe that by the spread of Vipassana, the strife, aversion and ill-will between different religions and communities will end and mutual love and affection will be produced in all people in this country and in the world.

Here Todd Martin's certainty that "the very idea of a God or Gods goes against everything the Buddha ever taught," gives way to S.N. Goenka's certainty that vipassana meditation as practiced between the years of 1967 and 1997 *completely proves* a fact about ancient history: twenty-five hundred years ago Śākyamuni Buddha did not intend to become Buddhism's founder, or even a specifically religious teacher.

Dharma collapses time: Goenka knows what the buddha taught and what the buddha intended. Thus too dharma erases temporal difference in its organization of social identity: fifth-century Śākyas and modern Buddhists are non-different insofar as they pursue dharma and practice vipassana. Insofar as members of these groups concern themselves with other matters they are hardly closer to eternal universal truth than Hindus or Christians, no matter what they call themselves. Of course, there is also little doubt that Hindus or Christians who wish to pursue universal truth through vipassana will, as an intermediate step in their journey at least, become Buddhists. After all, the Grand Vipassana Pagoda is located on Buddha Island off the Mumbai coast.

Dharmawise, karmafoolish

Let us now turn to Richard Hayes' *Land of No Buddha*, a book whose apologetic largely coincides with that of Goenka. Goenka looks back to the historical buddha as a source of transcendental value, and Hayes too uses phrases like "the original teachings and intentions of Buddhism" and "the original Sangha" as metaphors for absolute good.[48] But where Goenka would revivify Śākyamuni's ancient order in its pristine purity, Hayes describes his vision of how Buddhism ought to be in North America using words drawn from the social and intellectual history of the West. In other words, Goenka seems unaware that his Buddhist apocalypse is a distinctly modern vision, framed in dialectical opposition to a post-Enlightenment figment, *Buddhism*. I doubt that Goenka even cracked a smile at his own mischievous imagery, when he described the Grand Pagoda as herald to a "second coming." Hayes, by contrast, plays on ironies. He acknowledges the historicity of his own "Protestant values and attitudes," even as he argues for his model of religious authority *as if* it truly is timeless.[49] Likewise, where Goenka never wavers in his vision for the Grand Pagoda, Hayes presents himself as being of two minds about his book. The essays gathered as *Land of No Buddha* were written in the 1980s. A prefatory note explains that Hayes' views had changed, in some cases substantially, by 1998 when the collection was published. Although Hayes regretted his former strident tone and harsh polemic, friends persuaded him to publish *Land of No Buddha* anyway, to "chronicle" his growth as a Buddhist.[50] In light of these confessions, the book's title is a curious thing, for it is a cross-linguistic pun naming the book after Hayes himself. *No Buddha* translates a Korean word, *Mubul*, the Buddhist name that Hayes accepted from a Zen master.[51] The title displays Hayes' typical wit: Richard Hayes identifies the land of no buddha as his own eponymous territory, even as he disavows what he says there.

In matters of tone, style, and metaphor, Hayes and Goenka could not be more different. Yet an important parallel is clear: both take the critique of institutional Buddhism as a starting point for their presentations of *dharma* as a marker for Śākyamuni Buddha's true intentions—intentions about truth and how to spread truth.

> A couple of years ago someone asked me what I thought was missing in North American Buddhism, and without hesitation I found myself blurting out, "What is missing? Why, the Buddhism itself!" The word "Buddhism," of course, is mostly the invention of scholars of comparative religion, and does not really have very much meaning at all except as a convenient label. What I really meant in giving my answer is that the Dharma is missing, or at least is not yet here in its fullness.[52]

Hayes concurs with many of Goenka's views: the buddha was a rationalist and empiricist; the buddha was not a god or god's prophet; the buddha did not intend to found a religious sect but to teach dharma, that is, reality as it is; the buddha is best followed, not through worship, but through emulation; rituals are meaningless and have little to do with dharma; the dharma can be a source of benefit, happiness, and liberation for the entire world; the language of positive fact is the only language in which to represent the reality of dharma. Still, there are also two points (or doubtless more) at which they diverge. The first, really, is more a matter of emphasis. Hayes is a sometimes practitioner of vipassana, and a sometimes practitioner of zazen. In Hayes' text meditation is important, but he is not the partisan of one technique.

The second divergence goes to the nature and content of dharma as an index of reality. Goenka echoes Sanskrit and Pāli narratives of the buddha's enlightenment when he describes Śākyamuni as having "discovered and taught the operation of the natural laws of kamma (action) and the corresponding consequences of kamma as a result of his direct experience."[53] As we know, the *Mūlasarvāstivāda Vinaya* tells of the bodhisattva looking over his own and others' past lives, from which he discerns a pattern of actions and results, leading, ultimately, to his realization of the noble truths of suffering, its cause, and its cessation. And while the phrase "natural law" has no direct equivalent in classical Sanskrit or Pāli, it has become a common trope among Buddhist modernizers, since it coordinates Śākyamuni's enlightenment with the naturalistic positivism of the Enlightenment. Hayes, by contrast, not only does not represent karma as a law of nature, his book actively condemns karma as an "obstructive doctrine" that "serves more to impede Westerners than to help them acquire wisdom and become less self-centered."[54] A too-literal understanding of karma—and how can a natural law be anything but literal—contravenes the buddha-dharma, for it "dulls the mind and impairs the faculty of reason" by substituting myth in the place of reality as it is.

This is a curious position, given that academic histories of Buddhism always include karma in their glossaries of basic Buddhist terms. In fact, an author's note from the 1990s indicates that Hayes changed his mind, and regretted his earlier complete repudiation of karma. Still, Hayes' stridency is consistent with *Land of No Buddha's* other attempts to "fill" dharma with the dominant intellectual values of the Enlightenment. Hayes does not give *dharma* a single English equivalent, be it law, truth, Buddhist doctrine, religion, or wisdom. He is a Sanskritist, fluent in the problems of linguistic difference. To make dharma a living value for the West, Hayes needs to transubstantiate it: from exotic Sanskrit loan-word into Anglo-Buddhist scriptural seme. In the Land of No Buddha dharma is a self-authorizing source of exceptional universal value; dharma is a term that provides the key to its own true and proper interpretation; one harms oneself by rejecting true dharma or by misconstruing its truth. Let us see how.

In a sense, Goenka and Hayes give their audiences different Enlightenments. When Goenka calls karma a natural law, he speaks the Enlightened language of Newton and Hume; it is a law induced from empirical observation of regular occurrences in nature. But Goenka has forgotten Kant. The empirical faculty used and the elements of nature observed run afoul of the first *Critique*. Goenka presents Śākyamuni's ultimate insight into karma as being accomplished through unmediated "direct experience," the pure intellectual intuition of *noumenal* reality in itself. In Kantian terms, the claim to have attained enlightenment through direct realization of a thing in itself is itself a mark of unEnlightenment.

As an academic philosopher himself, Hayes is careful about whom he names as Śākyamuni's philosophical brethren. Men of the Enlightenment, Bacon, Newton, and Locke become the enlightened buddha's comrades-in-empiricism.[55] And Hayes, unlike Goenka, does not cross Kant's epistemological line, not least because he rejects karma as a myth. The Land of No Buddha's buddha is not the kind of buddha who intuits *noumena*. He is a philosopher and moralist whose dharma derives solely from duly circumscribed reason. Thus Hayes mobilizes a logic of equivalence whereby he fills dharma positively, associating it with values such as *wise* and *secular*, and exemplars such as Socrates and Thomas Jefferson. Likewise Hayes mobilizes a logic of difference to exclude the *myths* and *rituals* of the *masses*, who are always *fools*, from the ambit of dharma's positive meaning. This bears elaboration.

Wisdom is Hayes' favored equivalent for dharma. Hayes calls himself a Socratic Buddhist, and advises readers,

> What makes an awakened person (*buddha*) awakened, and therefore distinct from the masses of foolish people (*bāla-putujjana*), is just his wisdom Therefore the Buddha-dharma is the key virtue of the Buddha, and the key virtue of the Buddha is just his wisdom.... Being Dharma-centric...means making wisdom itself the very centre of one's life.

Though Hayes always marks wisdom as an ideological good, he is reluctant to grant it substantial or fixed doctrinal content. The truth of wisdom lies, rather, in the fact that it *cannot* be reduced to bumper-sticker slogans.

> True wisdom is always subtle and dynamic and rooted in very particular
> and concrete situations. It can never be successfully captured in static
> words and phrases and rules and formulas and creeds, because words deal
> only with broad generalizations and not with concrete situations.

An "essence of wisdom" does exist, though even the buddha's own words are
"awkward and clumsy" in their conveyance of it.[56]

As a dynamic mode of response, dharma/wisdom is predicated upon an
open-minded attitude that Hayes calls *secular*, pointing toward this-worldly
empiricism. Thus Śākyamuni and Thomas Jefferson are both secular in the sense
that their intellects are "rooted in this world that can be experienced directly
through the human senses rather than in mysterious other worlds that can be
known only through revelation and occult methods."[57] We might imagine a latter-day
Raphael painting, The School of Sarnath, with Śākyamuni flanked by Socrates on
the right and Jefferson on the left. Moreover, a secular dharma is an existentially
effective dharma. Hayes asserts, "The goal of every living thing is to be happy."[58]
He also gives us a specific definition thereof, "the only true form of lasting
happiness" is "the ability to see things as they truly are."[59] It would seem that
only an individual who understands dharma as secular wisdom can actually
accomplish life's universal goal, the full replacement of pain by peace.

Dharma, thus, is a scriptural seme that integrates rationality, religiosity, interpretability, certitude, and threat of danger. *Wise*, dharma is a self-authorizing
source of exceptional universal value. *Secular*, dharma is the key to its own true
and proper interpretation; dharma does not re-present reality—it is literal reality.
And no one who goes awry of dharma can realize life's goal, for the only true
happiness lies in knowing reality as it is, that is, in dharma's secular wisdom.
From this perspective, the Shorter Discourse to Mālunkya is a guide to dharma as
scripture. A wise secular man does not ask inappropriate questions when shot
with a poison arrow. He does not chant *om mani padme hum*, or offer *pūjā* to
gods. He ascertains the precise facts of the matter and assesses his prognosis with
dispassionate objectivity. Finally, he heeds Śākyamuni's command, *dhāretha*,
accept! Accept that I left certain matters unexplained, and that you can safely
ignore them. Accept that I did explain other matters, and that you should pursue
them, for that is how you will end suffering.

It is hardly surprising that *dharma* and *dhāretha* share the same verbal root,
dhr. *Dharma* names the cosmic order; *dhāretha* enjoins one's duty vis-à-vis that
order. Side-by-side *dharma* and *dhāretha* are a graphic reminder that the apolitical
is political, that necessary realities are contingent expressions of power. Hayes'
easy certainty, that every living being should strive to see things as they truly are,
only makes sense within the ambit of this e/Enlightenment hegemony. Hayes
envisions a humanity, much like that imagined by Edward Herbert, Lord of
Cherbury, in which universal rationality applied to matters of universal consensus
produces universal harmony. For Herbert, this required a scriptural humanity in
the image of god; for Hayes humanity is still scriptural, though the transcendental

basis is an impersonal dharma realized in rational enlightenment, and naturalized for his North American readers as *secular wisdom*. Yet, such assertions of universal rationality and universal harmony are contingent assertions. This point is absolutely clear for Herbert, whose five Common Notions concerning religion are now so self-evidently Christian particulars. Perhaps it is less easy to see hegemony at work in the Land of No Buddha, where the universal goal is happiness. After all, Śākya enlightenment and European Enlightenment converge on this ideal (if not on the substance of "happiness," or the means of its attainment). Both e/Enlightenments predict that a radical existential/social transformation will occur if secular rational wisdom replaces contingent power as the binding medium of the human social matrix.

The book's final chapter will note the political failure of this politics of rational consensus. It will look toward a wisdom that recognizes the secular facticity of struggle, suffering, and politics, yet responds *not* by projecting a chiliasm of politics transcended, but by articulating a politics compatible with irreducible pluralism; a wisdom that does not idealize the elimination of struggle, strife, and suffering, but that idealizes the ability to take responsibility for struggle, strife, and suffering as constitutive and productive dimensions of social/personal life. To reach that conclusion, however, necessitates a fuller explication of Hayes' endeavor to homologize enlightenment with Enlightenment.

Hayes is fluent in both dialects of the e/Enlightenment tongue, eastern and western. His articulation of an equivalence between the truths of enlightened Śākyamuni and those of the European Enlightenment is not ad hoc. Within Hayes' essays, a North American who truly adheres to the buddha-dharma is an individualist, rationalist, empiricist, universalist, who, accepting no authority other than buddha-dharma, is critical of ritual practices, of ecclesiastical institutions, and of spiritual hierarchies. Likewise this dharma-centrist pursues the four philosophical virtues as outlined by Socrates: wisdom, justice, patience, and moderation. Likewise, he shares Marxist outrage at the injustices of economic inequality. Likewise, his values are shared with the Puritans and Pietists who honor personal integrity and intellectual honesty. Likewise because, as a North American, he is a cultural Calvinist and mistrusts absolute temporal authority, he will have a "natural affinity" for the buddha's vision of social organization, since the buddha's "original Sangha was non-centralized, non-authoritarian, and non-absolutist." Indeed, he is a democrat in the tradition of Thomas Jefferson as well.[60]

Identities are formed on the leading edge of inclusion and exclusion, in the fluctuating assertions of equivalence and difference. Hayes eagerly expands the range of those meriting citizenship in his Land of No Buddha. The "essence of the Buddhist life" is to have an "all-or-nothing sense of dedication and commitment to wisdom."[61] One does not have to be a native, self-identified Buddhist to belong. Anybody who makes this commitment is a naturalized citizen. To make this commitment is to be a real Buddhist, whether or not one takes that name.

Of course, truth is also the margin of exclusion. Fools mistake myths, like karma and rebirth, for realities. But the myths that Hayes condemns most

176

frequently are myths about gods. And to the degree that a belief in god or gods is definitive of the category *religion*, Hayes is clear: Buddhism is no religion. "If we associate religion with obedience to divine commandment and restraint through fear of God, it is equally clear that Buddhism is not a religion in this sense and is even opposed to such ways of thinking."[62] Accordingly, devout Hindus and Catholics are barred from the Land of No Buddha. As for Protestants: fundamentalists and evangelicals will not make it in, though Deists and Unitarian Universalists well might. In fact, the huddled masses who are unwelcome in Hayes' Land of No Buddha, even as guest workers, include feminists, neo-romantics, sensualists, spiritualists, people stuck in the rut of romantic marriage, and ritualists.[63] The last-named group includes most Asian and North American Buddhists. They are too foolish to be allowed into his land, for institutional Buddhism is a mere religion of karma and system of rituals—"a haphazard assortment of benedictions, blessings, prayers for the dead, supplications for good fortune and prosperity, exorcisms of malicious forces, and awe-filled reverence for the supernatural accomplishments of saints"—that all but completely obscure dharma's spark of wisdom.[64]

Just as those who dedicate their lives to wisdom essentially are Buddhists, even if they do not take the name, so those who do not "discard all forms of revelation and celebrate reason above all else" are not real Buddhists, even if they do take the name.[65]

This brings us to the most egregious foolishness of all. Among Buddhism's many myths, superstitions, and empty rituals one stigmatizes dharma at its very core. Hayes calls this "the mythology of enlightenment."[66] This is enlightenment as a pathology of authority; this is dharma metastasized into social cancer. For where Hayes' dharma-centrist devotes himself to the legitimate task of imperfectly disseminating the inexpressible essence of a wisdom irreducible to static formulae, there are Zen masters and Tibetan lamas who claim (or, more importantly, whose devotees accept) that they are perfectly enlightened beings, more precious even than the buddha, the dharma, and the sangha. This mythology of enlightenment creates a hierarchy of spirituality, and fosters spiritual authoritarianism. Not only does it require students to trust, respect, and revere their teachers as their spiritual betters, but it requires students to scripturalize their teacher's every word and deed, no matter how capricious or self-serving it may appear. These Tibetan lamas and Zen masters narratize their actions in relation to heroes past—they tell the story of Naropa, who jumped off a cliff because his enlightened teacher asked him to do so; they tell the story of Nansen, who cut a cat in half to teach his students a lesson about their own ignorance—coercing students to accept that behavior, which an outsider might consider egregious or immoral, is, really, not an expression of power but, really, a deft strategy for shocking them into enlightenment. To criticize the master for being insensitive, malfeasant, or cruel, is to admit that one cannot see the emperor's clothes. In other words, the mythology of enlightenment uses dharma to authorize a community in which the acceptance of a subordinate position in a fixed power hierarchy is the condition for membership.

Among all the tomfoolery that Westerners have taken from Asian Buddhism, this is the most foolish, worse than karma, worse than the worship of this or that god. For the mythology of enlightenment transforms enlightenment itself into a predicate of divinity. The dharma-master becomes a supreme god, and dharma becomes a gift of divine grace rather than of human insight. And thus, this mythology substitutes an invalid scripture—the "enlightened" teacher's words and deeds—for the valid object—the dharma, the realization of which makes one an enlightened buddha.

Gods have everything to do with enlightenment

Hayes' mythology of enlightenment brings us full circle back to Todd Martin's exclusionary definition, "There are no gods in Buddhism. The very idea of a God or Gods goes against everything the Buddha ever taught." Though no one can say if we are now wiser, at least we have a better vocabulary. Indeed, that is why Hayes has been worth our time. He takes us past Todd Martin and S.N. Goenka, both because he recognizes that North Americans cannot conceptualize dharma except within an Enlightened Protestant imaginary, and because he reconceives dharma to fit that imaginary. Hayes gives us a native English vocabulary through which to talk about Buddhism as a discursive object, beyond the platitude that Buddhism is a post-Enlightenment category, and beyond its overt implications: scholars go awry when they treat Buddhism as a pre-nineteenth-century realia; Buddhists go awry when they focus on institutions rather than the truth of dharma.

As an Anglo-Sanskrit scriptural seme, *dharma* divides a dharmawise elect, whose members live peaceful lives in accord with rational explanation, from a karmafoolish unelect, whose members, to their peril, pursue unexplained revelation. Hayes models his social ideal on what he calls the "original Sangha," which he characterizes as "non-centralized, non-authoritarian, non-absolutist."[67] Despite the name, however, this original sangha owes as much to the Enlightenment's never-achieved "Elysium created by reason" as it does to any now-defunct community of Indian bauddha.[68] Note its likeness to the social model described by Laclau as quintessentially modern:

> Modernity started with the aspiration to a limitless historical actor, who would be able to ensure the fullness of a perfectly instituted social order. Whatever the road leading to that fullness—an "invisible hand" which would hold together a multiplicity of disperse individual wills, or a universal class who would ensure a transparent and rational system of social relations—it always implied that the agents of that historical transformation would be able to overcome all particularism and all limitation and bring about a society reconciled with itself. That is what, for modernity, true universality meant.[69]

Like the Proletarian "universal class" to which Laclau alludes, Hayes' "original sangha" reconciles all social particulars into a peaceful universal whole, brought about by rational men pursuing rational dharma via rational means following rational guidelines for behavior. Given all this rationality, Hayes creates real problems for himself when he suggests that "the model to be followed [in the creation of an ideal Buddhist society] should be the original blueprint as contained in the Vinaya."[70] For there is no evidence that an "original blueprint" ever existed, except as a matter of polemic; we have no reason to believe that an original vinaya ever existed. Hayes' vision of a harmonious Buddhist society patterned on an original vinaya is itself a revelation, a modern apocalypse. Still, he hopes that the dharmawise will someday organize themselves into this ideal community, though karmafools may never escape the abusive power-politics entailed by the mythology of enlightenment.

The first half of this chapter transformed Todd Martin's amazon.com review from an apophatic definition of Buddhism into a cataphatic assertion of hegemony. The second half explored that hegemony's subtleties and seductions, culminating in Hayes' social vision, which places a society founded in the mythology of enlightenment at antipodes to an ideal Buddhist society in which every person is wise, rational, equal, and free. Insofar as these two societies are *non-different* we have to wonder to what degree Hayes' negative valuation of the former contaminates the latter. Should we worry, for instance, when Hayes describes Buddhism as possessing "a unique potential to help mankind" since it "lays a stress on . . . positive moral guidelines that are valid for all men and women without exception"?[71] I have no doubt that Hayes' personal values are more to my taste than those of Congressman Tom Delay, discussed in the first chapter. But I take no greater solace in Hayes' representation of Buddhism as uniquely universal than I do in DeLay's parallel statement about Christianity: "Only Christianity offers a comprehensive worldview that covers all areas of life and thought, every aspect of creation. Only Christianity offers a way to live in response to the realities that we find in this world—only Christianity."[72] If dharma has an essence that is necessarily inexpressible and yet can be posited as a universally valid guideline for behavior; if dharma provides an absolute barrier, separating wisdom from foolishness, rationality from revelation, Buddhism-proper from debased-Buddhism, a non-institutional inchoate reality from clumsy institutional dogmas, personal enlightenment from a public mythology of enlightenment—then "fools" need fear this dharma as they would any sectarian revelation that comes from a source beyond experience and reason.

Indeed, as we move toward the book's conclusion, we should note the monstrous warning the mythology of enlightenment portends for dharma as a scriptural seme. To paraphrase from an earlier discussion in page 157, a scripture is a source of exceptional, universal value that does not re-present, but *is*, literal reality. This logic is predicated of an imbalance between surfaces (knowable and pragmatic) and depths (unfathomable but logically necessary). Thus the scriptural sleight-of-hand: surfaces are able to sustain the burden of reality because, in fact, they do re-present an occult reality. It is the anticipation of universal excess which guarantees that those particulars add up to more than their sum total. Hayes' treatment of dharma as contextual action that promotes happiness based upon this-worldly knowledge fits this pattern, for Hayes also posits a "true wisdom," an "essence of wisdom," associated with "the original teachings and intentions of Buddhism" and pursued by Śākyamuni's "original Sangha." Hayes requires the logical existence of dharma, transcending context, to ground judgements about the wise/secular/effective/moral character of specific contextual actions.

This dharma is internally split, however, for the contextualism that gives *wisdom* its dynamic charge is incongruous with the context-free rationalism that preordains the scope of what counts as properly *secular*. That is to say, Hayes accepts only the facts of this world that accord with empirical experience as secular; in a perfectly secular Land of No Buddha no one pursues mysteries or the occult. Hayes also imagines that secular wisdom participates in a universal economy of truth; even fools might become enlightened. Yet we also know that in Tom DeLay's parallel view it is evangelical Christianity that offers the only reasonable way to live in response to secular realities.

What do we learn? The act of delimiting the secular is always necessarily an exclusionary act. Dharma cannot be secular *and* rational *and* universal except as an empty signifier, as an *instrument* of hegemony. Thus dharma is not only split internally, it is externally divisive as well. On this point, as on most points, Hayes does not mince words: "Let's speak plainly. Buddhism is antisocial, if by society you mean the collective mentality of the half-awake masses who stumble their way unreflectively from cradle to grave, gaining nothing along the way but a superabundance of adipose tissue."[73] Hayes acknowledges only one definition of *the rational good*. There is only one legitimate way to be a human being: pursue Mubul's happiness through Mubul's truth, even if that means the Land of No Buddha is left devoid of inhabitants.

Now look at the *real* world. You see Zen Buddhists and Tibetan Buddhists, Hindus, Christians, and Muslims all taking recourse to occult mysteries. Of course, Mubul does as well, with his mythology of enlightenment as a state of existence in which no one makes myths and everyone is reasonable. Of course, the fact that he calls this "buddha-dharma" and "the buddha's dharma" is not inconsequential. The secular fact is, every community that organizes itself around a man whom it accepts as enlightened—including Śākyamuni—is a community grounded in the mythology of enlightenment. People see god and gods everywhere, including Bodh Gayā on the eve of Śākyamuni's enlightenment. Everyone always is somebody else's "fool." So the question cannot be, do we enlighten them to make them more like us (or, more like our ideal)? The question is, can we live with them just as they are? We need a dynamic, indeed wise, means for coexisting in a pluralistic world. The irreducible multiplicity of irreconcilable gods, fantasies, myths, ideologies, values, and goods is not just a *private* fact to be managed, it is the *res publica*, the ground of *public* action. Gods have everything to do with enlightenment—all of them. Vigorous public polytheism is secular wisdom for the modern age.

6

A BAROQUE CONCLUSION

I don't think you can hold anybody accountable for a situation that, maybe if you had done something different, maybe something would have occurred differently.

(Vice Admiral Albert T. Church, III, speaking at a
United States Department of Defense Briefing on
Detention Operations and Interrogation
Techniques, March 10, 2005)

Beyond Enlightenment has explored the political dimension of discursive objects that are commonly served up as apolitical: extraordinary universal value, original intentions, scripture, dharma. But these investigations have not advanced a model for positive engagement in a world where the apolitical is political. I shall endeavor to do so now. This final chapter will seek a wisdom that responds to the secular facticity of political struggle, *not* by projecting a chiliasm of politics transcended, but by articulating a politics compatible with irreducible pluralism; a wisdom that does not idealize the cessation of suffering, but idealizes the ability to take responsibility for suffering as a constitutive and productive dimension of life. And yes, it will be all the sweeter when we find a word for this wisdom in the Sanskrit of bauddha polemic—*icchantika*.

Ernesto Laclau has served as something of a *bête blanche* throughout this work. Here at the end, however, I take my lead from Chantal Mouffe, Laclau's longtime collaborator. If Laclau emphasizes hegemony and the structural contingency of power, Mouffe focuses more squarely upon the constructive potential opened up by contingency. If Laclau explains how identities, personal and collective, are formed in contingent assertions of power, structured through exclusion, entailing the potential for antagonism and conflict, Mouffe in turn explores how to manage these passions toward progressive political ends.

More to the point, Mouffe urges her readers "to discard the dangerous dream of perfect consensus, of harmonious collective will."[1] Indeed, Chapter 5 ended with a sense that *danger* might really lurk in Richard Hayes' e/Enlightened musings about an original sangha. But does not Mouffe's injunction force us to reach back into still earlier chapters, to weave their diverse threads into one simple question: If it is impossible to reach perfect consensus over the identification of an archaeological site—Ajanta is Buddhist—how much less likely is it that one set of personal values and daily needs can become the universal basis for a harmonious collective will? In more general terms, Mouffe argues that given the possibility of liberty, and the value placed on personal autonomy, along with the freedoms of conscience and thought, it is impossible for democratic unions to be free of strife. Any political theory that obviates or ignores the irreducible character of social antagonism, theorizing perfect reasonableness and/or neutrality as a viable foundation for perfect social concord, is necessarily anti-democratic:

> For democracy to exist, no social agent should be able to claim any mastery of the *foundation* of society. This signifies that the relation between social agents becomes more democratic only as far as they accept the particularity and the limitation of their claims; that is, only in so far as they recognize their mutual relation as one from which power is ineradicable. The democratic society cannot be conceived any more as a society that would have realized the dream of perfect harmony in social relations.[2]

Thus, for Mouffe, "the main question of democratic politics becomes . . . not how to eliminate power, but how to constitute forms of power which are compatible with democratic values."[3]

To translate Mouffe's concern into terms introduced in *Beyond Enlightenment*, we need a politics that does not presuppose a scriptural anthropology; that does not expect it can resolve multiplicity at the "literal" level into a higher-order unity through appeal to an occult transcendental. The varied arguments throughout this book have known Mouffe's call for a wise politics that does not reduce out the secular violence of social existence. The earlier chapters demonstrate why religious tropes (e.g., enlightenment; dharma) and religious institutions (e.g., Buddhism) deserve no special privilege in the modern social imaginary, since they, on the one hand, are incapable of eradicating the structural conditions that produce conflict, while, on the other hand, they are not suitable guides to managing conflict in a pluralistic world. The expectation that enlightenment or dharma or faith or secular wisdom or Buddhism or religion can resolve life's challenges—for you and me and everybody—may well be the "poison arrow" of modern times. The first chapter cited the Dalai Lama's affirmation, "there is every reason to appreciate and respect all forms of spiritual practice."[4] The DL is just plain wrong.

Yet the DL's affirmation of spiritual universalism also does point us forward. He used these words in 1996, when addressing a mixed audience of Christian and Buddhist monks. In the same year, speaking only to other Tibetans, however, the DL was less generous when he declared a spirit named Dorje Shugden to be a harmful spirit, and alleged that practices honoring this spirit threaten his own life and the cause of Tibetan political freedom more generally. The DL asked

Dorje Shugden's Tibetan devotees to dissociate themselves, either from the spirit, or from himself.[5] In fact, one can riffle through the bauddha literature of any land and any time, and find, as did Xuanzang in seventh-century India, "various viewpoints [being debated] as vehemently as crashing waves."[6] The bauddha always have been avid polemicists. This is hardly surprising since there is no Buddhism apart from the processes of hegemony. "Buddhist" is our name for people who treat enlightenment (dharma, etc.) as positive indices of meaningfulness, and who attempt to universalize and normalize their own particular values by filling these empty signifiers. The bauddha always have been avid polemicists, but in times past not all were loath to admit it.

So what I would like to do now is look back to the early centuries CE, to a polemic that provides extravagant allegorical possibilities for the present. I use *allegory* here in an elementary sense, as the trope of doubled reading. Allegory does not simply transfer value from one realm of meaning to another, as does metaphor. Allegory offers the opportunity to read a text simultaneously within two separate and distinct intertexts. My allegory is extravagant (recall Thoreau's use of this word, cited at the beginning of Chapter 4) because it "leaps the cowyard fence" of its Indian bauddha origin to seek new pastures in the latitude of contemporary politics.

Beyond enlightenment stands the *icchantika*. Several Mahāyāna texts theorize that not all living beings are capable of enlightenment. *Icchantika* is the name they give to someone who has not and will not become enlightened. Read in an allegorical mood, characterizations of the icchantika-figure allow us to reimagine e/Enlightenment as supporting a politics of irresolvable multiplicity, hybridity, and indeterminacy.

Traditionally, the icchantika played a minor role in the bauddha war of words. His interest lies now in the fact that he is a creature tied to polemic, the consummate outsider painted in shades of black. The *Mahāyāna Mahāparinirvāṇasūtra* (MNS) offers an open-ended condemnation: "An *icchantika* is one whose roots of goodness have been completely eradicated. His original mind is so devoid of any desire for good dharma that not a single thought of goodness will ever arise in him."[7] The icchantika seeks his own gratification, unabashedly and wholeheartedly. Thus "icchantika" came to designate the person who lacks higher values. And in some descriptions, the icchantika was not only uninterested but also unable to become enlightened. Again the MNS: "All sentient beings possess the Buddha-nature. Due to this nature, they can...attain the most perfect enlightenment. The only exceptions are the *icchantikas*."[8] On the path to perdition, in Robert Buswell's words, the icchantika falls short of even " 'the lowest common denominator' ... of the Buddhist spiritual equation."[9]

The icchantika will never escape saṃsāra, a condition *usually* explained by his moral, spiritual, and intellectual deficiencies. In most bauddha texts, that is the end of the matter. The *Laṅkāvatāra Sūtra*, however, adds a second explanation. The *Laṅkāvatāra's* discussion begins with a pun: "How is it that the wanters do not want to be liberated?"[10] The answer then distinguishes two types of icchantikas. One type, like that of the MNS, is devoid of merit. Lacking goodness, he cannot attain nirvāṇa, and is thus doomed to remain in saṃsāra. By contrast, the *Laṅkāvatāra's* second type of icchantika is entirely good. This is evidenced by his vow: "As long as all beings have not attained nirvāṇa, I will not attain nirvāṇa." Fully capable of liberation, the good icchantika nonetheless tries to emancipate beings who neither want nor value the emancipation he would proffer. He cuts a swath through the public sphere, speaking his truths, knowing that many of those to whom he speaks will not listen. Some might be moved at their very core by his words, and others will remain eternally unmoved. The good icchantika has embarked on an impossible task and has no illusions: he too will remain in saṃsāra forever.[11]

One might whiff an air of religious zealotry here. But the good icchantika of my allegory does not transmogrify into the Christian soldier or mujahideen or neoconservative, for he lacks recourse to an apolitical ground beyond contingency. He propounds an ideal that he himself has not experienced in the past and, by definition, will not experience in the future. Neither does he imagine an ultimate salvation; nor does he have faith in an invisible-but-beneficent hand. He does not expect and does not receive recompense for his struggles. There is no grace; no heaven; no bosom of Abraham; no 72 *houris*. No millennial land of milk and honey. No escape from Plato's cave. The good icchantika, in short, articulates ideals and pursues their realization with his attention fully on *this* world. He must fail—indeed, his title *icchantika* is eponymous with failure—yet he continues to strive. For all these reasons, the good icchantika acts the part of an adversary but never the part of an imperator. It is the bad icchantika who becomes so rapt in his own fervor for faith or truth or peace that he imagines that dharma/justice demands universal acceptance of his e/Enlightened ideal.

These two icchantika-types have a lexical symbiosis, not because they share the same desire, but because they both do desire; not because they share the same ultimate end, but because for both this world serves as an end in itself—and that end is never ending. Mahāyāna philosophers delighted in the paradoxical equation of opposites: nirvāṇa is saṃsāra, saṃsāra is nirvāṇa; form is emptiness, emptiness is form. Icchantika is icchantika. Is it not far more satisfying when both sides of the opposition have the same name? The word creates a unit without a unity. It conjoins the most debased with the most exalted without homologizing or equating the two. They belong together because they are eternally opposed.

Now, it is clear why the good icchantika is "good." But for this figure to serve allegorically within a progressive political imaginary we need also consider the quality of the bad icchantika's "badness." Fortunately, Robert Buswell has studied the icchantika in Pāli, Sanskrit, and Chinese sources, and gives us a firm starting point. At bottom, the bad icchantika is bad because he lacks generosity: "the very bedrock of Buddhist soteriology" is "the simple practice of charity, of giving (*dāna*)."[12] This brooks a straightforward doctrinal explanation: charity, in Buddhist terms, expresses detachment. Someone who can let go of a flower or dollar can eventually let go of saṃsāra. Someone who cannot practice detachment can never become a buddha. Buswell notes that this can be a matter of plain old avarice. But it is also possible the bad icchantika is greedy for enlightenment. Someone who does not engage in rituals of worship and giving because he sees them as hollow distractions from the pursuit of wisdom is as "bad" as someone who spends his wealth solely on sensual self-indulgence. Sapiential hedonism is little better than material. To foreshadow: salvational hedonism belongs on this list as well.

In nuce, the icchantika "worships his own desires" (per the MNS).[13] With this, now, let us shift this extravagant allegory's intertextual field, from the classical bauddha to the contemporary, in order to seek the bad icchantikas of our world. Given the icchantika-figure's doubling, insight into the bad should also reveal how now to be good. This will require a brief step away from the icchantikas, to the *mise en scène* of our moment.

Consider Vice Admiral Albert T. Church, III, whose words begin this chapter. As Naval Inspector General, Church investigated allegations of torture performed by US military interrogators from 2001 through 2004 in Afghanistan, Iraq, and Guantanamo Bay, Cuba. The unclassified version of the Church Report detailed 71 cases of abuse, involving 121 victims and six deaths.[14] The chapter's epigram comes, however, not from the report but from a press conference Church held upon its release. In both public fora, Church explained that although US interrogators abused Afghani and Iraqi prisoners, because the Department of Defense did not explicitly forbid such abuse, nobody could be held culpable for its occurrence.

Reread the quotation and consider Church's logic: A change of cause would have resulted in a change of effect. However, given that cause X inevitably produces effect Y, and given that X did occur, who can be blamed that Y followed? Church displaces the inevitability of a cause-and-effect chain from effect to cause. The cause itself becomes as if without origin. Where have we seen this before? This is how Leonard of the film *Memento*, a man without memory or scruples, experienced the world. And as Chapter 3 puzzled over Leonard's humanity, we must now wonder: what kind of man replaces the moral maxim that to act with choice is to act with responsibility, with the amoral principle that there is no responsibility *because* one's action is a matter of choice?

The MNS posits that bad icchantikas worship their own desires; they make a religion of self-interest. One can understand how this rubric might fit *Memento's* Leonard, who intentionally tricked himself into killing the "wrong" man for the "right" reasons. How about Church? Does the Vice Admiral also magnify his own self-serving amorality into a cosmic principle of life-and-death? The MNS speaks of worship: at whose altar does Church worship?

Blame Calvin! To find today's bad icchantikas look first to Calvin! Yes, all gods are the objectification of human ideals; all theists worship their own desires. But it was Calvin who took this construction to the limit: magnifying god into the greatest absolute monstrosity by diminishing humanity into the weakest servile dot. It is Calvin who gives stark expression to Feuerbach's theological dialectic: "that God may be all, man must be nothing."[15] It is Calvin's god who relieves men of the burden of responsibility for the consequences of their choices.

Chapter 4 cited Calvin: "It is the first business of an interpreter to let his author say what he does, instead of attributing to him what we think he ought to say."[16] In this spirit, let us follow a loose thread of citations from the *Institutes*.

> What for us seems a contingency, faith recognizes to have been a secret impulse from God.[17]
>
> What then? you will ask. Does nothing happen by chance, nothing by contingency? I reply ... "fortune" and "chance" are pagan terms. ... For if every success is God's blessing, and calamity and adversity his curse, no place now remains in human affairs for fortune or chance.[18]

If politics entails contingent expressions of power, then for today's bad icchantika nothing is political, even torture. Politics is not a matter of living, but of rhetoric; a word to stigmatize one's opponents with ulterior motives and hypocrisy. Hypocrisy! Why would not the Grand Inquisitor himself be numbered among the men of faith?

> Truly God claims, and would have us grant him, omnipotence—not the empty, idle, and almost unconscious sort ... but a watchful, effective, active sort, engaged in ceaseless activity. Not, indeed, an omnipotence that is only a general principle of confused motion ... but one that is directed towards individual and particular motions. ... For when, in The Psalms, it is said that "he does whatever he wills" [Psalms 115:3], a certain and deliberate will is meant.[19]

Beyond politics, Calvin's predication of god as absolutely autonomous and absolutely free requires human heteronomy and servitude. Moreover,

> God's will is so much the highest rule of righteousness that whatever he wills, by the very fact that he wills it, must be considered righteous. When, therefore, one asks why God has so done, we must reply: because he has willed it.[20]

How could torture be "wrong"? The abuse of Afghani and Iraqi prisoners, as a matter of "free choice" on the part of US soldiers, must be righteous. Indeed, there is little reason even to worry about whether individual Afghanis and Iraqis merit abuse, since god himself parcels out retribution apart from considerations of individual merit. A man is evil just because god wills him to damnation; a man is guilty just because the US military wills his detention.

> We call predestination God's eternal decree, by which he compacted with himself what he willed to become of each man. For all are not

created in equal condition; rather, eternal life is foreordained for some, eternal damnation for others.[21]

He who here seeks a deeper cause than God's secret and inscrutable plan will torment himself to no purpose.[22]

As the causeless cause of life and death, god's reasons for electing some and damning others are wholly his own. God gives life and god takes it: this knowledge is sufficient. So why seek culpability in the case of prisoner abuse? Yes, Jesus said, "Render unto Caesar." But here questions of legality merely confuse the issue. For the Church Report itself allows that "no specific guidance on interrogation techniques was provided to the commanders responsible for Afghanistan and Iraq." How can one ask responsible commanders to be responsible for guidelines they were not given? What seems to us to have been a contingent, even immoral choice, faith recognizes to have been a secret impulse from god, and thus infinitely glorious.

The very inequality of his grace proves that it is free.[23]

The doctrine of salvation...is falsely debased when presented as effectually profitable for all.[24]

The Lord wills that in election we contemplate nothing but his mere goodness.[25]

We never truly glory him unless we have utterly put off our own glory.[26]

For Calvin's god, the self-expression of autonomous freedom in the pursuit of his own unquestionable desires is the highest good. Anyone unwilling to worship at the altar of divine self-interest is thus damned. To doubt god's plan, righteousness, omnipotence, and universal providence, is to demonstrate one's own lack of election, for the only sure sign of election that god deigns to grant us is our ability to keep faith in faith itself.

God's unchangeable plan, by which he predestined for himself those whom he willed, was in fact intrinsically effectual unto salvation for these spiritual offspring alone.[27]

God...to show forth his glory, withdraws the effectual working of his Spirit from them [the wicked]. This inner call, then, is a pledge of salvation that cannot deceive us.[28]

Blessed is a United States' military that stands meekly before the Lord, for it shall inherit the earth.

Faith in faith is the core tenet of today's bad icchantika. How could any god be less charitable than an omnipotent, autonomous creator who saves and damns gratuitously precisely so that his slaves will recognize his freedom and their enslavement; so that they will praise him and condemn themselves...and in that self-abnegation hope for a sign of justification? Such a god relieves our world's bad icchantikas of the burden of generosity. Bad icchantikas, trusting providence, happily satisfy their own personal wants, no matter how terrible the consequence for others.

Where do we find these bad icchantikas? In 2005 we need not look far. Look for the scripturalization of selfishness: where even extreme expressions of self-interest are thought to serve a providential purpose, since an "invisible hand" will ensure that selfish intention functions as an instrument of the commonweal.

Look to the Christian Right, which opposes "Big Government" as a public source of financial assistance for those not blessed by providence, while it agitates for strict governmental regulations that compel citizens to be "moral" in their most intimate moments.

Look to Constitution in Exile: a libertarian movement dedicated to the elimination of all laws that impinge on property-ownership, from minimum-wage legislation, to laws protecting the environment, to measures that protect financial markets from fraud.[29]

Look to the conference, "Confronting the Judicial War on Faith," convened in Washington DC in April 2005. At this conference, US congressmen mingled with representatives of the Chalcedon Foundation.[30] This latter group's credo speaks the language of neoconservative liberty—"the role of the state is in essence to defend and protect, in the words of the early American Republic, life, liberty, and property"—which it then reframes in stringently Calvinist terms—

> we believe that the Bible should apply to all of life, including the state; and... we believe that the Christian state should enforce Biblical civil law; and finally,... we believe that the responsibility of Christians is to exercise dominion in the earth for God's glory.[31]

Is it any wonder that Tom DeLay was the conference's keynote speaker? Or that DeLay spoke thinly veiled words about the need to impeach judges who do not adhere to a Calvinist worldview? Or that other attendees stated this position explicitly?

Look to the main hive of bad icchantikas today: George W. Bush's White House. Its every piece of legislation is self-serving, yet who could doubt that the people working in the West Wing are convinced that their efforts at deregulation and privatization are fulfilling god's inscrutable plan? The bad icchantika worships his own desires. In our world, this describes the person who uses his faith in faith as an ultimate justification for self-serving behavior. Who does this describe more precisely than George W. Bush and Tom DeLay?

The chapter began with a promise: Bauddha speculation on enlightenment might yield a positive figure for contemporary progressivism. So, what is a good icchantika to do? Or to begin, what does he not do? First, definitively, the good icchantika does not take recourse to a rhetoric of apolitical ideals. If the good icchantika is "good," it is because he lacks faith in faith and thus does not seek solutions outside the sphere of politics, that is, contingent human relations. Because he does not claim transcendental freedom he does not then have to imagine a still-higher objective source of order—god; dharma—in order to constrain that freedom; to prevent liberty from becoming libertine. Thus the good icchantika can be a moral agent without taking recourse to a scriptural anthropology. He does not know a creator god and does not claim a natural right to accumulate property or treat the earth as his personal domain. He does not anticipate a next world and does not prophesy a chiliastic vision of ultimate reconciliation and redemption, for anybody. As they say in Las Vegas: What happens here, stays here.

Because the good icchantika has no world other than this one, he gives fully of himself right here, right now. Exchanging his time for others' benefit, he cultivates interpersonal bonds. This is how one improves a world fraught with antagonism. Yet, because he is determined to give to people who will not take, he also participates in, and perpetuates, the antagonisms endemic to human relations. Indeed, if this allegory has any pragmatic force, this is it: There is no single correct or proper way to be a good icchantika. Remember, the good icchantika exists in opposition to the bad. Human beings are impossibly infinite. So if bad icchantikas worship their own desires there must then be an endless number of gods for good icchantikas to both embrace and challenge.

Moreover, the diversity of desires/gods entails a diversity of means for political action. The various divisions that can lead to the inhibition of political involvement—theory versus practice; organized versus personal forms of resistance; revolution versus incremental change; working for change from within the "system" versus from without—are mooted. The good icchantika allows that his progressive cause is not everybody's progressive cause; that his agenda, ideology, and discourse are not for everybody. He does what he can, as he can, without demanding that all so-called "right-minded people" value what he values, understand what he understands, or act as he acts. How could he do otherwise? For the good icchantika too is beyond enlightenment.

What does it take to be a good icchantika? See every social encounter as an opportunity for adversarial giving. How do you begin? To circle back to the preface, here is one option. The next time you meet somebody on the road (or, for that matter, in a book), who says,

> Nobody is comparable to me.
> I am the only perfect buddha in the world.
> I have attained supreme enlightenment.
> I am conqueror over all.
> I am unrivaled in all realms, including those of the gods.

do not follow Upagu's lead and slink down another road. *Sapere aude!* You need not kill the buddha. Just slap him hard enough, so that he sees stars rather than enlightenment.

189

NOTES

PREFACE

1 Raniero Gnoli, ed., *The Gilgit Manuscript of the Saṅghabhedavastu* (Rome: ISMEO, 1977), 1:132.

1 A BENIGN INTRODUCTION

1 The 90 percent figure is not determined through scientific statistical methods. On April 23, 2002, Nancy Caciola and I combed through the Buddhism section of the Bodhi Tree Bookstore in West Hollywood, California. We each chose 100 books at random from throughout the section: Indian Buddhism, Tibetan Buddhism, Zen, and so on. Scholarly monographs, translations from Asian originals, as well as books directed toward a popular audience, were all included. The method was to scan each book's index, or failing that its pages, to determine whether its author used enlighten* or awaken* to describe the buddha and Buddhism.

2 Luis Gómez, *The Land of Bliss: The Paradise of the Buddha of Measureless* Light (Honolulu, HI: University of Hawai'i Press, 1996), 285.

3 David Snellgrove, *Indo-Tibetan Buddhism: Indian Buddhists and their Tibetan Successors* (Boston, MA: Shambala, 1987), 12.

4 David Snellgrove, *The Hevajra Tantra: A Critical Study* (Oxford: Oxford University Press, 1959), 1:97; akatvā kusalaṃ kammaṃ katvānākusalaṃ bahuṃ, kāyassa bhedā duppañño nirayaṃ so 'papajjatī (*Itivuttaka* 64).

5 John Olin, *A Reformation Debate: Sadoleto's Letter to the Genevans and Calvin's Reply* (New York: Harper & Row, 1966), 79.

6 Matthew Tindal, *Christianity as Old as the Creation* (London: Thomas Astley, 1730), 11.

7 Joinville, "On the Religion and Manners of the People of Ceylon," *Asiatick Researches* 7 (1801): 398.

8 William C. Mahony, "On *Singhala*, or *Ceylon*, and the Doctrines of the Bhoodha, from the Books of the *Singhalais*," *Asiatick Researches* 7 (1801): 33.

9 My investigation into this nineteenth century literature began with two bibliographies: Otto Kistner, *Buddha and His Doctrines: A Bibliographical Essay* (London: Trübner, 1869), and Philip Almond, *The British Discovery of Buddhism* (Cambridge: Cambridge University Press, 1988), 166–80. Just a sample of the sources will have to suffice. In 1819, H.H. Wilson's *A Dictionary in Sanscrit and English* defined *buddha* thus: "1. A generic name, for a deified teacher of the *Baudd'ha sect*... 2. A sage, a wise or learned man" ([Calcutta: Hindoostanee Press, 1819], 605). The 1832 second edition did not change this entry. In between those two editions, John Davy observed, "The term Boudou, or Boodhoo, is a generic term, signifying

wisdom, and applied to human beings of extraordinary faculties, attainments, and destiny" (*An Account of the Interior of Ceylon and of its Inhabitants: With Travels in that Island* [London: Longman *et al.*, 1821], 152); and William Francklin wrote, "The term Bood'h, or Boodhoo, is by the Singalese derived from the Pāli, and implies *wisdom*" (*Researches on the Tenets and Doctrines of the Jeynes and Boodhists; Conjectured to the Brahmanes of Ancient India* [London: William Francklin, 1827], 178–9). This pattern was repeated in French and German as well. Thus Abel Rémusat agreed that buddha is *connaissance*, or pure intelligence, or the Intelligent, but proposed to leave it untranslated ("Observations sur trois Mémoires de M. Deguignes," *Nouveau Journal Asiatique* 7 [1831]: 256). Likewise the *Allgemeine Encyclopädie* included the entry, "Bhoodha bedeutet nämlich Weisheit, Allwissenschaft und Heiligkeit" (*Allgemeine Encyclopädie der Wissenschaften und Künste in alphabetischer Folge* [Leipzig: J.F. Gieditsch, 1824], 13:330). As the century proceeded, translations became more diverse. Thus according to Félix Nève, "Il se disait BOUDDHA, c'est-à-dire, *éclairé* de la plus grand lumière"; at which point Nève added a footnote: "L'épithète devenant nom propre, on peut très-bien nommer Śākyamouni'le Bouddha,'le Sage par excellence" (*De l'état présent des études sur le bouddhisme et de leur application* [Gand: P. van Hifte, 1846], 11). So too John Gogerly's 1840 translation of the *Dhammapada* entitled chapter 14, "The Enlightened," and began verse 179, "The Buddha (or wise man) who is the unconquered conqueror of passions" (*Ceylon Buddhism: Being the Collected Works of Daniel John Gogerly* ed. Arthur Bishop [London: Kegan Paul, Trench, Trübner & Co., 1908], 2:281). This is not to say that the old standard was superceded. An anonymous article in *New Englander* for 1845 included, "Buddha, i.e., *Intelligence*" ("Buddhism," *New Englander* 3 [1845]: 185); Alexander Cunningham, the great archaeologist concurred, "*Buddha*, or Supreme Intelligence" ("Opening of the Topes or Buddhist Monuments of Central India," *Journal of the Royal Asiatic Society* 13 [1852]: 114); as did the Christian apologist, Fredrick Maurice, "The word Buddha, it seems to be admitted on all hands, means Intelligence. That men ought to worship pure Intelligence, must have been the first proclamation of the original Buddhists" (*The Religions of the World and their Relations to Christianity* [London: J.W. Parker, 1847], 90). For one final example let me note Viggo Fausböll's 1855 edition of the Pāli *Dhammapada*, with Latin translation. Because Latin is an inflected language, Fausböll usually did not translate buddha. The only exception is verse 59, where *sammasambuddha* became: "ita inter (vulgus) stercori simile (versans) occoecato vulgo praelucet intelligentiā plane sapientis (Buddhae) sāvakas (auscultator)" (*Dhammapadam* [London: Williams & Norgate, 1855], 11).

10   The translation of *bodhi* was rather more consistent than that of *buddha*, in part (I suppose) because the word *bodhi* was an object of significantly less interest. A short list of examples might begin with H.H. Wilson's *Sanscrit Dictionary*: "1. The holy fig tree. 2. A branch of holy study; keeping the mind awake to the knowledge of the true GOD... 3. Intellect, understanding...Wise, learned" (606). Here, *bodhi*'s first definition is the tree under which the buddha attained *bodhi*. In fact, that is the context within which the word was typically encountered. Thus, Abel Rémusat explained, "Le *génie de l'arbe Bodhi ou de l'intelligence*: il est constamment à veiller sur les lieux où les Tathāgatas accomplissent la doctrine, et c'est de là que vient son nom" (*Foĕ Kouĕ Ki, ou, Relation des Royaumes Bouddhiques* [Paris: L'Imprimerie Royale, 1836], 142). Likewise, Eugène Burnouf observed, "Le mot Bôdhi est le nom que les Buddhistes donnent au figuier (*ficus religiosa*) sous lequel Çãkya atteignit la *Bôdhi*, ou l'Intelligence, et d'une manière plus général, l'état de Buddha parfaitement accompli" (*Introduction à l'histoire du buddhisme indien* [Paris: Imprimerie Royale, 1844], 77). Another example might come from an article by Edward Neale,

"the bo-tree, *i.e.* the tree of wisdom, claimed to have attained the revelation of supreme intelligence, and came forth as Buddha, *i.e.* 'the all-knowing,' to reveal to mankind the path to the City of Peace" ("Buddha and Buddhism," *Macmillan's Magazine* 1 [1860]: 442). On occasion, *bodhi* is found in other discursive contexts. An article by Edward Salisbury, for instance, taught that a bodhisattva is, "*He who possesses the essence of Bodhi,* or the intelligence of Buddha." ("M. Burnouf on the History of Buddhism in India," *Journal of the American Oriental Society* 1 [1849]: 287).

11 Charles Friedrich Neumann, "Buddhism and Shamanism," *Asiatic Journal and Monthly Register* 16 (1835): 124. The French article is, "Coup d'oeil historique sur les peuples et la littérature de l'Orient," *Nouveau Journal Asiatique* 14 [1834]: 39–73, 81–114. The original reads: "Chākya ayant épuisé toute espèce de science reçut le nom de Bouddha, c'est-à-dire le sage ou l'illuminé. C'est d'aprés ce titre honorifique que ses sectateurs furent nommés bouddhas ou bouddhistes" (95).

12 Brian Hodgson, *Essays on the Languages, Literature, and Religion of Nepal and Tibet* (Amsterdam: Philo Press, 1972), 84, 83. The essay cited here was originally published in the *Journal of the Bengal Asiatic Society* 5 (1836). One sees a similar pattern in the citations from Gogerly's translation of the *Dhammapada* in note 9.

13 "Buddhist Pilgrims," *The Times* (April 17, 1857): 5, continued in (April, 20 1857): 6.

14 Max Müller, *Buddhism and Buddhist Pilgrims: A Review of M. Stanislas Julien's "Voyages des pèlerins bouddhistes,"* (London: Williams and Norgate, 1857).

15 Max Müller's influence is positively evidenced in two anonymous works: "Review of Paraméswarajnyána-góshthi," *The Christian Remembrancer* 35 (1858): 93, 97; "The Influence of Buddhism on Indian Society," *Bombay Quarterly Review* 7 (1858): 150. His critic is also anonymous: An Indian Missionary, *The Indian Religions: Or Results of the Mysterious Buddhism* (London: T.C. Newby, 1858), 2.

16 Max Müller, "Recent Researches on Buddhism," *The Edinburgh Review* 115 (1862): 379–408. The reprints are to be found in *Chips from a German Workshop*, Volume 1 (London: Longmans, Green, 1867), 235–78 and 181–234.

17 Henry Alabaster, *The Wheel of the Law* (London: Trübner, 1871), 162.

18 The tendentiousness of Müller's designation of the buddha as "the Enlightened" within his essays on the science of religion is foregrounded by the fact that his 1870 translation of the *Dhammapada* used the etymologically correct "Awakened." In fact, the essay Müller wrote as an introduction to his translation twice repeated the apposition: "the Buddha, the Enlightened." It was in the body of the translation itself that he entitled chapter 15, "The Awakened (Buddha)"; that he translated buddha as "the Awakened" in the verses; and that he added this footnote: "'Buddha,' the Awakened, is to be taken as an appellative rather than as the proper name of the 'Buddha.' It means anybody who has arrived at complete knowledge" ("Buddha's *Dhammapada*, Or 'Path of Virtue,'" in T. Rogers, ed., *Buddhaghosha's Parables* [London: Trübner, 1870], xxxviii, xxxix, cx). But it seems that Müller fell victim to his own influence. James d'Alwis' review of Müller's *Dhammapada* complained that Müller severely misrepresented several basic Buddhist tenets. Among Müller's many "errors" was the following: "In his anxiety to go into the radical meaning of words he has even rendered the name *Buddha* with the signification which it conveys, viz. 'the Awakened'" (*Buddhist Nirvána: A Review of Max Müller's Dhammapada* [Colombo: William Skeen, 1871], 69).

19 The most comprehensive work on Müller now available is Lourens van den Bosch's *Friedrich Max Müller: A Life Devoted to Humanities* (Leiden: Brill, 2002). Joseph Kitagawa and John Strong have authored a more circumscribed but no less excellent introduction to Müller ("Friedrich Max Müller and the Comparative Study of Religion," in Ninian Smart, ed. *Nineteenth Century Religious Thought in the West*, Volume 3 [Cambridge: Cambridge University Press, 1985], 179–213).

20 Müller, *Chips* (1867), x.
21 Ibid.
22 Ibid.
23 Ibid., x–xi.
24 Ibid.
25 Ibid., xii, xxiv.
26 Ibid., xxiii.
27 Ibid., xxv.
28 Ibid., xx.
29 Ibid., viii, ix, xxii.
30 Max Müller, *Lectures on the Science of Religion* (New York: Scribner, Armstrong, and Co., 1874), 45.
31 Müller, *Chips* (1867), xi.
32 This is added to the American version of *Chips from a German Workshop*, Volume 1, 2nd edition (New York: Scribner, 1869), xxviii.
33 Some of the wording here paraphrases, Müller, *Chips* (1867), xxiii–xxiv. The direct quote is from xx.
34 Max Müller, *Introduction to the Science of Religion* (New York: Scribner, Armstrong, and Co., 1874). In December of the year in which Müller published this *Introduction*, he also delivered a lecture in Westminster, on the occasion of the Day of Intercession for Missions. This lecture expresses Müller's value-hierarchy with particular clarity: "True Christianity lives, not in our belief, but in love—*in our love of God, and in our love of man, founded on our love of God*" ("Westminster Lecture on Missions," *Chips from a German Workshop*, Volume 4 [London: Longmans, 1875], 278).
35 Müller, *Chips* (1867), xxiii.
36 Max Müller, trans., *Critique of Pure Reason: In Commemoration of the Centenary of its First Publication* (New York: Macmillan, 1927 [1881]), xxxv.
37 Müller further describes Stilling as "one of the most religious and most honest of Kant's contemporaries" (ibid., lviii–lix).
38 Cited in Immanuel Kant, *Practical Philosophy* ed. and trans. Mary Gregor (Cambridge: Cambridge University Press, 1999), 13.
39 Immanuel Kant, "An Answer to the Question: What is Enlightenment?" [1784], in ibid., 17.
40 Ibid., 21.
41 Ibid.
42 The English "enlighten" has a history with several branches. The *Oxford English Dictionary* traces the literal matter of enlightening to the tenth century (*c*.975). Four centuries later (1382), John Wyclif transforms enlighten into a metaphor with Ephesians 1:18, "The yȝen of ȝoure herte inliȝtened." After another third-millennium (1732), this word becomes the denominator of open-mindedness, as when Berkeley praises "the select spirits of this enlightened age." For the adjectival, enlightened age, to become what we now commonly capitalize as the Age of Enlightenment, or simply, the Enlightenment, took only a little more than one century. The *OED* places the first usage in James Hutchison Stirling, *The Secret of Hegel* (London: Longman, Green, 1865), xxvii.
43 Several additional notes. First, Monier-Williams' 1851 English to Sanskrit dictionary included entries for "to enlighten" and "enlightened." In neither case does he list the verbal root *budh* among Sanskrit equivalents for the English. Moreover, the dictionary does not even have an entry for "enlightenment" (*A Dictionary, English and Sanskrit* [London: Wm.H. Allen, 1851], 230). Note further that in 1857 Karl Köppen published his *Die Religion des Buddha*, with the following note: "*Buddha, von der Wurzel budh* (erweckt werden, erkennen, wissen), bedeut der Erweckte order

Erwachte, Erleuchtete, Intelligente, Wissende, Ratonalis, Sapiens'" (Berlin: F. Schneider, 1857), 1:90. Erwachte = awakened; Erleuchtete = enlightened. Enlightened as aufgeklärten, and enlightenment as Aufklärung are not offered. In three earlier publications, Eugène Burnouf glossed buddha as "éveillé" and "l'éclairé," even though his stated preference was "intelligent" (Eugène Burnouf and Christian Lassen, *Essai sur le pali* [Paris: Dondey-Dupré, 1826], 131; Burnouf, *Introduction*, 71, 153, 484; Eugène Burnouf, *Le Lotus de la Bonne Loi* [Paris: L'Imprimerie Nationale, 1852], 797). As in German, so in French, Buddhist enlightenment and European Enlightenment are not homophones. Ulrich Im Hof discusses the multilingual history of Aufklärung, Lumières, Enlightenment, etc. (*The Enlightenment* [Oxford: Blackwell, 1994], 3–10).

44 Max Müller, *Essays: Erster Band. Beiträge zur vergleichenden Religionswissenschaft. Nach der zweiten englischen Ausgabe mit Aurotisation des Verfassers ins Deutsche Übertragen* (Leipzig: Wilhelm Engelmann, 1869), 190, 191, 214. These references correspond to *Chips* (1867), 217, 218, 246.

45 I would like to thank Betsy Bredeck for her clarification of the distinction between *erleuchten* and *aufklären* in German usage. The former gives the sense of increasing light or illumination, while the latter begins as a meteorological term for improving weather—the storm clears up; the fog lifts—and thus clearing up an inquiry, clarification, elucidation.

46 A brief note on capitalization. I will capitalize Enlightenment, Enlightened, and Enlighten whenever these words pertain to European intellectual history. When used for India's buddha or Buddhism, by contrast, enlightenment, enlightened, and enlighten will be rendered in lower case—except, of course, at the beginning of sentences.

47 Max Müller, *Natural Religion* (London: Longmans, Green, 1889), 571–2.

48 Peter Gay, *The Enlightenment: The Rise of Modern Paganism* (New York: Norton, 1995), 3.

49 Denis Diderot and Jean Le Rond d'Alembert, *Encyclopedia: Selections* trans. Nelly Hoyt and Thomas Cassirer (Indianapolis, IN: Bobbs-Merrill, 1965), 284.

50 Herbert Dieckmann, *Le Philosophe: Texts and Interpretation* (St Louis, 1948), 52.

51 This injunction is italicized in the original. Kant, "What is Enlightenment," 22.

52 Étienne Balibar, "Subjection and Subjectivation," in Joan Copjec, ed., *Supposing the Subject* (London: Verso, 1994), 6.

53 Ibid., 10.

54 Immanuel Kant, *Critique of Pure Reason* trans. Paul Guyer and Allen Wood (Cambridge: Cambridge University Press, 1999 [1781/1787]), 136.

55 Ibid., 362.

56 Immanuel Kant, *Critique of Practical Reason*, in Mary Gregor, ed. and trans., *Practical Philosophy* (Cambridge: Cambridge University Press, 1999 [1788]), 139.

57 Ibid., 199.

58 Ibid., 169.

59 Ibid., 241.

60 Ibid.

61 Immanuel Kant, "Religion Within the Boundaries of Mere Reason," in Allen Wood and George di Giovanni, eds and trans., *Religion and Rational Theology* (Cambridge: Cambridge University Press, 2001 [1793]), 89.

62 Ibid., 59–60.

63 Kant, *Critique of Practical Reason*, 243–4.

64 Ibid., 245, 238, 139–40.

65 Karl Marx, "On the Jewish Question" [1844], in *Karl Marx, Frederick Engels: Collected Works* trans. Clemens Dutt (Moscow: Progress Publishers, 1975), 3:155.

NOTES

66 Pierre Daniel Chantepie de la Saussaye, *Manual of the Science of Religion* trans. Beatrice Colyer-Fergusson (London: Longmans, Green, and Co., 1891), 14.
67 Peter Berger, "The Desecularization of the World: A Global Overview," in Peter Berger, ed., *The Desecularization of the World* (Grand Rapids, MI: Eerdmans, 1999), 13.
68 Czeslaw Milosz, "If There Is No God," *The New Yorker* (August 30, 2004): 94.
69 Ernesto Laclau, *Emancipation(s)* (London: Verso, 1996), 36.
70 Ernesto Laclau, "Identity and Hegemony: The Role of Universality in the Constitution of Political Logics," in Judith Butler, Ernesto Laclau, and Slavoj Zizek, eds, *Contingency, Hegemony, Universality* (London: Verso, 2000), 44.
71 Laclau, *Emancipation(s)*, 36–46.
72 Ferdinand de Saussure, *Course in General Linguistics* trans. Wade Baskin (New York: Philosophical Library, 1959 [1915]), 110.
73 Laclau, *Emancipation(s)*, 37.
74 Ibid.
75 Ibid., 38.
76 Voltaire, "Theist," *Philosophical Dictionary* trans. H.I. Woolf (London: George Allen & Unwin, 1923 [1764]), 301.
77 Laclau, *Emancipation(s)*, 38.
78 Cited in Bosch, *Friedrich Max Müller*, 418.
79 In a parallel vein, one might turn to the cover page of Matthew Tindal's *Christianity as Old as the Creation*, where Tindal cites Eusebius, Augustine, and fellow deist Thomas Sherlock as authorities for his premise: "the Religion of the Gospel, is the true original Religion of Religion and Nature."
80 On Müller's dialogue with the Brahmo Samaj, see Bosch, *Friedrich Max Müller*, 406ff.
81 Ibid., 418.
82 Cited in ibid., 420.
83 Cited in ibid., 373; Max Müller, *Chips* (1867), xx.
84 Laclau, *Emancipation(s)*, 44, 59.
85 Ibid., 38.
86 Laclau, "Identity and Hegemony," 44.
87 Antonio Gramsci, *Selections from the Prison Notebooks of Antonio Gramsci* ed. and trans. Quintin Hoare and Geoffrey Smith (New York: International Publishers, 1971), 12.
88 Alan Cooperman, "DeLay Criticized for 'Only Christianity' Remarks," *The Washington Post* (Saturday, April, 20 2002): A05.
89 Ibid.
90 Ibid.
91 Laclau, *Emancipation(s)*, 43.
92 Ian Hacking, *The Social Construction of What?* (Cambridge, MA: Harvard University Press, 2000), 1.
93 Ibid., 6.
94 Ibid., 33.
95 Richard Robinson and Willard Johnson, *The Buddhist Religion: A Historical Introduction* 4th edition (Belmont, CA: Wadsworth Publishing, 1997), 1.
96 Ibid., 7.
97 The phrase "anthropology of deception" comes from Russell McCutcheon. Unfortunately I no longer remember the exact source.
98 This oblique reference is, of course, to the theologian Friedrich Schleiermacher (1769–1834). Kant and Schleiermacher were Müller's intellectual parents. For Müller's inheritance from Schleiermacher see Bosch, *Friedrich Max Müller*, 304ff., 440–1.
99 Almond, *The British Discovery of Buddhism*; Jonathan Silk, "The Victorian Creation of Buddhism," *Journal of Indian Philosophy* 22 (1994): 171–96.

195

100 Almond, *British Discovery*, 12.
101 Ibid., 140.
102 Ibid., 5.
103 Ibid., 4.
104 Ibid., 6.
105 Silk, "Victorian Creation," 173–4.
106 Almond, *British Discovery*, 4; cited in Silk, "Victorian Creation," 173.
107 Ibid.
108 Dalai Lama, "Forward," in Donald Mitchell and James Wiseman, eds, *The Gethsemani Encounter: A Dialogue on the Spiritual Life by Buddhist and Christian Monastics* (New York: Continuum, 1997), ix.
109 Walter Spink. "The Archaeology of Ajaṇṭā," *Ars Orientalis* 21 (1992): 70.
110 Walter Spink, "Reply to K. Khandalavala, A. Jamkhedkar, [B. Deshpande," *Maharashtra Pathik* 3 (1992): 14.
111 Richard Lannoy, *The Speaking Tree: A Study of Indian Culture and Society* (London: Oxford University Press, 1975), 51; Kanaiyalal Vakil, *At Ajanta* (Bombay: D.B. Taraporevala Sons, 1929), 26.
112 This cartoon of Ajanta's history is based upon Walter Spink's voluminous work. In addition to the two articles cited, notes 109 and 110, see: "The Problem of Cave Eleven," *Ars Orientalis* 7 (1968): 155–68; "Ajaṇṭā's Chronology: The Crucial Cave," *Ars Orientalis* 10 (1975): 143–69; "Ajaṇṭā's Chronology: Politics and Patronage," in Joanna Williams, ed., *Kalādarśana* (New Delhi: Oxford and IBH Publishing, 1981), 109–26; "Ajaṇṭā's Chronology: Cave 7's Twice Born Buddha," in A.K. Narain, ed., *Studies in Buddhist Art of South Asia* (New Delhi: Kanak Publications, 1985), 103–16; "Ajanta's Chronology: Solstitial Evidence," *Ars Orientalis* 15 (1985): 97–119.
113 Xuanzang, *The Great Tang Dynasty Record of the Western Regions* trans. Li Rongxi (Berkeley, CA: Numata Center for Buddhist Translation and Research, 1996), 336–7.
114 M.K. Dhavalikar, "New Inscriptions from Ajaṇṭā," *Ars Orientalis* 7 (1968): 152.
115 This is not to say that India had completely forgotten Śākyamuni Buddha during this half-millennium. It still looked upon him as Viṣṇu's *avatāra*, and his name remained an entry in Sanskrit lexicons. Yet there seems to have been no memory that Śākyamuni Buddha was also supposed to have been the founder of a distinct and autonomous, though defunct, socio-religious institution. Claus Vogel makes this same point in his short but interesting essay, "On the Names of the Buddha as Found in Veṇīdatta and Glossed by Heinrich Roth," in Reinhold Grünendahl *et al.*, eds, *Studien zur Indologie und Buddhismuskunde* (Bonn: Indica et Tibetica Verlag, 1993), 289–92.
116 Walter Spink, "Before the Fall: Pride and Piety at Ajanta," in Barbara Stoler Miller, ed., *The Powers of Art: Patronage in Indian Culture* (Delhi: Oxford University Press, 1992), 67.
117 See Richard S. Cohen, "Setting the Three Jewels: The Complex Culture of Buddhism at the Ajanta Caves," (PhD dissertation, University of Michigan, 1995), figures 47 and 53 for tabular analyses of the inscriptions around the parameters of lay/monastic identity and the use of epithets.
118 See Richard S. Cohen, "Kinsmen of the Son: Śākyabhikṣus and the Institutionalization of the Bodhisattva Ideal," *History of Religions* 40 (2000): 1–31.
119 I would like to thank John Strong for calling my attention to the earlier work of Caroline Rhys Davids, who adopts a similar discursive strategy in her *Sakya or Buddhist Origins* (London: Kegan Paul, Trench, Trubner, 1931). Rhys Davids instructs her readers

> Put away... the word 'Buddhism' and think of your subject as 'Sakya.' This will at once place you for perspective at a truer point.... You are now concerned to learn less about 'Buddha' and 'Buddhism,' and more about him whom India has

ever known as Sakya-muni, and about his men who, as their records admit, were spoken of as the Sakya-sons, or men of the Sakyas (1).

120 This statement is based upon the uses for *bauddha* given in major Sanskrit dictionaries (Böhtlingk and Roth, Monier-Williams, Edgerton), as well as the two compendia of Indian Buddhist inscriptions (Masao Shizutani, *Indo Bukkyo Himei Mokuroku* [Kyoto: Heian Gakuen Kyoikin Kenkyukai, 1965]; Keisho Tsukamoto, *Indo Bukkyo Himei no Kenkyu* [Kyoto: Heirakuji Shoten, 1996–8]). In the latter, I found only one epigraphic use of *bauddha*, dating to the end of the eleventh century: J.F. Fleet, "Sanskrit and Old-Canarese Inscriptions," *Indian Antiquary* 10 (1881): 185–90, 273–4. Having not read India's bauddha literature in its entirety, I hardly expect this to be the final word.

121 James Burgess, *Notes on the Bauddha Rock-Temples of Ajanta, Their Paintings and Sculptures, and On the Paintings of the Bagh Caves, Modern Bauddha Mythology, &c.* (Bombay: Government Central Press, 1879).

122 See note 11.

2 A PLACE OF EXCEPTIONAL UNIVERSAL VALUE

1 Geoff Crowther *et al.*, *India: A Travel Survival Kit* 4th edition (Hawthorn, Australia: Lonely Planet Publications, 1990), 662.

2 A.P. Subramaniam and Y.S. Sahasrabudhe, *Geology of Greater Bombay and Aurangabad-Ellora-Ajanta Area* (New Delhi, 1964), 5.

3 The ICOMOS International Committee on Cultural Tourism, *Cultural Tourism: Tourism at World Heritage Cultural Sites: The Site Manager's Handbook* (Madrid: World Tourism Organization, 1993), 49.

4 "Operational Guidelines: Establishment of the World Heritage List," http://www.unesco.org/whc/- opgulist.htm (March 27, 2002).

5 ICOMOS, *Cultural Tourism*, 1.

6 Ibid., 9.

7 "Operational Guidelines."

8 Ibid.

9 David Hume, "An Enquiry Concerning Human Understanding" [1748], in Antony Flew, ed., *Hume on Human Nature and the Understanding* (New York: Macmillan, 1962), 94.

10 David Hume, *A Treatise of Human Nature* [1739], in ibid., 173.

11 Immanuel Kant, "Critique of Practical Reason," [1788], in Mary Gregor, ed., and trans. *Practical Philosophy* (Cambridge: Cambridge University Press, 1999), 269.

12 Ibid.

13 Claude-Adrien Helvétius, *A Treatise on Man; His Intellectual Faculties and His Education* trans. W. Hooper (New York: Burt Franklin, 1969 [1772]), 2:19; Augustine, *Confessions* trans. R.S. Pine-Coffin (New York: Penguin, 1961 [397]), 28.

14 Kant, *Critique Practical Reason*, 270.

15 Cited in Nancy Caciola, *Discerning Spirits: Divine and Demonic Possession in the Middle Ages* (Ithaca, NY: Cornell University Press, 2003), 299.

16 Thomas Paine, *The Age of Reason* (New York: Willey Book Company, n.d. [1795]), 12.

17 Ibid.

18 William Lipe, "Value and Meaning in Cultural Resources," in Henry Cleere, ed., *Approaches to the Archaeological Heritage* (Cambridge: Cambridge University Press, 1984), 10.

19 ICOMOS, *Cultural Tourism*, 62.

20 Jean-Antoine-Nicolas de Caritat, Marquis de Condorcet, *Sketch for a Historical Picture of the Progress of the Human Mind* trans. June Barraclough (New York: Noonday Press, 1955 [1795]), 173.

21 Ibid., 10.

22 Adam Smith, *An Inquiry into the Nature and Causes of the Wealth of Nations* (Oxford: Clarendon Press, 1976 [1776]), 456.

23 ICOMOS, *Cultural Tourism*, 59.

24 Ibid., 57.

25 Michel Foucault, "What is Enlightenment?," in Paul Rabinow, ed., *The Foucault Reader* (New York: Pantheon Books, 1984), 32–50.

26 Ibid., 38.

27 Kant's three questions are famously articulated in the *Critique of Pure Reason* A805/B833.

28 Foucault, "What is Enlightenment," 35.

29 Ibid., 40.

30 Foucault, "What is Enlightenment," 39.

31 Jean-Jacques Rousseau, *The Social Contract and The First and Second Discourses* trans. Susan Dunn (New Haven, CT: Yale University Press, 2002 [1762]), 158.

32 Ibid.

33 Ibid., 166; Foucault, "What is Enlightenment," 39.

34 Ibid.

35 Ibid., 41.

36 Ibid.

37 Wayne Begley, "The Identification of the Ajaṇṭā Fragment in the Boston Museum," *Oriental Art* 14 (1968): 33.

38 "Maharashtra at a Glance," http://www.maharashtra.gov.in/intranet/Deswebpage/maha.htm (July 15, 2004).

39 Foucault, "What is Enlightenment," 41.

40 Kant, *Critique of Practical Reason*, 198–211.

41 Janice Radway, "The Act of Reading the Romance: Escape and Instruction," in Juliet Schor and Douglas Holt, eds, *The Consumer Society Reader* (New York: The New Press, 2000), 172.

42 Ibid.

43 James Edward Alexander, "Notice of a Visit to the Cavern Temples of Adjunta in the East-Indies," *Transactions of the Royal Asiatic Society of Great Britain and Ireland* 2 (1830): 362–4.

44 Ibid., 368.

45 Ibid., 370. Alexander cites lines 3–5 of Horace's Ode 3.30: "It cannot be destroyed by gnawing rain or wild north wind, by the procession of unnumbered years or by the flight of time" (*The Complete Odes and Epodes* trans. David West [Oxford: Oxford University Press, 1997], 108).

46 Alexander, "Notice," 370.

47 James Prinsep, "Facsimiles of Various Ancient Inscriptions," *Journal of the Asiatic Society of Bengal* 5 (1836): 557.

48 A Subaltern, *A Description of the Ruined City of Mandu, the Ancient Capital of Malwa* (Bombay: Bombay Times' Press, 1844), 121, 107. This is a revision of a work published under the pseudonym "Selim" in several issues of the *Bombay Courier* in 1839: April 9, April 20, April 23, April 27, April 30. *The Cave Temples of India* identifies this wily Subaltern/Selim as one Lieutenant Blake (James Fergusson and James Burgess, *The Cave Temples of India* [London: W.H. Allen, 1880], 281).

49 See Subaltern, *Description*, 105–25.

50 Begley, "Identification," 25.

51 Prinsep, "Facsimiles," 560.

52 Ibid., 561.

53 James Bird, *Historical Researches on the Origin and Principles of the Bauddha and Jaina Religions* (Bombay: American Mission Press, 1847), iii.

54 Ibid.

55 Ibid., v.

56 Ibid., iv.

57 James Fergusson, "On the Rock-Cut Temples of India," *Transactions of the Royal Asiatic Society of Great Britain and Ireland* 8 (1846): 90–1.

58 Cited in John Griffiths, *The Paintings in the Buddhist Cave-Temples of Ajanta, Khandesh, India* (London: W. Griggs, 1896–7), 1:2.

59 Hossain Syed Bilgrami and C. Willmott, *Historical and Descriptive Sketch of His Highness the Nizam's Dominions* (Bombay: Times of India Steam Press, 1884), 2:258.

60 Ibid., 2:259.

61 John Cumming, ed., *Revealing India's Past*: A *Co-operative Record of Archeological Conservation and Exploration in India and Beyond* (London: The India Society, 1939), 254–5.

62 Ibid., 255.

63 Darryl D'Monte, "Conservation Questions at Ajanta," *Frontline* 15 (November 20, 1998): 65–70.

64 Dulari Gupte Qureshi, *Tourism Potential in Aurangabad (With Ajanta, Ellora, Daulatabad Fort)* (Delhi: Bharatiya Kala Prakashan, 1999), 155.

65 Ibid.

66 Dean MacCannell, *The Tourist: A New Theory of the Leisure Class* (Berkeley, CA: University of California Press, 1999), 2.

67 Ibid., 3.

68 Ibid., 41; Jonathan Z. Smith, *To Take Place: Toward Theory in Ritual* (Chicago, IL: University of Chicago Press, 1987), 109–10.

69 MacCannell, *Tourist*, 37; Smith, *To Take Place*, 109–10.

70 MacCannell, *Tourist*, 102–3.

71 Abdul Qadir, "Mega Plan for Mahabodhi Temple," *Times of India* (June 29, 2002) http://timesofindia.indiatimes.com/articleshow.asp?artid=14403657&sType = 1 (July 22, 2002).

72 "Operational Guidelines, for the Implementation of the World Heritage Convention," http://www.unesco.org/whc/nwhc/pages/doc/main.htm (March 26, 2002)

73 Myra Shackley, "Introduction: World Cultural Heritage Sites," in Myra Shackley, ed., *Visitor Management: Case Studies from World Heritage Sites* (Oxford: Butterworth-Heinemann, 1998), 1.

74 http://www.unesco.org/whc/opgulist.htm (March 27, 2002).

75 Shackley, *Visitor Management*, xiii.

76 Thomas Hine, *The Total Package*: *The Secret History and Hidden Meanings of Boxes, Bottles, Cans, and Other Persuasine Containers* (Boston, MA: Little Brown, 1995), 46–8.

77 Ibid., 54.

78 Jean-Noël Kapferer, *Strategic Brand Management* (London: Kogan Page, 1997), 23.

79 Ibid.

80 Tom Peters, *The Circle of Innovation*: *You Can't Shrink your Way to Greatness* (New York: Vintage Books, 1997), 337.

81 Ibid., 308–9.

82 See Tom Peters, *The Pursuit of Wow!* (New York: Random House, 1994).

83 Rita Clifton and Esther Maughan, eds, *The Future of Brands: Twenty-Five Visions* (New York: New York University Press, 2000), xiii.

84 Thomas Gad, *4-D Branding: Cracking the Corporate Code of the Network Economy* (London: Financial Times Prentice Hall, 2001), 180–1.

85 Shackley, *Visitor Management*, xiii.

86 Lipe, "Value and Meaning," 2.

87 Wolfgang Haug, *Critique of Commodity Aesthetics: Appearance, Sexuality and Advertising in Capitalist Society* trans. Robert Bock (New York: Polity Press, 1986), 16–17.
88 Holt and Schor, *Consumer Society*, xxi.
89 Shackley, *Visitor Management*, 1.
90 James Twitchell, *Lead Us Into Temptation: The Triumph of American Materialism* (New York: Columbia University Press, 1999), 20.
91 Karl Marx, "Economic and Philosophic Manuscripts of 1844," in *Karl Marx, Frederick Engels: Collected Works* trans. Clemens Dutt (Moscow: Progress Publishers, 1975), 3:307.
92 Peters, *Circle*, 295–6.
93 See Gary Cross, *An All-Consuming Century: Why Consumercialism Won in Modern America* (New York: Columbia University Press, 2000), 193–232.
94 Kalle Lasn, *Culture Jam: How to Reverse America's Suicidal Consumer Binge—And Why We Must* (New York: HarperCollins, 1999), xii–xiii.
95 Holt and Schor, *Consumer Society*, ix.
96 Robert Bork, *Slouching Toward Gomorrah* (New York: Regan Books, 1996), 8–9.
97 Twitchell, *Lead Us*, 271–86; Lasn, *Culture Jam*, xiii.
98 Immanuel Kant, "An Answer to the Question: What is Enlightenment?," in Mary Gregor, ed. and trans., *Practical Philosophy* (Cambridge: Cambridge University Press, 1999 [1784]), 20.
99 Edward, Lord Herbert of Cherbury, *De Veritate* trans. Meyrick Carré (Bristol: J.W. Arrowsmith, 1937 [1624]), 295.
100 Voltaire, "Sect," *Philosophical Dictionary* trans. H.I. Woolf (London: George Allen & Unwin, 1923 [1764]), 270.
101 Immanuel Kant, "Religion Within the Boundaries of Mere Reason," in Allen Wood and George di Giovanni, eds and trans., *Religion and Rational Theology* (Cambridge: Cambridge University Press, 2001 [1793]), 140.
102 Twitchell, *Lead Us*, 54.
103 Ibid., 57.
104 Holt and Schor, *Consumer Society*, ix.
105 Ibid.
106 Lasn, *Culture Jam*, 212, xiv.
107 Ibid., 107–8.
108 Ibid., 108.
109 Ibid., xiii.
110 See Bernard Faure, *The Rhetoric of Immediacy: A Cultural Critique of Chan/Zen Buddhism* (Princeton, NJ: Princeton University Press, 1991).
111 Robert Scharf, "The Zen of Japanese Nationalism," in Donald Lopez, ed., *Curators of the Buddha: The Study of Buddhism Under Colonialism* (Chicago, IL: University of Chicago Press, 1995), 107.
112 Lasn, *Culture Jam*, 106.
113 Chögyam Trungpa, *Cutting Through Spiritual Materialism* (Berkeley, CA: Shambhala, 1973), 16.
114 Lasn, *Culture Jam*, xii–xiii.
115 Ibid., xv.
116 Twitchell, *Lead Us*, 286.
117 Maharashtra, Directorate of Tourism, *Ajanta* (Bombay: Tata McGraw-Hill, 1976), 1–2.
118 Caritat, *Sketch*, 201.
119 Directorate of Tourism, *Ajanta*, 2.
120 Jean-Marie Dru, *Disruption: Overturning Conventions and Shaking up the Marketplace* (New York: John Wiley, 1996).

3 A TALE OF TWO HISTORIES

1 Ashis Nandy, "History's Forgotten Doubles," *History and Theory* 34 (1995): 63.
2 Ibid., 47.
3 Ashis Nandy, "Homing in on History," *The Statesman* (Sunday, June 21, 1992): Miscellany section.
4 Nandy, "Forgotten Doubles," 47.
5 Ibid.
6 Nandy, "Homing."
7 Ibid.
8 "WHC Convention," http://whc.unesco.org/nwhc/pages/doc/main.htm (August 3, 2002).
9 See William Pietz, "The Problem of the Fetish, I," *Res* 9 (1985): 7–17; "The Problem of the Fetish, II: The Origin of the Fetish," *Res* 13 (1987): 23–45; "The Problem of the Fetish, IIIa: Bosman's Guinea and the Enlightened Theory of Fetishism," *Res* 16 (1988): 105–23; "Fetishism and Materialism: The Limits of Theory in Marx," in Emily Apter and William Pietz, eds, *Fetishism as Cultural Discourse* (Ithaca, NY: Cornell University Press, 1993), 119–51.
10 Pietz, "Fetish, I," 14.
11 Pietz, "Fetish, II," 24.
12 Ibid., 24–5.
13 Bruno Latour and Steve Woolgar, *Laboratory Life: The Social Construction of Scientific Facts* (Beverly Hills, CA: Sage Publications, 1979), 182.
14 Ibid., 240.
15 Ibid.
16 A.K. Ramanujan, "Is There an Indian Way of Thinking? An Informal Essay," *Contributions to Indian Sociology* 23 (1989): 41–58.
17 Ibid., 46.
18 See Immanuel Kant, "On a Supposed Right to Lie from Philanthropy," in Mary Gregor, ed., *Practical Philosophy* (Cambridge: Cambridge University Press, 1999 [1797]), 611–15.
19 Ramanujan, "Indian Way," 46.
20 Ibid.
21 This question is patterned on Kant's definition of truth—which he calls "nominal... granted and presupposed"—namely, "the agreement of cognition with its object" (*Critique of Pure Reason* trans. Paul Guyer and Allen Wood [Cambridge: Cambridge University Press, 1999 [1781/1787]], 197). I will return to this definition throughout the chapter.
22 Dipesh Chakrabarty, *Provincializing Europe: Postcolonial Thought and Historical Difference* (Princeton, NJ: Princeton University Press, 2000), 41.
23 Ibid., 36, 37.
24 Ibid., 41.
25 Mukul Chandra Dey, *My Pilgrimages to Ajanta & Bagh* (New York: George Doran, 1925), 27; Richard Lannoy, *The Speaking Tree: A Study of Indian Culture and Society* (London: Oxford University Press, 1975), 50.
26 Richard S. Cohen, "Setting the Three Jewels: The Complex Culture of Buddhism at the Ajanta Caves," (PhD dissertation, University of Michigan, 1995), 376–7.
27 Alan Moorehead, "Lovers upon the Walls," *The New Yorker* 30 (May 1, 1954): 63.
28 M.K. Dhavalikar, "New Inscriptions from Ajaṇṭā," *Ars Orientalis* 7 (1968): 152.
29 Ibid.
30 Dey, *Pilgrimages*, 45–6.
31 http://www.agencyfaqs.org/newcamp/maharashtra_24092001.html (June 6, 2003).
32 Dhavalikar, "New Inscriptions," 152.

33 Cohen, "Setting," 371, 362.
34 James Fergusson and James Burgess, *The Cave Temples of India* (London: W.H. Allen, 1880), 299.
35 Walter Spink, "The Archaeology of Ajaṇṭā," *Ars Orientalis* 21 (1992): 70.
36 Ibid., 69.
37 This point has been noted by many scholars. For a clear statement see Vidya Dehejia, "The Collective and Popular Basis of Early Buddhist Patronage: Sacred Monuments, 100 B.C.–A.D. 250," in Barbara Stoler Miller, ed., *The Powers of Art: Patronage in Indian Culture* (Delhi: Oxford University Press, 1992), 35–45.
38 I must apologize for not treating this matter further. For although Spink's morphological and motival analyses are trustworthy, he uses faulty translations of Ajanta's major inscriptions to set those relative facts into a historical narrative. For a discussion of where Spink has gone awry in his historical reconstruction see my "Problems in the Writing of Ajanta's History: The Epigraphic Evidence," *Indo-Iranian Journal* 38 (1995): 125–48. For a tentative alternative reconstruction, see Cohen, "Setting," 63–77.
39 Spink, "Archaeology," 81.
40 Walter Spink, "Before the Fall: Pride and Piety at Ajanta," in Miller, *Powers*, 67.
41 Abū al-Fazl ibn Mubārak, *A'in-I-Ākbari* trans. H.S. Jarrett and Sarkar Jadu-Nath (Calcutta: Royal Asiatic Society of Bengal, 1949 [1598]), 2:239.
42 "Very extensive excavations have recently been discovered both at the top and bottom of the Ajunta-pass. They have been little visited, on account of the difficulty of approaching them. The only information regarding them, which I possess, is contained in a Memorandum of Captain Morgan's, of the Madras establishment, which states, that 'they were described by the officers who visited them in 1819 as having sitting figures with curled wigs. No traces of Brahminical religion were discovered. The paintings were in a decent state of preservation. There is, near one of the caves, a long inscription, apparently Shanscrit, engraved on a rock, which may throw some light on the excavations.' If the conjectures already hazarded are correct, these inscriptions will probably be found to be in the Maghadhi or Prakrit tongue" (William Erskine, "Observations on the Remains of the Bouddhists in India," *Transactions of the Bombay Literary Society* 3 [1823]: 520).
43 Walter Spink, "Ajanta in a Historical and Political Context," *Maharashtra Pathik* 2 (September 1990): 5.
44 Ibid.
45 Moorehead, "Lovers," 65.
46 Hans Bakker, *The Vakatakas: An Essay in Hindu Iconology* (Groningen: Egbert Forsten, 1997), 40.
47 Cohen, "Setting," 3.
48 Sheila Weiner, *Ajanta: Its Place in Buddhist Art* (Berkeley, CA: University of California Press, 1977), 2–3.
49 Ibid., 3.
50 Ibid., 35.
51 Ibid., 7.
52 Ibid.
53 al-Fazl, *A'in-I-Ākbari*, 2:239.
54 See ibid., 3:223–7.
55 Dipesh Chakrabarty, "The Time of History and the Times of Gods," in Lisa Lowe and David Lloyd, eds, *The Politics of Culture in the Shadow of Capital* (Durham, NC: Duke University Press, 1997), 36; Chakrabarty, *Provincializing Europe*, 37.
56 R.G. Collingwood, *The Idea of History* (London: Oxford University Press, 1956), 215.
57 Nandy, "Forgotten Doubles," 64.

58 Christopher Nolan and Jonathan Nolan, *Memento*. Directed by Christopher Nolan. 113 min. Columbia Tri-Star, 2000. DVD.

59 Étienne Balibar, "Subjection and Subjectivation," in Joan Copjec, ed., *Supposing the Subject* (London: Verso, 1994), 6.

60 Kant, *Critique of Pure Reason*, 178–84.

61 Ibid., 306–7.

62 Ibid., 298.

63 Nandy, "Forgotten Doubles," 65.

64 Ibid.

65 Kant, *Critique of Pure Reason*, 197.

66 Chakrabarty, *Provincializing Europe*, 45.

67 Weiner, *Ajanta*, 108.

68 Geoff Crowther, Hugh Finlay, Prakash A. Raj and Tony Wheeler, *India: A Travel Survival Kit*, 4th edition (Hawthorn, Australia: Lonely Planet Publications, 1990), 663.

69 ...not too short either, for the white outline of a trident can be discerned in a photographic plate in James Fergusson's *The Rock-Cut Temples of India Illustrated by Seventy-Four Photographs Taken on the Spot by Major Gill* (London: John Murray, 1864), 13. I would advise the intrepid reader to locate a first edition. The trident is in a deep shadow, and will probably be lost in later reproductions.

70 John Griffiths, *The Paintings in the Buddhist Cave-Temples of Ajanta, Khandesh India* (London: W. Griggs, 1896–7), 1:2.

71 Myra Shackley, *Visitor Management: Case Studies from World Heritage Sites* (Oxford: Butterworth-Heinemann, 1998), xiii.

72 Griffiths, *Paintings*, 1:2.

73 Ibid.

74 Ibid.

75 Ibid. Citation is lightly edited.

76 Published under the pseudonym *Selim*, Lieutenant Blake's account is first found in the *Bombay Courier* over a series of issues in 1839: April 9, 20, 23, 27, 30. He then revised these articles, and included them in an anonymous collection of essays: A Subaltern, *A Description of the Ruined City of Mandu, the Ancient Capital of Malwa* (Bombay: The Bombay Times' Press, 1844). I thank *The Cave Temples of India* for identifying this wily Selim/Subaltern as Lieutenant Blake (281).

77 Subaltern, *Description*, 125. Citation is lightly edited.

78 Ibid., 124. Citation is lightly edited.

79 Ibid., 117.

80 Griffiths, *Paintings*, 1:1.

81 Ibid., 1:7.

82 Chakrabarty, *Provincializing Europe*, 45.

83 Ibid., 46.

84 James Fergusson, "On the Rock-Cut Temples of India," *Transactions of the Royal Asiatic Society of Great Britain and Ireland* 8 (1846): 30.

85 Ibid.

86 Ibid.

87 Ibid., 32.

88 Spink, "Archaeology," 70.

89 Fergusson, "On Rock-Cut Temples," 36.

90 Ibid., 44, 55.

91 Cited in Gregory Schopen, *Bones, Stones, and Buddhist Monks: Collected Papers on the Archaeology, Epigraphy and Texts of Monastic Buddhism in India* (Honolulu, HI: University of Hawai'i Press, 1997), 42.

92 Fergusson, "On Rock-Cut Temples," 44, 55.

93 Fergusson, "On Rock-Cut Temples," 44, 55–6.
94 Ibid., 32.
95 Ibid., 45.
96 Ibid., 46.
97 Fergusson, *Rock-Cut Temples*, xvi.
98 Fergusson and Burgess, *Cave Temples*, 295.
99 Ibid., 170, 297.
100 Weiner, *Ajanta*, 3, 7.
101 Fergusson and Burgess, *Cave Temples*, 528, 539.
102 Philip Almond, *The British Discovery of Buddhism* (Cambridge: Cambridge University Press, 1988), 95.
103 Fergusson and Burgess, *Cave Temples*, 179.
104 Ibid., 179, 297.
105 Ibid., 297, 298.
106 Douglas Holt and Juliet Schor, *The Consumer Society Reader* (New York: The New Press, 2000), xxi.
107 François Truffaut, *Hitchcock* (New York: Simon and Schuster, 1984), 138.
108 Ibid., 138, 168–9.
109 Ibid., 139.

4 THE ANTHROPOLOGY OF ENLIGHTENMENT

1 Henry David Thoreau, *Walden; Or, Life in the Woods* (New York: Harper & Row, 1966 [1854]), 428. Thanks to Jeremy Zwelling for calling this passage to my attention.
2 James Fergusson, "On the Rock-Cut Temples of India," *Transactions of the Royal Asiatic Society of Great Britain and Ireland* 8 (1846): 44; James Fergusson and James Burgess, *The Cave Temples of India* (London: W.H. Allen, 1880), 283.
3 Fergusson, "Rock-Cut Temples," 33.
4 Fergusson and Burgess, *Cave Temples*, 16.
5 James Fergusson, *The Rock-Cut Temples of India Illustrated by Seventy-Four Photographs Taken on the Spot by Major Gill* (London: John Murray, 1864), 58.
6 Fergusson, "Rock-Cut Temples," 55.
7 Fergusson, *Rock-Cut Temples, Illustrated*, 33.
8 Fergusson and Burgess, *Cave Temples*, 317.
9 Jane Rendall, "Scottish Orientalism: From Robertson to James Mill," *The Historical Journal* 25 (1982): 43.
10 William Erskine, "Observations on the Remains of the Bouddhists in India," *Transactions of the Bombay Literary Society* 3 (1823): 495.
11 Ibid., 494.
12 Ibid.
13 Ibid., 507.
14 Richard Davis, "The Story of the Disappearing Jains: Retelling the Śaiva–Jain Encounter in Medieval South India," in John Cort, ed., *Open Boundaries: Jain Communities and Cultures in Indian History* (Albany, NY: SUNY Press, 1998), 223.
15 Thoreau, *Walden*, 428.
16 Richard Gombrich, *Theravāda Buddhism: A Social History from Ancient Benares to Modern Colombo* (London: Routledge & Kegan Paul, 1988), 1–2.
17 Richard S. Cohen, "Setting the Three Jewels: The Complex Culture of Buddhism at the Ajanta Caves," (PhD dissertation, University of Michigan, 1995), 384–5.
18 Sigmund Freud, *The Interpretation of Dreams* trans. James Strachey (New York: Avon Books, 1965 [1900]), 317.
19 Ibid., 182.

20 Ernesto Laclau and Chantal Mouffe, *Hegemony and Socialist Strategy: Towards a Radical Democratic Politics* (London: Verso, 1985), 104.

21 Raniero Gnoli, ed., *The Gilgit Manuscript of the Saṅghabhedavastu* (Rome: ISMEO, 1977), 1:113.

22 Cohen, "Setting," 380.

23 This analysis of the mural is based upon the version of the story found in Gnoli, *Gilgit*, 1:113–19.

24 Cave Twenty Six's image of the Earth goddess is somewhat unusual. Typically this deity is a serene figure, half-emerging from the ground. Ajanta's goddess—with her vigorous footwork, billowing scarf, and call to war—belongs to a sub-genre of wrathful Earth goddesses. Janet Leoshko discusses this iconography in, "The Case of the Two Witnesses to the Buddha's Enlightenment," in Pratapaditya Pal, ed., *A Pot-Pourri of Indian Art* (Bombay: Marg Publications, 1988), 39–52.

25 These descriptions are taken from two of the earliest modern published records about Ajanta: James Edward Alexander, "Notice of a Visit to the Cavern Temples of Adjunta in the East-Indies," *Transactions of the Royal Asiatic Society of Great Britain and Ireland* 2 (1830): 362–70; and James Prinsep, "Facsimiles of Various Ancient Inscriptions," *Journal of the Asiatic Society of Bengal* 5 (1836): 348–9, 556–61.

26 John Zephaniah Holwell, *Interesting Historical Events, Relative to the Provinces of Bengal, and the Empire of Indostan* (London: T. Becket and P.J. De Hondt, 1766–71), 1:9.

27 Ibid., 1:9–10.

28 Erskine, "Observations," 520.

29 Alexander, "Notice," 365.

30 Prinsep, "Facsimiles," 560.

31 James Bird, *Historical Researches on the Origin and Principles of the Bauddha and Jaina Religions* (Bombay: American Mission Press, 1847), 13–18.

32 Prinsep, "Facsimiles," 559.

33 Dieter Schlingloff, *Studies in the Ajanta Paintings: Identifications and Interpretations* (Delhi: Ajanta Publications, 1988), 35.

34 Immanuel Kant, "Critique of Practical Reason," in Mary Gregor, ed., and trans., *Practical Philosophy* (Cambridge: Cambridge University Press, 1999 [1788]), 269.

35 Ibid., 270.

36 Ibid., 270–1.

37 Christopher Berry, *Social Theory of the Scottish Enlightenment* (Edinburgh: Edinburgh University Press, 1997), 4–5.

38 Pierre Simon, Marquis de Laplace, *A Philosophical Essay on Probabilities* trans. Frederick Truscott and Frederick Emory (New York: Dover Publications, 1951 [1814]), 4.

39 Karl Popper, *The Open Universe: An Argument for Indeterminism* (Totowa, NJ: Rowman and Littlefield, 1982), 5.

40 Roger Hausheer, "Introduction," in Isaiah Berlin, ed., *Against the Current: Essays in the History of Ideas* (London: Hogarth Press, 1979), xxvi.

41 Popper, *Open Universe*, 5. Though I cite Popper here, the best, most complete exploration of this connection is found in Amos Funkenstein, *Theology and the Scientific Imagination From the Middle Ages to the Seventeenth Century* (Princeton, NJ: Princeton University Press, 1986).

42 Martin Luther, *The Bondage of the Will* trans. J.I. Packer and O.R. Johnston (Grand Rapids, MI: Fleming H. Revell, 2003 [1525]), 40.

43 Ibid., 216–7.

44 Ibid., 101.

45 Ibid., 317.

46 Peter Gay, *The Enlightenment: The Rise of Modern Paganism* (New York: Norton, 1995), 368.

47 Gregory Schopen, *Bones, Stones, and Buddhist Monks: Collected Papers on the Archaeology, Epigraphy and Texts of Monastic Buddhism in India* (Honolulu, HI: University of Hawai'i Press, 1997), 2.

48 Ibid., 2, 1.

49 Ibid., 13.

50 Ibid., 7.

51 Erskine, "Observations," 507.

52 Ibid., 503.

53 Schopen, *Bones*, 9.

54 Ibid., 14.

55 Ibid., 2.

56 Ibid., 114.

57 Mircea Eliade, *The Sacred and the Profane: The Nature of Religion* trans. Willard Trask (San Diego, CA: Harcourt Brace, 1987), 20.

58 Ibid., 22.

59 Ibid.

60 Ibid., 21.

61 Ibid., 42.

62 Ibid.

63 Although India had no sense of tragedy parallel to that found in classical Greece, Aristotle's description of the tragic drama is appropriate to this narrative. Figures who, for Greece, would be deemed "tragic heroes" are in India always treated as villains. Māra is no exception. Though he is called the Evil One, in fact he is an "intermediate kind of personage," noble but flawed (Aristotle, "De Poetica," 1453a). Māra is responsible for his own misery, not because he is depraved but because he is in error. Thus he is the source for the audience's "pleasure...of fear and pity" (1453b). This is an Indian story. In the long run, Māra is redeemed, a fate that distinguishes him from the likes of Creon or Pentheus (see John Strong, *The Legend of King Aśoka: A Study and Translation of the Aśokāvadāna* [Princeton, NJ: Princeton University Press, 1983], 185–98).

64 Richard Lannoy, *The Speaking Tree: A Study of India Culture and Society* (London: Oxford University Press, 1975), 49–50.

65 Bernard Faure, "The Buddhist Icon and the Modern Gaze," *Critical Inquiry* 24 (1998): 768–813.

66 Following the lead of Pran Gopal Paul, we have one more interpretation to consider. In an article on the *varada mudrā's* iconology, Paul proposes that this gesture first indicated the buddha's gift of knowledge, rather than blessings of a material nature. The *mudrā* thus began as something of a visual pun, referring back to a specific incident in the buddha's life. Śākyamuni is remembered as having suffered cramps off and on during the his final months, not unusual for an eighty year old man. After one severe bout, his attendant Ānanda voiced the expectation that the buddha would remain alive at least long enough to give final instructions. Not a little angry, Śākyamuni replied that no such instruction was needed, for he had never concealed any teachings within a "closed fist." Every relevant truth had been revealed. According to Paul, the *varada mudrā's* open palm "crystallized ostensibly as an antithesis of the proverbial [teacher's closed fist]" ("From Ācaryamuṣṭi to Varadamudrā: Antithetical Transformation of a Literary Concept into Visual Art," in Ellen Raven and Karel Van Kooij, eds, *Indian Art and Archaeology* [Leiden: Brill, 1992], 74). In this way, we might regard the relief as a whole as the buddha's teaching. The act of overcoming Māra itself reprises Śākyamuni's "quintessential role as a preacher" (73).

This interpretation is attractive in that it starts from the overt materiality of the mural, the open-handed gesture of generosity. Additionally, Paul's interpretation of the *mudrā* is less likely to offend the pious than some suggested in the main text, including the possibility that Śākyamuni doubles as a pimp. Nevertheless, Paul does not give us a determinative key to the relief's significance. His interpretation does not logically contravene the others, but neither does it necessarily coordinate them. Paul's reduction of a complex biography to a "quintessential role" also represents the relief's significance as a calculus of value within a distinct economy of meaning, a referential network that invigorates the eyes and enlivens the stone.

At best, Paul defers the issue. Let us stipulate that his interpretation *is* accurate. What truths are pushed forward by this teacher's open hand? Again, multiple possibilities can be read into the palm's characteristic lines. The metaphysics underlying the MSV is a kind of realism, somewhat magical, which allows that there are real bodhisattvas and real gods, and that one really can read the mind of the other. However, the MSV was not the only text known to Ajanta's community. Belonging to the *vinaya* genre, the MSV focuses upon monastic discipline; its conceptualization of buddhahood as an abstract state is largely implicit. Other texts known to Ajanta were expressly concerned with theorizing buddhahood. And some of these were not as "naive" as the MSV. In the fifth century, Ajanta was a center for Mahāyāna, a form of Buddhism whose normative buddhology is magical and *not* realist. According to Mahāyāna mythology, Śākyamuni himself created Māra in order to stage a drama of conflict and resolution. Māra was in Bodh Gayā, not because he *really* is an Evil One, but because the story needed a villain to hold its audience's imagination. By challenging the bodhisattva, this Māra assisted the buddha. Indeed for Mahāyāna, Śākyamuni's entire life on earth was an elaborate charade: he was enlightened in the infinite past, not the fifth century BCE; his enlightenment took place in a heaven, not on earth; he realized enlightenment in a single blinding moment of insight after a ritual consecration, not after a laborious process of rational analysis. To take such bauddha tenets seriously is to read a new intentionality within the creases of this buddha's open palm. His *varada mudrā* does not offer teachings (only) about drying out the mire of ignorance and evil that keeps one stuck in saṃsāra, rather it (also) gives instruction on Śākyamuni's cosmic supremacy. Perhaps viewers are meant to learn that buddhas are all-powerful, all-knowing, virtually eternal, thoroughly compassionate, and ever-present superdivinities. Buddhas are not dazed by saṃsāra's swirl, nor confused in any circumstance, for they have conquered every imp of doubt. Perhaps we are meant to learn that however lost we feel—dazed and confused for so long by samsara's swirling eddy—however many choices we have to make without a good, solid basis for knowing what is right, we know a being exists who solves all confusion. Perhaps the final irony here is that even the promise of absolute certainty also adds to our perplexity.

67 Ernesto Laclau, *New Reflections on the Revolution of Our Time* (London: Verso, 1990), 27.

68 Schopen, *Bones*, 13–14.

69 Ibid., 14.

70 Ibid., 13. Emphasis mine.

71 Martin Luther, "The Last sermon at Wittenberg, 17 January 1546," in John Doberstein, ed. and trans., *Luther's Works*, Volume 51 (Philadelphia, PA: Muhlenberg Press, 1959), 374.

72 Luther, *Bondage*, 170.

73 Schopen, *Bones*, 114.

74 Ibid.

75 Martin Luther, cited in Frederic Farrar, *History of Interpretation* (New York: Dutton, 1886), 329.

76 Martin Luther, cited in Siegbert Becker, *The Foolishness of God: The Place of Reason in the Theology of Martin Luther* (Milwaukee, WI: Northwestern Publishing, 1982), 172.

77 David Hume, *Enquiries Concerning the Human Understanding and Concerning the Principles of Morals* (Oxford: The Clarendon Press, 1966 [1748]), 127.

78 Peter Berger, "The Desecularization of the World: A Global Overview," in Peter Berger, ed., *The Desecularization of the World* (Grand Rapids, MI: Eerdmans, 1999), 13.

79 In the interest of full disclosure, I have had work published by Eerdmans as well. See "Shakyamuni: Buddhism's Founder in Ten Acts," in David Noel Freedman and Michael McClymond, eds, *The Rivers of Paradise: Moses, Buddha, Confucius, Jesus and Muhammad As Religious Founders* (Grand Rapids, MI: Eerdmans, 2000), 121–232, 663–71.

80 J.D. Paterson, "Of the *Origin* of the *Hindu Religion,*" *Asiatic Researches* 8 (1808): 44.

81 William Jones, "On the Gods of Greece, Italy and India," *Asiatick Researches* 1 (1788): 221.

82 Holwell, *Historical Events*, 3:3–4.

83 John Leland, *A View of the Principal Deistical Writers* (New York: Garland Publishing, 1978 [1757]), 7.

84 Edward, Lord Herbert of Cherbury, *De Veritate* trans. Meyrick Carré (Bristol: J.W. Arrowsmith, 1937 [1624]), 303.

85 Cited in Ronald Bedford, *The Defence of Truth: Herbert of Cherbury and the Seventeenth Century* (Manchester: Manchester University Press, 1979), 166.

86 Herbert, *De Veritate*, 295.

87 Ibid., 83.

88 Ibid., 83–4.

89 Herbert, *De Veritate*, 301.

90 Bedford, *Defence*, 182, 254.

91 Herbert, *De Veritate*, 116, 118.

92 Ibid., 69.

93 Jean Calvin, *Institutes of the Christian Religion* trans. Ford Battles (Philadelphia, PA: Westminster Press, 1960 [1535]): 2: 920–97.

94 "Canons of Dordrecht," http://www.iclnet.org/pub/resources/text/ipb-e/epl-01/candt-01.txt (June 12, 2004).

95 Herbert, *De Veritate*, 136.

96 Ibid.

97 Ibid., 150.

98 Ibid., 123.

99 Ibid., 17.

100 Ibid., 91.

101 Ibid.

102 Ibid., 289.

103 Ibid., 119–30.

104 Ibid., 34.

105 Ibid., 289–307.

106 Ibid., 295.

107 Ibid., 151.

108 Ibid.

109 Ibid., 299–300.

110 Luther, *Bondage*, 170.

111 Ibid.

112 Ibid., 170–1.

113 Ibid.

114 David Steinmetz, *Luther in Context* (Bloomington, IN: Indiana University Press, 1986), 1.

115 Robert Grant, *A Short History of the Interpretation of the Bible* (Philadelphia, PA: Fortress Press, 1984), 129.

116 Luther is cited in ibid., 131; Calvin, *Institutes*, 1:74.

117 Ibid., 1:40.

118 Steinmetz, *Luther*, 96.

119 Luther, *Bondage*, 128.

120 Ibid., 192.

121 Cited in Edward Dowey, *The Knowledge of God in Calvin's Theology* (New York: Columbia University Press, 1952), 33.

122 This is from Calvin's Preface to the Romans, cited in Farrar, *History of Interpretation*, 347.

123 Calvin, *Institutes*, 1:580.

124 Ibid., 2:921.

125 Ibid., 2:967.

126 Ibid., 2:980.

127 Cited in Dowey, *Knowledge*, 187–8.

128 Edward Herbert, *Pagan Religion: A Translation of De Religion Gentilium* trans. John Butler (Binghamton, NY: MRTS, 1996), 16.

129 Herbert, *De Veritate*, 302.

130 John Locke, *An Essay Concerning Human Understanding* (Amherst, NY: Prometheus Books, 1995 [1693]), 44.

131 Ibid., 50. Not a little ironically, Herbert sought to problematize the equation of religious rationalism with revealed Christianity, while Locke's *The Reasonableness of Christianity* claimed that faith, special revelation, and the mysterious "wisdom of God" are what make Christianity *more reasonable* than other religions. See for instance the discussion of the "wisdom of God" in which Locke argued that reason consists precisely in proportioning one's own expectations of knowledge to one's subordinate position vis-à-vis god (John Locke, *The Reasonableness of Christianity, As Delivered in the Scriptures* (Bristol, UK: Thoemmes Press, 1997 [1695]), 134).

132 For an excellent survey see, Peter Byrne, *Natural Religion and the Nature of Religion: The Legacy of Deism* (London: Routledge, 1989).

133 Immanuel Kant, "What Does It Mean to Orient Oneself in Thinking," in Allen Wood and George di Giovanni, eds and trans., *Religion and Rational Theology* (Cambridge: Cambridge University Press, 2001 [1786]), 17–18.

134 Ibid., 12.

135 Ibid., 15.

136 Voltaire, "Prejudices," *Philosophical Dictionary* trans. H.I. Woolf (London: George Allen & Unwin, 1923 [1764]), 251.

5 WHAT DO GODS HAVE TO DO WITH ENLIGHTENMENT?

1 Rupert Gethin, *The Foundations of Buddhism* (New York: Oxford University Press, 1998).

2 Online reviews often seem to have be written in haste, without careful editing. Todd Martin's is no exception. I have not edited or corrected his infelicities of spelling, punctuation, and grammar. "Amazon.com: Books: The Foundations of Buddhism," http://www.amazon.com/exec/obidos/tg/detail/-/0192892231/qid%3D1050590100/ 102–0880043–9102565 (June 16, 2004). I should also note that, as of this date, all of amazon.com's other lay reviewers assess Gethin's book as worthy of five stars.

3 Richard S. Cohen, "Setting the Three Jewels: The Complex Culture of Buddhism at the Ajanta Caves," (PhD dissertation, University of Michigan, 1995), 378–81.
4 Cited in Henri du Lubac, *La rencontre du bouddhisme et de l'Occident* (Paris: Aubier, 2000), 99.
5 This list of countries is taken from Fannie Roper Feudge, "The Mammoth Religion of the World," *Galaxy* 16 (1873): 342.
6 James Clarke, "Buddhism: Or, the Protestantism of the East," *The Atlantic Monthly* 23 (1869): 713–28; Lydia Child, "Resemblances Between the Buddhist and Roman Catholic Religions," *The Atlantic Monthly* 26 (1870): 660–5.
7 Monier Monier-Williams, *The Holy Bible and the Sacred Books of the East* (London: Seely, 1887), 31.
8 Anonymous, "French Missionaries in Tartary and Thibet," *Fraser's Magazine* 45 (1852): 37.
9 Samuel Beal, *Buddhism in China* (London: Society for Promoting Christian Knowledge, 1884), 98.
10 Frederick Maurice, *The Religions of the World and their Relations to Christianity* (London: J.W. Parker, 1847), 93.
11 Edward Conze, *Buddhism: Its Essence and Development* (New York: Harper Torchbooks, 1975), 12.
12 Ibid., 76–7.
13 See note 2. The paragraph attached to note 2 is the first of Martin's review. That paragraph is followed by the two cited here. Given the web's ephemerality, let me preserve the review's fourth and concluding paragraph: "Do not buy this book. Buy 'What the Buddha Taught' by Walpola Rahula. It's generally considered the standard introduction to Buddhism in the west." Finis. Finally, lest I leave an incorrect impression, I myself have published a review of Gethin's book, in which I describe it as lucid and cogent. In fact, the review asserts my preference for Gethin's work over that old standard, *What the Buddha Taught (Religious Studies Review* 25 [1999]: 322).
14 Cited in Gethin, *Foundations*, 66. The *Cūla-Māluṅkyasutta* is sutta #63 in the Pāli *Majjhima Nikāya*.
15 Raniero Gnoli, ed., *The Gilgit Manuscript of the Saṅghabhedavastu* (Rome: ISMEO, 1977), 1:117–19.
16 V. Treckner, ed., *The Majjhima-Nikāya* (London: Pali Text Society, 1935), 1:432.
17 Richard Robinson and Willard Johnson, *The Buddhist Religion: A Historical Introduction* 4th edition (Belmont, CA: Wadsworth Publishing, 1997), 1.
18 See Gethin, *Foundations*, 2–3.
19 David Steinmetz, *Luther in Context* (Bloomington, IN: Indiana University Press, 1986), 96.
20 Edward, Lord Herbert of Cherbury, *De Veritate* trans. Meyrick Carré (Bristol: J.W. Arrowsmith, 1937 [1624]), 302.
21 Denis Diderot and Jean Le Rond d'Alembert, *Encyclopedia: Selections* trans. Nelly Hoyt and Thomas Cassirer (Indianapolis, IN: Bobbs-Merrill, 1965), 285.
22 Martin Luther, *The Bondage of the Will* trans. J.I. Packer and O.R. Johnston (Grand Rapids, MI: Fleming H. Revell, 2003 [1525]), 73, 128.
23 Ernesto Laclau, *Emancipation(s)* (London: Verso, 1996), 103, 90.
24 Gethin, *Foundations*, 2.
25 Laclau, *Emancipation(s)*, 88.
26 Ibid., 78.
27 Ernesto Laclau, "Identity and Hegemony: The Role of Universality in the Constitution of Political Logics," in Judith Butler, Ernesto Laclau, and Slavoj Zizek, eds, *Contingency, Hegemony, Universality* (London: Verso, 2000), 50.
28 Laclau, *Emancipation(s)*, 38.

29 Philip Almond, *The British Discovery of Buddhism* (Cambridge: Cambridge University Press, 1988), 12.

30 Ibid., 10.

31 Rodney Needham, "Polythetic Classification: Convergence and Consequences," *Man* 10 (1975): 349–69.

32 Robert Sokal and Peter Sneath, *Principles of Numerical Taxonomy*, cited in ibid., 356.

33 Donald Lopez, ed., *A Modern Buddhist Bible: Essential Readings from East and West* (Boston, MA: Beacon Press, 2002), ix–xi.

34 Laclau, *Emancipation(s)*, 78.

35 The earliest and best known articulation of this myth is that of the *Viṣṇu Purāṇa* 3:18, see verse 20 in particular. To find additional instances, open Wendy Doniger O'Flaherty's *The Origins of Evil in Hindu Mythology* (Berkeley, CA: University of California Press, 1976). Be advised that Doniger focuses on Śākyamuni as an incarnation of Viṣṇu or Śiva; she is less concerned with the terms used to categorize his followers. When we open medieval mythological and astrological treatises, however, we will see that they do not treat *Śākya* as the name of a distinct or separate religion, but rather as what we might now call a cult or sect. Śākya does not bear that same institutional weight in the context of early medieval India as they often do today. This is not to say that the Śākyas were wayward Hindus, but that terms like "Buddhism" and "Hinduism" obscure the social and ideological divisions active in that period. For instance, the seventh-century *Bṛhatsamhitā* treats *Śākya* as a social taxon equivalent to *Bhāgavata* and *Pāśupata*, sects devoted to Viṣṇu and Śiva respectively (Varāhamihira, *Bṛhatsaṃhitā* trans. M. Ramakrishna Bhat [Delhi: Motilal Banarsidass, 1981], 571–2). Likewise, the fifth/sixth-century *Brahmāṇḍa Purāṇa* (v. 2.3.14.38) lists heretical groups created by demons; these include the Śākyas, Vṛddhaśrāvakīs, Nirgranthas, Jīvaskas, and Kārpaṭas (Ganesh Vesudeo Tagare, trans., *The Brahmāṇḍa Purāṇa* [Delhi: Motilal Banarsidass, 1983]), 1:541; K.V. Sharma, ed., *The Brahmānna Mahāpurāṇam* [Varanasi: Krishnadas Academy, 2000], 130). The Vṛdhaśrāvakīs are devotees of Śiva, now called "Hindus," while the Nirgranthas are now called "Jains." A later text, the *Padma Purāṇa* (circa twelfth century) is even more expansive on the equivalences between the bauddha and sects usually lumped together as Hindu. Here Śiva explains that, at the bidding of Viṣṇu, he "created the reviled sects of the outcastes by proclaiming the Śaiva, Pāśupata, Nyāya, Sānkhya, Materialist, and Buddhist heresies" (Doniger, *Origins of Evil*, 287).

36 Jayadeva, trans., *The Gītagovinda of Jayadeva: Love Song of the Dark Lord* trans. Barbara Stoler Miller (New York: Columbia University Press, 1977), 71.

37 Sarvepalli Radhakrishnan, "Forward," in P.V. Bapat, ed., *2500 Years of Buddhism* (Delhi: Ministry of Information and Broadcasting, 1971), ix.

38 Maitreya, *Buddha-Mimansa, Or, The Buddha and His Relation to the Religion of the Vedas* (London: Thacker, 1925), 32, 45.

39 Slavoj Zizek, *The Sublime Object of Ideology* (London: Verso, 1989), 95–6.

40 In July 2000, for instance, I was discussing Ajanta's origins with a tour-group from Rajasthan. One man told me, "Just as Krishna built the city of Dwarka—one, two, three!—like that Vishwakarma built this place." Another informed me, "According to our Ved-Purana, written by the rshi-munis, the Karmacharya Vishwakarma Dev made this [Ajanta] as an ashram for the gods to live in."

41 Lopez, *Modern Buddhist Bible*, xi.

42 T.W. Rhys Davids, *Buddhist India* (London: T. Fisher Unwin, 1903), 294; T.W. Rhys Davids, *Buddhism: Its History and Literature* (New York: G.P. Putnam's Sons, 1896), 38.

43 "Richard Hayes' Research Activities," http://www.unm.edu/~rhayes/interest.html (May 10, 2004).

44 "Foundation Plaque of the Grand Pagoda," http://www.vri.dhamma.org/general/pgplaque.html (May 10, 2004).

45 S.N. Goenka, "Why the Grand Vipassana Pagoda?" *The Vipassana Newsletter: Dhammagiri Edition* 7/8 (October 1997), http://www.vri.dhamma.org/newsletters/pnl9710.html (April 5, 2004). All subsequent citations of Goenka come from this article, unless otherwise indicated.
46 Al Ries and Jack Trout, *The Twenty Two Immutable Laws of Marketing: Violate Them At Your Own Risk*! (New York: HarperCollins, 1993), 27.
47 Almond, *British Discovery*, 4.
48 Richard Hayes, *Land of No Buddha: Reflections of a Sceptical Buddhist* (Birmingham: Windhorse Publications, 1998), 56, 88.
49 Ibid., 87.
50 Ibid., 2.
51 Ibid., 7–8.
52 Ibid., 83–4.
53 Goenka, "Why the Grand Vipassana Pagoda?"
54 See Hayes, *Land*, 60–5 for his discussion of karma and rebirth, as well as the sources of the citations here and to follow.
55 Ibid., 35.
56 Ibid., 34–5.
57 Ibid., 35.
58 Ibid., 148.
59 Ibid., 156.
60 Ibid., 45, 57, 49, 88, 43.
61 Ibid., 149.
62 Ibid., 144.
63 See ibid., 156, 164, 168, 183, 229.
64 Ibid., 36.
65 Ibid., 130.
66 Ibid., 89–90.
67 Ibid., 88. Allow me to clarify this "original sangha." According to Hayes, ancient Indian men and women who were driven to realize the buddha-dharma and willing to be guided by the rules of discipline as taught by the buddha (*vinaya*) organized themselves into a network of monastic communities supported by a generous laity. By contrast with the mythology of enlightenment, which places the guru at the center of the spiritual universe, this monastic network was decentralized. These original Buddhists were peripatetic. They would move from place to place in search of new teachers to train them in the vinaya or to better explain the dharma. Teachers were not expected to be buddhas, or even their students' spiritual superiors; they were mere monks still on the path to their own perfection. If a student found fault with his teacher, he was allowed to call attention to that failing and offer corrective instruction. Yet there was no overarching Inquisition enforcing orthodoxy and orthopraxy. "The consensus of a community guided by the Dharma and the Vinaya itself," and thus by reason, would re-establish the ailing community "in a more healthy practice" (89). In this way, Hayes' original sangha cohered as an integral community even though its institutions were non-centralized, non-authoritarian, and non-absolutist. For the monastic "us" total consensus was the sine qua non of social life. A group of monks could not accomplish a formal monastic act—for instance, advancing a novice to full monkhood—unless every individual in the community present at that time in that place gave his assent; unanimity was necessary; if one man dissented, the motion failed.
68 Jean-Antoine-Nicolas de Caritat, Marquis de Condorcet, *Sketch for a Historical Picture of the Progress of the Human Mind* trans. June Barraclough (New York: Noonday Press, 1955 [1795]), 202.
69 Laclau, *Emancipation(s)*, 51.

70 Hayes, *Land*, 88.
71 Ibid., 116.
72 Alan Cooperman, "DeLay Criticized for 'Only Christianity' Remarks," *The Washington Post* (Saturday, April 20, 2002): A05.
73 Hayes, *Land*, 49.

6 A BAROQUE CONCLUSION

1 Chantal Mouffe, "Radical Democracy or Liberal Democracy," *Socialist Review* 20 (1990): 58–9.
2 Chantal Mouffe, *The Democratic Paradox* (London: Verso, 2000), 21.
3 Ibid., 22.
4 Dalai Lama, "Forward," in Donald Mitchell and James Wiseman, eds, *The Gethsemani Encounter: A Dialogue on the Spiritual Life by Buddhist and Christian Monastics* (New York: Continuum, 1997), ix.

Hegemonic ecumenism is not just a contemporary phenomenon. Early medieval Sanskrit literature provides a wonderful example. King Harṣavardhana (r. 606–47 CE) was one of India's preeminent rulers. Bāṇabhaṭṭa, a member of Harṣa's court, wrote the *Deeds of Harṣa* in celebration of his patron's youthful adventures. The scene that concerns us has Harṣa wandering through a jungle wilderness. He happens upon the hermitage of Divākaramitra, a brahmin who exchanged his Vedic garments for bauddha robes. In Divākaramitra's jungly glade, Harṣa sees:

> Among the trees were men from many nations sitting all over the place.... Free of passion, those men included: Digambara Jains, Pāśupatas, Śvetāmbara Jains, Ājīvakas, Bhāgavatas, Naiṣṭhika Brahmacārins, ascetics who pull their hair out, Sāṃkhyas, Lokāyatas, Bauddhas, Vaiśeṣikas, Vedantins, Naiyāyikas, alchemists, scholars of the Dharmaśastras, scholars of the Purāṇas, Mimāṃsakas, Śaivas, grammarians, Pāñcarātras, and others. Each was diligently studying his own sectarian tenets (*sva-sva-siddhānta*)—pondering, urging objections, raising doubts, resolving them, giving etymologies, disputing, studying, and explaining. All were avowed students [of Divākaramitra].
>
> (This passage needs a note of its own. See * on page 214 for supporting details.)

Who are these men? Who is Divākaramitra? To answer the first: These are men one normally sees presented as philosophical and religious rivals. The assembly includes partisans of Śiva and of Viṣṇu, atheists and pantheists, materialists and fatalists, ritualists and people who ridicule ritual, scholars of the law and antinomians. Or, to update the image, there are neo-Marxists and neo-Straussians, Secular Humanists and Southern Baptists, Wiccans and Wahabis. This sylvan harmony is staggering. Moreover, Bāṇabhaṭṭa does not simply describe bitter rivals tolerating each other. Śaivas and Vaiṣṇavas, Lokāyatas and Bauddhas follow their own truths while actively striving to "convert" the others. Note the term *siddhānta*, literally "established conclusion." *Siddhāntas* are the doxa and dogmas that differentiate sects; the axiomatic truths without which there is no sectarian identity; the every-man's-land of antagonism.

Note that *siddhānta* is prefixed by *sva*, "own"; doubled, *sva-sva* indicates plurality and particularity. Whatever it means for each man to avow himself as a student of Divākaramitra, it does not mean he has to stop worshiping his own deity, or to give up his own distinct sectarian identity, practices, or beliefs. Bāṇabhaṭṭa describes a kind of doctrinal state of nature—an intellectual war of all against all—civilized through Divākaramitra's presence.

So who is Divākaramitra? Bāṇabhaṭṭa calls Divākaramitra a supreme follower of buddha; names him as the bodhisattva Avalokiteśvara; describes him as somebody worthy of the buddha's reverence and of the dharma's worship. Now if one wonders how this divine man's disciples can hold such diverse sectarian views, Bāṇabhaṭṭa provides the answer. Divākaramitra's physical body has a unique atomic composition, namely it is comprised of the syllables of all sectarian treatises. In short, Divākaramitra embodies the *coincidentia oppositorum* of all theological truths *as well as* all theological disputes.

Divākaramitra is many and one: he embodies all sects at the same time that he is a supreme bauddha. Because of Divākaramitra's constitution, individual disciples may accept Divākaramitra as guru for diverse, idiosyncratic reasons, and yet remain unified as a group. Divākaramitra's followers happily pursue distinct sectarian aims precisely because that is the way to proceed toward a universal good. But Divākaramitra is also a brahmin who renounced the Vedas to become a bauddha. As the concrete embodiment of pure religious positivity, Divākaramitra hegemonically validates all truths as bauddha truths, all gods as bauddha gods, all "spiritual practices" as bauddha practices.

* The complete account of Divākaramitra's hermitage is found in Bāṇabhaṭṭa, *Bāṇabhaṭṭa's Biography of King Harshavardhana of Sthāṇīśvara with Śaṅkara's Commentary, Saṅketa* ed. A.A. Führer (Bombay: Government Central Press, 1909), 316–18; Bāṇabhaṭṭa, *The Harsa-carita of Bāna* trans. E.B. Cowell and F.W. Thomas (London: Royal Asiatic Society, 1897), 236–7. The translation of Cowell and Thomas is unsatisfactory on several accounts. My text is less a literal translation than it is a gloss, which substitutes the better-known names of sects for those used by Bāna. For these identifications, I have taken the suggestions of Vasudeva Agrawala's *The Deeds of Harsha: Being a Cultural Study of Bāna's Harshacarita* (Varanasi: Prithivi Prakashan, 1969), 225–6. I do not want to belabor this point since the precise delineation of these sectarian identities is not important for my purposes, as long as we recognize the general fact of their theological and doctrinal diversity. The same cannot be said for the inclusion of *Bauddha* on this list, so let me discuss that point further. Bāna does not use "bauddha" in this passage, he uses "jaina." In classical Sanskrit, however, the word "jina," conqueror, was given to any spiritual teacher who had overcome ignorance and/or death—including Śākyamuni Buddha. A follower of any *jina* might be called a *jaina*. Unlike today, these terms had no special connection to the people we call Jains or their religion, Jainism. Bāṇabhaṭṭa uses *jaina* three times in the body of his text. In the first instance, the *Harṣacarita*'s fourteenth-century commentary glosses *jaina* as *Śākya*. In the second instance, the commentary gives *bauddha* as the gloss. No gloss is given in the third instance, and no gloss is necessary, since Bāṇabhaṭṭa uses *jaina* in this third instance as a direct characterization of Śākyamuni Buddha's followers (Bāṇabhaṭṭa, *Bāṇabhaṭṭa's Biography*, 97, 316, 325).

5 To investigate this Dorje Shugden incident in greater depth, begin with the Tibetan government's official document: *The Worship of Shugden: Documents Related to a Tibetan Controversy* (Dharamsala, India: Department of Religion and Culture, Central Tibetan Administration, 1998).

6 Xuanzang, *The Great Tang Dynasty Record of the Western Regions* trans. Li Rongxi (Berkeley, CA: Numata Center for Buddhist Translation and Research, 1996), 57.

7 Cited in Ming-Wood Liu, "The Problem of the *Icchantika* in the Mahāyāna *Mahāparinirvāṇa Sūtra*," *Journal of the International Association of Buddhist Studies* 7 (1984): 64.

8 Ibid.

9 Robert E. Buswell, Jr, "The Path to Perdition: The Wholesome Roots and their Eradication," in Robert Buswell and Robert Gimello, eds, *Paths to Liberation: The*

Marga and Its Transformations in Buddhist Thought (Honolulu, HI: University of Hawai'i Press, 1992), 108.

10 Bunyiu Nanjio, ed., *The Laṅkāvatāra Sūtra* (Kyoto: Otani University Press, 1956), 65–6; D.T. Suzuki, trans., *The Lankavatara Sutra* (London: Routledge & Kegan Paul, 1956), 58–9. The pun works because the word *icchantika* derives from a present active participle *icchant*, "desiring." An *icchantika*, literally, is a wanter, desirer, or hedonist.

11 Note, the *Laṅkāvatāra* does not draw these conclusions. After offering its icchantika-typology, the sūtra then invokes a *deus ex machina*. It explains that, although the good icchantika cannot liberate the bad, the buddha does have the power to compel a bad icchantika to seek enlightenment. Thus, for the *Laṅkāvatāra*, everybody eventually does become a buddha. My extravagant allegorization of the icchantika ignores this most unsatisfactory denouement.

12 Buswell, "Perdition," 108.

13 Cited in Liu, "Problem," 61.

14 Albert T. Church, III, "Unclassified Executive summary." http://www.defenselink.mil/news/Mar2005/d20050310exe.pdf (April 20, 2005).

15 Ludwig Feuerbach, *The Essence of Christianity* trans. George Eliot (New York: Harper, 1957 [1841]), 26.

16 Calvin, cited in Frederic Farrar, *History of Interpretation* (New York: Dutton, 1886), 347.

17 Jean Calvin, *Institutes of the Christian Religion* trans. Ford Battles (Philadelphia, PA: Westminster Press, 1960 [1535]), 210.

18 Ibid., 207.

19 Ibid., 200.

20 Ibid., 949

21 Ibid., 926.

22 Ibid., 978.

23 Ibid., 929.

24 Ibid., 944.

25 Ibid., 943.

26 Ibid., 764.

27 Ibid., 931.

28 Ibid., 967.

29 Jeffery Rosen, "The Unregulated Offensive," *The New York Times Magazine* (Sunday, April 17, 2005): 42.

30 For an account of the conference see, Michelle Goldberg, "In Theocracy They Trust," http://www.salon.com/news/feature/2005/04/11/judicial_conference (April 20, 2005). Thanks to Michele Greenstein for bringing this to my attention.

31 "The Chalcedon Foundation—Faith For All Life," http://www.chalcedon.edu/credo.php (April 20, 2005).

BIBLIOGRAPHY

Abū al-Fazl ibn Mubārak, *A'in-I-Ākbari*. trans. H.S. Jarrett and Sarkar Jadu-Nath (Calcutta: Royal Asiatic Society of Bengal, 1949 [1598]).

Agrawala, Vasudeva S., *The Deeds of Harsha: Being a Cultural Study of Bāṇa's Harshacarita*. ed. Prithvi K. Agrawala (Varanasi: Prithivi Prakashan, 1969).

Alabaster, Henry, *The Wheel of the Law* (London: Trübner, 1871).

Alexander, James Edward, "Notice of a Visit to the Cavern Temples of Adjunta in the East-Indies," *Transactions of the Royal Asiatic Society of Great Britain and Ireland* 2 (1830): 362–70.

Allgemeine Encyclopädie de Wissenschaften und Künste in alphabetischer Folge, Volume 13 (Leipzig: J.F. Gieditsch, 1824).

Almond, Philip C., *The British Discovery of Buddhism* (Cambridge: Cambridge University Press, 1988).

Alwis, James de, *Buddhist Nirvána: A Review of Max Müller's Dhammapada* (Colombo: William Skeen, 1871).

"Amazon.com: Books: The Foundations of Buddhism," http://www.amazon.com/exec/obidos/tg/detail/-/0192892231/qid%3D1050590100/102–0880043–9102565 (June 16, 2004).

Amberley, John R., "Recent Publications on Buddhism," *The Theological Review* 9 (July 1872): 293–318.

Anon, "Buddhism," *New Englander* 3 (1845): 182–91.

—— "French Missionaries in Tartary and Thibet," *Fraser's Magazine* 45 (1852): 33–45.

—— "The Influence of Buddhism on Indian Society," *Bombay Quarterly Review* 7 (1858): 143–64.

—— "Review of *Paraméswara-jnyána-góshthi. A Dialogue of the Knowledge of the Supreme Lord, in which are compared the Claims of Christianity and Hindúism, and various Questions of Indian Religion and Literature are fairly discussed* (Cambridge: Deighton, Bell & Co., 1856)," *The Christian Remembrancer* 35 (1858): 81–129.

Augustine, *Confessions*. trans. R.S. Pine-Coffin (New York: Penguin, 1961 [397]).

Bakker, Hans, *The Vakatakas: An Essay in Hindu Iconology* (Groningen: Egbert Forsten, 1997).

Balibar, Étienne, "Subjection and Subjectivation," in Joan Copjec, ed., *Supposing the Subject* (London: Verso, 1994).

Bāṇabhaṭṭa, *The Harsa-carita of Bāna*. trans. E.B. Cowell and F.W. Thomas (London: Royal Asiatic Society, 1897).

—— *Bāṇabhaṭṭa's Biography of King Harshavardhana of Sthāṇīśvara with Śaṅkara's Commentary, Saṅketa.* ed. A.A. Führer (Bombay: Government Central Press, 1909).

Beal, Samuel, *Buddhism in China* (London: Society for Promoting Christian Knowledge, 1884).

Becker, Siegbert W., *The Foolishness of God: The Place of Reason in the Theology of Martin Luther* (Milwaukee, WI: Northwestern Publishing, 1982).

Bedford, Ronald D., *The Defence of Truth: Herbert of Cherbury and the Seventeenth Century* (Manchester: Manchester University Press, 1979).

Begley, Wayne, "The Identification of the Ajaṇṭā Fragment in the Boston Museum," *Oriental Art* 14 (1968): 25–33.

Berger, Peter, "The Desecularization of the World: A Global Overview," in Peter Berger, ed., *The Desecularization of the World: Resurgent Religion and World Politics* (Grand Rapids, MI: Eerdmans, 1999).

Berry, Christopher J., *Social Theory of the Scottish Enlightenment* (Edinburgh: Edinburgh University Press, 1997).

Bilgrami, Hossain Syed and C. Willmott, *Historical and Descriptive Sketch of His Highness the Nizam's Dominions* (Bombay: Times of India Steam Press, 1884).

Bird, James, *Historical Researches on the Origin and Principles of the Bauddha and Jaina Religions* (Bombay: American Mission Press, 1847).

Bork, Robert, *Slouching Toward Gomorrah* (New York: Regan Books, 1996).

Burgess, James, *Notes on the Bauddha Rock-Temples of Ajanta, Their Paintings and Sculptures, and on the Paintings of the Bagh Caves, Modern Bauddha Mythology, &c.* (Bombay: Government Central Press, 1879).

Burnouf, Eugène, *Introduction à l'histoire du buddhisme indien* (Paris: Imprimerie Royale, 1844).

—— *Le Lotus de la Bonne Loi* (Paris: L'Imprimerie Nationale, 1852).

Burnouf, Eugène and Christian Lassen, *Essai sur le pali* (Paris: Dondey-Dupré, 1826).

Buswell, Robert E., Jr, "The Path to Perdition: The Wholesome Roots and their Eradication," in Robert Buswell and Robert Gimello, eds, *Paths to Liberation: The Marga and Its Transformations in Buddhist Thought* (Honolulu, HI: University of Hawai'i Press, 1992).

Byrne, Peter, *Natural Religion and the Nature of Religion: The Legacy of Deism* (London: Routledge, 1989).

Caciola, Nancy, *Discerning Spirits: Divine and Demonic Possession in the Middle Ages* (Ithaca, NY: Cornell University Press, 2003).

Calvin, Jean, *Institutes of the Christian Religion.* trans. Ford Battles (Philadelphia, PA: Westminster Press, 1960 [1535]).

"Canons of Dordrecht," http://www.iclnet.org/pub/resources/text/ipb-e/epl-01/candt-01.txt (June 12, 2004).

Chakrabarty, Dipesh, "The Time of History and the Times of Gods," in Lisa Lowe and David Lloyd, eds, *The Politics of Culture in the Shadow of Capital* (Durham, NC: Duke University Press, 1997).

—— *Provincializing Europe: Postcolonial Thought and Historical Difference* (Princeton, NJ: Princeton University Press, 2000).

"The Chalcedon Foundation—Faith For All Life," http://www.chalcedon.edu/credo.php (April 20, 2005).

Chantepie de la Saussaye, Pierre Daniel, *Manual of the Science of Religion.* trans. Beatrice Colyer-Fergusson (London: Longmans, Green, and Co., 1891).

Child, Lydia, "Resemblances Between the Buddhist and Roman Catholic Religions," *The Atlantic Monthly* 26 (1870): 660–5.

Church, Albert T., III, "Unclassified, Executive Summary," http://www.defenselink.mil/news/Mar2005/d20050310exe.pdf (April 20, 2005).

Clarke, James, "Buddhism: Or, the Protestantism of the East," *The Atlantic Monthly* 23 (1869): 713–28.

Clifton, Rita and Esther Maughan, eds, *The Future of Brands: Twenty-Five Visions* (New York: New York University Press, 2000).

Cohen, Richard S., "Problems in the Writing of Ajanta's History: The Epigraphic Evidence," *Indo-Iranian Journal* 38 (1995): 125–48.

—— "Setting the Three Jewels: The Complex Culture of Buddhism at the Ajanta Caves," (PhD dissertation, University of Michigan, 1995).

—— "Kinsmen of the Son: Śākyabhikṣus and the Institutionalization of the Bodhisattva Ideal," *History of Religions* 40 (2000): 1–31.

—— "Shakyamuni: Buddhism's Founder in Ten Acts," in David Noel Freedman and Michael McClymond, eds, *The Rivers of Paradise: Moses, Buddha, Confucius, Jesus and Muhammad As Religious Founders* (Grand Rapids, MI: Eerdmans, 2000).

Collingwood, Robin G., *The Idea of History* (London: Oxford University Press, 1956).

Condorcet, Jean-Antoine-Nicolas de Caritat, and Marquis de, *Sketch for a Historical Picture of the Progress of the Human Mind* trans. June Barraclough (New York: Noonday Press, 1955 [1795]).

Conze, Edward, *Buddhism: Its Essence and Development* (New York: Harper Torchbooks, 1975).

Cooperman, Alan, "DeLay Criticized for 'Only Christianity' Remarks," *The Washington Post* (Saturday, April 20, 2002): A05.

Cross, Gary S., *An All-Consuming Century: Why Commercialism Won in Modern America* (New York: Columbia University Press, 2000).

Crowther, Geoff, Hugh Finlay, Prakash A. Raj, and Tony Wheeler, *India: A Travel Survival Kit*, 4th edition (Hawthorn, Australia: Lonely Planet Publications, 1990).

Cumming, John, ed., *Revealing India's Past: A Co-operative Record of Archaeological Conservation and Exploration in India and Beyond* (London: The India Society, 1939).

Cunningham, Alexander, "Opening of the Topes or Buddhist Monuments of Central India," *Journal of the Royal Asiatic Society* 13 (1852): 108–14.

Dalai Lama, "Forward," in Donald Mitchell and James Wiseman, eds, *The Gethsemani Encounter: A Dialogue on the Spiritual Life by Buddhist and Christian Monastics* (New York: Continuum, 1997).

Davis, Richard, "The Story of the Disappearing Jains: Retelling the Śaiva–Jain Encounter in Medieval South India," in John Cort, ed., *Open Boundaries: Jain Communities and Cultures in Indian History* (Albany, NY: State University of New York Press, 1998).

Davy, John, *An Account of the Interior of Ceylon and of its Inhabitants: With Travels in that Island* (London: Longman, Hurst, Rees, Orme, and Brown, 1821).

Dehejia, Vidya, "The Collective and Popular Basis of Early Buddhist Patronage: Sacred Monuments, 100 B.C.–A.D. 250," in Barbara Stoler Miller, ed., *The Powers of Art: Patronage in Indian Culture* (Delhi: Oxford University Press, 1992).

Dey, Mukul Chandra, *My Pilgrimages to Ajanta & Bagh* (New York: George Doran, 1925).

Dhavalikar, M.K., "New Inscriptions from Ajaṇṭā," *Ars Orientalis* 7 (1968): 147–53.

Diderot, Denis and Jean Le Rond d'Alembert, *Encyclopedia: Selections.* trans. Nelly Hoyt and Thomas Cassirer (Indianapolis, IN: Bobbs-Merrill, 1965).

Dieckmann, Herbert, *Le Philosophe: Texts and Interpretation* (St Louis, MO: 1948).

D'Monte, Darryl, "Conservation Questions at Ajanta," *Frontline* 15 (November 20, 1998): 65–70.

Dowey, Edward, *The Knowledge of God in Calvin's Theology* (New York: Columbia University Press, 1952).

Dru, Jean-Marie, *Disruption: Overturning Conventions and Shaking up the Marketplace* (New York: John Wiley, 1996).

Eliade, Mircea, *The Sacred and the Profane: The Nature of Religion*. trans. Willard Trask (San Diego, CA: Harcourt Brace, 1987).

Erskine, William, "Observations on the Remains of the Bouddhists in India," *Transactions of the Bombay Literary Society* 3 (1823): 494–537.

Farrar, Frederic, *History of Interpretation* (New York: Dutton, 1886).

Faure, Bernard, *The Rhetoric of Immediacy: A Cultural Critique of Chan/Zen Buddhism* (Princeton, NJ: Princeton University Press, 1991).

—— "The Buddhist Icon and the Modern Gaze," *Critical Inquiry* 24 (1998): 768–813.

Fausböll, Viggo, ed., *Dhammapadam* (London: Williams & Norgate, 1855).

Fergusson, James, "On the Rock-Cut Temples of India," *Transactions of the Royal Asiatic Society of Great Britain and Ireland* 8 (1846): 30–92.

—— *The Rock-Cut Temples of India Illustrated by Seventy-Four Photographs Taken on the Spot by Major Gill* (London: John Murray, 1864).

Fergusson, James and James Burgess, *The Cave Temples of India* (London: W.H. Allen, 1880).

Feudge, Fannie Roper, "The Mammoth Religion of the World," *Galaxy* 16 (1873): 342–54.

Feuerbach, Ludwig, *The Essence of Christianity*. trans. George Eliot (New York: Harper, 1957 [1841]).

Fleet, J.F., "Sanskrit and Old-Canarese Inscriptions," *Indian Antiquary* 10 (1881): 185–90, 273–4.

Foucault, Michel, "What is Enlightenment?" in Paul Rabinow, ed., *The Foucault Reader* (New York: Pantheon Books, 1984).

Francklin, William, *Researches on the Tenets and Doctrines of the Jeynes and Boodhists; Conjectured to be the Brachmanes of Ancient India* (London: William Francklin, 1827).

Freud, Sigmund, *The Interpretation of Dreams*. trans. James Strachey (New York: Avon Books, 1965 [1900]).

Funkenstein, Amos, *Theology and the Scientific Imagination From the Middle Ages to the Seventeenth Century* (Princeton, NJ: Princeton University Press, 1986).

Gad, Thomas, *4-D Branding: Cracking the Corporate Code of the Network Economy* (London: Financial Times Prentice Hall, 2001).

Gay, Peter, *The Enlightenment: The Rise of Modern Paganism* (New York: Norton, 1995).

Gethin, Rupert, *The Foundations of Buddhism* (Oxford: Oxford University Press, 1998).

Gnoli, Raniero, ed., *The Gilgit Manuscript of the Saṅghabhedavastu* (Rome: Istituto Italiano per il Medio ed Estremo Oriente, 1977).

Goenka, S.N., "Why the Grand Vipassana Pagoda?" *The Vipassana Newsletter: Dhammagiri Edition* 7/8 (October 1997), http://www.vri.dhamma.org/newsletters/pnl9710.html (April 5, 2004).

—— "Foundation Plaque of the Grand Pagoda," http://www.vri.dhamma.org/general/pgplaque.html (May 10, 2004).

Gogerly, Daniel John, *Ceylon Buddhism: Being the Collected Works of Daniel John Gogerly*. ed. Arthur Bishop (London: Kegan Paul, Trench, Trübner & Co., 1908).

Goldberg, Michelle, "In Theocracy They Trust," http://www.salon.com/news/feature/2005/04/11/judicial_conference (April 20, 2005).

Gombrich, Richard, *Theravāda Buddhism: A Social History from Ancient Benares to Modern Colombo* (London: Routledge & Kegan Paul, 1988).

Gómez, Luis O., *The Land of Bliss: The Paradise of the Buddha of Measureless Light* (Honolulu, HI: University of Hawai'i Press, 1996).

Gramsci, Antonio, *Selections from the Prison Notebooks of Antonio Gramsci*. ed. and trans. Quintin Hoare and Geoffrey Smith (New York: International Publishers, 1971).

Grant, Robert, *A Short History of the Interpretation of the Bible* (Philadelphia, PA: Fortress Press, 1984).

Griffiths, John, *The Paintings in the Buddhist Cave-Temples of Ajanta, Khandesh, India* (London: W. Griggs, 1896–7).

Hacking, Ian, *The Social Construction of What?* (Cambridge, MA: Harvard University Press, 2000).

Haug, Wolfgang Fritz, *Critique of Commodity Aesthetics: Appearance, Sexuality and Advertising in Capitalist Society*. trans. Robert Bock (New York: Polity Press, 1986).

Hausheer, Roger, "Introduction," in Isaiah Berlin, ed., *Against the Current: Essays in the History of Ideas* (London: Hogarth Press, 1979).

Hayes, Richard P., *Land of No Buddha: Reflections of a Sceptical Buddhist* (Birmingham: Windhorse Publications, 1998).

—— "Richard Hayes' Research Activities," http://www.unm.edu/~rhayes/interest.html (May 10, 2004).

Helvétius, Claude-Adrien, *A Treatise on Man; His Intellectual Faculties and His Education*. trans. W. Hooper (New York: Burt Franklin, 1969 [1772]).

Herbert, Edward, Lord of Cherbury, *De Veritate*. trans. Meyrick H. Carré (Bristol: J.W. Arrowsmith, 1937 [1624]).

—— *Pagan Religion: A Translation of De Religione Gentilium*. trans. John Butler (Binghamton, NY: Medieval & Renaissance Texts & Studies, 1996 [1663]).

Hine, Thomas, *The Total Package: The Secret History and Hidden Meanings of Boxes, Bottles, Cans, and Other Persuasive Containers* (Boston, MA: Little Brown, 1995).

Hodgson, Brian, *Essays on the Languages, Literature, and Religion of Nepal and Tibet* (Amsterdam: Philo Press, 1972).

Holwell, John Zephaniah, *Interesting Historical Events, Relative to the Provinces of Bengal, and the Empire of Indostan* (London: T. Becket and P.J. De Hondt, 1766–71).

Horace, *The Complete Odes and Epodes*. trans. David West (Oxford: Oxford University Press, 1997).

Hume, David, *Hume on Human Nature and the Understanding*. ed. Antony Flew (New York: Macmillan, 1962).

—— *Enquiries Concerning the Human Understanding and Concerning the Principles of Morals* (Oxford: The Clarendon Press, 1966).

The ICOMOS International Committee on Cultural Tourism, *Cultural Tourism: Tourism at World Heritage Cultural Sites: The Site Manager's Handbook* (Madrid: World Tourism Organization, 1993).

Im Hof, Ulrich, *The Enlightenment* (Oxford: Blackwell, 1994).

An Indian Missionary, *The Indian Religions: Or Results of the Mysterious Buddhism* (London: T.C. Newby, 1858).

Jayadeva, *The Gītagovinda of Jayadeva: Love Song of the Dark Lord.* trans. Barbara Stoler Miller (New York: Columbia University Press, 1977).

Joinville, "On the Religion and Manners of the People of Ceylon," *Asiatick Researches* 7 (1801): 339–446.

Jones, William, "On the Gods of Greece, Italy and India," *Asiatick Researches* 1 (1788): 221–75.

Kant, Immanuel, *Critique of Pure Reason.* trans. Paul Guyer and Allen Wood (Cambridge: Cambridge University Press, 1999 [1781/1787]).

—— "An Answer to the Question: What is Enlightenment?" in Mary Gregor, ed. and trans., *Practical Philosophy* (Cambridge: Cambridge University Press, 1999 [1784]).

—— "What Does It Mean to Orient Oneself in Thinking," in Allen Wood and George di Giovanni, eds and trans., *Religion and Rational Theology* (Cambridge: Cambridge University Press, 2001 [1786]).

—— "Critique of Practical Reason," in Mary Gregor, ed. and trans., *Practical Philosophy* (Cambridge: Cambridge University Press, 1999 [1788]).

—— "Religion Within the Boundaries of Mere Reason," in Allen wood and George di Giovanni, eds and trans., *Religion and Rational Theology* (Cambridge: Cambridge University Press, 2001 [1793]).

—— "On a Supposed Right to Lie From Philanthropy," in Mary Gregor, ed. and trans., *Practical Philosophy* (Cambridge: Cambridge University Press, 1999 [1797]).

Kapferer, Jean-Noël, *Strategic Brand Management* (London: Kogan Page, 1997).

Kistner, Otto, *Buddha and His Doctrines: A Bibliographical Essay* (London: Trübner, 1869).

Kitagawa, Joseph and John Strong, "Friedrich Max Müller and the Comparative Study of Religion," in Ninian Smart, ed., *Nineteenth Century Religious Thought in the West*, Volume 3 (Cambridge: Cambridge University Press, 1985).

Köppen, Karl Friedrich, *Die Religion des Buddha* (Berlin: F. Schneider, 1857–9).

Laclau, Ernesto, *New Reflections on the Revolution of Our Time* (London: Verso, 1990).

—— *Emancipation(s)* (London: Verso, 1996).

—— "Identity and Hegemony: The Role of Universality in the Constitution of Political Logics," in Judith Butler, Ernesto Laclau, and Slavoj zizek, eds, *Contingency, Hegemony, Universality* (London: Verso, 2000).

Laclau, Ernesto and Chantal Mouffe, *Hegemony and Socialist Strategy: Towards a Radical Democratic Politics* (London: Verso, 1985).

Lannoy, Richard, *The Speaking Tree: A Study of Indian Culture and Society* (London: Oxford University Press, 1975).

Laplace, Pierre Simon and Marquis de, *A Philosophical Essay on Probabilities.* trans. Frederick Truscott and Frederick Emory (New York: Dover Publications, 1951 [1814]).

Lasn, Kalle, *Culture Jam: How to Reverse America's Suicidal Consumer Binge—And Why We Must* (New York: HarperCollins, 1999).

Latour, Bruno and Steve Woolgar, *Laboratory Life: The Social Construction of Scientific Facts* (Beverly Hills, CA: Sage Publications, 1979).

Leland, John, *A View of the Principal Deistical Writers* (New York: Garland Publishing, 1978 [1757]).

Leoshko, Janet, "The Case of the Two Witnesses to the Buddha's Enlightenment," in Pratapaditya Pal, ed., *A Pot-Pourri of Indian Art* (Bombay: Marg Publications, 1988).

Lipe, William D., "Value and Meaning in Cultural Resources," in Henry Cleere, ed., *Approaches to the Archaeological Heritage* (Cambridge: Cambridge University Press, 1984).

Liu, Ming-Wood, "The Problem of the *Icchantika* in the Mahāyāna *Mahāparinirvāṇa Sūtra*,*" *Journal of the International Association of Buddhist Studies* 7 (1984): 57–81.

Locke, John, *An Essay Concerning Human Understanding* (Amherst, NY: Prometheus Books, 1995 [1693]).

—— *The Reasonableness of Christianity, As Delivered in the Scriptures* (Bristol, UK: Thoemmes Press, 1997 [1695]).

Lopez, Donald S., Jr, ed., *A Modern Buddhist Bible: Essential Readings from East and West* (Boston, MA: Beacon Press, 2002).

Lubac, Henri du, *La rencontre du bouddhisme et de l'Occident* (Paris: Aubier, 2000).

Luther, Martin, "The Last Sermon at Wittenberg, 17 January 1546," in John Doberstein, ed. and trans., *Luther's Works*, Volume 51 (Philadelphia, PA: Muhlenberg Press, 1959).

—— *The Bondage of the Will.* trans. J.I. Packer and O.R. Johnston (Grand Rapids, MI: Fleming H. Revell, 2003 [1525]).

MacCannell, Dean, *The Tourist: A New Theory of the Leisure Class* (Berkeley, CA: University of California Press, 1999).

"Maharashtra at a Glance," http://www.maharashtra.gov.in/intranet/Deswebpage/maha.htm (July 15, 2004).

Maharashtra, Directorate of Tourism, *Ajanta* (Bombay: Tata McGraw-Hill, 1976).

Mahony, William C., "On *Singhala*, or *Ceylon*, and the Doctrines of the Bhoodha, from the Books of the *Singhalais,*" *Asiatick Researches* 7 (1801): 32–56.

Maitreya, *The Buddha-Mimansa, Or, The Buddha and His Relation to the Religion of the Vedas* (London: Thacker, 1925).

Marx, Karl, *Karl Marx, Frederick Engels: Collected Works.* trans. Clemens Dutt, Volume 3 (Moscow: Progress Publishers, 1975).

Maurice, Fredrick D., *The Religions of the World and their Relations to Christianity* (London: J.W. Parker, 1847).

Milosz, Czeslaw, "If There Is No God," *The New Yorker* (August 30, 2004): 94.

Monier-Williams, Monier, *A Dictionary, English and Sanskrit* (London: W.H. Allen, 1851).

—— *The Holy Bible and the Sacred Books of the East* (London: Seely, 1887).

Moorehead, Alan, "Lovers upon the Walls," *The New Yorker* 30 (May 1, 1954): 39–69.

Mouffe, Chantal, "Radical Democracy or Liberal Democracy," *Socialist Review* 20 (1990): 56–66.

—— *The Democratic Paradox* (London: Verso, 2000).

Müller, Max, *Buddhism and Buddhist Pilgrims: A Review of M. Stanislas Julien's "Voyages des pèlerins bouddhistes"* (London: Williams & Norgate, 1857).

—— "Buddhist Pilgrims," *The Times* (Friday, April 17, 1857): 5; (Monday, April 20, 1857): 6.

—— "Recent Researches on Buddhism," *The Edinburgh Review* 115 (1862): 379–408.

—— *Chips from a German Workshop*, Volume 1 (London: Longmans, Green, 1867).

—— *Chips from a German Workshop*, Volume 1, 2nd edition (New York: Scribner, 1869).

—— *Essays: Erster Band. Beiträge zur vergleichenden Religionswissenschaft. Nach der zweiten englischen Ausgabe mit Aurotisation des Verfassers ins Deutsche Übertragen* (Leipzig: Wilhelm Engelmann, 1869).

—— "Buddha's Dhammapada, Or 'Path of Virtue'," in T. Roger, ed., *Buddhaghosha's Parables* (London: Trübner, 1870).

—— *Introduction to the Science of Religion* (New York: Scribner, Armstrong, and Co., 1874).

—— *Lectures on the Science of Religion* (New York: Scribner, Armstrong, and Co., 1874).

—— *Chips from a German Workshop*, Volume 4 (London: Longmans, 1875).

—— trans., *Critique of Pure Reason: In Commemoration of the Centenary of its First Publication* (New York: Macmillan, 1927 [1881]).

—— *Natural Religion* (London: Longmans, Green, 1889).

Nandy, Ashis, "Homing in on History," *The Statesman* (Sunday, June 21, 1992): Miscellany section.

—— "History's Forgotten Doubles," *History and Theory* 34 (1995): 44–66.

Nanjio, Bunyiu, ed., *Laṅkāvatāra Sūtra* (Kyoto: Otani University Press, 1956).

Neale, Edward, "Buddha and Buddhism," *Macmillan's Magazine* 1 (1860): 439–48.

Needham, Rodney "Polythetic Classification: Convergence and Consequences," *Man* 10 (1975): 349–69.

Neumann, Charles Friedrich, "Coup d'oeil historique sur les peuples et la littérature de l'Orient," *Nouveau Journal Asiatique* 14 (1834): 39–73, 81–114.

—— "Buddhism and Shamanism," *Asiatic Journal and Monthly Register* 16 (1835): 124–6.

Nève, Félix, *De l'état présent des études sur le bouddhisme et de leur application* (Gand: P. van Hifte, 1846).

"NEW CAMPAIGNS–Maharashtra," http://www.agencyfaqs.org/newcamp/maharashtra_24092001.html (June 6, 2003).

Nolan, Christopher and Jonathan Nolan, *Memento*. Directed by Christopher Nolan. 113 min. Columbia Tri-Star, 2000. DVD.

O'Flaherty, Wendy Doniger, *The Origins of Evil in Hindu Mythology* (Berkeley, CA: University of California Press, 1976).

Olin, John C., *A Reformation Debate: Sadoleto's Letter to the Genevans and Calvin's Reply* (New York: Harper & Row, 1966).

"Operational Guidelines: Establishment of the World Heritage List," http://www.unesco.org/whc/- opgulist.htm (March 27, 2002).

"Operational Guidelines, for the Implementation of the World Heritage Convention," http://www.unesco.org/whc/nwhc/pages/doc/main.htm (March 26, 2002).

Paine, Thomas, *The Age of Reason* (New York: Willey Book Company, n.d. [1795]).

Paterson, J. D., "Of the Origin of the Hindu Religion," *Asiatic Researches* 8 (1808): 44–87.

Paul, Pran Gopal, "From Ācaryamuṣṭi to Varadamudrā: Antithetical Transformation of a Literary Concept into Visual Art," in Ellen Raven and Karel Van Kooij, eds, *Indian Art and Archaeology* (Leiden: Brill, 1992).

Peters, Tom, *The Pursuit of Wow!* (New York: Random House, 1994).

—— *The Circle of Innovation: You Can't Shrink Your Way to Greatness* (New York: Vintage Books, 1997).

Pietz, William. "The Problem of the Fetish, I," *Res* 9 (1985): 7–17.

—— "The Problem of the Fetish, II: The Origin of the Fetish," *Res* 13 (1987): 23–45.

—— "The Problem of the Fetish, IIIa: Bosman's Guinea and the Enlightened Theory of Fetishism," *Res* 16 (1988): 105–23.

—— "Fetishism and Materialism: The Limits of Theory in Marx," in Emily Apter and William Pietz, eds, *Fetishism as Cultural Discourse* (Ithaca, NY: Cornell University Press, 1993).

Popper, Karl, *The Open Universe: An Argument for Indeterminism* (Totowa, NJ: Rowman and Littlefield, 1982).

Prinsep, James, "Facsimiles of Various Ancient Inscriptions," *Journal of the Asiatic Society of Bengal* 5 (1836): 348–9, 556–61.

Qadir, Abdul, "Mega Plan for Mahabodhi Temple," *Times of India* (June 29, 2002), http://timesofindia.indiatimes.com/articleshow.aspartid=14403657&sType=1 (July 22, 2002).

Qureshi, Dulari Gupte, *Tourism Potential in Aurangabad (With Ajanta, Ellora, Daulatabad Fort)* (Delhi: Bharatiya Kala Prakashan, 1999).

Radhakrishnan, Sarvepalli, "Forward," in P V. Bapat, ed., *2500 Years of Buddhism* (Delhi: Ministry of Information and Broadcasting, 1971).

Radway, Janice, "The Act of Reading the Romance: Escape and Instruction," in Juliet Schor and Douglas Holt, eds, *The Consumer Society Reader* (New York: The New Press, 2000).

Ramanujan, A.K., "Is There an Indian Way of Thinking? An Informal Essay," *Contributions to Indian Sociology* 23 (1989): 41–58.

Rémusat, Abel, "Observations sur trois Mémoires de M. Deguignes, insérés dans le tome XL de la *Collection de l'Academie des Inscriptions et Belles-Lettres*, et relatifs à la religion samanéenne," *Nouveau Journal Asiatique* 7 (1831): 241–301.

—— *Foĕ Kouĕ Ki; ou, Relation des Royaumes Bouddhiques: voyage dans la Tartarie, dans l'Afghanistan et dans l'Inde, exécuté, à la fin du IVe siècle, par Chỹ Fă Hian* (Paris: Imprimerie Royale, 1836).

Rendall, Jane. "Scottish Orientalism: From Robertson to James Mill," *The Historical Journal* 25 (1982): 43–69.

Rhys Davids, Caroline, *Sakya or Buddhist Origins* (London: Kegan Paul, Trench, Trubner, 1931).

Rhys Davids, T.W., *Buddhism: Its History and Literature* (New York: G.P. Putnam's Sons, 1896).

—— *Buddhist India* (London: T. Fisher Unwin, 1903).

Ries, Al and Jack Trout, *The Twenty Two Immutable Laws of Marketing: Violate Them At Your Own Risk!* (New York: HarperCollins, 1993).

Robinson, Richard and Willard Johnson, *The Buddhist Religion: A Historical Introduction*. 4th edition (Belmont, CA: Wadsworth Publishing, 1997).

Rosen, Jeffery, "The Unregulated Offensive," *The New York Times Magazine* (Sunday, April 17, 2005).

Rousseau, Jean-Jacques, *The Social Contract and The First and Second Discourses*. trans. Susan Dunn (New Haven, CT: Yale University Press, 2002).

Salisbury, Edward, "M. Burnouf on the History of Buddhism in India," *Journal of the American Oriental Society* 1 (1849): 275–98.

Saussure, Ferdinand de, *Course in General Linguistics*. trans. Wade Baskin (New York: Philosophical Library, 1959 [1915]).

Scharf, Robert, "The Zen of Japanese Nationalism," in Donald S. Lopez, Jr, ed., *Curators of the Buddha: The Study of Buddhism Under Colonialism* (Chicago, IL: University of Chicago Press, 1995).

Schlingloff, Dieter, *Studies in the Ajanta Paintings: Identifications and Interpretations* (Delhi: Ajanta Publications, 1988).

Schopen, Gregory, *Bones, Stones and Buddhist Monks: Collected Papers on the Archaeology, Epigraphy and Texts of Monastic Buddhism in India* (Honolulu, HI: University of Hawai'i Press, 1997).

Schor, Juliet B. and Douglas B. Holt, "Introduction," in Juliet Schor and Douglas Holt, eds, in *The Consumer Society Reader* (New York: The New Press, 2000).

Selim, "Correspondence: The Caves of Adjunta," *Bombay Courier* (Tuesday, April 9, 1839): 162; (Saturday, April 20, 1839): 173–4; (Tuesday, April 23, 1839): 177; (Saturday, April 27, 1839): 182; (Tuesday, April 30, 1839): 185.

Shackley, Myra, "Introduction: World Cultural Heritage Sites," in Myra Shackley, ed., *Visitor Management: Case Studies from World Heritage Sites* (Oxford: Butterworth-Heinemann, 1998).

Sharma K.V., ed., *The Brahmāṇḍa Mahāpurāṇam* (Varanasi: Krishnadas Academy, 2000).

Shizutani, Masao, *Indo Bukkyo Himei Mokuroku* (Kyoto: Heian Gakuen Kyoikin Kenkyukai, 1965).

Silk, Jonathan, "The Victorian Creation of Buddhism," *Journal of Indian Philosophy* 22 (1994): 171–96.

Smith, Adam, *An Inquiry into the Nature and Causes of the Wealth of Nations* (Oxford: Clarendon Press, 1976 [1776]).

Smith, Jonathan Z., *To Take Place: Toward Theory in Ritual* (Chicago, IL: University of Chicago Press, 1987).

Snellgrove, David, *The Hevajra Tantra: A Critical Study* (Oxford: Oxford University Press, 1959).

—— *Indo-Tibetan Buddhism: Indian Buddhists and their Tibetan Successors* (Boston, MA: Shambala, 1987).

Spink, Walter M. "The Problem of Cave Eleven," *Ars Orientalis* 7 (1968): 155–68.

—— "Ajaṇṭā's Chronology: The Crucial Cave," *Ars Orientalis* 10 (1975): 143–69.

—— "Ajaṇṭā's Chronology: Politics and Patronage," in Joanna Williams, ed., *Kalādarśana* (New Delhi: Oxford and IBH Publishing in collaboration with the American Institute of Indian Studies, 1981).

—— "Ajaṇṭā's Chronology: Cave 7's Twice Born Buddha," in A.K. Narain ed., *Studies in Buddhist Art of South Asia* (New Delhi: Kanak Publications, 1985).

—— "Ajanta's Chronology: Solstitial Evidence," *Ars Orientalis* 15 (1985): 97–119.

—— "Ajanta in a Historical and Political Context," *Maharashtra Pathik* 2 (September 1990): 5–17.

—— "The Archaeology of Ajaṇṭā," *Ars Orientalis* 21 (1992): 67–94.

—— "Before the Fall: Pride and Piety at Ajanta," in Barbara Stoler Miller, ed., *The Powers of Art: Patronage in Indian Culture* (Delhi: Oxford University Press, 1992).

—— "Reply to K. Khandalavala, A. Jamkhedkar, B. Deshpande." *Maharashtra Pathik* 3 (1992): 16–25.

Steinmetz, David C., *Luther in Context*, (Bloomington, IN: Indiana University Press, 1986).

Stirling, James Hutchison, *The Secret of Hegel* (London: Longman, Green, 1865).

Strong, John S., *The Legend of King Aśoka: A Study and Translation of the Aśokāvadāna* (Princeton, NJ: Princeton University Press, 1983).

A Subaltern, *A Description of the Ruined City of Mandu, The Ancient Capital of Malwa with a Sketch of its History During the Period of its Independence, Under the Muhammadan Kings; and Explanatory Notes. Also, an Account of the Buddhist Cave Temples of Ajanta, in Khandes* (Bombay: The Bombay Times' Press, 1844).

Subramaniam, A.P. and Y.S. Sahasrabudhe, *Geology of Greater Bombay and Aurangabad-Ellora-Ajanta Area* (New Delhi, 1964).

Suzuki, D.T., trans., *Lankavatara Sutra* (London: Routledge & Kegan Paul, 1956).

Tagare, Ganesh V., trans., *The Brahmāṇḍa Pūrāṇa* (Delhi: Motilal Banarsidass, 1983).

Thoreau, Henry David, *Walden; Or, Life in the Woods* (New York: Harper & Row, 1966 [1854]).

Tindal, Matthew, *Christianity as Old as the Creation* (London: Thomas Astley, 1730).

Treckner. V., ed., *Majjhima-Nikāya* (London: Pali Text Society, 1935).

Truffaut, François, *Hitchcock* (New York: Simon and Schuster, 1984).

Trungpa, Chögyam, *Cutting Through Spiritual Materialism* (Berkeley, CA: Shambhala, 1973).

Tsukamoto, Keisho, *Indo Bukkyo Himei no Kenkyu* (Kyoto: Heirakuji Shoten, 1996–8).

Twitchell, James B., *Lead Us Into Temptation: The Triumph of American Materialism* (New York: Columbia University Press, 1999).

Vakil, Kanaiyalal, *At Ajanta* (Bombay: D.B. Taraporevala Sons, 1929).

Van den Bosch, Lourens, *Friedrich Max Müller: A Life Devoted to Humanities* (Leiden: Brill, 2002).

Varāhamihira, *Brhatsaṃhitā*. trans. M. Ramakrishna Bhat (Delhi: Motilal Banarsidass, 1981).

Vogel, Claus, "On the Names of the Buddha as Found in Veṇīdatta and Glossed by Heinrich Roth," in Grünendahl Reinhold Heinz Bechert, Jens-Uwe Hastmann, and Petra Kieffer- Pülz, eds, *Studien zur Indologie und Buddhismuskunde* (Bonn: Indica et Tibetica Verlag, 1993).

Voltaire, *Philosophical Dictionary.* trans. H.I. Woolf (London: George Allen & Unwin, 1923 [1764]).

Weiner, Sheila, *Ajanta: Its Place in Buddhist Art* (Berkeley, CA: University of California Press, 1977).

"WHC Convention," http://whc.unesco.org/nwhc/pages/doc/main.htm (August 3, 2002).

Wilson, Horace H., *A Dictionary in Sanscrit and English*, 1st edition (Calcutta: Hindoostanee Press, 1819).

—— *A Dictionary in Sanscrit and English*, 2nd edition (Calcutta: Education Press, 1832).

The Worship of Shugden: Documents Related to a Tibetan Controversy (Dharamsala, India: Department of Religion and Culture, Central Tibetan Administration, 1998).

Xuanzang, *The Great Tang Dynasty Record of the Western Regions.* trans. Li Rongxi (Berkeley, CA: Numata Center for Buddhist Translation and Research, 1996).

Zizek, Slavoj, *The Sublime Object of Ideology* (London: Verso, 1989).

INDEX

Note: Page numbers in italics indicate illustrations.

Devadatta 116
Dey, M.C. 74, 78, 201 nn.25, 30
dharma (Sanskrit) (Pāli *dhamma*) 168,
170, 171, 172, 173; as empty signifier
174, 180; as scriptural 174, 175, 178,
180; and the Vinaya 212 n.67; as
wisdom 174–5, 177, 180
Dhavalikar, M.K. 77, 78, 80, 196 n.114,
201 nn.28, 32
Diderot, D. 9, 194 n.49; 210 n.21; and
d'Alembert's *Encyclopédie* 156
Dieckmann, H. 194 n.49
Divākaramitra 213 n.4
Divine Universal Providence 141
D'Monte, D. 199 n.63
Dorje Shugden 183, 214 n.5
Dowey, E. 209 nn.121, 127
dream-elements 147
Dru, J.-M. 68, 200 n.120
duḥkha (suffering, imperfection) 7,
153–4, 155, 157

Edgerton, F. 197 n.120
Eerdmans press 137
Elephanta 99
Eliade, M. 128, 129, 132, 206 nn.57–62;
crypto-theological vocabulary 130;
schematization of sacred space 130
Eliot, G. 215 n.15
empty signifier 18, 20, 160; *Christian*, as
18–19; defined 15; *dharma*, as 174,
180; *enlightenment*, as 16, 19; *theist*, as
17–18; theorization of 15–17; *see also*
hegemony
Encyclopédie 9, 156
England, Civil War in 138
e/Enlightenment 15, 66, 68, 121, 156,
124, 183, 193 n.42, 194 n.46; discursive
power of 8, 15–22; hegemony 175,
213 n.4; as the recognition of
exceptional universal value 57, 156–7;
tongue, eastern and western 176
enlightenment (*bodhi*) xii, 65, 113, 136,
153–4, 161, 171, 180, 182; as basis of
Buddhism 2, 6–7, 26, 112, 136, 147–8;
as discursive object 22–5, 30, 113, 148,
160; as event 1, 25, 114–18, 147; as
instrument of hegemony xiii, 19, 151,
156, 167; mythology of enlightenment
152, 177–80, 180; as religious
experience 113; as translation 1–5,
190 n.9, 191 n.10, 193 nn.42–43;
see also e/Enlightenment

Enlightenment (European) 9–10, 57, 176,
174; Ajanta as authentic repository of
values 61; anthropology 136–7;
assumptions of anthropology 40;
Aufklärung, translation as 7–9;
citizenship 14; conception of history
69–70, 74, 85–6, 88, 90, 96, 105;
epistemology 10–12, 122–4, 125, 127;
history, alternatives to 85–6;
humanism 39, 40, 57, 62; perspective
on Ajanta 38–42; philosophical
anthropology 42, 62; political context
9–15; political thought 10; religious
humanism 62–4; semantic field 15;
theories of time 86–9; universalism 42,
52, 86, 96, 181–2; *see also*
e/Enlightenment
enlightenment (Protestant) 2, 6, 144–5,
157, 186–8
Erskine, W. 122, 127, 136, 202 n.42,
204 nn.10–13, 205 n.28, 206 nn.51–52;
1821 paper on Ajanta to Literary
Society of Bombay 82, 110, 111, 119,
120, 146; on identity of civilization in
Ajanta 111, 113, 126, 135, 146
Europe: during Thirty Years War 138;
intellectual developments during the
seventeenth and eighteenth centuries 9;
intellectual or economic presence 69;
intellectuals 64
Eusebius 195 n.79
Exceptional Universal Value 35, 49, 55,
57, 61, 66, 133, 145, 152, 175, 181
exchange-value 58, 59

fact, construction of 72, 96
Farrar, F. 215 nn.16–28
Faure, B. 129, 130, 200 n.110,
206 n.65
Fergusson, J. 49, 50, 57, 81, 97, 98, 99,
102, 109, 110, 127, 136, 198 n.48,
199 n.57, 202 n.34, 203 nn.84–87, 89,
92–93, 204 nn.2–8, 94–99, 101,
103–105; 1843 paper 99, 105; 1863
plan of Cave Eleven 97, 107; as
historian of architectural India 100;
observations about Ajanta's religious
provenance 135
fetishism 71, 72, 96, 125
Feudge, F.R. 210 n.5
Feuerbach, L. 215 n.15
Fleet, J.F. 197 n.120
Flew, A. 197 n.9